JavaScript:
A Beginner's Guide

John Pollock

Osborne/**McGraw-Hill**

New York   Chicago   San Francisco
Lisbon   London   Madrid   Mexico City   Milan
New Delhi   San Juan   Seoul   Singapore   Sydney   Toronto

Osborne/**McGraw-Hill**
2600 Tenth Street
Berkeley, California 94710
U.S.A.

To arrange bulk purchase discounts for sales promotions, premiums, or fund-raisers, please contact Osborne/**McGraw-Hill** at the above address. For information on translations or book distributors outside the U.S.A., please see the International Contact Information page immediately following the index of this book.

JavaScript: A Beginner's Guide

234567890 DOC DOC 01987654321

ISBN 0-07-213140-3

Publisher   Brandon A. Nordin
Vice President & Associate Publisher   Scott Rogers
Acquisitions Editor   Rebekah Young
Project Editor   Elizabeth Seymour
Acquisitions Coordinator   Paulina Pobocha
Technical Editors   Pankaj Kamthan, Vincent Puglia
Copy Editors   Karyn DiCastri, Chrisa Hotchkiss, Marilyn Smith
Proofreader   Linda Medoff
Indexer   James Minkin
Computer Designers   Roberta Steele, Jean Butterfield
Illustrators   Beth E. Young, Lyssa Sieben-Wald, Michael Mueller
Series Design   Gary Corrigan
Cover Series Design   Gregg Scott
Cover Illustration   Kevin Curry

This book was composed with Corel VENTURA™ Publisher.

To Bruce and Joy Anderson

In memory of James D. Anderson;
and in memory of John William and Edith Hopkins

Contents

Acknowledgments

I'd like to begin by thanking my parents, Bruce and Joy Anderson, for always being there for me and supporting all of my endeavors.

In addition I would like to thank John and Betty Hopkins (grandparents), James D. and Livian Anderson (grandparents), Richard Pollock (brother) and family, Misty Castleman (sister) and family, Warren Anderson (brother) and family, Lisa and Julian Owens (aunt/uncle) and family, and every aunt, uncle, cousin, or other relation in my family. All of you have been a great influence in my life.

I would like to thank all of my editors at McGraw-Hill for their outstanding help and support throughout the writing of this book. Thanks to Rebekah Young, Elizabeth Seymour (and her crew—I didn't get to know all of you, unfortunately), and Paulina Pobocha. Thanks to my two technical editors Pankaj Kamthan (module 1 and modules 8-17) and Vincent Puglia (modules 2-7) for editing and checking the technical aspects of the book, and helping me provide clear explanations of the topics that are covered.

I would like to thank my English professors at Sam Houston State University in Huntsville, Texas for guiding me toward a better understanding of the English language. Thanks to James J. Dent, Helena Halmari, Douglas Krienke, Julie Hall, Tracy Bilsing, Phillip Parotti, Ralph Pease, Paul Ruffin, and Jack Kerr. In addition, I thank all of my other professors at the university for helping me gain knowledge in so many areas.

I want to thank my friends for putting up with me and for giving me encouragement when I needed it. Thanks to Don Sargent (of course, given *ceteris paribus*!) and family, Sammy Delgado (Super Sam!), Cammie Flanagan, Brenda Galdamez, Lane Arnold, Lisa Cisneros, everyone from GP and Friday Night Live, Caislanders, GzazJim, Arielladog, Voicebox and to all my friends out there for your support and guidance.

I would like to thank God for the ability he has given me to help and teach people through my writing. "In all your ways acknowledge Him, and He shall direct your paths." (Proverbs 3:6)

Introduction

Welcome to *JavaScript: A Beginner's Guide*! Years ago, I was surfing the Web and noticed that people were publishing pages about themselves and calling them homepages. After viewing a number of these, I decided to create a homepage myself. I had no idea where to begin but, through trial and error, I figured out how to code HTML and publish my documents on a Web server. Over time, I saw some interesting effects used on other homepages (like alert messages that popped up out of nowhere or images that would magically change when I moved my mouse over them). I was curious and just *had* to know what was being done to create those effects. Were these page creators using HTML tags I didn't know about?

Eventually, one site revealed what they were using to create those effects: **JavaScript**. I went in search of information on it, and came across a few tutorials and scripts on the Web. Since I had programmed in other languages (I remember a language called Ada), I was able to catch on to JavaScript fairly quickly by looking at these tutorials and scripts.

I learned enough that I decided to create a Web site that would teach HTML and JavaScript to beginners. As soon as I began the project, I received questions from visitors that were way over my head—forcing me to dig deeper and learn more about JavaScript. As a result, I became completely familiar with this programming language and what it can do. Not only can you add fun effects to a Web page, you can create scripts that will perform useful tasks, like validate form input or add navigational elements to documents.

The goal of this book is to help you to learn the basics of the JavaScript language with as little hair pulling and monitor smashing as possible. You do not need any prior programming experience to learn JavaScript from this book. All you need is knowledge of HTML and how to use your favorite text editor and Web browser (see Module 1 for more information).

What This Book Covers

This book is divided into 17 chapters, or **modules**, which cover specific topics on the JavaScript language. The first two modules cover the most basic aspects of the language: what it is, what you need, and how to place JavaScript into an

HTML file. The middle of the book (Modules 3-15) covers beginning JavaScript topics from variables all the way to using JavaScript with frames. The final two chapters (Modules 16-17) introduce some advanced techniques, and point you toward resources if you want to learn more about JavaScript once you have completed the book.

Special Features

This book includes a number of special features in each module to assist you in learning JavaScript. These features include:

- **Goals:** Each module begins with a set of goals that outline the topics that you will want to understand when you complete the module.

- **Notes and Hints:** Notes and Hints call your attention to noteworthy statements that you will find helpful as you move through the modules.

- **1-Minute Drill:** The drills allow you to practice topics by asking you a few questions on what has just been discussed. The questions are brief so that you will be able to answer them quickly and continue with the module.

- **Ask The Expert:** The Ask the Expert Sections lets you see what type of questions are commonly asked about certain topics, with responses from the author.

- **Projects:** Projects let you practice what you have learned using a hands-on approach. Each project will have you code a script through step-by-step directions on what you need to do to in order to accomplish the goal. You can find solutions to each project on the Osborne Web site at www.osborne.com.

- **Mastery Check:** Each module ends with a Mastery Check, which is a series of four or five questions that will determine whether you have mastered the topics covered in the module. The answers to each Mastery Check can be found in Appendix A.

That's it! You are now familiar with the organization and special features of this book and you can begin your journey through JavaScript. If you find that you are stuck and need help, feel free to get online and visit the JavaScript discussion forums on my Web site at http://www.javascriptcity.com/forums. The forums will allow you to interact with other JavaScript coders who may be able to help you with your questions.

Now it is time to learn JavaScript. Get ready, get set, and have fun!

Module 1

Introduction to JavaScript

The Goals of This Module

- Understand the role of text editors in using JavaScript
- Understand the role of Web browsers in using JavaScript
- Review which types of text editors and Web browsers are recommended for coding with JavaScript
- Introduce the JavaScript language
- Understand how to use HTML with JavaScript

Welcome to *JavaScript: A Beginner's Guide*! You're obviously interested in learning JavaScript, but perhaps you're not sure what you need to know to use it. This module answers some basic questions about what JavaScript is, discusses its advantages and limitations, explains how you can use it to create more dynamic and inviting Web pages, and provides a brief history of the language.

JavaScript is ubiquitous on the World Wide Web. It can help your pages become more interactive, allowing them to react to a viewer's actions or allowing you to have some special effects (visual or otherwise) on your pages.

JavaScript often gets thrown in with Hypertext Markup Language (HTML) as one of the recommended languages for beginning Web developers (whether you build Web sites for business or pleasure). Of course, you can build a Web page by using only HTML, but JavaScript allows you to add additional features that a static page of HTML can't provide without some sort of scripting or programming help.

What You Need to Know

Before you begin learning about JavaScript, you should have a basic knowledge of the following:

- HTML

- Text editors

- Web browsers

- The different versions of JavaScript

If you have this basic knowledge (and most likely you do), then you'll do just fine as you work through this book. Knowing another programming/scripting language or having previous experience with JavaScript isn't required. This book is a *beginner's* guide to JavaScript.

If you think you don't have enough experience in one of the aforementioned areas, a closer look at each one may help you decide what to do.

Basic HTML Knowledge

While you don't need to be an HTML guru, you will need to know
where to place certain elements (like the head and body elements) and
how to add your own attributes. This book will often reference scripts in
the head section (between the <HEAD> and </HEAD> tags) and the
body section (between the <BODY> and </BODY> tags).

Occasionally, you will also need to add an attribute to a tag for a script
to function properly. For example, you may need to name a form element
using the *name* attribute, as shown in the following code:

```
<INPUT type="text" name="thename">
```

If you know the basics of using tags and attributes, the HTML portion
shouldn't pose any problems to learning JavaScript.

If you don't have a basic knowledge of HTML, you can learn it
fairly quickly through a number of mediums. For example, you can buy
a book or look for some helpful information on the Web. A good book
is *HTML: A Beginner's Guide* by Wendy Willard (Osborne, 2000). To
find information about HTML on the Web, check out these sites: http://
www.pageresource.com/html/ and http://htmlgoodies.earthweb.com.

Basic Text Editor and Web Browser Knowledge

Before jumping in and coding with JavaScript, you must be able to use a
text editor or HTML editor, and a Web browser. You'll use these tools to
code your scripts.

Text Editors

A number of text editors and HTML editors support JavaScript. If you
know HTML, you've probably already used an HTML editor to create
your HTML files, so you might not have to change.

However, some HTML editors have problems related to adding
JavaScript code (such as changing where the code is placed or altering
the code itself when you save the file). You may need to use a simpler
editor or look for an HTML editor that handles the addition of your
own JavaScript code easily. Some examples of text editors are Notepad,
TextPad, and Simple Text.

Web Browsers

Again, if you've been coding in HTML, you probably won't need to change your browser. However, some browsers have trouble with the newer versions of JavaScript. The choice of Web browser is ultimately up to you, as long as it's compatible with JavaScript. I recommend one of the following browsers to test your JavaScript code:

● Microsoft Internet Explorer version 4.0 or later

● Netscape Navigator version 4.0 or later

New versions of these browsers continue to be produced. At the time of this writing, nonbeta versions of Internet Explorer 5.5 and Netscape Navigator 4.7 are available.

To give you an idea of what each browser looks like, Figure 1-1 shows a Web page when viewed in Microsoft Internet Explorer. Figure 1-2 shows the same page when viewed in Netscape Navigator.

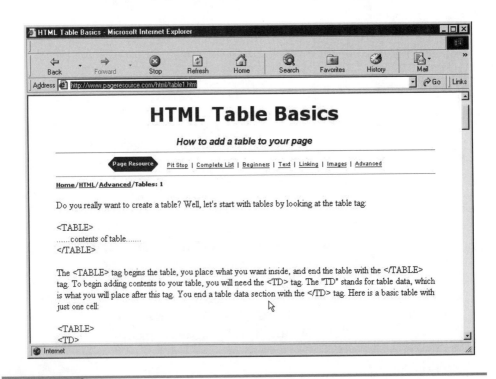

| **Figure 1-1** | **A Web page viewed in Microsoft Internet Explorer** |

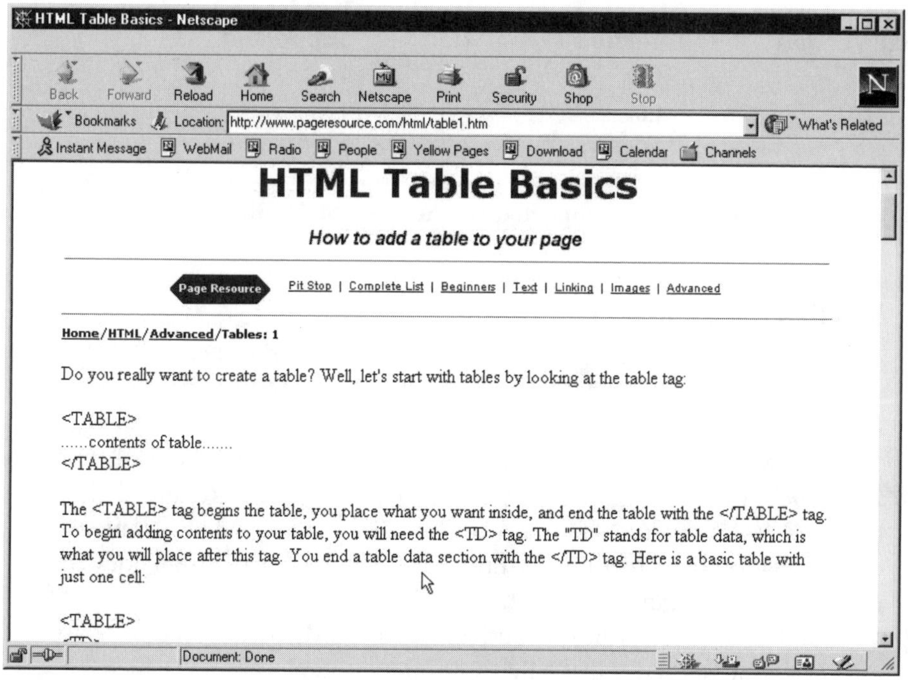

Figure 1-2 A Web page viewed in Netscape Navigator

If you have an older browser and you can't upgrade, a number of features (mostly discussed later in the book) may not work in that browser. Even so, the book can still help you learn the JavaScript language itself, so you don't need to give up if you have an older browser.

The two major browsers mentioned and the versions of JavaScript they support are shown in Table 1-1.

The next section, "Which Version," explains what the version numbers mean in more detail. For a complete listing (which includes a number of popular browsers, and addresses platform issues like which version is used in Windows or a Macintosh in the same browser), see this excellent online reference: http://www.webreview.com/browsers/browsers.shtml.

Once you've determined that you meet the basic requirements, you're ready to begin learning the language.

Microsoft Internet Explorer Version	Netscape Navigator Version	JavaScript Version Supported
5.0	4.5	1.3
4.0	4.0	1.2
3.0	3.0	1.0/1.1

Table 1-1 JavaScript Versions Supported by the Two Major Browsers

Which Version?

At the time of this writing, the browsers recommended earlier in this module should support at least JavaScript 1.2. (Some of the newer ones will likely support JavaScript 1.3.)

A browser version of 3.0 or earlier may support only JavaScript 1.0 or 1.1, which is why I suggested version 4.0 or later of the recommended browsers. JavaScript 1.4 is currently in the works and already has some documentation from Netscape at http://developer.netscape.com/docs/manuals/js/core/jsguide/index.htm.

You may also see or hear about JScript or ECMAScript. JScript is the version of JavaScript that Microsoft Internet Explorer uses (which has additional features because it is implemented as a Windows Script engine; it can use server-side languages to perform more complex tasks like updating databases). For more information on JScript, see http://msdn.microsoft.com/scripting/default.htm.

ECMAScript is the international standard name and specification for the JavaScript language, so it's not a new language but a standard that is set for JavaScript and JScript. For more on ECMAScript, see http://www.jsworld.com/ecmascript.

Remember, It's Not Java

JavaScript and Java are two different languages. Java is a full programming language that must be compiled before a program (often called a Java *applet*) can be executed. Java is more powerful but also more complex. JavaScript doesn't need a compiler and is more lenient in a number of areas, such as syntax.

Similarities to Other Languages

JavaScript does have similarities to other programming and scripting languages. If you have experience with Java, C++, or C, you'll notice some similarities in the syntax, which may help you learn more quickly. Because it's a scripting language, JavaScript also has similarities to languages like Perl—it, too, can be run through an interpreter rather than being compiled.

If you have programming or scripting experience in any language, it will make learning JavaScript easier—but it isn't required.

Ask the Expert

Question: You mentioned that I could use a text editor or HTML editor of my choice, but I'm not quite sure what that means. What is a text editor and where can I find one?

Answer: A text editor is a program that you can use to save and edit written text. Text editors range from simple to complex, and a number of choices are available: Notepad, Wordpad, Simple Text, Microsoft Word, and Corel WordPerfect Millennium Edition, to name a few. You can also purchase and download some from the Web, like NoteTab or TextPad.

An HTML editor is either a more complex text editor, or it's an editor that allows you to add code by clicking buttons or by other means—often called a What You See Is What You Get (WYSIWYG) editor. I recommend a plain text editor or an HTML editor that doesn't change any code you add to it manually. Some examples of HTML editors are Microsoft FrontPage, Allaire HomeSite, and Macromedia Dreamweaver.

Question: What exactly do I need to know about using a text editor?

Answer: Basically, you only need to know how to type plain text into the editor, save the file with an .html or .htm extension, and be able to open it again and edit it if necessary. Special features aren't needed because HTML files are made up of plain text.

Question: **What do I need to know about using a browser?**

Answer: All you absolutely need to know is how to open a local HTML file on your computer (or on the Web) and how to reload a page. If you don't know how to open an HTML file from your own computer, open your browser and go to the File menu. Look for an option that says something like Open or Open File, and select it. You should be able to browse for the file you want to open like you would with other programs. This shows where the option is in Microsoft Internet Explorer 5.5:

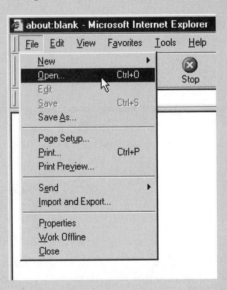

Question: **Where do I get those browsers you mentioned?**

Answer: Microsoft Internet Explorer: http://www.microsoft.com/ie Netscape Navigator: http://home.netscape.com/computing/download

Introduction to JavaScript

JavaScript came about as a joint effort between Netscape Communications Corporation and Sun Microsystems, Inc. The news release of the new language came on December 4, 1995, back when Netscape Navigator 2.0

was still in its beta version. (See http://home.netscape.com/newsref/pr/
newsrelease67.html for the news release.) JavaScript version 1.0 became
available with the new browser. (Before its release as JavaScript, it was
called LiveScript.)

JavaScript is an object-based, client-side scripting language that you
can use to make Web pages more dynamic. To make sense of such a
definition, let's look at its important parts one by one.

Object Based

Object based means that JavaScript can use items called *objects*. However,
the objects are not *class based* (meaning no distinction is made between a
class and an instance); instead, they are just general objects. You'll learn
how to work with JavaScript objects in Module 8. You don't need
to understand them in any detail until you know a few other features of
the language.

Client Side

Client side means that JavaScript runs in the *client* (software) that the viewer
is using, rather than on the Web server of the site serving the page. In this
case, the client would be a Web browser. To make more sense of this,
let's take a look at how a server-side language works and how a client-side
language works.

Server-Side Languages

A *server-side language* needs to get information from the Web page or the
Web browser, send it to a program that is run on the host's server, and
then send the information back to the browser. Therefore, an intermediate
step must send and retrieve information from the server before the results
of the program are seen in the browser.

A server-side language often gives the programmer options that a
client-side language doesn't have, such as saving information on the Web
server for later use, or using the new information to update a Web page
and save the updates.

However, a server-side language is likely to be limited in its ability to
deal with special features of the browser window that can be accessed with
a client-side language (like the content seen in the status bar of a browser
window or the contents of a form *before* it's submitted to the server).

Client-Side Languages

A client–side language is run directly through the client being used by the viewer. In the case of JavaScript, the client is a Web browser. Therefore, JavaScript is run directly in the Web browser and doesn't need to go through the extra step of sending and retrieving information from the Web server.

With a client–side language, the browser reads and interprets the code, and the results can be given to the viewer without getting information from the server first. This process can make certain tasks run more quickly.

A client–side language can also access special features of a browser window that may not be possible with a server–side language. However, a client–side language lacks the ability to save files or updates to files on a Web server like a server–side language can.

A client–side language is most useful for tasks that deal with parts of the browser or that allow information to be validated before it is sent to a server–side program or script. For instance, JavaScript can open a new window with specific dimensions, specific features (such as a toolbar or status bar), and its point of placement on the screen.

JavaScript can also be used to check the information entered into a form before it is sent to a server–side program to be processed. The information can prevent strain on the Web server by preventing submissions with inaccurate or incomplete information. Rather than running the program on the server until the information is correct, that data can be sent to the server just once with correct information.

Scripting Language

A *scripting language* doesn't require a program to be compiled before it is run. All the interpretation is done on the fly by the client.

With a regular programming language, you must write the code; compile it using a special compiler to be sure there are no syntax errors; and then, after that, you can run the program. With a scripting language, the code is interpreted as it is loaded in the client. Thus, you can test the results of your code more quickly.

However, errors won't be caught before the script is run and could cause problems with the client if it can't handle the errors well. In the case of JavaScript, the error handling is up to the browser being used by the viewer.

Putting It All Together

1

With all this in mind, you might wonder how JavaScript is run in a browser. You might wonder where to write your JavaScript code and what tells the browser it is different than anything else on a Web page. The answers are general for now, but the next module provides more details.

JavaScript runs in the browser by being added directly into an existing HTML document. You can add special tags and commands to the HTML code that will tell the browser that it needs to run a script. Once the browser sees these, it interprets the JavaScript commands and will do what you have directed it to do with your code. Thus, by simply editing an HTML document, you can begin using JavaScript on your Web pages and see the results.

For example, the following code adds some JavaScript to an HTML file that writes some text onto the Web page. Notice the addition of <SCRIPT> and </SCRIPT> tags. The code within them is JavaScript:

```
<HTML>
<BODY>
<SCRIPT language="JavaScript">
document.write("This writes text to the page");
</SCRIPT>
</BODY>
</HTML>
```

This tag tells the browser that JavaScript follows

This line writes the text inside the quote marks on the page

This line tells the browser that this is the end of the script

The next module looks at how to add JavaScript in an HTML file by using the <SCRIPT> and </SCRIPT> HTML tags. This will be your first step on the road to becoming a JavaScript coder!

Online Resources

To find additional information online to help you with JavaScript, here are some useful resources:

● A place to find tutorials with working examples of the results: http://www.pageresource.com/jscript

- An excellent tutorial site that includes cut-and-paste scripts: http://www.wsabstract.com

- A place where you can address questions about JavaScript to fellow coders: http://www.javascriptcity.com/forums

1-Minute Drill

- **What is JavaScript?**
- **Are objects in JavaScript class based?**
- **Can JavaScript save a file on a Web server?**

pr1_1.html

Project 1-1: Using JavaScript to Write Text

This project shows you JavaScript in action by loading an HTML document in your browser. The script writes a line of text in the browser using JavaScript.

Step-by-Step

1. Copy and paste the code shown here into your text editor:

```
<HTML>
<BODY>
<SCRIPT language="JavaScript">
<!--
document.write("This text was written with JavaScript!");
//-->
</SCRIPT>
</BODY>
</HTML>
```

2. Save the file as pr1_1.html and open it in your Web browser. You should see a single line of text that was written with JavaScript.

- **JavaScript is an object-oriented, client-side scripting language that can be used to make Web pages more dynamic**
- **No**
- **No**

☑ *Mastery Check*

1. You must know which of the following to be able to use JavaScript?

    A. Perl

    B. C++

    C. HTML

    D. SGML

2. Which of the following is something you should have to use JavaScript?

    A. A Web browser

    B. A C++ compiler

    C. A 50GB hard drive

    D. A CD-RW drive

3. How can a client-side language help when using forms on a Web page?

    A. It can save the information on the server.

    B. It can validate the information before it is sent to the server.

    C. It can update a file and save the file with the new information.

    D. It can't help at all.

4. How is JavaScript added to a Web page?

    A. It is written into a special editor in the browser.

    B. It is taken from a compiled program on the server.

    C. You place the code in a file by itself and open that file.

    D. It is added to an HTML document.

Module 2

Placing JavaScript in an HTML File

The Goals of This Module

- Understand the functions of SCRIPT tags
- Insert scripts into HTML documents
- Run external JavaScript files from HTML documents
- Add JavaScript comments to code

Now that you have been introduced to JavaScript, you're ready to start coding. Since JavaScript code is run from HTML documents, you need to know how to tell browsers to run your scripts. The most common way to set off a script is to use the HTML <SCRIPT> and </SCRIPT> tags in your document. You can place your script in either the HEAD or BODY section of an HTML document.

This module looks at the use of SCRIPT tags to begin and end a segment of JavaScript code. Then you will get started creating and running your first scripts. At the end of the module, you will learn how to add JavaScript comments to document your scripts.

Using the HTML SCRIPT Tags

SCRIPT tags are used to tell the browser where some type of scripting language will begin and end in an HTML document. In their most basic form, SCRIPT tags appear just like any other set of HTML tags:

```
<SCRIPT>  ◄─────────────  Tells the browser where script code begins
JavaScript code here
</SCRIPT>  ◄─────────────  Tells the browser where script code ends
```

As you can see, there is the opening <SCRIPT> tag, the JavaScript code, and then the closing </SCRIPT> tag. When you use just the basic opening and closing tags like this, many browsers will assume that the scripting language to follow will be JavaScript. However, some browsers may need to be told which scripting language is being used.

Besides distinguishing where a script begins and ends for the browser, SCRIPT tags can also tell the browser which scripting language will be used and define the address for an external JavaScript file. These additional functions are achieved through the language and src (source) attributes.

Identifying the Scripting Language

The scripting language between the opening and closing SCRIPT tags could be JavaScript, VBScript, or some other language. Even though JavaScript is usually set as the default scripting language in browsers, there may be some browsers that do not default to JavaScript. To be safe, it is a good idea to explicitly identify the language as JavaScript. You do this by adding the language attribute with the value of "JavaScript" to the opening SCRIPT tag:

```
<SCRIPT language="JavaScript">    Tells the browser the scripting
JavaScript code here              language will be JavaScript
</SCRIPT>
```

Since the SCRIPT tag is an HTML tag, it is not case sensitive. You can put the entire tag, including the script language name, in all lowercase, uppercase, or mixed case—whatever you prefer. The following form works the same as the previous example:

```
<script language="javascript">
JavaScript code here
</script>
```

However, unlike HTML, JavaScript is case sensitive, and you will need to be more careful with it. Until we look at XHTML in a later module, I will use uppercase for HTML tag names and lowercase for the attribute names. The JavaScript code will use the case that is needed in order for it to function correctly.

The opening SCRIPT tag can be expanded a little further if you are writing code that works only in or above a certain version of JavaScript. For instance, if you use code that works with only JavaScript 1.2 or later, you can add the version number right after the word "JavaScript" in the language attribute with no space between them:

```
<SCRIPT language="JavaScript1.2">    Browser will execute this
JavaScript code here                 code only if it can handle
</SCRIPT>                             JavaScript 1.2 or later
```

This means that browsers that support JavaScript 1.2 or later should run the script; other browsers should ignore it. You will want to specify a version if you write scripts that use options available in only the latest versions of JavaScript.

Calling External Scripts

SCRIPT tags are also useful if you wish to call an external JavaScript file in your document. An *external JavaScript file* is a text file that contains nothing but JavaScript code, and it is saved with the .js file extension. By calling an external file, you can save the time of coding long lines of script into each page in which the script is needed. Instead, you can use a single line that points to the JavaScript file with all of the code.

You can call external scripts by adding an src (source) attribute to the opening SCRIPT tag:

```
<SCRIPT language="JavaScript" src="yourfile.js"></SCRIPT>
```

This example calls a JavaScript file named yourfile.js from any page on which you place the line.

If the script is extremely long, using the src attribute can be much quicker than inserting the entire code on each page. However, this method is best used with Netscape Navigator or Microsoft Internet Explorer in version 4 or later because other browsers often do not support external files or only partially support them (causing JavaScript errors or display errors).

Hiding JavaScript Code from Older Browsers

What happens when someone visits your page with an older browser that does not support JavaScript? If you're not careful, the entire contents of your JavaScript code might be dumped on the page as plain text. To prevent this from occurring, you can tell the browser to ignore what follows by placing HTML comments between the opening and closing SCRIPT tags.

After the opening SCRIPT tag, you insert the opening HTML comment code (<!--). Just before the closing SCRIPT tag in the document, place the closing HTML comment code, preceded by two forward slashes (//-->).

```
<SCRIPT language="JavaScript">
<!--
JavaScript code here
//-->
</SCRIPT>
```

Begins the HTML comment to hide the code from older browsers

Ends the HTML comment to hide the code from older browsers

The two forward slashes in front of the ending HTML comment are the code for a JavaScript comment. JavaScript knows to ignore the opening of an HTML comment, but not the closing of one. To be sure that the closing HTML comment does not cause an error in the script, use the pair of forward slashes to form a single-line JavaScript comment, telling JavaScript to ignore what follows. You will learn more about JavaScript comments later in this module, in the "Using JavaScript Comments" section.

1-Minute Drill

● **Why should you use the language attribute in the opening SCRIPT tag?**

● **What filename extension is used for an external JavaScript file?**

● **Why should HTML comments be used between the <SCRIPT> and </SCRIPT> tags?**

● To be sure the browser does not interpret your JavaScript as another scripting language and become confused
● The .js filename extension
● To prevent old browsers from displaying JavaScript code as text on a Web page

Creating Your First Script

Now that you know how to use the HTML SCRIPT tags to tell browsers about the JavaScript in a document, you're ready to learn how to add the actual JavaScript code between those SCRIPT tags. The first coding example often given to teach any language is one that writes some sort of text to the default output area, commonly known as a basic "Hello World" script. Following that convention, your first script will write a string of text to a Web page.

Writing a "Hello World" Script

Rather than write "Hello World," you'll use another line of text for this script: "Yes! I am now a JavaScript coder!" This requires only a single line of code, using the document.write method, which writes a string of text to the document:

```
<SCRIPT language="JavaScript">
<!--
document.write("Yes! I am now a JavaScript coder!");
//-->
</SCRIPT>
```

Notice the parentheses and the quotation marks around the text. The parentheses are required because the document.write method is a JavaScript *function*, which takes an *argument* contained in parentheses. You will learn more about JavaScript functions in Module 4.

The quotation marks denote a *string* of text. A string is a type of variable that is defined in JavaScript by placing it inside quotation marks. Module 3 provides details on strings and other types of JavaScript variables.

The last thing to notice about your script is the semicolon at the end of the line. The semicolon signals the end of a JavaScript statement. A statement is a portion of code that does not need anything added to it to be complete in its syntax (its form and order). A statement can be used to perform a single task, multiple tasks, or to make calls to other parts of the script that perform several statements. Most JavaScript statements end with a semicolon, so it is a good idea to get in the habit of remembering to add one.

Note

In later modules, you will see various lines that do not end in semicolons because they open or close a block of code. Also, many scripts you encounter may not end statements with semicolons. JavaScript is lenient about the use of a semicolon in most cases; however, it is best to use the semicolon to end a statement because it can prevent possible errors and aid in debugging (removing errors from) the script later.

So, to write a text string to the page, you use the document.write method, followed by the text, surrounded by quotation marks and enclosed in parentheses. End the line (the statement) with a semicolon. JavaScript will handle the rest of the job.

Creating an HTML Document for the Script

In order to make this example complete and test the script, you need to insert it into an HTML document. First, create the following HTML document with the basic tags (using any text editor you prefer):

```
<HTML>
<HEAD>
<TITLE>My First JavaScript</TITLE>
</HEAD>
<BODY>
</BODY>
</HTML>
```

Save the document as test1.html in your text editor. You will call it later with a Web browser to see the results of the script. Next, you'll add the script to this HTML document, so leave the file open.

Inserting the Script into the HTML Document

Now you need to insert the script in the document. Where should it go? You can place a script between the <HEAD> and </HEAD> tags, or between the <BODY> and </BODY> tags. If the script is going to write something directly to the page, it is normally placed in the BODY section of the document, where you want the results to appear. Scripts that do not write to the page directly, such as those that change elements or define variables, are normally placed in the HEAD section.

Since this example writes a text string directly to the page, you want to insert the script between the <BODY> and </BODY> tags, wherever you want the text string to appear. It can come before, after, or between any HTML code on the page.

To make it clear how the script results appear, you'll add HTML code to write lines of bold text before and after the script. The SCRIPT tags and the script itself are inserted between those lines. Add the lines shown next between the BODY tags:

```
<HTML>
<HEAD>
<TITLE>My First JavaScript</TITLE>
</HEAD>
<BODY>
<B>This is the first line, before the script results.</B>
<BR>
<SCRIPT language="JavaScript">
<!--
document.write("Yes! I am now a JavaScript coder!");
//-->
</SCRIPT>
<BR>
<B>This line comes after the script.</B>
</BODY>
</HTML>
```

Save the test1.html document again. You should now be able to open the document in your Web browser to see the results of the script. Figure 2-1 shows how the text should look in your browser when you load the Web page.

Congratulations, you have now finished your first script!

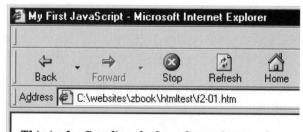

Figure 2-1   The test.html file in a Web browser

Ask the Expert

Question: Do I always need to use SCRIPT tags to add JavaScript to a page?

Answer: When you are just starting out, you need to use SCRIPT tags in your HTML documents. However, it's possible to use *event handlers* that allow you to write short bits of script outside the SCRIPT tags or to call parts of scripts that are within SCRIPT tags. You'll learn about event handlers in Module 7.

Question: Are the attributes and comments really necessary when using SCRIPT tags? Why not just use <SCRIPT> and </SCRIPT>?

Answer: While using the basic SCRIPT tags will often work just fine, some older browsers may have problems with this. By using the language attribute and the comments, you can make sure that users of older browsers don't see errors or the code itself written on the page.

Question: Why is there a dot (.) in the document.write()
command?

Answer: Document is one of JavaScript's predefined objects, and write()
is a predefined method of the document object. The dot puts the object
and the method together to make the function work. Module 8 explains
JavaScript objects, and Module 9 is devoted to the document object.

Question: How do I know when to add the script inside the
HEAD section and when to add it inside the BODY section?

Answer: The main reason to add a script to the BODY section of a
document is when you are writing something directly to the page using the
document.write() command. As you will learn in later modules, in many
cases, most of the scripting can be accomplished in the HEAD section,
since you can use functions to call the code in the BODY section. This
will become clearer as you create more scripts.

pr2_1.html

Project 2-1: Insert a Script into an HTML Document

The following project will give you practice adding a script to your
page. You will create an HTML document and insert a script that
displays a short sentence in the browser window when the page loads.

Step-by-Step

1. Set up an HTML document so that you have a simple file with
   nothing between the <BODY> and </BODY> tags yet.

2. Put the following line of text into the Web page, and make it bold.

I am part of the HTML document!

3. Insert a <P> (paragraph) tag after this line.

4. After the <P> tag, insert a script that will write the following line on the page.

This came from my script, and it is now on the page!

5. Place a <P> tag after the script code.

6. Put the following line of text into the Web page after the last <P> tag, and make it bold.

I am also part of the HTML document, after the script results!

7. Here is what your HTML document should look like:

```
<HTML>
<BODY>
<B>I am part of the HTML document!</B>
<P>
<SCRIPT language="JavaScript">
<!--
document.write("This came from my script, and is now on the page!");
//-->
</SCRIPT>
<P>
<B>I am also part of the HTML document, after the script results!</B>
</BODY>
</HTML>
```

8. Save the file as pr2_1.html and view the page in your browser to see the results.

Revisiting "Hello World" in External Form

Now suppose that you want to use your "Hello World" script (the one you created earlier in this module) on more than one page, but you do not want to write it out on each page. You can do this by putting the script in an external script file and calling it with the src attribute of the SCRIPT tag. For this method, you need to create a JavaScript text file to hold your script. You also need one or more HTML files into which you will place the SCRIPT tags to call your external script file.

Note

If you do not have either Netscape Navigator or Microsoft Internet Explorer at version 4 or later, you may not be able to view the external script file examples. However, you can still learn to code the external file and the HTML files by reading the information.

Creating a JavaScript File

For this example, you will create a JavaScript file that contains only one line. For practical applications, you would use this approach for lengthier scripts—the longer the script is, the more useful this technique becomes.

Open a new file in your text editor and insert only the JavaScript code (the document.write statement) itself. The SCRIPT tags and HTML comments are not needed in the external JavaScript file. The file should appear like this:

```
document.write("Yes! I am now a JavaScript coder!");
```

Save the file as jsfile1.js in your text editor. To do this, you may need to use the Save As option on the File menu and place quotation marks around your filename, as shown in Figure 2-2 (using Notepad with Windows).

Once the file has been saved, you can move onto the next step, which is creating the HTML files in which to use the script.

2

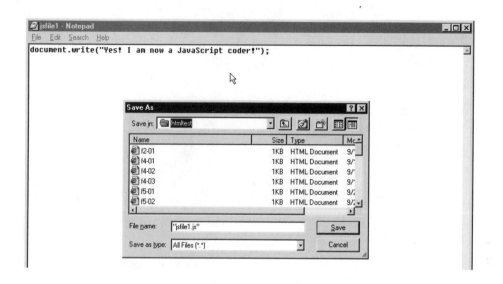

Figure 2-2 An example of saving a file with a .js extension using quote marks so that it will be saved with the correct file extension

Creating the HTML Files

You will create two files in which to place your script. The technique should work for any number of HTML files, though, as long as you add the required SCRIPT tags to each file.

For the first file, insert the SCRIPT tags into the BODY section of the document, using the src attribute to point to the jsfile1.js file, and add some HTML text to the body of the page to identify it as the first HTML document:

```
<HTML>
<HEAD>
<TITLE>External .js File- Page 1</TITLE>
</HEAD>
<BODY>
<SCRIPT language="JavaScript" src="jsfile1.js"></SCRIPT>
<P>
<B>This is page 1, and the script works here!</B>
</BODY>
</HTML>
```

Save this file as jsext1.html in your text editor. Be sure to save it in the same directory as your jsfile1.js file.

The second HTML document looks the same as the first one, except that the HTML text says that it's page 2:

```
<HTML>
<HEAD>
<TITLE>External .js File- Page 2</TITLE>
</HEAD>
<BODY>
<SCRIPT language="JavaScript" src="jsfile1.js"></SCRIPT>
<P>
<B>This is page 2, and the script also works here!</B>
</BODY>
</HTML>
```

Save this file as jsext2.html in your text editor. Again, be sure to place it in the same directory as the other files.

Viewing the Pages in Your Browser

Open the jsext1.html file in your Web browser. It should appear as shown in Figure 2-3, with the JavaScript inserted in the page from the external script file.

Next, open the jsext2.html file in your Web browser. It should appear as shown in Figure 2-4, with only the small difference of the text you

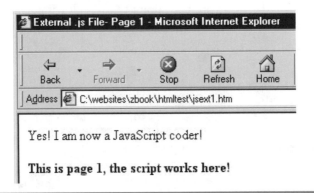

Figure 2-3 | The result of calling the script in the jsext1.html file, the first HTML page

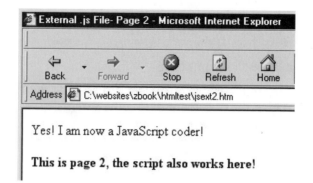

| **Figure 2-4** | The result of calling the script on the jsext2.html file, the second HTML page |

added to the HTML file to say that this is page 2. The JavaScript should write the same text to this page as it did to the first HTML page.

Although we used a short script in this example, it should give you an idea of how using an external file could be a great time-saver when you have a large script.

htm1, prjs2_2.js

Project 2-2: Call an External Script from an HTML Document

This project will allow you to practice creating external JavaScript files and using them to insert a script into a Web page.

Step-by-Step

1. Set up a simple HTML document with nothing between the <BODY> and </BODY> tags.

2. Place the following line of text between the BODY tags of the page.

   This text is from the HTML document!

3. Place a <P> tag after this text. If you need to save this file now, save it as pr2_2.html.

4. Create an external .js file that will write the following line when it is executed.

   I love writing JavaScript and using external files!

5. Here is how your .js file should look:

```
document.write("I love writing JavaScript, and using external files!");
```

6. Save the .js file as prjs2_2.js.

7. Go back to the HTML document. Place the SCRIPT tags after the <P> tag in the document so that the external .js file will write its sentence on the page.

8. Your HTML document should look like this:

```
<HTML>
<BODY>
This text is from the HTML document!
<P>
<SCRIPT language="JavaScript"
SRC="prjs2_2.js"></SCRIPT>
</BODY>
</HTML>
```

9. Save this file as pr2_2.html and view the results in your browser.

Using JavaScript Comments

You may need to make notes in your JavaScript code, such as to describe what a line of code is supposed to do. It's also possible that you will want to disable a line of the script for some reason. For instance, if you are looking for an error in a script, you may want to disable a line in the script to see if it is the line causing the error. You can accomplish these tasks by using JavaScript comments. You can insert comments that appear on one line or run for numerous lines.

Inserting Comments on One Line

If you want to add commentary on a single line in your code, place a pair of forward slashes before the text of the comment:

```
// Your comment here
```

In this format, anything preceding the two slashes on that line is "live" code—code that will be executed—and anything after the slashes on that line is ignored. For example, suppose that you wrote this line in your code:

```
document.write("This is cool!"); // writes out my opinion
```

The document.write method will be run by the browser, so the text "This is cool!" will be written to the page. However, the comment after the slashes will be ignored by the browser.

　　If you place the forward slashes at the beginning of a line, the browser will ignore the entire line. Suppose that you move the slashes in the

Hint

Single-line comments are very useful for adding short notes into your code. By writing a brief description of the purpose of a line using comments, you make your code easier to understand (when you or someone else looks at it later) and to debug.

previous example to be the first items on the line:

```
// document.write("This is cool!");
```

In this format, the entire line is ignored, since it begins with the two slashes that represent a JavaScript comment. The text will not be written to the page, since the code will not be executed by the browser. In effect, you are disabling the document.write statement. You may wish to do this if the script containing this line has an error and you want to know whether or not this line is causing the problem.

Adding Multiple-Line Comments

Comments denoted by a pair of forward slashes apply only to the line on which they appear; their effects are cut off at the end of the line. To add comments that span any number of lines, you use a different comment format: a forward slash followed by an asterisk at the beginning of the comment, then the text of the comment, and then an asterisk followed by a forward slash at the end the comment. Here's an example:

```
/*
My script will write some text into my HTML document!
```

```
All of this text is ignored by the browser.
*/
document.write("You can see me!");
```

Using this format, you can begin the comment on one line and end it on another line.

Multiple-line comments can be handy when you want to insert lengthier descriptions or other text, but you need to be careful when you use them. Look at this example to see if you can find a problem with it:

```
<SCRIPT language="JavaScript">
<!--
/*
This code won't work for some reason.
document.write("I want someone to see me!");
//-->
</SCRIPT>
```

Did you notice that the closing JavaScript comment symbols are missing? When you use multiple-line comments, you need to be careful to close them. Otherwise, you might accidentally comment out code you need executed! In this example, the comment just keeps going on with no end in sight. To fix this, you need to close the JavaScript comments before the document.write method is used:

```
<SCRIPT language="JavaScript">
<!--
/*
The JavaScript code is now working! This text is hidden.
*/
document.write("Now everyone can see me!");
//-->
</SCRIPT>
```

In the preceding examples, you saw how comments can be used to provide some documentation of what to expect from each script. In Module 16, you will learn how using comments can help you debug your JavaScript code. For now, you should get in the habit of adding comments to your scripts as short documentation or instructions.

☑ *Mastery Check*

1. What is the purpose of the <SCRIPT> and </SCRIPT> tags?

   A. To tell the browser where a script begins and ends

   B. To let the browser know the scripting language to be used

   C. To point to an external JavaScript file

   D. All of the above

2. Why would you use HTML comments within the <SCRIPT> and </SCRIPT> tags?

   A. To tell the browser there is HTML in your JavaScript

   B. To keep the JavaScript code inside the tags from rendering as plain text in older Web browsers

   C. To help you make special notes in your script

   D. There is no reason to use the HTML comments

3. When would it be a good idea to use an external JavaScript file?

   A. When the script is short or going to be used in only one HTML document

   B. When your Web site viewers have older browsers

   C. When the script is very long or needs to be placed in more than one HTML document

   D. External files are not a good idea

4. JavaScript comments can be very useful for the purposes of _____ and _____ your code.

Module 3

Using Variables

The Goals of This Module

- Understand the purpose of variables
- Declare and assign values to variables
- Understand the different JavaScript variable types
- Use variables in your scripts

Now that you have learned the basics of adding JavaScript to a Web page, it is time to get into the inner workings of the language. Since variables are an important part of JavaScript coding, you will need to know as much as possible about what they are and why they are useful in your scripts. Once you have an understanding of how variables work and what they can do, you will be able to move on to other topics that build on the use of the various types of variables.

In this module, you will begin by learning what variables are and why they are useful. We will then move on to the methods used to declare variables and how to assign a value to a variable. Finally, you will see how to use variables in your scripts.

What Is a Variable?

A *variable* represents or holds a value. The actual value of a variable can be changed any time. To understand what a variable is, consider a basic statement that you may recall from algebra class:

```
x=2
```

The letter x is used as the name of the variable. It is assigned a value of 2. To change the value, you simply give x a new assignment:

```
x=4
```

The name of the variable stays the same, but now it represents a different value.

Taking the math class example one step further, you probably had to solve a problem like this one:

```
If x=2, then 3+x=?
```

To get the answer, you put the value of 2 in place of the variable x in the problem, for $3+2=5$. If the value of x changes, so does the answer to the problem. So, if $x=7$, then the calculation turns into $3+7$, and now the result is 10.

Variables in JavaScript are much like those used in mathematics. You give a variable a name, and then assign it values based on your needs. If the value of the variable changes, it will change something that happens within the script.

Why Are Variables Useful?

Using variables offers two benefits:

- They can save you time in writing and updating your scripts.

- They can make the purpose of your code clearer.

Variables as Time-Savers

Variables speed up script writing because their values can change. When you assign a value to a variable at the beginning of a script, the rest of the script can simply use the variable in its place. If you decide to change the value later, you need to change the code in only one place—where you assigned a value to the variable—rather than in numerous places.

For instance, suppose that back in math class, you were asked to solve this problem:

```
If x=2, then 3+x-1+2-x=?
```

You know that you need to substitute the value of 2 for each x that appears, for 3+2–1+2–2=4. Now if the teacher wants you to do this problem again with a different value for x, the whole problem does not need to be rewritten. The teacher can just give you the following instruction:

```
Solve the above problem for x=4.
```

The longer and more complex the problem gets, the more useful the variable becomes. Rather than rewriting the same thing over and over, you can change one variable to offer an entirely new result.

Variables as Code Clarifiers

Since variables represent something, and you can give them meaningful names, they are often easier to recognize when you read over (and debug) your scripts. If you just add numbers, you may forget what they stand for. For example, consider this line of code:

```
TotalPrice=2.42+4.33;
```

Here, the numbers could mean almost anything. Instead, you might assign 2.42 as the value of a variable named CandyPrice and 4.33 as the value of a variable named OilPrice:

```
TotalPrice=CandyPrice+OilPrice;
```

Now, rather than trying to remember the meaning of the numbers, you can see that the script is adding the price of some candy to the price of some oil. This is also useful in debugging, because the meaningful variable names make it easier to spot errors.

1-Minute Drill

● **What does a variable do?**

● **How can changing the value of a single variable be useful?**

● **What is the advantage of assigning numbers to variables with names?**

Defining Variables for Your Scripts

Now that you understand what variables are and why you want to use them, you need to learn how to make them work in your scripts. You

---

● A variable represents or holds a value
● Changing a variable can make it easier to repeat a task using different values without rewriting the script
● The names can describe the meaning or purpose of the numbers

create variables by *declaring* them. Then you assign values to them using the JavaScript *assignment operator.* When you name your variables, you need to follow the rules for naming variables in JavaScript, as well as consider the meaningfulness of the name.

Declaring Variables

To declare text as a variable, you use the *var* keyword, which tells the browser that the text to follow will be the name of a new variable:

```
var variablename;
```

For example, to name your variable "coolcar," the declaration looks like this:

```
var coolcar;
```

In this example, you have a new variable with the name "coolcar". The semicolon ends the statement. The variable "coolcar"does not have a value assigned to it yet. As described in the next section, you can give your new variable a value at the same time that you declare it, or you can assign it a value later in your script.

The code for giving a variable a name is simple, but there are some restrictions on words that you can use for variables and the cases of the letters. You'll learn more about JavaScript naming rules after you see how to assign a value to a variable.

Assigning Values to Variables

To assign a value to a variable, you use the JavaScript assignment operator, which is the equal to (=) symbol. If you want to declare a variable and assign a value to it on the same line, use this format:

```
var variablename=variablevalue;
```

For example, to name your variable "paycheck" and give it the numeric value 1200, use this statement:

```
var paycheck=1200;
```

3

The statement begins with the keyword *var*, followed by the variable "paycheck," just as in the plain variable declaration described in the previous section. Next comes the assignment operator (=), which tells the browser to assign the value on the right side of the operator to the variable on the left side of the operator. To the right of the assignment operator is 1200, which is the numeric value being assigned to the variable "paycheck." The line ends with a semicolon to mark the end of the statement.

Caution

Be careful not to think of the assignment operator (=) as having the meaning "is equal to." This operator only assigns a value. The operator for "is equal to" is two equal signs together (==), as you'll learn in Module 5.

To declare and assign another variable, you use the same format, placing the statement on a new line. For example, to set up a variable named "spending" to track the amount of money you are spending from the paycheck variable, use these statements:

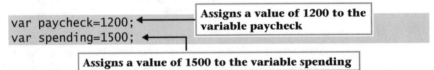

```
var paycheck=1200;
var spending=1500;
```

Assigns a value of 1200 to the variable paycheck

Assigns a value of 1500 to the variable spending

Of course, you will also notice that this financial situation is headed for trouble, since the money being spent in the spending variable is more than what is being brought in with the paycheck variable. Oddly, it is starting to look like the budget for my Web site!

The examples you've seen illustrate the proper and safe way to code variable declarations and assignments. However, the truth is that JavaScript allows a certain amount of flexibility when it comes to variables. In many cases, the declaration statement will work without using the *var* keyword at the beginning of the line or the semicolon at the end. For example, you may see some scripts written without the *var* keyword:

```
paycheck=1200;
```

You may also see a script that leaves off the ending semicolon:

```
var paycheck=1200
```

And in some scripts, both features are left out of the variable assignment:

```
paycheck=1200
```

In fact, sometimes JavaScript variables can be used without ever being declared as variables!

All of these shortcuts may seem handy, but it is best to go ahead and define each variable before using it, use the *var* keyword, and include the semicolon. Not doing so can cause errors in some browsers and may give people the impression the code was not written well. Also, any of these omissions can be really troublesome if you need to debug the script. Giving variables the correct assignments will avoid problems, and your code will be easier to read and understand.

Naming Variables

Before you start naming your own variables, you need to be aware of JavaScript's naming rules. The factors you need to consider when choosing names are case sensitivity, invalid characters, and the names that are reserved by JavaScript. Additionally, you should try to give your variables names that are both easy to remember and meaningful.

Using Case in Variables

JavaScript variables are case sensitive—paycheck, PAYCHECK, Paycheck, and PaYcHeCk are four different variables. When you create a variable, you will need to be sure to use the same case when you write that variable's name later in the script. If you change the capitalization at all, JavaScript will see it as a new variable or will return an error. Either way, it can cause problems with your script.

Here are a couple of suggestions for using case in your variables:

- If you are using a variable with only one word, it is probably easiest to keep it all in lowercase. It will be quicker to type, and you will know when you use it later to type it all in lowercase.

- For a variable name with two words, you might decide to capitalize the first letter of each word. For example, you may name a variable MyCar or My_Car (we will see more on the underscore (_) character in the next section.

The capitalization of variables is entirely up to you, so you should use whatever style you are most comfortable with. It is best that you adopt a convention and continue to use it. For instance, if you name a variable only with lowercase characters, you should do the same throughout the script to avoid accidentally switching the case when using the variable later. In this book I will be using variable names all in lowercase to keep the code clear.

Using Allowed Characters

An important rule to remember is that a variable name must begin with a letter or an underscore character (_). The variable name cannot begin with a number or any other character that is not a letter (other than the underscore). The other characters in the variable name can be letters, numbers, or underscores. Blank spaces are not allowed in variable names. So, the following variable names would be valid:

- paycheck

- _paycheck

- pay2check

- pay_check

- pay_245

However, the following variable names are not valid:

- #paycheck

- 1paycheck

- pay check

- pay_check 2

- _pay check

The hardest rule to remember may be that you cannot begin the name with a number (it's the one I forget most often). While such a name seems reasonable, JavaScript doesn't allow it.

Avoiding Reserved Words

Another rule to keep in mind when naming your variables is to avoid the use of JavaScript reserved words. These are special words that are used for a specific purpose in JavaScript. For instance, you've learned that the reserved word *var* is used to declare a JavaScript variable. Using it as a variable name can cause numerous problems in your script, since this word is meant to be used in a different way.

The following table lists the reserved words in JavaScript. Note that all of these words are in all lowercase letters. In later modules, you will learn how these reserved words are used, so they will become more familiar over time.

abstract	delete	function	null	throw
boolean	do	goto	package	throws
break	double	if	private	transient
byte	else	implements	protected	true
case	enum	import	public	try
catch	export	in	return	typeof
char	extends	instanceof	short	var
class	false	int	static	void
const	final	interface	super	volatile
continue	finally	long	switch	while
debugger	float	native	synchronized	with
default	for	new	this	

Giving Variables Meaningful Names

Although *x* is an acceptable variable name, it is unlikely to help you remember what it stood for if you need to debug the program later. It would also make it harder if you have someone else try to help you debug the code.

You should try to give your variables names that describe what they represent as clearly as possible. Suppose that you want to use a variable to hold a number of an example on a page. Rather than use *x, ex,* or another short variable, use something more descriptive:

```
var example_number=2;
```

The variable example_number will be easy for you to recognize later, and other coders will be more likely to understand its use quickly.

The more variables you use in a script, the more important it becomes to use meaningful and memorable names.

1-Minute Drill

- **What is used as the assignment operator in JavaScript?**
- **What type of words should not be used as JavaScript variables?**
- **Why is it important to give your variables memorable names?**

Understanding Variable Types

So far, you've seen examples of variable values that are numbers. In JavaScript, the variable values, or *types*, can include numbers, strings, Booleans, and nulls.

Unlike stricter programming languages, JavaScript does not force you to declare the type of variable when you define it. Instead, JavaScript allows virtually any value to be assigned to any variable. Although this gives you flexibility in coding, you need to be careful because you can end up with some unexpected results—especially when adding numbers.

- **The = symbol**
- **Reserved words**
- **When you need to debug the program, it will be easier to recognize what the variable represents**

3

Numbers

Number variables are just that—numbers. JavaScript does not require numbers to be declared as integers, floating-point numbers, or any other number type. Instead, any number is seen as just another number, whether it is 7, −2, 3.453, or anything else. The number will remain the same type unless you perform a calculation to change the type. For instance, if you use an integer in a variable, it won't suddenly have decimal places unless you perform a calculation of some sort to change it (dividing unevenly, for instance).

As you've seen, you define a number variable by using the keyword *var*.

```
var variablename=number;
```

Here are some examples:

```
var paycheck=1200;
var phonebill=29.99;
var savings=0;
var sparetime=-24.5;
```

If you need to use a particularly long number, JavaScript has exponential notation. To denote the exponent, use a letter *e* right after the base number and before the exponent. For example, to create a variable named "bignumber" and assign it a value of 4.52×10^5 (452,000), put the letter *e* in place of everything between the number and the exponent (to represent the phrase "times 10 to the power of"):

```
var bignumber=4.52e5;
```

Note

JavaScript may return an answer to a calculation using exponential notation (like many calculators).

Strings

String variables are variables that represent a string of text. The string may contain letters, words, spaces, numbers, symbols, or most anything you like. Strings are defined in a slightly different way than numbers, using this format:

```
var variablename="stringtext";
```

Here are some examples of string variables:

```
var mycar="Corvette";
var oldcar="Big Brown Station Wagon";
var mycomputer="Pentium 3, 500 mHz, 128MB RAM";
var oldcomputer="386 SX, 40 mHz, 8MB RAM";
var jibberish="what? cool! I am @ home 4 now. (cool, right?)";
```

As you can see, strings can be short, long, or anything in between. You can place all sorts of text and other characters inside of string variables. However, there are the quotation marks, some special characters, and the case sensitivity of strings to consider.

Matching the Quotation Marks

In JavaScript, you define strings by placing them inside quotation marks (quotes, for short), as you saw in the examples. JavaScript allows you to use either double quotes or single quotes to define a string value. The catch is that if the string is opened with double quotes, it must be closed with double quotes:

```
var mycar="Red Corvette";
```

The same goes for single quotes:

```
var myhouse='small brick house';
```

Trying to close the string with the wrong type of quotation mark, or leaving out an opening or closing quotation mark, will cause problems.

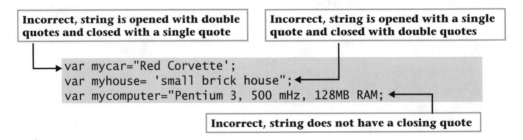

Incorrect, string is opened with double quotes and closed with a single quote

Incorrect, string is opened with a single quote and closed with double quotes

```
var mycar="Red Corvette';
var myhouse= 'small brick house";
var mycomputer="Pentium 3, 500 mHz, 128MB RAM;
```

Incorrect, string does not have a closing quote

These mistakes will result in an "Unterminated String" error in the Web browser.

Watching the Case

JavaScript strings are case-sensitive. This may not seem important now, but it matters when you need to compare strings for a match. It only takes one character having a different case to make the strings different:

```
"My car is fun to drive!"
"my car is fun to drive!"
```

You'll learn more about string comparisons in Module 5.

Using Special Characters

Special characters enable you to add things to your strings that could not be added otherwise. For example, suppose that you need a tab character between each word in a string. If you press the TAB key on the keyboard, JavaScript will probably see it as a bunch of spaces. Instead, use the special character code \t, which places a tab in the string, as in this example:

```
var mypets="dog\tcat\tbird";
```

In each spot where the special character code \t appears, JavaScript interprets tab characters.

The special codes all begin with a backslash character (\). Thus, if you want a single backslash character in your string, you will need to use the special code for a backslash: \\. For instance, suppose you wish to write the following sentence on a Web page: "Go to the directory c:\javascript on your computer." If you use the string as it is written, your code would look like this:

The single backslash won't be printed to the browser

```
<SCRIPT language="JavaScript">
<!--
document.write("Go to the directory c:\javascript on your computer.");
//-->
</SCRIPT>
```

The problem is that the single backslash would not be printed on the Web page. It would appear as

```
Go to the directory c:javascript on your computer
```

Unless the backslash is followed with the code for a special character, JavaScript prints the character after the slash as it appears (you will see this in the escape technique discussed in the next section). To fix this, use the \\ special code to print a single backslash on the page:

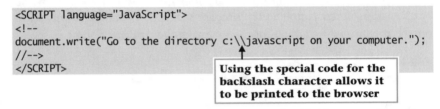

```
<SCRIPT language="JavaScript">
<!--
document.write("Go to the directory c:\\javascript on your computer.");
//-->
</SCRIPT>
```

Using the special code for the backslash character allows it to be printed to the browser

Now you get the sentence you want printed to the browser, like this:

```
Go to the directory c\:javascript on your computer.
```

The special characters used in JavaScript are shown in Table 3-1.

The special code used most often is probably the newline (\n) character. For example, the newline code (\n) can be handy here if you want the HTML code to appear on different lines when your JavaScript code is viewed from a browser.

Suppose that you want to print a sentence on a Web page in bold type. JavaScript allows you to print HTML code to the page as part of a string in the document.write method (which you used for your first scripts

Output Character	Special Code to Use
Backslash (\)	\\
Backspace	\b
Form feed	\f
Newline	\n
Carriage return	\r
Tab	\t

Table 3-1   Special JavaScript Characters

in Module 2). To print in bold type, you could just add in the <B> and </B> tags from HTML, as in this sample code:

```
<SCRIPT language="JavaScript">
<!--
document.write("<B>JavaScript Rules!</B> This is fun.");
//-->
</SCRIPT>
```

> **Note the HTML <B> and </B> tags within the JavaScript string**

Now suppose that you want the code itself to appear on two lines when it is viewed as the page source code, like this:

```
<B>JavaScript Rules!</B>
This is fun.
```

You can do this by adding the newline special character to the code:

```
<SCRIPT language="JavaScript">
<!--
document.write("<B>JavaScript Rules!</B>\n This is fun.");
//-->
</SCRIPT>
```

The \n special code is only a newline in JavaScript; it will not result in an HTML line break. The JavaScript newline code adds a new line only to the HTML *source code,* not to the result of the code shown in the browser display. So, the end result of the preceding code is a sentence like this one:

```
JavaScript Rules! This is fun.
```

If you want to add a line break in the browser display, you need to use the HTML BR tags to produce it.

Keep in mind that the JavaScript newline affects only the appearance of the source code; it does not play a factor in the end result. However, it does help later when you want to format the output of JavaScript alert boxes and various other JavaScript constructions.

Escaping Characters

JavaScript allows you to *escape* certain characters, so that they will show up correctly and avoid causing errors. Like special character codes, escape sequences use the backslash character (\), which precedes the character that needs to be escaped.

As noted earlier, if JavaScript sees a backslash character within a string, it will ignore the backslash and print the following character. This is useful if you want to have a quote within a string. For example, suppose that you want to print the following sentence on a Web page:

```
John said, "JavaScript is easy."
```

What would happen if you just threw it all into a document.write command?

```
<SCRIPT language="JavaScript">
<!--
document.write("John said, "JavaScript is easy."");
//-->
</SCRIPT>
```

The extra set of quote marks here will cause an error

If you look near the end of the document.write line, you will see that the two double quotes together could cause trouble, but the browser will actually get upset before that point. When the double quote is used before the word *JavaScript*, the browser thinks you have closed the string used in the document.write command and expects the ending parenthesis and semicolon. Instead, there is more text, and the browser gets confused.

To avoid problems with quotes, use the backslash character to escape the quotation marks inside the string. By placing a backslash in front of each of the interior double quote marks, you force them to be seen as part of the text string, rather than as part of the JavaScript statement:

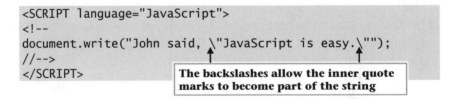

```
<SCRIPT language="JavaScript">
<!--
document.write("John said, \"JavaScript is easy.\"");
//-->
</SCRIPT>
```

The backslashes allow the inner quote marks to become part of the string

This fixes the problem with the string, and the sentence will print with the quotation marks.

Caution

Also watch for single quotes and apostrophes within strings. Escaping these is required for strings enclosed within single quotes.

The escape technique also works for HTML code in which you need quotation marks. For instance, if you want to put a link on a page, you use the anchor tag and place the URL in quotes. If you escape the quotes in the anchor tag, JavaScript allows you to write the HTML code to the page within the document.write method, as in this example:

```
<SCRIPT language="JavaScript">
<!--
document.write("<A HREF=\"http://someplace.com\">Text</A>");
//-->
</SCRIPT>
```

This does the job, but there is also an easier way to make this work if you do not want to escape quotation marks all of the time.

To avoid escaping the quotes in the preceding code, you could use single quotes around the URL address instead, as in this code:

```
<SCRIPT language="JavaScript">
<!--
document.write("<A HREF='http://someplace.com'>Text</A>");
//-->
</SCRIPT>
```

Single quotes within double quotes are okay

You can also do this the other way around if you prefer to use single quotes on the outside, as in this example:

```
<SCRIPT language="JavaScript">
<!--
document.write('<A HREF="http://someplace.com">Text</A>');
//-->
</SCRIPT>
```

Double quotes inside singles quotes are also okay

The important point to remember here is to be sure that you do not use the same type of quotation marks inside the string as you use to enclose the string. If you need to go more than one level deep with the quotes, you will need to start escaping the quotes; this is because if you switch again, it will terminate the string. For example, look at this code:

```
document.write("John said, 'Jeff says, \"Hi!\" to someone.'");
document.write("John said, 'Jeff says, "Hi!" to someone.'");
```

The first one would work, since the quotes are escaped to keep the string going. However, the second line only switches back to double quotes when inside the single quotes within the string. Placing the double quotes there without escaping them causes the string to terminate and gives an error.

As you can see, quotation marks can be a real pain when you need to use a large number of them within a string. However, remembering to use the backslash to escape the quotes when necessary will save you quite a few headaches looking for a missing quote. I've had to look for missing quotes in my code a number of times, and my head was spinning after a few of those encounters! Later in this module, you will see that you can add strings together, which can simplify the use of quotes for you.

Boolean

A *Boolean* variable is one with a value of true or false. Here are examples:

```
var JohnCodes=true;
var JohnIsCool=false;
```

Notice that the words *true* and *false* do not need to be enclosed in quotes. This is because they are reserved words, which JavaScript recognizes as Boolean values.

Instead of using the words *true* and *false*, JavaScript also allows you to use the number 1 for true and the number 0 (zero) for false, as shown here:

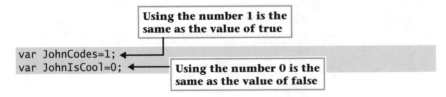

Using the number 1 is the same as the value of true

```
var JohnCodes=1;
var JohnIsCool=0;
```

Using the number 0 is the same as the value of false

Boolean variables are useful when you need variables that can only have values of true and false, such as in event handlers (covered in Module 7).

Note

When we talk about the concept of a *Boolean* variable, the first letter of the word *Boolean* is capitalized. However, the JavaScript reserved word *boolean* is written in all lowercase letters when you use the keyword in a script.

3

Null

Null means that the variable has no value. It is not a space, nor is it a zero; it is simply nothing. If you need to define a variable with a value of null, use a declaration like this:

```
var variablename=null;
```

As with the Boolean variables, you do not need to enclose this value in quotation marks as you do with string values, because JavaScript recognizes null as a keyword with a predefined value (nothing).

Null variables are useful when you test for input in scripts, as you'll learn in later modules.

Ask the Expert

Question: Why do I need to learn about variables? Couldn't I just put in the number or text I want to use right where I'm going to use it?

Answer: You can do that; however, it will make longer scripts much harder to write, read, and debug. It also makes it much more difficult to update your scripts because, in order to change that number or text, you would need to change every line where it appears. When you use variables, you can modify just one line of code to change the value of a variable every place it is used. As you gain more experience with JavaScript, you will see just how useful variables are.

Question: Why don't I need to define the type of number I am using (such as float or integer) when I declare a numeric variable?

Answer: JavaScript doesn't require this, which can be a good or bad feature depending on your perspective. To JavaScript, any number is just a number and can be used as a number variable.

Question: Why do I need to put quotation marks around the text in a string?

Answer: This is so JavaScript knows where a string begins and ends. Without it, JavaScript would be unsure what should be in a string and what should not.

Question: But doesn't a semicolon end a statement? Why not use that and lose the quote marks?

Answer: A variable declaration or any command involving strings can become more complex using the addition operator to add two strings and/or variables together. When this happens, JavaScript needs to know when one string stops and another begins on the same line.

Question: What does the backslash (\) character do, in general?

Answer: If the backslash is followed by a code to create a special character, the special character is rendered in its place. Otherwise, the first character after a single backslash is seen "as-is" by JavaScript and treated as part of the string in which it resides.

`pr3_1.html`

Project 3-1: Declare Variables

This project will give you the opportunity to practice declaring variables with various values. It will also print a short line of text on the page.

Step-by-Step

1. Create an HTML page, leaving the space between the <BODY> and </BODY> tags open.

2. Between the <BODY> and </BODY> tags, add the <SCRIPT> and </SCRIPT> tags, with the HTML comments between them, as you learned in Module 2.

3. Create a numeric variable named *chipscost* and give it the value 2.59.

4. Create a Boolean variable named *istrue* and give it the value false.

5. Create a variable named *nada* and give it the value null.

6. Create a JavaScript statement to write the string value that follows to appear in the browser. Remember to escape quotation marks when necessary:

John said, "This project is fun!"

7. The HTML document should look like this when you are finished:

```
<HTML>
<BODY>
<SCRIPT language="JavaScript">
<!--
var chipscost=2.59;
var istrue=false;
var nada=null;
document.write("John said, \"This project is fun!\"");
//-->
</SCRIPT>
</BODY>
</HTML>
```

8. Save the file as pr3_1.html and view it in your Web browser.

You should see only the text that you output with the document.write command. The variable definitions won't be printed on the browser screen. You can view the page source code to see how the variable definitions look in the code.

Using Variables in Scripts

To make a variable useful, you need to do more than just declare it in the script. You need to use it later in the script in some way, perhaps to print its value or even just to change its value. To use a variable, you make the call to a variable after it has been declared.

Making a Call to a Variable

The following code shows how to write the value of a variable to a Web page using the document.write method:

```
<SCRIPT language="JavaScript">
<!--
var mycar="Corvette";
document.write(mycar);
//-->
</SCRIPT>
```

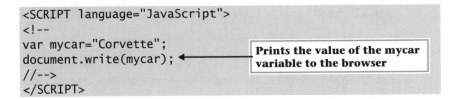

Prints the value of the mycar variable to the browser

The script begins by declaring a variable "mycar" and giving it a value of Corvette. Then, in the document.write command, you see that just the variable name mycar is enclosed within the parentheses. The result of this script is simply to write "Corvette" to the browser.

There are no quotation marks around what is being written to the page. The reason for this is that the mycar variable has already been given a string value, so it does not need to be within quotes to print its value to the page in the document.write command. Already, you can see how using a variable has the advantage of making a short document.write command easier to code.

Adding Variables to Text Strings

The preceding code just prints the value of the variable in the browser. If you want that variable to print along with some other text in a string, the document.write command becomes more complex. The text string needs quotes around it if it has not been defined as a variable, and the variable needs to be on its own. You use the addition operator (+) to add the value of the variable to the string, as shown in this example:

```
<SCRIPT language="JavaScript">
<!--
var mycar="Corvette";
document.write("I like driving my "+mycar);
//-->
</SCRIPT>
```

A variable is added to the string that is written to the browser

This code prints the following sentence in the browser window:

```
I like driving my Corvette.
```

Notice the space after the word "my" in the code. This ensures that a space appears before the variable is added to the string. If you used the line

```
document.write("I like driving my"+mycar);
```

the result would be

```
I like driving myCorvette.
```

When adding strings, you need to be careful to add the spaces you want to appear in the output.

The addition operator enables you to place a variable onto the beginning, the end, or even the middle of a string. To insert a variable into the middle of a string (so that it shows with text on both sides of it), just use another addition operator to add whatever you need to the right of the variable, as in this example:

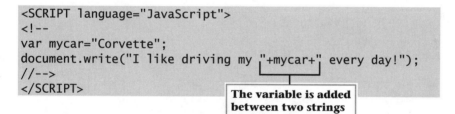

```
<SCRIPT language="JavaScript">
<!--
var mycar="Corvette";
document.write("I like driving my "+mycar+" every day!");
//-->
</SCRIPT>
```

The variable is added between two strings

Now the variable sits inside two text strings, putting a single string together from three pieces. This code prints the following sentence to the browser:

```
I like driving my Corvette every day!
```

When using the variable, you need to make sure that the variable and addition operators are not inside the quotation marks of a string.

If they are, you will not get the results you intended. For example, look at this code:

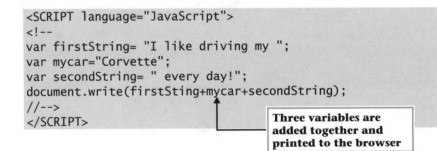

```
<SCRIPT language="JavaScript">
<!--
var mycar="Corvette";
document.write("I like driving my +mycar+ every day!");
//-->
</SCRIPT>
```

The addition operator must also be outside the quote marks to work

JavaScript will not recognize the operators and variables here; they are seen only as part of the text string because they are inside the quotes. Instead of using the variable, JavaScript takes everything literally and prints this sentence in the browser:

```
I like driving my +mycar+ every day!
```

To make this code easier to write, you could place every string involved into a variable, so that you only need to add the variable values together rather than dealing with the quotes, like this:

```
<SCRIPT language="JavaScript">
<!--
var firstString= "I like driving my ";
var mycar="Corvette";
var secondString= " every day!";
document.write(firstSting+mycar+secondString);
//-->
</SCRIPT>
```

Three variables are added together and printed to the browser

This prints the same sentence but allows you to change its parts later without needing to edit the document.write command.

The techniques you've learned in this section will become useful as your strings become more complex, especially when you use HTML code within the strings.

1-Minute Drill

- **What operator is used to add a variable to a string?**
- **Why does a variable need to be added to a string outside the quotation marks?**
- **What happens if you leave a variable name inside a set of quotation marks for a string?**

3

Writing a Page of JavaScript

Now that you know how to use variables and write basic HTML code to the page using JavaScript, you will create a page that is almost entirely written with JavaScript (everything inside the <BODY> and </BODY> tags), as a way to reinforce the techniques you have learned up to this point.

Creating the Framework

The first thing you need is a basic framework for the page so that you know where to insert your script. Since you are going to create everything within the <BODY> and </BODY> tags with JavaScript, your HTML page should look similar to this:

```
<HTML>
<HEAD>
<TITLE>A Page of JavaScript</TITLE>
</HEAD>
<BODY>
<SCRIPT language="JavaScript">
<!--
Script will go here        ◄——— Variable declarations and
//-->                              other JavaScript code will
</SCRIPT>                          be inserted here
```

- The addition (+) operator
- Because the variable has already been given a string value and, therefore, does not need to be within quotes
- The variable name will print as part of the string, rather than the value of the variable that you want to use

```
</BODY>
</HTML>
```

The code you place between the SCRIPT tags will determine what shows up in the browser when you have finished.

Defining the Variables

To begin your script, add a heading to the page. You could write the code as a string directly into the document.write command, as shown here:

```
document.write("<H1>A Page of JavaScript</H1>");
```

On the other hand, you could place the string inside a variable and use the variable inside the document.write command:

```
var headingtext="<H1>A Page of JavaScript</H1>";
document.write(headingtext);
```

For this example, you will go with the second method, since it makes use of a variable. You will see how this can be a handy feature as you get further into the script.

In fact, along with the headingtext variable, you'll create a bunch of variables to hold the strings of HTML code to add to the page. The next one will add a short sentence of introduction to the page. The variable declaration for the introduction will look like this:

```
var myintro="Hello, welcome to my JavaScript page!";
```

Next, you'll add a link to the page. The variable declaration for the link looks like this:

```
var linktag="<A HREF='http://www.pageresource.com'>Link to a Site</A>";
```

Next, you'll put in some red text to add a little color. Here's the redtext variable definition:

```
var redtext="<FONT COLOR='red'>I am so colorful today!</FONT>";
```

Finally, you'll add in some variables that give you just the opening and
closing boldface tags and a paragraph tag:

```
var begineffect="<B>";
var endeffect= "</B>";
var beginpara="<P>";
```

The code for all of the variables is as follows:

```
var headingtext="<H1>A Page of JavaScript</H1>";
var myintro="Hello, welcome to my JavaScript page!";
var linktag="<A HREF='http://www.pageresource.com'>Link to a Site</A>";
var redtext="<FONT COLOR='red'>I am so colorful today!</FONT>";
var begineffect="<B>";
var endeffect= "</B>";
var newsection="<P>";
```

Adding the Commands

Now you can add some document.write commands to create a small Web
page with the items you have:

```
document.write(headingtext);
document.write(begineffect+myintro+endeffect);
document.write(newsection);
document.write(linktag);
document.write(newsection);
document.write(redtext);
```

This writes the heading at the top of the page. Adding the begineffect
and endeffect variables to the left and right of the myintro variable writes
the introductory text in bold under the heading. After that is a new
paragraph, followed by a link, and then another new paragraph, followed
by the red text message.

Here is the entire code for the page up to this point:

```
<HTML>
<HEAD>
<TITLE>A Page of JavaScript</TITLE>
</HEAD>
<BODY>
```

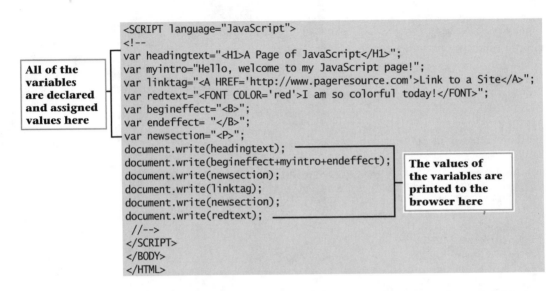

All of the variables are declared and assigned values here

```
<SCRIPT language="JavaScript">
<!--
var headingtext="<H1>A Page of JavaScript</H1>";
var myintro="Hello, welcome to my JavaScript page!";
var linktag="<A HREF='http://www.pageresource.com'>Link to a Site</A>";
var redtext="<FONT COLOR='red'>I am so colorful today!</FONT>";
var begineffect="<B>";
var endeffect= "</B>";
var newsection="<P>";
document.write(headingtext);
document.write(begineffect+myintro+endeffect);
document.write(newsection);
document.write(linktag);
document.write(newsection);
document.write(redtext);
  //-->
</SCRIPT>
</BODY>
</HTML>
```

The values of the variables are printed to the browser here

The end result of this code in the browser is shown in Figure 3-1. Note the bold introduction text and the use of paragraphs between sections.

Modifying the Page

Now suppose that you do not like the layout as it appeared on the Web page. Instead, you want the bold introduction to be in italics and the

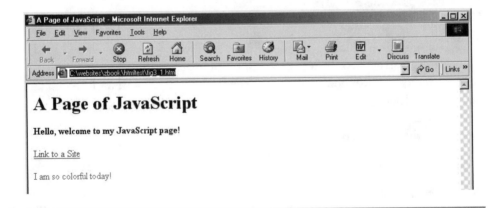

Figure 3-1   The result of the JavaScript code in a Web browser

paragraphs to be only single-line breaks. If you had written the document.write commands with plain strings rather than variables, you would need to search through the code to find the bold tags and change them to italic tags. Then, you would need to find every spot where you placed a paragraph tag and replace those tags with line break tags.

However, since you used the variables, all you need to do is change the values of the appropriate variables at the top of the script. You only need to change that paragraph tag once, and you don't need to look for the bold tags inside a bunch of code.

The code that follows shows the changes that you could make to the script to get the new effects. Notice how you only need to change the values of the begineffect, endeffect, and newsection variables to change the format of the text on the page:

```
<HTML>
<HEAD>
<TITLE>A Page of JavaScript</TITLE>
</HEAD>
<BODY>
<SCRIPT language="JavaScript">
<!--
var headingtext="<H1>A Page of JavaScript</H1>";
var myintro="Hello, welcome to my JavaScript page!";
var linktag="<A HREF='http://www.pageresource.com'>Link to a Site</A>";
var redtext="<FONT COLOR='red'>I am so colorful today!</FONT>";
var begineffect="<I>";  ◄
var endeffect= "</I>";  ◄
var newsection="<BR>";  ◄
document.write(headingtext);
document.write(begineffect+myintro+endeffect);
document.write(newsection);
document.write(linktag);
document.write(newsection);    Changed from <P> to <BR>
document.write(redtext);
 //-->                         Changed from </B> to </I>
</SCRIPT>
</BODY>                        Changed from <B> to <I>
</HTML>
```

Figure 3-2 shows how these changes affect the display of the page in a Web browser.

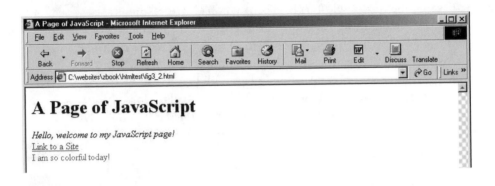

Figure 3-2 The page after changing some JavaScript variables

pr3_2.html, pr3_2_1.html

Project 3-2: Create an HTML Page with JavaScript

In this project, you will create an HTML page with JavaScript, similar to the one you created in this module. The variables will be given new values, and the differences should be noticeable.

Step-by-Step

1. Create an HTML page, leaving the space between the <BODY> and </BODY> tags open.

2. Between the <BODY> and </BODY> tags, add the <SCRIPT> and </SCRIPT> tags, with the HTML comments between them, as you learned in Module 2.

3. Create a variable named *myheading* and give it this value:

   This is My Web Page!

4. Create a variable named *linktag* and give it this value:

   <A HREF='http://www.javascriptcity.com'>Web Site Link!</A>

5. Create a variable named *sometext* and give it this value:

   This text can be affected by other statements.

6. Create a variable named *begineffect* and give it the value <U>.

7. Create a variable named *endeffect* and give it the value </U>.

8. Create a variable named *newsection* and give it the value <BR>.

9. Write the value of each variable to the Web browser in this order:

> myheading
> newsection
> begineffect
> sometext
> endeffect
> newsection
> linktag
> newsection
> sometext

When you have finished, the HTML document should look like this:

```
<HTML>
<BODY>
<SCRIPT language="JavaScript">
<!--
var myheading="This is My Web Page!";
var linktag="<A HREF='http://www.javascriptcity.com'>Web Site Link!</A>";
var sometext="This text can be affected by other statements.";
var begineffect="<U>";
var endeffect="</U>";
var newsection="<BR>";
document.write(myheading);
document.write(newsection);
document.write(begineffect);
document.write(sometext);
document.write(endeffect);
document.write(newsection);
document.write(linktag);
document.write(newsection);
document.write(sometext);
//-->
</SCRIPT>
</BODY>
</HTML>
```

10. Save the file as pr3_2.html and view the page in your Web browser.

11. Change the value of begineffect to \<B>.

12. Change the value of endeffect to \</B>.

13. Change the value of newsection to \<P>. When you have finished, the HTML document should look like this:

```
<HTML>
<BODY>
<SCRIPT language="JavaScript">
<!--
var myheading="This is My Web Page!";
var linktag="<A HREF='http://www.javascriptcity.com'>Web Site Link!</A>";
var sometext="This text can be affected by other statements.";
var begineffect="<B>";
var endeffect="</B>";
var newsection="<P>";
document.write(myheading);
document.write(newsection);
document.write(begineffect);
document.write(sometext);
document.write(endeffect);
document.write(newsection);
document.write(linktag);
document.write(newsection);
document.write(sometext);
//-->
</SCRIPT>
</BODY>
</HTML>
```

14. Save the file as pr3_2_1.html and view the page in your Web browser. Notice the differences resulting from the changes in the variable values.

☑ *Mastery Check*

1. Which of the following declares a variable named *pagenumber* and gives it a value of 240?

   A. var PageNumber=240;

   B. pagenumber=220;

   C. var pagenumber=240;

   D. var integer named Pagenumber=240;

2. Which of the following variable declarations uses a variable with a valid variable name in JavaScript?

   A. var default;

   B. var my_house;

   C. var my dog;

   D. var 2cats;

3. Which of the following string declarations is invalid?

   A. var mytext="Here is some text!";

   B. var mytext='Here is some text!';

   C. var mytext= "Here is some text!';

   D. var mytext= "Here is \n some text!";

4. Which of the following statements would be valid in JavaScript?

   A. document.write("John said, "Hi!"");

   B. document.write('John said, "Hi!"");

   C. document.write("John said, "Hi!");

   D. document.write("John said, \"Hi!\"");

☑ Mastery Check

5. Which of the following successfully prints a variable named *myhobby* by adding it to a set of strings?

A. document.write("I like to +myhobby+ every weekend");

B. document.write("I like to" +myhobby+ "every weekend");

C. document.write("I like to myhobby every weekend");

D. document.write("I like to 'myhobby' every weekend");

Module 4

Using Functions

The Goals of This Module

- Understand the purpose of functions
- Declare and properly structure a JavaScript function
- Use parameters and return statements in functions
- Call functions in scripts

As a JavaScript coder, you need to know how to use functions in your scripts. Functions can make your scripts more portable and easier to debug.

This module covers the basics of using functions. It begins with explanations of what functions are and why they are useful. Then you will learn how to define and structure functions. Finally, you will learn how to call functions in your scripts.

What Is a Function?

A *function* is basically a little script within a larger script. Its purpose is to perform a single task or a series of tasks. What a function does depends on what code you place inside it. For instance, a function might write a line of text to the browser or calculate a numeric value and return that value to the main script.

As you may recall from math class, a function can be used to calculate values on a coordinate plane. You may have seen calculations like these:

```
f(x)=x+2
y=x+2
```

Both are commonly used to calculate the *y* coordinate from the value of the *x* coordinate. If you need the *y* coordinate when *x* is equal to 3, you substitute 3 for *x* to get the *y* value: 3+2=5. Using the function, you find that when *x*=3, *y*=5.

The function itself is just sitting on the paper (or, in our case, the script) until you need to use it to perform its task. And you can use the function as many times as you need to, by calling it from the main script.

Why Are Functions Useful?

Functions help organize the various parts of a script into the different tasks that must be accomplished. By using one function for writing text and another for making a calculation, you make it easier for yourself and others to see the purpose of each section of the script, and thus debug it more easily.

Another reason functions are useful is their portability. They can be used more than once within a script to perform their task. Rather than rewriting the entire block of code, you can simply call the function again.

Consider the simple function $y=x+2$. If you use it only once, the function doesn't serve much purpose. If you need to get several values, however, the function becomes increasingly useful. Rather than writing out the formula for each calculation, you can just substitute the x values each time you need to get the y value. So, if you need the y value when x is 3, 4, and 5, you can use the function three times to get the y values. The function will calculate 5, 6, and 7, respectively. Instead of writing the content of the function three times, it only needs to be written once to get three answers.

Functions can perform complex tasks and can be quite lengthy. In the examples in this and later modules, you'll see just how useful and time-saving they are in JavaScript.

1-Minute Drill

● **Basically, what is a function?**

● **What are two reasons a function can be useful?**

● **Why does a function become more useful as it is used more often?**

● A little script within a larger script that is used to perform a single task or a series of tasks
● They provide a way to organize the various parts of a script into the different tasks that must be accomplished, and they are portable, so they can be reused
● Instead of writing the content of the function numerous times, it needs to be written only once to get many answers

Structuring Functions

Now that you understand what functions are and why you want to use them, you need to learn how to structure them in your scripts. A function needs to be declared with its name and its code. There are also some optional additions you can use to make functions even more useful. You can import one or more variables into the function, which are called *parameters*. You can also return a value to the main script from the function using the *return statement*.

Let's begin by looking at how the function begins.

Declaring Functions

On the first line of a function, you declare it as a function, name it, and indicate whether it accepts any parameters. To declare a function, you use the reserved word *function*, followed by its name, and then a set of parentheses:

```
function functionname()
```

The reserved word *function* tells the browser that you are declaring a function and more information will follow. The next piece of information is the function's name. After that, the set of parentheses indicates whether the function accepts any parameters.

For example, to name your function "reallycool" and say that it does not use any parameters, the first line looks like this:

```
function reallycool()
```

Because the function does not use any parameters, the parentheses are left empty. As with variable names, there are some special considerations for naming variables. You'll learn about those considerations after the discussion of the function structure.

You may have noticed that this line does not end with a semicolon, as do the other code lines you've seen so far in this book. This is because you use a different technique to show where the function's code begins and ends, as described next. However, each of the separate lines of code within the function does end with a semicolon, as you will see in the examples in this module.

Defining the Code for Functions

Curly brackets ({ }) surround the code inside the function. The opening curly bracket marks the beginning of the function's code; then comes the code; and, finally, the closing curly bracket marks the end of the function, in this format:

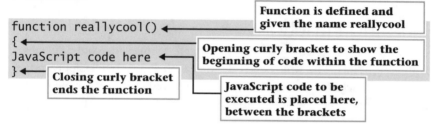

4

The browser will execute all of the code inside the curly brackets when the function is called (as you will learn later in this module). When the browser gets to the closing curly bracket, it knows the function has ended. The browser will move to the next line of code or continue whatever it was doing before the function was called.

You have some flexibility in formatting the curly brackets. There are two common ways to place the curly brackets into a script. The format shown in the preceding example "lines up" the brackets so that the opening and closing of the function are seen on the left margin of the code. This method is handy if you use other statements that need curly brackets (you will see some other statements that use curly brackets in later modules). By indenting each set of brackets, you make it easy to see which brackets are nested within the function and which ones begin and end the function itself.

The other common format is to put the opening bracket on the same line as the function declaration, rather than on the next line:

```
function reallycool() {      Opening bracket is on the
JavaScript code here         first line with the declaration
}                            of the function
```

In this format, the opening brackets of code blocks are seen to the right, and closing brackets appear on the left. This can be a useful technique if you wish to count how many brackets have been opened and/or closed within a segment of code.

The format you choose will likely depend on your background in programming and how you like to see the code. Either style is acceptable, so use the one that you feel most comfortable viewing and editing. In the examples in this book, I will place the curly brackets on their own lines (as in the first example format from this section).

Naming Functions

As with variables, functions need to be named carefully to avoid problems with your scripts. The same basic rules that applied to variables apply to the naming of functions: case-sensitivity, using allowed characters, avoiding reserved words, and giving functions memorable and meaningful names.

Note

If you already know the rules for naming variables, you may wish to skip this section, since the function-naming rules are essentially the same. However, there are some details about choosing names for functions that you may find useful.

Using Case in Function Names

Function names are case-sensitive, just like variable names. This means that reallycool, REALLYCOOL, and ReallyCool represent different functions. Remember that you need to call your functions using the same letter cases as you used in their declarations.

Using Allowed Characters and Avoiding Reserved Words

The characters that are allowed for function names are the same as those you can use for variable names:

- The function name must begin with a letter or an underscore character (_)
- The function name cannot contain any spaces

Also as with variable names, you cannot use JavaScript reserved words for function names. Doing so can cause the function to fail, which can cause real problems within a script. See Table 3-1 in Module 3 for a complete list of JavaScript reserved words.

Giving Functions Meaningful Names

Your functions will be easier to remember and to debug if you choose names that reflect their purpose. As you learned in Module 3, for a variable, you should use a name that represents its value, such as example_number to stand for the number of an example on a page. A function name should tell you something about what the function will do.

For example, suppose that you create a function that writes some text to the page. It could contain the following line of code:

```
document.write("<B>This is a bold statement!</B>");
```

4

You could just name the function *text*; but that might not be descriptive enough, because you could have other functions that also write text to the page. Instead, you might name it something like print_bold_text, so that you know that the function is used to print a piece of bold text to the browser. The full function is shown here:

```
function print_bold_text()
{
document.write("<B>This is a bold statement!</B>");
}
```

This name helps describe the purpose of the function

This line is the code that will be executed when the function is called

As with variables, the more functions you use in a script, the more important it becomes to use meaningful and memorable names for them.

Adding Parameters to Functions

Parameters are used to allow a function to import one or more values from somewhere outside the function. Parameters are set on the first line of the function inside the set of parentheses, in this format:

```
function functionname(variable1, variable2)
```

Any value brought in as a parameter becomes a variable within the function, using the name you give it inside the parentheses.

For example, here is how you would define a function reallycool with the parameters (variables) coolcar and coolplace:

```
function reallycool(coolcar,coolplace)◄——— Parameters are
{                                              added to the first
JavaScript code here                           line within the
}                                              parentheses
```

Notice that in JavaScript, you do not use the *var* keyword when you set the parameters for a function. JavaScript declares the variables automatically when they are set as parameters to a function, so the *var* keyword is not used here. For example, a line like this one could cause problems when the function is executed:

```
function reallycool(var coolcar, var coolplace)
```

Where do the parameters come from in the first place? They are obtained from outside the function when you make the function call. You will see how this works later in this module. For now, you just need to know how they are used as parameters to JavaScript functions.

Note

In other languages, it is often required that a variable have a declaration when set as a parameter, but JavaScript will do this for you. However, when you declare variables anywhere else, you need to use the var keyword.

Using Function Parameter Values

When you assign parameters to a function, you can use them like any other variables. For example, you could give the coolcar variable value to another variable by using the assignment operator, as in this example:

```
function reallycool(coolcar,coolplace)
{                                    The value of the coolcar
var mycar=coolcar;◄——————————        variable is assigned to
}                                    the mycar variable
```

This assigns the value of the coolcar parameter to a variable named "mycar. "

Instead of assigning its value to another variable, you could just use the coolcar parameter in the function, as in this example:

```
function reallycool(coolcar,coolplace)
{
document.write("My car is a "+coolcar);
}
```

> The value of the coolcar variable is used in a document.write() command

If the value of coolcar is Corvette, then the function would print this line to the browser when it is called:

```
My car is a Corvette
```

Notice that we gave the coolcar parameter a value out of the blue here. In actual use, the value must come from somewhere in the main script or another function, or the variable will have no value.

Using Multiple Parameters

You may have noticed that the previous example had two parameters but used only one parameter. A function can have as few or as many parameters as you wish. When you assign multiple function parameters, the function doesn't need to use all of them. It can use one parameter, a few, or none. How many are used depends on what the function does and how it is called.

The only rule is that if you have more than one parameter, you need to separate each parameter with a comma, so that the browser knows what to do.

In the previous example, the second parameter was not used. Here is how you could change the function to use both parameters:

```
function reallycool(coolcar,coolplace)
{
document.write("My car is a "+coolcar+" and I drive it to "+coolplace);
}
```

> Both parameters are used as variables in this document.write() command

Now, if the value of coolcar is Corvette and the value of coolplace is Las Vegas, the function would print the following line to the browser when it is called:

```
My car is a Corvette and I drive it to Las Vegas
```

You can place as many parameters as your function needs within the parentheses on the first line of the function. Here is an example with three parameters:

```
function reallycool(coolcar,coolplace,coolfood,coolbreeze)
```

Remember to separate each parameter with a comma when you have more than one.

Adding Return Statements to Functions

A return statement is used to be sure that a function returns a specific value to the main script, to be used in the main script. You place the return statement as the last line of the function before the closing curly bracket and end it with a semicolon. Most often, the value returned is the value of a variable, using the following format:

```
return variablename;
```

For example, to return the value of a variable cooltext, the return statement looks like this:

```
return cooltext;
```

This returns the value of cooltext to the place in the main script where the function was called.

Suppose that you want to write a function that returns the result of adding two strings together. You could use a return statement, as in this example:

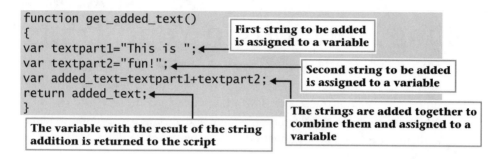

```
function get_added_text()
{
var textpart1="This is ";
var textpart2="fun!";
var added_text=textpart1+textpart2;
return added_text;
}
```

First string to be added is assigned to a variable

Second string to be added is assigned to a variable

The strings are added together to combine them and assigned to a variable

The variable with the result of the string addition is returned to the script

In this function, the first two variables are assigned string values, and the added_text variable is given the value of the addition of those two strings. The new value is sent back to the script where it was called. It returns this string:

```
This is fun!
```

This returned value is then used in the main script. As it is, this function is not very useful, because the strings were just defined in the function rather than being brought in as parameters.

You will see examples of more useful functions that use parameters and return statement in the next section.

1-Minute Drill

- **Which style should you use when you set up your curly brackets to enclose the content of a function?**

- **Why do the rules for naming functions seem familiar?**

- **What are parameters used for in a function?**

- The style you are comfortable viewing and using
- The rules for naming functions are similar to those for naming variables
- To allow a function to import one or more values from somewhere outside the function

Calling Functions in Your Scripts

Now that you know how the function itself works, you need to learn how to call a function in your script. A call to a function in JavaScript is simply the function name along with the set of parentheses (with or without parameters between the opening and closing parentheses), ending with a semicolon, like a normal JavaScript statement:

```
functionname();
```

You can call functions in the HEAD section of a page, or you can call them in the BODY section of the page. You can even call a function inside of another function.

A good rule to follow is to have the function definition come before the function call in the script. The easiest way to be sure that your function definition comes before your function call is to place all of your function definitions between the <HEAD> and </HEAD> tags on the page, as close to the beginning of the script as possible.

Defining a function before calling it is a suggestion for good coding practice, not a strict rule. A function can be called anywhere in JavaScript, but the function code must be loaded by the browser before the function will work. This is why it is suggested that you define your functions before calling them. If you were to call a function that is defined near the bottom of a document, there is a chance it would not load in time to be executed. Thus, it is normally best to define a function before it is called.

Calling a Function in the HEAD Section

When you build a function that you can call inside the HEAD section of the document, you need only one set of SCRIPT tags to complete the task. As an example, you will create a script that sends an alert message to the viewer as soon as the page is opened in the browser. To have a message pop up in a small message box, you use a JavaScript method called *window.alert*.

First, you'll learn how to create a JavaScript alert, and then you'll see how to build a function that uses that method and call the function in a script.

Creating a JavaScript Alert

Rather than writing something to the screen with the document.write method, you can create a JavaScript alert that pops up in a message box by using the window.alert method. Like the document.write method, the window.alert method takes the text string for the alert as a parameter, using this format:

```
window.alert("alert_text");
```

4

The string of text will be displayed in the alert pop-up box.

For example, suppose that you want to display "This is an alert!" in the pop-up box. You would write the command like this:

```
window.alert("This is an alert!");
```

Hint

The window.alert() method is often shortened to just alert() in scripts. You will learn more about using shortened commands in later modules. For now, the examples will use the full command.

Now you know how to make the alert pop up, but how can you get it to appear right as the page is opened? You can do this by making sure the window.alert method is called before the body of the Web page is loaded. By placing the script inside the <HEAD> and </HEAD> tags of the document, as shown next, you ensure that it will be executed before the rest of the page is loaded.

```
<HTML>
<HEAD>
<TITLE>Functions</TITLE>
<SCRIPT language="JavaScript">
<!--
window.alert("This is an alert!");        This line sends a
//-->                                      pop-up alert before
</SCRIPT>                                   the page is displayed
</HEAD>
<BODY>
HTML code here         The HTML for the
</BODY>                page would be here
</HTML>
```

As you can see, this would certainly be an easy way to show an alert when the page opens. However, because you are learning about functions, you will take another approach.

Using a Function for a JavaScript Alert

The following code uses a function to pop up an alert box as soon as the page opens:

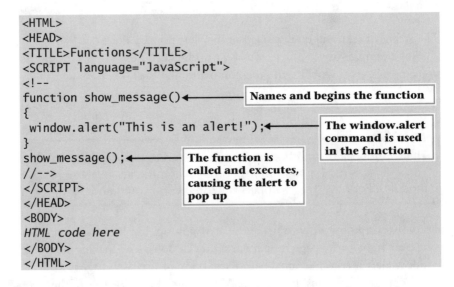

```
<HTML>
<HEAD>
<TITLE>Functions</TITLE>
<SCRIPT language="JavaScript">
<!--
function show_message()          Names and begins the function
{
  window.alert("This is an alert!");   The window.alert
}                                       command is used
show_message();                         in the function
//-->                    The function is
</SCRIPT>                 called and executes,
</HEAD>                   causing the alert to
<BODY>                    pop up
HTML code here
</BODY>
</HTML>
```

This example creates a function named show_message() to do the job of showing the alert. The alert will be shown only if you call the show_message() function somewhere after it is defined. In this case, the function is called right after its definition. The result is a small alert box with the message "This is an alert!"

Note

When an alert box appears, you may see the page pause until you click the OK button, or it may continue to load while waiting for you to click OK. This depends on your browser.

Even though the function is defined first, it doesn't mean it will be executed first. A function is not executed until it is called; in other words, JavaScript will not use the function until it gets to the function call in the script.

Any commands that come before the function call (and that are not part of the function definition) will be executed before the function. For instance, look over this code:

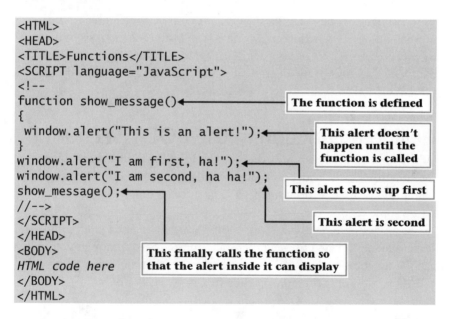

```
<HTML>
<HEAD>
<TITLE>Functions</TITLE>
<SCRIPT language="JavaScript">
<!--
function show_message()          ──────── The function is defined
{
  window.alert("This is an alert!");  ──── This alert doesn't
}                                          happen until the
window.alert("I am first, ha!");    ──────  function is called
window.alert("I am second, ha ha!");
show_message();                     ──────  This alert shows up first
//-->
</SCRIPT>                            ──────  This alert is second
</HEAD>
<BODY>
HTML code here      This finally calls the function so
</BODY>             that the alert inside it can display
</HTML>
```

This example defines the same function, show_message(), on the first line. The function definition line is followed by two lone window.alert commands, and then the line that calls the function.

4

The two lone alert commands are the first executable statements JavaScript will see, and they will come first. The call to our function is seen last, so the function is executed last. The result is three alerts, in this order:

● The user will get an alert, saying "I am first!," and will need to click the OK button to get rid of it.

● Then the alert that displays "I am second!" will appear, and the viewer will need to click the OK button again.

● Finally, the function is executed, and the viewer sees the alert "This is an alert!" and will need to click OK a third time to end the alert frenzy.

Although this example goes overboard with its alerts, it helps you understand how a function call works in the HEAD section, since it can be executed there. Next, you will learn how to make a function call in the BODY section of the document while the function is defined in the HEAD section.

Calling a Function in the BODY Section

When the entire script is placed inside the HEAD section, that's where the function call is made. However, you may need to call a function within the BODY section of a page. This is often done when your script writes some text on the page.

As an example, you will create a short function named *print_text* to write the text "I came from a function!" on the page. Although you will call the function in the BODY section, the function definition goes in the HEAD section of the document, like this:

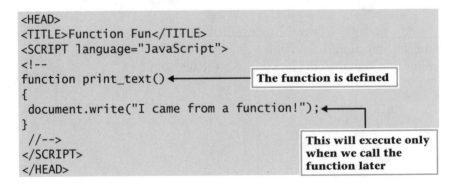

```
<HEAD>
<TITLE>Function Fun</TITLE>
<SCRIPT language="JavaScript">
<!--
function print_text()          The function is defined
{
  document.write("I came from a function!");
}
  //-->
</SCRIPT>                       This will execute only
</HEAD>                         when we call the
                               function later
```

This code creates the function print_text(), which will print a message on the page when it is called. Since calling it in the HEAD section could cause display problems (likely it would just show up at the top of the page, but that may not be where you want it to appear), you want to place the function call inside the <BODY> and </BODY> tags of the page.

But how do you call the function in another section of the script? You have already used SCRIPT tags in the HEAD section. Can you use them again? The answer is that you can use as many sets of SCRIPT tags as you need on a page. You just need to be sure that you don't have scripts that conflict with each other. In this case, the two sections could be thought of as part of the same script that are executed in different parts of the HTML: the HEAD section and the BODY section.

To make this example more interesting, you will add some HTML code on both sides of your script. You will place the script below a link and above some bold text on the page. Here is the code for the BODY of the page:

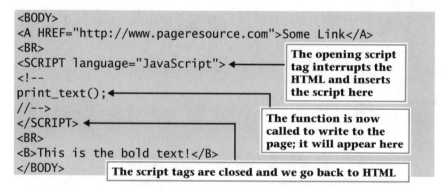

The BODY section begins with the code for a link, which is followed by a line break tag. This is where you insert your SCRIPT tags in order to call your function, since this is where you want the text from the function printed on the page. Then the only thing you need to do in the SCRIPT section is to call the function. The function is able to handle the rest, and it is executed at this time.

After the script, you see another line break tag and then the bold text. This is what will appear after the text that has been written from your script.

Let's put both pieces together to form the entire page. The code should look like this:

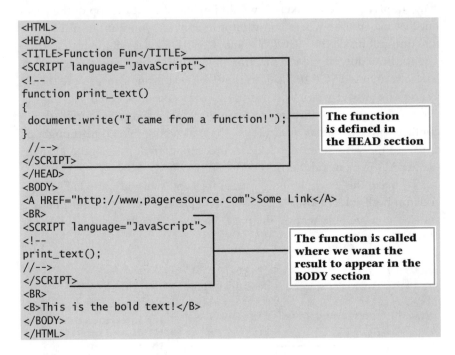

```
<HTML>
<HEAD>
<TITLE>Function Fun</TITLE>
<SCRIPT language="JavaScript">
<!--
function print_text()
{
 document.write("I came from a function!");
}
 //-->
</SCRIPT>
</HEAD>
<BODY>
<A HREF="http://www.pageresource.com">Some Link</A>
<BR>
<SCRIPT language="JavaScript">
<!--
print_text();
//-->
</SCRIPT>
<BR>
<B>This is the bold text!</B>
</BODY>
</HTML>
```

The function is defined in the HEAD section

The function is called where we want the result to appear in the BODY section

With all of this together, the result is the link, the function result, and the HTML text, appearing in that order.

Now that you know how to call a function in the BODY section, let's look at how to call one function from within another function.

Calling a Function from Another Function

Calling a function within another function can be a useful way to organize your sequence of events that will occur. Usually, the function is placed inside another function that has a larger task to finish.

When you place a function call within a function, you should define the function that will be called before you define the function that calls it. This is so you can follow the suggestion that a function should be defined before it is called.

Here is an example of two functions inside the HEAD section, where the second function calls the first one:

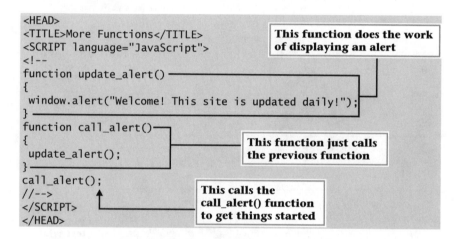

```
<HEAD>
<TITLE>More Functions</TITLE>
<SCRIPT language="JavaScript">
<!--
function update_alert()
{
 window.alert("Welcome! This site is updated daily!");
}
function call_alert()
{
 update_alert();
}
call_alert();
//-->
</SCRIPT>
</HEAD>
```

This function does the work of displaying an alert

This function just calls the previous function

This calls the call_alert() function to get things started

Notice that the update_alert() function is where all the real action happens. Everything else is a function call. The call_alert() function does nothing more than call the update_alert() function so that it is executed. Finally, you see the command that starts the entire sequence, which is the call to the call_alert() function.

Since this is the first JavaScript statement outside a function, it is executed first. When it is executed, it just calls the update_alert() function, which does the work of displaying the alert.

Note

Most browsers would execute the preceding example without a problem even if you defined the update_alert() function after you called it. However, there is a chance that some older browsers may not be as lenient and will want the function defined before it is called. Also, if the function definition is too far down the page to be loaded in time, it will not work correctly. Thus, it is normally best to define a function before it is called.

Now suppose that you want to create three functions to perform three tasks. To make sure that they occur in the correct sequence, you can call them in order from within another function. Here is an example of this technique with three functions that call alerts for various purposes:

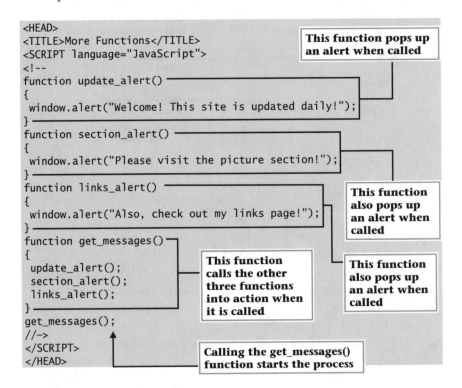

```
<HEAD>
<TITLE>More Functions</TITLE>
<SCRIPT language="JavaScript">
<!--
function update_alert()
{
 window.alert("Welcome! This site is updated daily!");
}
function section_alert()
{
 window.alert("Please visit the picture section!");
}
function links_alert()
{
 window.alert("Also, check out my links page!");
}
function get_messages()
{
 update_alert();
 section_alert();
 links_alert();
}
get_messages();
//-->
</SCRIPT>
</HEAD>
```

This function pops up an alert when called

This function also pops up an alert when called

This function also pops up an alert when called

This function calls the other three functions into action when it is called

Calling the get_messages() function starts the process

The code begins by defining the three functions to show each alert. Then it defines the get_messages() function, which just calls the previous three functions. Of course, the get_messages() function must be called to actually put this into action. This call happens as the first statement outside of a function.

Of course, creating a script that pops up message after message is not something you typically want to do. Although the example demonstrates the correct use of function calls, a script that does this would likely annoy your viewers! You'll see examples of practical uses of functions in later modules.

Calling Functions with Parameters

The previous example used three different functions to show three alerts. While it works, it would be nice if you did not need to write a new function for each alert. You can do this by using parameters. You can create a function to be used multiple times to do the same thing, but with the new information from the parameters each time.

As mentioned earlier in the module, variables are commonly used as parameters. However, you can also use a value as a parameter. You'll learn about the different types of variable parameters first, and then take a look at value parameters.

If you want to send the values of certain variables to the function, you must first declare the variables and then be sure that they have the values you need before you send them. Here, the *scope* of a variable becomes important. The scope of a variable determines where it can and cannot be changed. JavaScript has global and local variables.

Using Global Variables

Global variables are the variables that you learned about in Module 3. They are defined outside any functions, and so they can be changed anywhere in the script—inside or outside of functions. A global variable is declared anywhere outside a function, as in the following code:

```
<SCRIPT language="JavaScript">
<!--
var mycar="Honda";        These are global
var paycheck="1200";      variables being
//-->                     declared
</SCRIPT>
```

The variables in this example can be changed anywhere in the script. This means that they can even be accidentally overwritten or changed by a function.

To understand how global variables can be affected by a function, consider an example that shows two alerts. You want one alert to tell you how much money you need to get a certain car, and you want the other one to tell you how much money you currently have and what type of car you now own. What would happen if you used the following code?

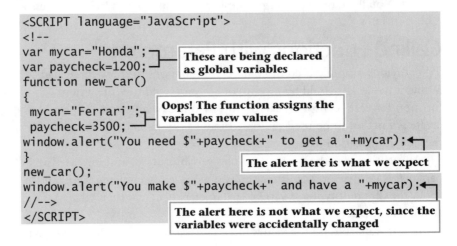

```
<SCRIPT language="JavaScript">
<!--
var mycar="Honda";
var paycheck=1200;                    These are being declared
function new_car()                    as global variables
{
  mycar="Ferrari";                    Oops! The function assigns the
  paycheck=3500;                      variables new values
window.alert("You need $"+paycheck+" to get a "+mycar);
}                                     The alert here is what we expect
new_car();
window.alert("You make $"+paycheck+" and have a "+mycar);
//-->                                 The alert here is not what we expect, since the
</SCRIPT>                             variables were accidentally changed
```

It may look as if you created new variables inside the function, even though they had the same name. However, the script would output the following text in the two alerts:

```
You need $3500 to get a Ferrari
You make $3500 and have a Ferrari
```

Obviously this isn't right.

This example demonstrates why you need to use the *var* keyword when declaring variables. Without the *var* keyword, you are not creating new variables inside the function (which would be local). Instead, you are changing the value of our global variables—you are issuing a reassignment command rather than a new variable command. To clear this up, you need to either change one set of variable names or use local variables, as described in the next section.

Using Local Variables

A *local variable* can be used only within the function in which it is declared. It does not exist outside that function, unless you pass it along to another function using a parameter.

The key to creating a local variable in a function is to be sure that you declare it using the *var* keyword. Otherwise, any global variables by that name could be changed, as you saw in the previous example. To declare a local variable, you must place it inside a function and use the *var* keyword, as shown in this code:

```
<SCRIPT language="JavaScript">
<!--
function new_car()
{
  var mycar="Honda";
  var paycheck="1200";
}
//-->
</SCRIPT>
```

These variables are declared as local variables, using the var keyword inside a function

4

The mycar and paycheck variables are now local variables, which can only be seen and changed by the new_car() function.

Therefore, in order to correct the script in the previous section, you just need to add the *var* keyword to declare the local variables inside the function, like this:

```
<SCRIPT language="JavaScript">
<!--
var mycar="Honda";
var paycheck=1200;
function new_car()
{
  var mycar="Ferrari";
  var paycheck=3500;
window.alert("You need $"+paycheck+" to get a "+mycar);
}
new_car();
window.alert("You make $"+paycheck+" and have a "+mycar);
//-->
</SCRIPT>
```

Adding the var keyword ensures that variables are declared locally and do not change the global variables by the same name

Now the alerts should appear as you intended:

```
You need $3500 to get a Ferrari
You make $1200 and have a Honda
```

As you can see, the scope of a variable can be important when you can send certain variables as parameters to a function.

Using Variables As Function Parameters

The following example uses variable parameters. It sends a global variable along to the function. It then assigns its value to a local variable to avoid any accidental changes.

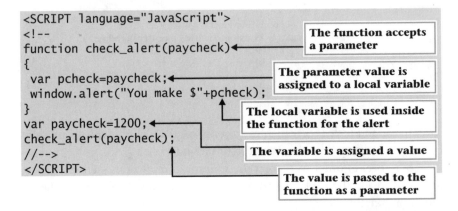

The script begins with the check_alert() function, which takes in the parameter paycheck. The line of code in the function assigns the value of paycheck to a local variable, pcheck. This way, you can use pcheck within the function to avoid changing the global paycheck variable. The function is then used to display an alert that uses the value of pcheck. After the function, in the outside script, the global variable paycheck is assigned a value of 1200. Then the code calls the check_alert() function and sends it the value of the paycheck variable.

The previous example shows a rather long way to keep from changing a global variable. Since function parameters are sent as values of variables, you can change the variable name the function accepts inside the parentheses in the function definition. This creates a local variable from the parameter that is sent to the function. Here is an example:

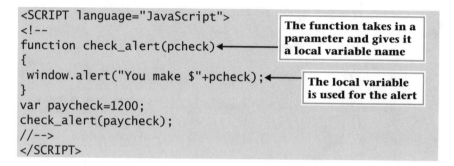

```
<SCRIPT language="JavaScript">
<!--
function check_alert(pcheck)◄─────  The function takes in a
{                                    parameter and gives it
                                     a local variable name
 window.alert("You make $"+pcheck);◄─── The local variable
}                                        is used for the alert
var paycheck=1200;
check_alert(paycheck);
//-->
</SCRIPT>
```

When this code calls the check_alert() function, it sends that function the value of the paycheck variable. The value is pulled in from the function itself. Rather than naming the value "paycheck" here and assigning it to another variable, you simply use another name within the parentheses: pcheck. The pcheck variable becomes a local variable inside the check_alert() function. Since the code sends paycheck a value of 1200, pcheck will be 1200, unless you change it later in the function.

Using Value Parameters

You can also send a value as a parameter directly. Instead of needing to declare a global variable in order to send a parameter, you can just send a value that will be turned into a local variable inside the function. This allows you to send a value on the fly rather than needing to have a global variable handy.

The important thing to remember is that if you send a string value, you need to enclose it in quotes. The following function call sends a string value of "something" to a function named *text_alert()*:

```
text_alert("something");
```

For example, the example in the previous section can be modified to add more information while using one less line by using value parameters:

```
<SCRIPT language="JavaScript">
<!--
function check_alert(pcheck,car)
{
  window.alert("You make $"+pcheck+" and have a "+car);
}
check_alert(1200,"Corvette");
//-->
</SCRIPT>
```

The function is sent a numeric value and a string value instead of variable values

In this example, the function call sends two parameters to the function. The first one is a numeric value and does not need quotes. The second value is a string and needs to be enclosed in quotes. These values are then sent to the function, where they are read in as the local variables pcheck and car, respectively. They can now be used in the function to display this sentence in an alert:

```
You make $1200 and have a Corvette
```

As you can see, the script used one less line than it did before the modification. The extra line was used to declare a global variable; but since you sent values, you did not need to have any additional variables.

By using parameters, you will be able to create more useful and portable functions within your scripts. This will be helpful when you start to create longer and more complex functions.

Calling Functions with Return Statements

To call a function and make use of a return statement in the function, you can assign the result of the function to a variable. In this way, the variable gets the value returned from the function and can be used later in the script. This is the format for declaring a variable that has the value returned by a function:

```
var variableame=functionname();
```

Consider the previous example, which had a function that returned the value of two text strings added together. You can modify it so that the function result is assigned to a variable, as follows:

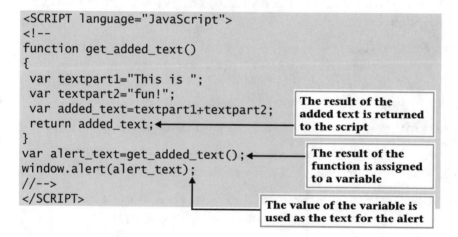

```
<SCRIPT language="JavaScript">
<!--
function get_added_text()
{
 var textpart1="This is ";
 var textpart2="fun!";
 var added_text=textpart1+textpart2;
 return added_text;          The result of the
}                            added text is returned
var alert_text=get_added_text();    to the script
window.alert(alert_text);
//-->                        The result of the
</SCRIPT>                     function is assigned
                             to a variable

                   The value of the variable is
                   used as the text for the alert
```

As you can see, the function returns the value of the added text variable to the script. By assigning the result of the get_added_text() function to the alert_text variable, you can use the added text later in the script. The variable is used to send an alert to the user with the result of the added text. The alert message reads

```
This is fun!
```

Now, isn't this fun? You'll see some more practical applications of return methods when you learn about form validation in Module 14.

Ask the Expert

Question: What if I put a function into my script but decide not to call it in the script? Will it matter?

Answer: No, because the function won't be executed unless it is called. The only things that it will do is take up extra space in your text editor and make the script longer than it has to be.

Question: What happens if I decide to remove a function from my script later?

Answer: This can cause trouble if you do not also remove any calls you made to the function. The script may cause a JavaScript error; or it may run, but give you unexpected results. Also, before you remove a function, make sure that it does not perform a necessary task someplace in the script.

Question: So, what happens if I call a function that doesn't exist?

Answer: Either you will get a JavaScript error or the browser will do nothing when the function is called, since it cannot find the function.

Question: What is the best way to know when to use a function and when to just code what I want right into the script?

Answer: For the most part, you will want to use a function if the code within the function will be reusable in some way. For instance, a function that performs a specific calculation might be useful in more than one spot in the script. Also, if you just like the idea of organizing the code a little more, a function helps with that. If you decide the code will be used just once in the script, you may just want to put the code right into the script as it is, rather than creating a function for it.

pr4_1.html

Project 4-1: Create an HTML Page with Functions

This project will create an HTML page with two JavaScript functions. One function will use parameters sent to it to pop up an alert box with a message. The other function will use a return statement to send a value back to the script. That returned value will then be used in an alert message to the viewer.

Step-by-Step

1. Create an HTML page, leaving the space between the <HEAD> and </HEAD> tags open.

2. Between the <HEAD> and </HEAD> tags, add the <SCRIPT> and </SCRIPT> tags.

3. Create a function named *car_cost()* that takes two parameters, mycar and paycheck. Create a window.alert command that will send a line like this one to the alert box:

```
You have a <mycar variable here> and make $<paycheck
variable here>
```

4. Create a function named get_added_text() that returns the value of two strings added together inside the function. The two strings to add are these two separate lines:

```
This project<space here>
is almost fun!
```

5. In the main script, call the car_cost() function, and send it the values of "Mustang" and 1500 as parameters.

6. In the main script, assign the result of the get_added_text() function to a variable named *alert_text*. Create an alert that pops up with the value of that variable.

4

7. When you have finished, your HTML document should look like this:

```
<HTML>
<HEAD>
<SCRIPT language="JavaScript">
<!--
function car_cost(mycar,paycheck)
{
 window.alert("You have a "+mycar+" and make $"+paycheck);
}
function get_added_text()
{
 var textpart1="This project ";
 var textpart2="is almost fun!";
 var added_text=textpart1+textpart2;
 return added_text;
}
car_cost("Mustang",1500);
var alert_text=get_added_text();
window.alert(alert_text);
//-->
</SCRIPT>
</HEAD>
<BODY>
</BODY>
</HTML>
```

8. Save the file as pr4_1.html and view it in your browser to see the result.

When you run this script, you should see two alert messages:

```
You have a Mustang and make $1500
This project is almost fun!
```

Putting It All Together

Now that you have learned the basics of using functions, take a look at the rather long page that follows. This page has some JavaScript added to the HTML document. Try to follow it through to see how it works and what it will do.

```
<HTML>
<HEAD>
<TITLE>Function Frenzy</TITLE>
<SCRIPT language="JavaScript">
<!--
function get_added_text(textpart1,textpart2)
{
 var added_text=textpart1+" "+textpart2;
 return added_text;
}
function print_text()
{
 var myfood=get_added_text("cheese","bread");
 document.write(myfood);
}
var alert_text=get_added_text("soup","crackers");
window.alert(alert_text);
//-->
</SCRIPT>
</HEAD>
<BODY>
<H1>"Welcome to my Function Page," I said.</H1>
<P>
<SCRIPT language="JavaScript">
<!--
print_text();
//-->
</SCRIPT>
<P>
<FONT COLOR="red">I'm seeing red!</FONT>
</BODY>
</HTML>
```

4

First, you see that there are two functions defined. The get_added_text() function is used to add two pieces of text, put a space between them, and return that value to where it was called. The print_text() function is used to send some text as parameters to the get_added_text() function, assign the result to a variable named "myfood", and print the result to the page itself.

The first command executed is the one right after all the function definitions in the HEAD section. It is this line:

```
var alert_text=get_added_text("soup","crackers");
```

This line is declaring a variable named *alert_text* and assigning it the value that is returned from the get_added_text() function when the function receives "soup" and "crackers" as the parameters. The result will be the two parameter values with a space between them. The returned string of "soup crackers" is now assigned to the alert_text variable.

The next line executed is the line directly afterward, shown here:

```
window.alert(alert_text);
```

This line is in the HEAD section, so it sends an alert message to the viewer before the rest of the page loads. The alert has the text assigned to the alert_text variable, which is the added string returned from the get_added_text() function.

After this, there is no more action until after the BODY section is opened. Here, you see there is some HTML code for a heading, and then a new paragraph. Next, there is another set of SCRIPT tags, which are used to call the print_text() function into action.

The first thing the print_text() function does is declare a variable named "myfood" and assign it the value returned from the get_added_text() function. It is sent the values of "cheese" and "bread" as parameters. So, the value returned is the string "cheese bread," which will be assigned to the myfood variable. The print_text() function then takes that value and writes it to the screen using the document.write() method.

4

Figure 4-1 | The alert box that appears before or while the page loads

Figures 4-1 and 4-2 show the results of this script when run in a browser. Figure 4-1 shows the alert box that pops up first, and Figure 4-2 shows the page the viewer sees after clicking OK in the alert box.

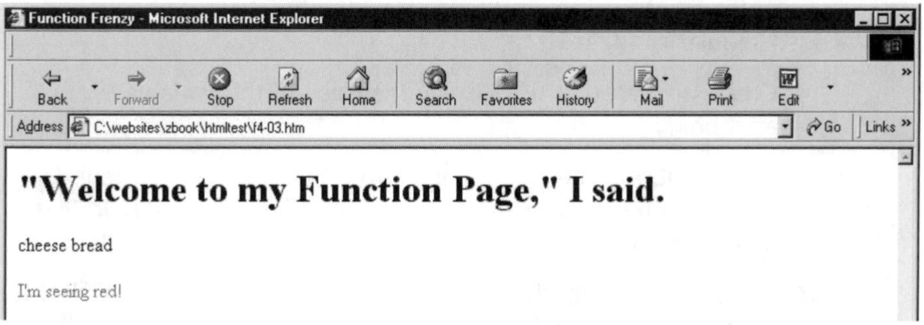

Figure 4-2 | The page that appears once the OK button in the alert box is clicked

`pr4_2.html`

Project 4-2: Write Your Own Functions

This project will create an HTML page with two JavaScript functions. For this project, you can use your own variable and function names and create your own version of the script.

Step-by-Step

1. Create one function that takes in two strings as parameters. Have it return the value of the two strings added together, but with a space between them.

2. Create a second function that will get the result of the first function and assign it to a variable. Write the value of this variable directly into the HTML document. The parameters to send to the first function are the strings "Hi" and "there!"

3. In the main script, create a new variable and assign it the result of the first function. This time, send the function the two strings "Regular" and "text!"

4. Create an alert that will display the value of this variable in an alert box.

5. In the BODY of the HTML page, write the result of the second function after a line of bold text reading "This is some bold text" and a new paragraph.

6. When you have finished, save the page as pr4_2.html and view it in your browser to see how it works.

The results should be an alert that says "Hi there!" followed by the page opening when OK is clicked in the alert box. The page should display a bold line of text reading "This is some bold text." On the next line, there should be text reading "regular text!"

☑ *Mastery Check*

1. In general, a function is a little _____ within a larger _____ that is used to perform a single _____ or a series of _____.

2. Which of the following would be a valid function name in JavaScript?

   A. function my function()

   B. function if()

   C. function get_text()

   D. function 24hours()

3. Which of the following is a valid use of the window.alert() method?

   A. win.alt("This is text");

   B. window.alert("This is text);

   C. window.alert('This is text");

   D. window.alert("This is text");

4. Which of the following correctly calls a function named *some_alert()* and sends it two string values as parameters?

   A. some_alert();

   B. some_alert("some","words");

   C. some_alert("some",words);

   D. SOME_alert("some","words")

5. Which of the following correctly assigns the result of a function named *get_something()* to a variable named *shopping*?

   A. var shopping=get_something();

   B. var shopping="get_something";

   C. var Shopping=get_Something();

   D. shopping=get_something;

4

Module 5

JavaScript Operators

The Goals of This Module

- Understand the purpose of JavaScript operators
- Explore the mathematical operators
- Find out about the assignment operators
- Understand the comparison operators
- Learn about the logical operators
- Recognize the bitwise operators

Operators do much of the work in scripts. In the previous modules, you have seen examples of the use of the assignment (=) and addition (+) operators. JavaScript offers many other types of operators to perform various operations.

This module begins with an introduction to the different types of JavaScript operators. Then you will learn about each operator and its use in scripts. Finally, you will learn about the order of precedence for operators, which determines which operations are performed before others.

Understanding the Operator Types

An *operator* is a short symbol in JavaScript that performs some sort of calculation, comparison, or assignment on one or more values. In some cases, an operator provides a shortcut to shorten the code so you need to type less.

Common calculations include finding the sum of two numbers, combining two strings, or dividing two numbers. Some common comparisons might be to find out if two values are equal or to see if one value is greater than the other. A shortcut assignment operator might be used to assign a new value to a variable without the need to type the variable name twice.

JavaScript uses several different types of operators:

- **Mathematical** These operators are most often used to perform mathematical calculations on two or more values. The mathematical operators will probably be the most familiar to you. They use symbols such as +, −, and *.

- **Assignment** These operators are used to assign new values to variables. As you learned in Module 3, the assignment operator is the symbol =.

- **Comparison** These operators are used to compare two values, two variables, or perhaps two longer statements. They use symbols such as > (for "is greater than") and < (for "is less than").

- **Logical** These operators are used to compare two conditional statements to see if one or more of the statements is true and to proceed accordingly. They use symbols such as && (returns true if the statements on both sides of the operator are true) and || (returns true if a statement on either side of the operator is true).

- **Bitwise** These are logical operators that work at the bit level (ones and zeros). They use symbols like << (for left shifting bits) and >> (for right shifting bits).

   In this module, you will learn about each of these types of operators. This will be a general overview of the function of each type of operator, so that you will better know the purpose of them when you put them to use later. To begin, you'll look at the mathematical operators in JavaScript.

1-Minute Drill

- **What is an operator?**
- **What sort of symbols might you see for mathematical operators?**
- **What are some uses of JavaScript operators?**

- A short symbol in JavaScript that allows you to perform some sort of calculation, comparison, or assignment on one or more values
- Symbols such as +, –, *, and others
- To perform calculations, comparisons, or assignments, or to shorten the code

5

Mathematical Operators

For a mathematical calculation, you use a mathematical operator. The values used can be any sort of values you like. For instance, you could use two variables, two numbers, or a variable and a number. A few of these operators are able to perform a task on a single variable's value.

As a quick example, you will remember that you used the addition operator (+) to add two strings together in previous modules. Here is an example of two string values being combined with the addition operator:

```
window.alert("I begin and "+"this is the end.");
```

You can also use the addition operator when one of the values is a variable, as in this example:

```
var part2="this is the end."
window.alert("I begin and "+part2);
```

The addition operator also works when both values are variables, as in the next example:

```
var part1="I begin and ";
var part2="this is the end."
window.alert(part1+part2);
```

These examples illustrate how you can use many of the mathematical operators with a number of values and/or variables. This allows you some flexibility in the way you code your scripts.

The three operators that work on single values are the increment, decrement, and unary negation operators. The increment and decrement operators are actually shortcuts to adding or subtracting one, so learning how to use them could save you some coding time.

The mathematical operators and their functions are summarized in Table 5-1. The following sections discuss each operator in more detail.

Operator	Symbol	Function
Addition	+	Adds two or more values
Subtraction	–	Subtracts one value from another
Multiplication	*	Multiplies two or more values
Division	/	Divides one value by another
Modulus	%	Divides one value by another and returns the remainder
Increment	++	Shortcut to add 1 to a single number
Decrement	– –	Shortcut to subtract 1 from a single number
Unary negation	–	Makes a positive negative or a negative positive

Table 5-1	**The Mathematical Operators**

5

The Addition Operator (+)

As you have seen, the addition operator can be used for combining two strings. It is also used to add numbers in mathematical calculations.

Variables for Addition Results

When adding numerical values, you often assign the result to a variable and use the variable later to make use of the result. For example, to calculate the value of 4 plus 7 and show the result, you could code it like this:

```
var thesum=4+7;        ← Two numbers are added with the addition operator
window.alert(thesum);  ← The result of the addition is
                          shown as an alert to the viewer
```

The result is an alert that says "11."

To make the example a little more complex, you could change one of the numbers to a variable:

```
var num1=4;             ← A number is assigned to a variable
var thesum=num1+7;      ← A number is added to the variable and
window.alert(thesum);      the total is assigned to a new variable
```

The result is the same as the previous example's code: an alert that says "11."

Taking the example one step further, you could make both of the numbers variables:

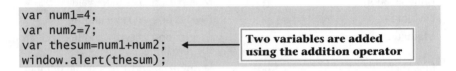

```
var num1=4;
var num2=7;
var thesum=num1+num2;
window.alert(thesum);
```

Two variables are added using the addition operator

This example allows for the most flexibility, since you can change the values of the two number variables and get a new result without needing to dig deeper into the script to make the change.

Type Conversions in Addition Calculations

When you use the addition and other mathematical operators, you need to be aware that JavaScript will automatically convert different values (like an integer and a float) to the appropriate type. For instance, you might place the following code in the HEAD section of a document:

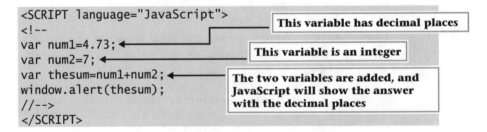

```
<SCRIPT language="JavaScript">
<!--
var num1=4.73;
var num2=7;
var thesum=num1+num2;
window.alert(thesum);
//-->
</SCRIPT>
```

This variable has decimal places

This variable is an integer

The two variables are added, and JavaScript will show the answer with the decimal places

When the script is run, you will see an alert with the result.

Microsoft Internet Explorer ⊠

⚠ 11.73

OK

JavaScript added the integer and the float together and gave back a float: 11.73. JavaScript does this often, so you need to make sure that you have the right sort of values when you begin adding.

For example, if you add a number and a string, the result will come out as though you had added two strings. Look at this example:

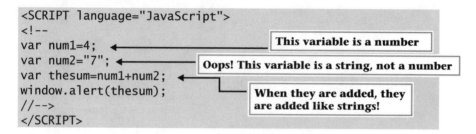

```
<SCRIPT language="JavaScript">
<!--
var num1=4;          ◄───── This variable is a number
var num2="7";        ◄───── Oops! This variable is a string, not a number
var thesum=num1+num2;  ◄───── When they are added, they
window.alert(thesum);          are added like strings!
//-->
</SCRIPT>
```

This looks as if it would be adding the numbers 4 and 7, since they both appear to be numbers. The trouble is that the 7 is a string in this case, not a number, because it has quotes around it. This causes the 4 to be converted to a string, and then the two strings are added (combined). The result that appears in the alert box may surprise you.

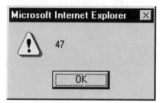

Rather than the expected answer of 11, you get 47. When the two values are added as strings, they are strung together rather than added mathematically. With strings, "4"+"7"=47.

The other mathematical operators also do conversions, much like the addition operator. You'll see how this can be important later, when you learn how to take user input in your scripts.

The Subtraction Operator (–)

The subtraction operator is used to subtract the value on its right side from the value on its left side, as in mathematics. Here is an example:

```
var theresult=10-3;    ◄───── Two numbers are subtracted
window.alert(theresult);        using the subtraction operator
```

This code simply subtracts 3 (the number on the right of the operator) from 10 (the number on the left of the operator). The result is an alert that says "7."

As with the addition operator, you can use variables to hold the numbers you are working with, as in this example:

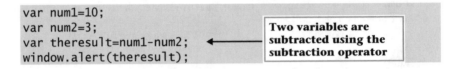

```
var num1=10;
var num2=3;
var theresult=num1-num2;      Two variables are
window.alert(theresult);       subtracted using the
                               subtraction operator
```

The result is the same as the previous example: an alert that says "7."

The use of variables with mathematical operators also works with the multiplication, division, and modulus operators, which are described in the next sections.

The Multiplication Operator (*)

The multiplication operator multiplies the two values on each side of the operator by each other. Again, this is just like mathematical multiplication. The next example shows this operator in action:

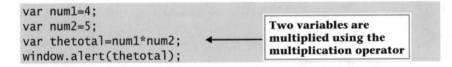

```
var num1=4;
var num2=5;
var thetotal=num1*num2;       Two variables are
window.alert(thetotal);        multiplied using the
                               multiplication operator
```

Here, you get an alert that says "20", the result of 4 times 5. This operator shouldn't give you too many surprises, so let's move onto the division operator.

The Division Operator (/)

The division operator is used to divide the value on its left side by the value on its right side. For example, the code 4/2 means 4 divided by 2 and gives the result of 2.

For a JavaScript example of this in action, take a look at this code:

```
var num1=10;
var num2=2;
var theresult=num1/num2;     ◄─────  Two numbers are divided using
window.alert(theresult);            the division operator
```

This will give us an alert that says "5", the result of dividing 10 by 2.

Division by Zero

When you use the division operator, you need to be careful that you do not end up dividing by zero in some way. If you do, the result is either going to be infinity or undefined, depending on your browser. The code that follows shows an example of this happening (although it is unlikely to occur exactly in this way):

5

```
<SCRIPT language="JavaScript">
<!--
var num1=10;
var num2=0;
var theresult=num1/num2;     ◄─────  Oh no! On this line we
window.alert(theresult);     ◄─────  are dividing by zero!

//-->                                This alert won't
</SCRIPT>                            be a number
```

If you placed this code in the HEAD section of a document, you might see an alert box like this:

To avoid dividing by zero, be careful about what numbers or variables are placed on the right side of the division operator.

Type Conversions in Division Calculations

Another thing to remember with division is that if you have two values that do not divide evenly, the result is converted into a float, and thus will have decimal places. The code that follows shows an example:

```
var num1=3;
var num2=4;
var theresult=num1/num2;
window.alert(theresult);
```

The result in this case is 0.75, which is what you see in the alert box. Some browsers may not show the zero before the decimal, and display just ".75" in the alert box instead.

This example showed a simple calculation; but the result can get much longer, depending on the numbers used. In later modules, you will learn some techniques for formatting the output, so that the viewer doesn't end up seeing something like .75664421004.

The Modulus Operator (%)

The modulus operator is used to divide the number on its left side by the number on its right side, and then give a result that is the integer remainder of the division. Think back to when you learned long division and used remainders as part of the answer rather than converting to decimals or fractions. Dividing 11 by 2 gives 5 with a remainder of 1. The remainder of 1 is what the modulus operator gives you when you write 11%2.

In order to see an example in JavaScript, let's look at this code:

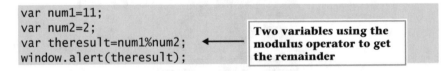

```
var num1=11;
var num2=2;
var theresult=num1%num2;     ←——  Two variables using the
window.alert(theresult);           modulus operator to get
                                   the remainder
```

The result is an alert box that shows the value of the remainder, which is 1. If the calculation had no remainder, the result would be zero.

This is the last of the mathematical operators that work on two or more values at the same time. The next operators work on only one value at a time.

The Increment Operator (++)

The increment operator can be used on either side of the value on which it operates. It increases the value it is operating on by 1, just like adding 1 to the value. The actual result depends on whether the operator is used before or after the value it works on, called the *operand*. This operator is often used with variables, and often within loops (covered in Module 6).

The Increment Operator Before the Operand

When the increment operator is placed before the operand, it increases the value of the operand by 1, and then the rest of the statement is executed. Here is an example:

```
var num1=2;
var theresult=++num1;
```

In this case, the variable num1 begins with a value of 2. However, when the code assigns the value to the variable theresult, it increments the value of num1 before the assignment takes place. The increment occurs first because the increment operator is in front of the operand. So, the value of num1 is set to 3 (2+1) and is then assigned to the variable theresult, which gets a value of 3.

The Increment Operator After the Operand

If you place the increment operator after the operand, it changes the result of an assignment. Consider this example:

```
var num1=2;
var theresult=num1++;
```

As in the previous example, num1 begins with the value of 2. On the next line, the increment operator is used after the operand. This means that the code assigns the current value of num1 to the variable theresult, and *after* that is done, it increments the value of num1. So, only after this assignment is complete do you have a new value for num1. The variable theresult is given a value of 2, and then num1 is changed to 3. If we use num1 after this, it will have a value of 3.

5

Another way to see how the increment operator works before and after the operand is to run the following script in your browser. You can place it in the HEAD section of your HTML code. Notice what the values are in the first alert and what they are in the second alert.

```
<SCRIPT language="JavaScript">
<!--
num1=2;
result= ++num1;
alert("num1= "+num1+" result= "+result);
num1=2;
result= num1++;
alert("num1= "+num1+" result= "+result);
//-->
</SCRIPT>
```

In the first alert box, you will see num1= 3 result= 3. Since the ++ operator is used before the operand here, the value of num1 is increased by 1 and then assigned to the result variable. In the second alert box, you will see num1= 3 result= 2. This is because the ++ operator is used after the operand, so the value of num1 is increased after it has been assigned to the result variable. The result variable gets a value of 2, but num1 will be increased to 3.

Note

Don't worry if the difference between using the increment operator before and after the operand is still not clear to you. When you learn how to use loops in later modules, you will see how the placement of this operator can be quite important.

The Decrement Operator (−−)

The decrement operator works in the same way as the increment operator, but it subtracts 1 from the operand rather than adding 1 to it. As with the increment operator, its placement before or after the operand is important.

If you place the decrement operator before the operand, the operand is decremented, and then the remainder of the statement is executed. Here is an example:

```
var num1=2;
var theresult=--num1;
```

Here, the variable num1 is given a value of 2. In the next line, the code subtracts 1 from num1 and then assigns the result to the variable theresult. Thus, the variable theresult ends up with a value of 1 (2–1).

When you place the operator after the operand, as in the next example, the rest of the statement is executed and the operand is decremented afterward.

```
var num1=2;
var theresult=num1--;
```

This time, the variable theresult is assigned a value of 2, and then num1 is decremented to 1. If you use num1 after this line, it will have a value of 1.

As with the increment operator, the decrement operator becomes important when you work with loops, as you will learn in later modules.

The Unary Negation Operator (–)

Unary negation is the use of the subtraction sign on only a single operand. This operator creates a negative number or negates the current sign of the number (positive or negative).

Here is an example of assigning a negative value to a number:

```
var negnum=-3;
```

This defines a variable with a value of negative 3. Basically, the operator tells the browser that the 3 is "not positive," because it negates the default sign of positive by placing the negation operator ahead of the number.

You can also use the unary negation operator to help show the addition or subtraction of a negative number, as in this example:

```
var theresult=4+(-3);
```

Notice the parentheses around the −3 portion of the statement. As in math, you can use parentheses to set the order of operations (as you'll learn later in this module) or just to clarify the order visually. Here, the parentheses aren't necessary, but they help organize that code so that you can see that it is adding −3 to 4. You could have written this code as well:

```
var theresult=4+-3;
```

This doesn't look as nice, but it still works.

You may be thinking that an even easier way to write the same thing looks like this:

```
var theresult=4-3;
```

You're right, this is the simplest way to write it; but it uses subtraction rather than unary negation.

Now that you've learned about the mathematical operators, let's turn to the assignment operators.

Assignment Operators

Assignment operators assign a value to a variable. They do not compare two items, nor do they perform logical tests.

When you learned about variables in Module 3, you saw how the basic assignment operator, the single equal sign (=), is used to give an initial value or a new value to a variable, as in this example:

```
var mytime=0;
```

As you know, this assigns a value of zero to a variable mytime.

The other assignment operators also give new values to variables, but they do so in slightly different ways because they perform a simple calculation as well. These operators are particularly useful within loops, as you'll learn in later modules.

Table 5-2 summarizes the assignment operators, which are each discussed in more detail in the following sections.

Operator	Symbol	Function
Assignment	=	Assigns the value on the right side of the operator to a variable
Add and assign	+=	Adds the value on the right side of the operator to the variable on the left side, and then assigns the new value to the variable
Subtract and assign	−=	Subtracts the value on the right side of the operator from the variable on the left side, and then assigns the new value to the variable
Multiply and assign	*=	Multiplies the value on the right side of the operator by the variable on the left side, and then assigns the new value to the variable
Divide and assign	/=	Divides the variable on the left side of the operator by the value on the right side, and then assigns the new value to the variable
Modulus and assign	%=	Takes the integer remainder of dividing the variable on the left side by the value on the right side, and assigns the new value to the variable

Table 5-2   The Assignment Operators

The Assignment Operator (=)

You have been using the direct assignment operator since Module 3. It assigns the value on the right side of the operator to the variable on the left side, as in this example:

```
var population=4500;
```

This assigns the value of 4500 to the variable population.

The more complex assignment operators come next, so let's begin with the operator used to add to a variable and assign it a new value.

The Add-and-Assign Operator (+=)

The += operator adds the value on the right side of the operator to the variable on its left side and then assigns the variable that new value. In essence, it is a shortcut to writing the type of code shown here:

```
var mymoney=1000;
mymoney=mymoney+1;
```

Here, the variable mymoney is created and assigned a value of 1000. The code then changes the value by assigning it a value of itself plus 1. The value assigned to the mymoney variable is 1001.

Instead of writing the variable name an extra time, you can use the add-and-assign operator to shorten the code. The following code gives the same result as the previous example, but saves a little typing:

```
var mymoney=1000;
mymoney+=1;
```

Using the add-and-assign operator, this code adds 1 (the value on the right) to mymoney (the variable on the left), assigning the new value of 1001 to the variable mymoney.

This operator can be used to add any value, not just 1. For example, you could add 5 in the assignment, as in this example:

```
var mymoney=1000;
mymoney+=5;
```

This time, mymoney ends up with a value of 1005.

You can even use a variable rather than a plain number value on the right side, as in this example:

```
var mymoney=1000;
var bonus=300;
mymoney+=bonus;
```

Here, bonus has a value of 300, which is added to the variable mymoney, and then mymoney is assigned the result of 1300. In this way, the value of the bonus variable can be changed to affect the result of the assignment.

The Subtract-and-Assign Operator (−=)

The −= operator works like the += operator, except that it subtracts the value on the right side from the variable on the left side. This value is then assigned to the variable. Here is an example of this operator in action:

```
var mymoney=1000;
var bills=800;
mymoney-=bills;
```

This example subtracts the value of the bills variable (800) from
the mymoney variable and assigns the result to mymoney. In the end,
mymoney has a value of 200. Since this is so similar to the add-and-assign
operator, let's move on to the next one (which is also very similar).

The Multiply-and-Assign Operator (*=)

The *= operator multiples the value on the right side of the operator by
the variable on the left side. The result is then assigned to the variable.
The next example shows this operator at work:

```
var mymoney=1000;
var multby=2;
mymoney*=multby;
```

Here, the variable mymoney is multiplied by the value of the multby
variable, which is 2. The result of 2000 is then assigned to the variable
mymoney.

The Divide-and-Assign Operator (/=)

The /= operator divides the variable on the left side of the operator by the
value on the right side. The result is then assigned to the variable. Here is
an example:

```
var mymoney=1000;
var cutpayby=2;
mymoney/=cutpayby;
```

In this example, the variable mymoney is divided by the value of the
variable cutpayby, which is 2. The result of 500 is then assigned to
the mymoney variable.

5

The Modulus-and-Assign Operator (%=)

Like the other assignment variables that also perform math, the %= operator does a calculation for the variable assignment. It divides the variable on the left side of the operator by the value on the right side, takes the integer remainder of the division, and assigns the result to the variable. Here is how you might assign a value to the mymoney variable using the modulus–and–assign operator:

```
var mymoney=1000;
var cutpayby=2;
mymoney%=cutpayby;
```

Here, the variable mymoney is divided by the value of the variable cutpayby, which is 2. The result of that is 500 with no remainder, meaning that the end result of the calculation is zero. Thus, zero is the value that gets assigned to the variable mymoney. (If they start cutting pay like this anyplace, it is probably time to leave!)

1-Minute Drill

● **Why is a mathematical operator used?**

● **Why shouldn't you divide by zero in JavaScript?**

● **What does an assignment operator do?**

● To perform a mathematical calculation on two or more values
● The answer will be infinity or undefined, depending on the browser
● It assigns a new value to a variable

pr5_1.html

Project 5-1: Adjust a Variable Value

This project will create a page that makes use of some of the mathematical and assignment operators, and writes the results on an HTML page.

There is more than one solution that can be used for many of these steps, so feel free to use the method you prefer. You can also try to see which method requires the least typing. Be sure to write the results of each change to the page using the document.write command.

Step-by-Step

1. Create an HTML page, leaving the space between the <BODY> and </BODY> tags open. This is where you will insert your SCRIPT tags and the script within the SCRIPT tags.

2. Create a variable named *paycheck*, and give it an initial value of 2000.

3. Using only an assignment operator, increase the value of paycheck to 4000.

4. Using a mathematical operator, decrease the value of paycheck to 3500.

5. Using a mathematical operator, decrease the value of paycheck to 0 (zero).

6. Using a mathematical operator, increase the value of paycheck to 500.

7. Finally, using an assignment operator, decrease the value of paycheck to 420.

8. After you perform each action, write the value of the paycheck variable on the page.

5

9. A possible solution is shown in the following code, but keep in mind there are several ways to achieve the same results:

```
<HTML>
<BODY>
<SCRIPT language="JavaScript">
<!--
var paycheck=2000;
document.write(paycheck+"<BR>");
paycheck+=2000;
document.write(paycheck+"<BR>");
paycheck=paycheck-500;
document.write(paycheck+"<BR>");
paycheck=paycheck*0;
document.write(paycheck+"<BR>");
paycheck=paycheck+500;
document.write(paycheck+"<BR>");
paycheck-=80;
document.write(paycheck+"<BR>");
//-->
</SCRIPT>
</BODY>
</HTML>
```

Comparison Operators

Comparison operators are often used with conditional statements and loops in order to perform actions only when a certain condition is met. Since these operators compare two values, they return a value of either true or false, depending on the values on either side of the operator. In later modules, you will learn how to create a block of code to be performed only when the comparison returns true.

Table 5-3 summarizes the comparison operators, and they are discussed in more detail in the following sections.

Operator	Symbol	Function
Is equal to	==	Returns true if the values on both sides of the operator are equal to each other
Is not equal to	!=	Returns true if the values on both sides of the operator are not equal to each other
Is greater than	>	Returns true if the value on the left side of the operator is greater than the value on the right side
Is less than	<	Returns true if the value on the left side of the operator is less than the value on the right side
Is greater than or equal to	>=	Returns true if the value on the left side of the operator is greater than or equal to the value on the right side
Is less than or equal to	<=	Returns true if the value on the left side of the operator is less than or equal to the value on the right side

Table 5-3　The Comparison Operators

The Is-Equal-To Operator (==)

For the == operator to return true, the values or statements on each side must be equal. They cannot just be close; they must be exactly the same. If they are not exactly equal, the == operator returns false. Table 5-4 shows examples of statements that use the is-equal-to operator, their return values, and the reason why they return true or false.

Comparison	Return Value	Reason
4==4	True	Two equal numbers
(4+2)==(3+3)	True	Result on both sides is 6, and 6 is equal to 6
"my socks"=="my socks"	True	Both strings are exactly the same

Table 5-4　Examples of == Statements

Comparison	Return Value	Reason
("my "+ "socks")==("my"+" socks")	True	Results of string additions return equal string values
4==5	False	4 and 5 are not equal numbers
(4+3)==(2+2)	False	Result on the left side is 7, result on the right side is 4, and these are not equal
"My socks"=="my socks"	False	Strings are not exactly alike (capitalization)
("my"+"socks")==("my "+"socks")	False	Result on left has no space character; result on right does, causing the strings to be unequal

Table 5-4   Examples of == Statements *(continued)*

Note

You will notice the addition of parentheses around some of the statements in Table 5-4, as well as in some of the tables that come later. Here, they are used mainly for readability. You will learn more about parentheses and the order of operations near the end of this module.

As with the other operators, you can use variables with comparison operators. If the values of the variables are equal, the comparison will return true. Otherwise, it will return false. Suppose that you have declared the following variables:

```
var num1=2;
var num2=5;
var num3=5;
```

The following comparison would return true:

```
num2==num3
```

The next comparison would return false:

```
num1==num3
```

Caution

Remember that the is-equal-to operator (==) is for comparison. Be careful not to accidentally use the assignment operator (=) in its place, because it can cause your scripts to work incorrectly.

The Is-Not-Equal-To Operator (!=)

The != operator is the opposite of the == operator. Instead of returning true when the values on each side of the operator are equal, the != operator returns true when the values on each side of it are *not* equal. The only way to return a false value with this operator is when it finds that the values on both sides of the operator are equal. Table 5-5 shows some examples of statements that use the != operator, their return values, and the reason they return true or false.

The Is-Greater-Than Operator (>)

When the greater-than operator is used, the comparison returns true only if the value on the left side of the operator is greater than the value on the right side. Like the other operators, the > operator works with string values as well as numeric ones. But how can one string be greater than another string?

In the case of strings, a lowercase letter is greater than a capital letter, and a capital letter is greater than a number. When comparing strings, JavaScript first checks the first letter of the string for a difference. If there is no difference, it moves on to the next character, then the next one, and so on, until it finds a difference or reaches the end of the string. If the two values on each side of the > operator are equal, it returns false. If the value on the right side is greater, this also returns false. Table 5-6 shows some examples of statements that use the greater-than operator.

Comparison	Return Value	Reason
4!=3	True	4 and 3 are not equal numbers
"CooL"!="cool"	True	Strings do not have the same capitalization, so they are not equal
4!=4	False	4 is equal to 4, so this returns false
"cool"!="cool"	False	Strings are exactly alike, so they are equal

Table 5-5 Examples of != Statements

Comparison	Return Value	Reason
5>2	True	5 is a larger number than 2
0>–2	True	0 is larger than negative numbers, such as –2
"a">"A"	True	Lowercase letters are greater than capital letters in strings
"A"> "1"	True	Letters in strings are greater than numbers in strings
5>7	False	5 is less than 7, not greater
–1>0	False	Negative numbers are less than zero, not greater
"Q">"q"	False	Capital letters are less than lowercase letters in strings
"3">"B"	False	Letters are greater than numbers, not less than numbers
2>2	False	These are equal, so the value on the left is not greater

Table 5-6   Examples of > Statements

The Is-Less-Than Operator (<)

The less–than operator works in reverse from the greater–than operator. Rather than returning true when the value on the left is greater, the less–than operator returns true when the value on the left side of the operator is less than the value on the right side of the operator. This comparison operator will return false if the value on the left side of the operator is greater than or equal to the value on the right side. Again, you can see how this works by looking at the examples in Table 5–7.

Comparison	Return Value	Reason
2<10	True	2 is a smaller number than 10
"A"<"a"	True	Capital letters are less than lowercase letters in strings

Table 5-7   Examples of < Statements

Comparison	Return Value	Reason
10<2	False	10 is greater than 2, not less
"a"<"A"	False	Lowercase letters are greater than capital letters in strings, not less
10<10	False	These are equal, so the value on the left is not less

Table 5-7 Examples of < Statements *(continued)*

The Is-Greater-Than-or-Equal-To Operator (>=)

The >= operator is slightly different from the comparison operators you've read about so far. This operator adds an option for the values on both sides to be equal and still have the comparison return true. So, to return true, the value on the left side of the operator must be greater than or equal to the value on the right side. A greater-than-or-equal-to comparison will return false only if the value on the left side is less than the value on the right side. Table 5-8 shows some examples of statements that use that greater-than-or-equal-to operator.

Comparison	Return Value	Reason
5>=2	True	5 is a larger number than 2
2>=2	True	2 is equal to 2
"a">="A"	True	Lowercase letters are greater than capital letters
"A">="A"	True	The strings are equal
1>=2	False	1 is less than 2
"A">="a"	False	Capital letters are less than lowercase letters, not greater or equal to

Table 5-8 Examples of >= Statements

The Is-Less-Than-or-Equal-To Operator (<=)

Much like the >= operator, the <= operator adds the possibility for the values on each side to be equal. With the less-than-or-equal-to operator, a value of true is returned if the value on the left side of the operator is less than or equal to the value on the right side of the operator. Table 5-9 shows examples of statements that use the less-than-or-equal-to operator.

You'll get some practice using this and the other comparison operators when you learn about conditional statements and loops in Module 6. Next up are the logical operators, which are also used to check conditions.

Logical Operators

The three logical operators allow you to compare two conditional statements to see if one or more of the statements is true and to proceed accordingly. They can be useful if you want to check on more than one condition at a time and make use of the results. Like the comparison operators, the logical operators return either true or false, depending on the values on either side of the operator.

Table 5-10 summarizes the logical operators, which are discussed in the following sections.

Comparison	Return Value	Reason
2<=5	True	2 is a smaller number than 5
2<=2	True	2 is equal to 2
"A"<="a"	True	Capital letters are less than uppercase letters
"A"<="A"	True	The strings are equal
5<=2	False	5 is greater than 2, not less than or equal
"a"<="A"	False	Lowercase letters are greater than capital letters, not less than or equal

Table 5-9   Examples of <= Statements

Operator	Symbol	Function
AND	&&	Returns true if the statements on both sides of the operator are true
OR	||	Returns true if a statement on either side of the operator is true
NOT	!	Returns true if the statement to the right side of the operator is not true

Table 5-10   The Logical Operators

5

The AND Operator (&&)

The logical operator AND returns true if the comparisons on both sides of the && operator are true. If one or both comparisons on either side of the operator are false, a value of false is returned. Table 5-11 shows some statements that use the AND operator.

Statement	Return Value	Reason
(1==1)&&(2==2)	True	Comparisons on both sides are true: 1 is equal to 1, and 2 is equal to 2
(2>1)&&(3<=4)	True	Comparisons on both sides are true: 2 is greater than 1, and 3 is less than 4
("A"<="A")&&("c"!="d")	True	Comparisons on both sides are true: "A" is equal to "A", and "c" is not equal to "d"
(1==1)&&(2==3)	False	Comparison on the right is false
("a"!="a")&&("b"!="q")	False	Comparison on the left is false
(2>7)&&(5>=20)	False	Comparisons on both sides are false

Table 5-11   Examples of && Statements

The OR Operator (||)

The logical operator OR will return true if the comparison on either side of the operator returns true. So, for this to return true, only one of the statements on one side needs to evaluate to true. To return false, the comparisons on both sides of the operator must return false. Table 5-12 shows some examples of comparisons using the OR operator.

The NOT Operator (!)

The logical operator NOT can be used on a single comparison to say, "If this is not the case, then return true." Basically, it can make an expression that would normally return false return true, or make an expression that would normally return true return false. Table 5-13 shows some examples of this operator at work.

Now that we have the logical operators down, let's take a quick look at the bitwise operators.

Statement	Return Value	Reason
(2==2)||(3>5)	True	Comparison on the left is true
(5>17)||(4!=9)	True	Comparison on the right is true
(3==3)||(7<9)	True	Both comparisons are true
(4<3)||(2==1)	False	Both comparisons are false
(3!=3)||(4>=8)	False	Both comparisons are false

Table 5-12 Examples of || Statements

Comparison	Return Value	Reason
!(3==3)	False	3 is equal to 3 is true, but the NOT operator makes this statement false
!(2>5)	True	2 is not greater than 5 is false; the NOT operator makes the statement true

Table 5-13   Examples of ! Statements

The Bitwise Operators

Bitwise operators are logical operators that work at the bit level, where there are a bunch of ones and zeros. You will not be using them in the examples presented in this book, but you may see them in some scripts on the Web. Table 5-14 lists some of the bitwise operators and their symbols. This list is by no means complete, but it should help you spot a bitwise operator if you see one.

Operator	Symbol
AND	&
XOR	^
OR	|
NOT	~
Left Shift	<<
Right Shift	>>
Right Shift (Zero-Fill)	>>>

Table 5-14   The Bitwise Operators

Ask the Expert

Question: Why are there so many assignment operators? If I can write $x=x+1$ instead of $x+=1$, why do I need to know about the extra assignment operators?

Answer: They are provided as shortcuts, so you don't need to type the variable name a second time in the same line. They also cut down the overall size of the script a bit, which helps with the loading time of the Web page. You can use either method; it just depends on how much you want to trim the script size or avoid extra typing. Also, it is good to know what these assignment operators do, so that you can recognize their purpose in scripts.

Question: Can I use more than one operator at a time in a statement? What will happen if I do that?

Answer: Yes, you can use multiple operators in a single statement. The operators will be executed according to their precedence in the order of operations, which is covered in the next section.

Question: What is with all of the parentheses? Why are they used in some cases but not in others? Is there a reason for them?

Answer: The parentheses used so far have been added for the readability of the statements. In some cases, it is necessary to use parentheses to get a desired result. This is something else that is covered in the next section.

Question: Are there any common typos that are made with all of these operators?

Answer: Often, the assignment operator (=) gets used in place of the comparison operator (==) because the second equal sign is left off by accident. Also, forgetting to use && and typing just & is another common typo that can cause trouble in a script. The same sort of mistake can occur with the logical OR (||) and bitwise OR (|) operators.

Order of Operations

In JavaScript, the operators have a certain order of precedence. In a statement with more than one operator involved, one may be executed before another, even though it is not in that order in the statement. For instance, look at this example:

```
var answer=8+7*2;
```

If you remember how this works in mathematics, you will know that the multiplication is performed first on the 7*2 part of the statement, even though it does not look like that is the right order when you read from left to right. The reason the multiplication is performed first is that the multiplication operator has a higher precedence in the order of operations than the addition operator. So, any multiplication done within a statement will be performed before any addition, unless you override it somehow.

As with math problems, in JavaScript, the way to override the order of operations is through the use of parentheses to set off the portion of the statement that should be executed first. Thus, if you wanted to be sure the addition was performed first in the preceding example, you would write it as shown here instead:

```
var answer=(8+7)*2;
```

If you use more than one set of parentheses or operators of the same precedence on the same level, then they are read from left to right, as in this example:

```
var answer=(8+7)-(4*3)+(8-2);
```

Since the parentheses are all on the same level (not nested), they are read from left to right. The addition and subtraction operators outside the parentheses have the same precedence, and thus are also read from left to right.

The precedence of the JavaScript operators is shown in Table 5-15, ranked from highest precedence (done first) to lowest precedence (done last).

5

Type of Operator	Example of Operators
Parentheses (overrides others)	( )
Unary (mathematical, logical, or bitwise)	– ++ –– ! ~
Multiplication, division, modulus	* / %
Addition, subtraction	+ –
Shifts (bitwise)	>>> >> <<
Relational comparison	> >= < <=
Equality comparison	== !=
AND (bitwise)	&
XOR (bitwise)	^
OR (bitwise)		
AND (logical)	&&
OR (logical)	||
Assignment	= += –= *= /= %=

Table 5-15 Operator Precedence, from Highest to Lowest

As you can see in Table 5-15, parentheses override the other operators. Parentheses are handy when you are unsure of the precedence of various operators or if you want to make something more readable.

pr5_2.html

Project 5-2: True or False?

This project will allow you to experiment with some of the comparison operators to see how they work. You will create a script that shows an alert stating whether or not a statement or comparison will return true. The script will use a conditional if/else statement, which is explained in detail in the next module.

Step-by-Step

1. Insert the code that follows between the <HEAD> and </HEAD> tags of your page.

```
<SCRIPT language="JavaScript">
<!--
var num1=0;
```

```
var num2=0;
if(num1==num2) {
 window.alert("True");
}
else {
 window.alert("False");
}
//-->
</SCRIPT>
```

2. Save the page as pr5_2.html and open it in your browser. You should instantly see an alert saying "True."

3. Change the value of the variable num1 to 5. Resave the file and refresh your browser. You should now get an alert saying "False."

4. In the following line of code, change the == operator to the > operator:

```
if(num1==num2) {
```

5. Resave the file and refresh your browser. You should get "True" again.

6. Change the value of the variable num2 to 7.

7. Resave the file and refresh your browser. You should now get "False" again.

8. In the following line (which you changed in step 4), change the operator to the < operator.

```
if(num1>num2) {
```

9. Resave the file and refresh your browser. You should get "True" again.

10. Try to change the value of the num1 variable so that you get an alert that says "False" instead.

11. Try your own tests with the other comparison operators to see what the results will be.

5

✓ *Mastery Check*

1. Which of the following is not a JavaScript operator?

   A. =

   B. ==

   C. &&

   D. $#

2. What does an assignment operator do?

   A. Assigns a new value to a variable

   B. Gives a variable a new name

   C. Performs a comparison

   D. Assignment operators do nothing because they are useless

3. What does a comparison operator do?

   A. Performs a mathematical calculation

   B. Deals with bits and is not important right now

   C. Compares two values or statements, and returns a value of true or false

   D. Compares only numbers, not strings

4. Which of the following statements will return true?

   A. (3==3)&&(5<1)

   B. !(17>=20)

   C. (3!=3)||(7<2)

   D. (1==1)&&(2<0)

5. Which of the following statements will return false?

   A. !(3<=1)

   B. (4>=4)&&(5<=2)

   C. ("a"=="a")&&("c"!="d")

   D. (2<3)||(3<2)

Module 6

Conditional Statements and Loops

The Goals of This Module

- Learn about conditional statements and their structure
- Learn about loops and their structure
- Identify the various types of conditional statements and loops
- Know how conditional statements and loops are used in scripts

Now that you have seen how the various operators work in JavaScript, this module will instruct you in how to put them to good use. Conditional statements and loops enable us to make use of the mathematical, comparison, and logical operators because they enable us to do things only when a condition is met (conditional statements) or to do things repeatedly (loops).

We will begin by introducing conditional statements. We will see why they are useful, and we will learn about each of the conditional statement blocks and how to use them. After that, we will move on to the topic of loops. We will learn what they are and why they are useful to us in scripts. Finally, we will cover each type of loop and learn how to make use of it within our scripts. To get started, let's take a look at conditional statements.

Defining Conditional Statements

In order to use conditional statements, we need to know what they are and why they are useful to us in our scripts.

What Is a Conditional Statement?

A conditional statement is a statement that we can use to execute a bit of code based on a condition or to do something else if that condition is not met. You can think of a conditional statement as being a little like cause and effect. Perhaps a good way to parallel it would be to use something a parent might say, as in the following text:

```
"If your room is clean, you will get dessert. Otherwise, you will go to bed
early."
```

The first cause would be a clean room, which would have the effect of getting dessert. The second cause would be an unclean room, which would have the effect of an early bedtime. In our scripts, we may want to create a similar statement. Perhaps something more like the following line:

```
"If a variable named mymoney is greater than 1000, send an alert that says
my finances are OK. Otherwise, send an alert saying I need more money!"
```

In this case, the first cause would be a variable having a value greater than 1000, which would have the effect of an alert that says things are OK. The second cause is the variable being less than 1000. If this happens, we get an alert saying we need more money.

As you can see, if we can create statements like these in our scripts, we will be able to do quite a bit more than we have with our scripts in the past.

Why Conditionals Are Useful

As we saw in the previous section, a conditional statement can be quite useful to us. Rather than executing every single line of code in the script as is, we could have certain sections of the script only be executed when a particular condition is met. We could even expand that single condition into a combination of conditions that need to be met for parts of the code to run.

With conditionals, we can tell JavaScript to do things such as the following:

- If a variable named "yourname" is equal to John, then write a line to the page that says hello to John. Otherwise, write a line to the page that says hello to Unknown Surfer and have it be in bold type.

- If a variable named "mycar" is equal to Corvette or Mustang, then send an alert saying "Cool Car" to the browser. Otherwise, send an alert that says "My car is cooler" to the viewer.

- If a variable named "yourname" is equal to John and a variable named "mycar" is equal to Corvette or Mustang, then send an alert that says "John drives a cool car" to the browser. Otherwise, send an alert that says "Unknown surfer drives a car of some sort" to the viewer.

I don't really drive a Corvette or a Mustang, so that leaves me out of the cool crowd here; however, these examples do show how we can make our scripts more useful by adding a way to check for certain conditions before an action takes place in the script.

We can make statements (such as the preceding statements) as simple or complex as we need them; however, the trick is in how to code all these statements so that JavaScript will interpret them as we mean them to be interpreted. We will learn how to do this shortly, when we move on to the various types of conditional statements we can use in our scripts.

6

1-Minute Drill

- **What is a conditional statement?**
- **A conditional statement can be thought of as being similar to what?**
- **Why are conditional statements useful?**

Conditional Statements

Now that we know what conditional statements are, it's time to look at them in more detail and learn how to code them. We will be looking at the two types of conditional statement blocks used in JavaScript: the if/else statement blocks and the switch statement blocks. To begin, we will look at the if/else statement blocks, which are used quite often in JavaScript.

Using If/Else Statement Blocks

While using conditional statements, we will see that they are similar to functions in some ways. Most notable are the curly brackets ({}) that surround the sections of code that will be executed given a condition. To see more on how this works, let's look at the basic structure of an if/else statement block.

If/Else Statement Block Structure

The first thing we must deal with in an if/else statement is the first line, which tells the browser to continue or move along. We begin an if/else statement with the JavaScript keyword if, followed by a comparison in parentheses. The following line shows a sample of the format of the first line:

```
if (comparison here)
```

- A conditional statement is a statement that we can use to execute a bit of code based on a condition or to do something else if that condition is not met
- A conditional statement is similar to cause and effect
- Rather than executing every single line of code in the script as is, certain sections of the script may only be executed when a particular condition is met

We will replace the comparison here text with an actual comparison. To do this, we need to remember the comparison operators from the previous module. Suppose we want to see if a variable named "boats" is equal to 3. The following is how we write the first line of the if/else block:

```
if (boats==3)
```

Remember that a comparison will return a value of true or false. This is where the return value becomes useful. If the comparison of boats==3 returns true, we can go on to the next line. If it returns false, the browser begins looking for the else keyword, or the first line of script after the block following the if line is completed.

If the comparison returns true, we need to make a block of statements after the if line that will be executed. To do this, we use the curly brackets similarly to the way we enclosed commands for a function. The following code shows how to add the brackets to enclose the code that will execute if the comparison returns true:

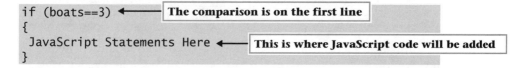

```
if (boats==3)  ◄──────  The comparison is on the first line
{
 JavaScript Statements Here  ◄───  This is where JavaScript code will be added
}
```

If the comparison of boats==3 returns true, the code we place within the brackets will be executed. If it returns false, the code inside the brackets is ignored and the line of code after the closing curly bracket is executed.

If we wish to use an else block to execute a certain bit of code when the comparison returns false, we place the else keyword on the next line and then follow it with its own set of curly brackets, as in the following code:

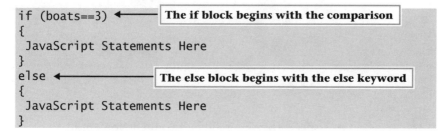

```
if (boats==3)  ◄──────  The if block begins with the comparison
{
 JavaScript Statements Here
}
else  ◄────────  The else block begins with the else keyword
{
 JavaScript Statements Here
}
```

6

Now we can see the entire if/else block, and we can see how it works to execute one of the two blocks of code within curly brackets. If the comparison returns true, the block of code following the if statement is executed. If the comparison returns false, the block of code following the else keyword is executed.

We can now create an entire block with code. Let's say we want to send an alert that says "You have the right number of boats" if the variable boats is equal to three. If it is not, we want to send an alert that says "You do not have the right number of boats" instead. The code for this is shown in the following example:

```
if (boats==3)
{
  window.alert("You have the right number of boats");
}
else
{
  window.alert("You do not have the right number of boats");
}
```

This alert is executed if the comparison on the first line returns true

This alert is executed if the comparison on the first line returns false

Now that we have the statements set up, we need to know whether or not the comparison returns true so we can determine which block of code is executed.

To do so, let's declare the boats variable and assign it a value before the comparison takes place. This will give us the value to determine what happens in the script. See if you can guess which block of code is executed (first or second) if we use the following code:

```
var boats=3;
if (boats==3)
{
  window.alert("You have the right number of boats");
}
else
{
  window.alert("You do not have the right number of boats");
}
```

If you guessed the first code block would be executed, you got it! Since the variable boats is equal to 3, the comparison boats==3 returns true.

Since it returns true, the first code block is executed and the code block after the else keyword is ignored. We get the alert that says "You have the right number of boats" and nothing else.

Now we will set it up so that we have the opposite result. The following code will cause the comparison to return false:

```
var boats=0;  ◀──────── Assigning the variable a value of zero will
if (boats==3)            cause the comparison to return false
{
 window.alert("You have the right number of boats");
}
else
{
 window.alert("You do not have the right number of boats");
}
```

6

With the value of the variable boats at 0, the comparison boats==3 will return false; thus, the first code block is ignored and the code block after the else statement is executed instead. This time we get the alert that says "You do not have the right number of boats," while the alert in the first block is ignored.

Now that we know the basic structure of the if/else statement block, we need to look at the technique of nesting one block within another.

Block Nesting

If we decide to nest something, we are basically putting one structure inside another structure of the same or a similar nature. With the if/else statement blocks, we are able to nest other if/else statements within the first block after the comparison (we'll call it the "if" block) or within the second block after the else keyword (we'll call it the "else" block).

For example, maybe we would like the browser to execute a statement such as the one following: "If a variable named 'have_cookbook' is equal to yes, and if a variable named 'meatloaf_recipe' is equal to yes, send an alert that says 'Recipe found' to the browser. If have_cookbook is equal to yes, but meatloaf_recipe is not equal to yes, then alert 'Have the book but no recipe' to the viewer; otherwise, send an alert that says 'You need a cookbook' to the browser."

This is a somewhat long and complex statement, but we can accomplish what we are after by nesting an if/else statement within the if block of another if/else statement.

To see how this works, let's put the previous statement into JavaScript form. The example code follows:

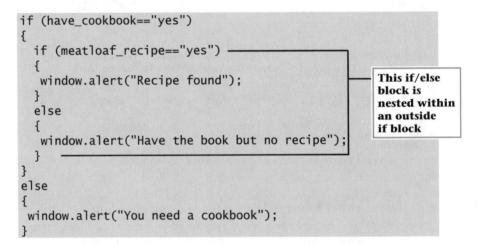

```
if (have_cookbook=="yes")
{
  if (meatloaf_recipe=="yes")
  {
  window.alert("Recipe found");
  }
  else
  {
  window.alert("Have the book but no recipe");
  }
}
else
{
 window.alert("You need a cookbook");
}
```

This if/else block is nested within an outside if block

Oh no, by nesting an if block we used a ton of curly brackets all over the place! Let's see if we can break this down to figure out what is going on with this piece of code.

The first thing we get is the main (first, or outermost) if block. We use it to find out whether the variable have_cookbook is equal to yes or not. If this comparison returns true, we move along into the if block; however, the next thing we find is another if block! This is the nested if block, which means it is inside the outside if block. In the nested block, we check whether the variable meatloaf_recipe is equal to yes or not. If this returns true, we finally are able to do something, which is to send the "Recipe found" alert.

When the nested if block is finished, we see that it had an else block to go with it in case the comparison meatloaf_recipe=="yes" returned false. If it had returned false, the browser would then go to this else block and execute the code within it. In the preceding code example, the comparison on the outside block (have_cookbook=="yes") returned true, but the comparison on the nested block (meatloaf recipe=="yes") returned false. So, the nested else block is executed, sending the "Have the book but no recipe" alert.

After this nested else block, we see what looks like an extra closing curly bracket; however, this closing bracket is actually used to close the outside if block that contains all of this nested code. Looking at how the code is indented will help you see which brackets are closing which blocks. This is where using indentions or tabs can be helpful in your code, because—as opposed to the code being all in a straight line up and down—indentions can make the code easier to read.

Finally, we get to the outside else block. This is the block that is executed only if the first comparison (have_cookbook=="yes") returns false. If that comparison returns false, all the code within that outside if block is ignored (we never get to the nested if/else block) and the browser moves on to this outside else block. In this case, we get the "You need a cookbook" alert sent to the viewer.

Let's try the same if/else code we used in the preceding code example, but this time let's define the variables that will be used by the conditional statements. We will give both variables a value of yes. See if you can follow the code and name the alert that will show up on the screen when it is executed:

```
var have_cookbook="yes";
var meatlof_recipe="yes";

if (have_cookbook=="yes")
{
  if (meatloaf_recipe=="yes")
  {
   window.alert("Recipe found");
  }
  else
  {
   window.alert("Have the book but no recipe");
  }
}

else
{
 window.alert("You need a cookbook");
}
```

The alert you should have chosen is the "Recipe found" alert. When the first comparison returns true, we are sent to the nested if block. Since the comparison for the nested if block also returns true, we execute the code within that block, which is to send the "Recipe found" alert to the browser.

We can nest if/else statements within the outside else block, or we can even nest statements inside both the outside if block and the outside else block. If we want nested statements inside both blocks, we could expand our script a bit. The following example code expands on the code we already have, but adds an additional nested if/else statement within the outside else block:

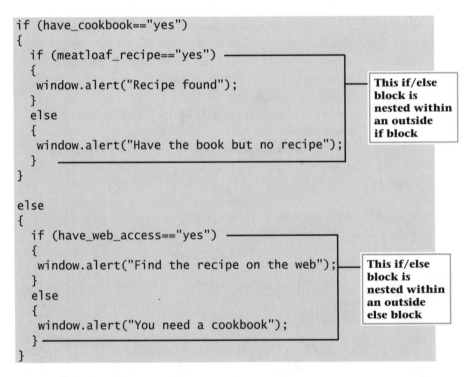

```
if (have_cookbook=="yes")
{
  if (meatloaf_recipe=="yes")
  {
   window.alert("Recipe found");
  }
  else
  {
   window.alert("Have the book but no recipe");
  }
}

else
{
  if (have_web_access=="yes")
  {
   window.alert("Find the recipe on the web");
  }
  else
  {
   window.alert("You need a cookbook");
  }
}
```

This if/else block is nested within an outside if block

This if/else block is nested within an outside else block

Although it hasn't been declared, you will notice the addition of a new variable: have_web_access. This is used to see whether or not the script should tell the viewer to find the recipe on the Web or to buy a cookbook. Keep in mind that in a live script, all the variables will need to be declared before being used.

This time, if the first comparison (have_cookbook=="yes") returns false, we are sent to the outside else block; however, the outside else block now has a nested if/else statement within it, so the browser now goes to the inside if block and looks at that comparison (have_web_access= "yes"). If it returns true, the code within the nested if block is executed and we get the "Find the recipe on the Web" alert. If the comparison returns false, the browser moves on to the nested else block and executes that code instead. In that case, we would get the "You need a cookbook" alert.

The last thing we should know about nesting is that we can nest as many blocks as we want inside of other blocks. Rather than just nesting one if/else statement inside another, we could have a second nesting inside that statement, a third, or as many as we can track without going insane. To keep the example from getting out of hand, we will just nest one more time within the if block of our previous code:

```
if (have_cookbook=="yes")
{
  if (meatloaf_recipe=="yes")
  {
    if (is_moms_meatloaf=="yes")
    {
    window.alert("Recipe found");
    }
    else
    {
    window.alert("Recipe found, but not like what mom makes");
    }
  }
  else
  {
    window.alert("Have the book but no recipe");
  }
}

else
{
  if (have_web_access=="yes")
  {
    window.alert("Find the recipe on the web");
  }
  else
  {
    window.alert("You need a cookbook");
  }
}
```

This if/else block is nested within a nested if block

6

Now there is an if/else block within an if block within an if block. We added yet another variable, is_moms_meatloaf, to check for an even more specific recipe. We could keep going on and on like this, until we cannot take it anymore; however, this should be enough to allow us to build on it later if we need to do so.

Now that we know a bit about nesting, we will want to look at one more detail before we leave the if/else topic in this section. We need to learn about making more complex comparisons in our if/else statements.

Complex Comparisons

Rather than making a simple comparison such as $x==2$ or $y<3$, we are also able to build more complex comparisons using the logical operators we discussed in the previous module. You may recall that we had built some of these in a form similar to the following example:

```
(2==2)||(3<5)
```

At the time, we were only concerned with whether it would return true or false, and not with how to add it to an if/else statement. Notice that we have parentheses around each comparison. They are there mainly for organization; but given the order of operations, we could write the comparison as

```
2==2||3<5
```

The problem here is that this is harder to read, so it would be difficult to determine whether there is a problem with the code if we need to debug it later.

Recall that the first line of the if/else statement uses parentheses to enclose the comparison. If we write our complex comparisons without the organizational parentheses, as in the previous example, we could have the first line look like the line of code shown here:

```
if (2==2||3<5)
```

This is easy to type, but pretty difficult to read because we are not sure if it should be read as "if 2 is equal to 2 or 3 and is less than 5" or as "if (2 is equal to 2) or (3 is less than 5)." If we add the parentheses for organization, it becomes easier to read; but we must be careful that we nest them correctly. The following example code shows the addition of parentheses for organization:

```
if ((2==2)||(3<5))
```

Which form you use will come down to personal preference. For now, we are going to use the method with the extra parentheses for organization. It should make reading the code from the book easier for you.

Now we can create scripts that allow for more values to be included or allow a specific range of values that will return true. Suppose we want to show an alert when a variable named "num1" is greater than 2 but less than 11, and another when num1 is not in that range. We could use the following code:

```
if ((num1>2)&&(num1<11))    ◄——————————  This complex
{                                        comparison allows a
  window.alert("Cool number");           specific range of values
}                                        to return true
else
{
  window.alert("Not a cool number");
}
```

Our comparison is saying, "If num1 is greater than 2 and num1 is less than 11." If that comparison returns true, then we see the "Cool number" alert. If it returns false, we get the "Not a cool number" alert instead.

Of course, we can make the comparison line as complex as we want it to be. We can add *and* and *or* logical operators in one long line until we get what we need or have a nervous breakdown. In the following example, we add an extra stipulation to the comparison to see if num1 is equal to 20:

```
if ((num1>2)&&(num1<11)||(num1==20))  ◄——  This complex
{                                          comparison adds an
  window.alert("Cool number");             additional number
}                                          that would cause
else                                       the comparison to
{                                          return true
  window.alert("Not a cool number");
}
```

Now, the comparison allows the numbers greater than two, the numbers less than 11, and the number 20 to give the "Cool number" alert. The comparison now reads, "If num1 is greater than 2 *and* num1 is less than 11 *or* num1 is equal to 20." We could keep adding information to create

6

more numbers that will return true, or even additional number ranges that will return true.

Of course, to see the preceding code in action we would need to declare the num1 variable and assign it a value. See if you can figure out which alert will show up if the following code is used:

```
var num1=1;

if ((num1>2)&&(num1<11)||(num1==20))
{
 window.alert("Cool number");
}
else
{
 window.alert("Not a cool number");
}
```

Yes, we are stuck with the "Not a cool number" alert because the number 1 just doesn't cut it here (1 is not within the accepted range of numbers for the condition to return true). Of course, we can change it to something that fits to get the "Cool number" alert instead.

Now that we have the if/else statement down, let's take a look at another conditional block we can use to make some things a bit easier.

Using the switch Statement

The switch statement allows us to take a single variable value and execute a different line of code based on the value of the variable. If we wish to check for a number of different values, this can be an easier method than the use of a set of nested if/else statements.

The first line of a switch statement would have the following syntax:

```
switch (varname)
```

We replace *varname* with the name of the variable we are testing. We could also replace it with some other sort of expression, such as the addition of two variables or some similar calculation, and have it evaluate. For now, we will just use a variable that has been assigned a value before the switch statement begins. In our later scripts, we may use some more complex switch statements.

Now, we need to see the general syntax for a full switch statement. The following code is an example of how a switch statement looks:

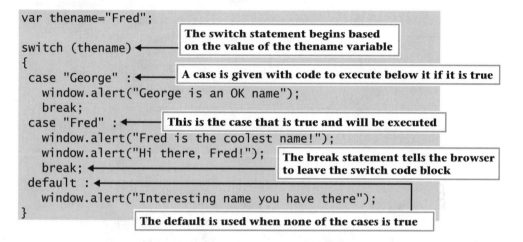

```
var thename="Fred";

switch (thename)          The switch statement begins based
{                         on the value of the thename variable
  case "George" :         A case is given with code to execute below it if it is true
    window.alert("George is an OK name");
    break;
  case "Fred" :           This is the case that is true and will be executed
    window.alert("Fred is the coolest name!");
    window.alert("Hi there, Fred!");     The break statement tells the browser
    break;                               to leave the switch code block
  default :
    window.alert("Interesting name you have there");
}
                          The default is used when none of the cases is true
```

First, we declared and assigned a variable named "thename." We gave it a value of Fred. Now the switch statement begins, using the variable thename as the basis for comparison. We then open the block with a curly bracket, and we see our first case statement.

Written like this, it is saying, "If thename is equal to George then execute the commands after the colon at the end of this line." If thename were equal to George we would get an alert. Then we see the break statement.

The break statement tells the browser to exit the code block and move on to the next line of code after the block. We use the break statement in the switch block to be sure only one of the case sections is executed; otherwise, we run the risk of having all the cases executed following the one that returned true. This is because, by default, the browser would simply move on to the next line after the statements in a case section once one of the cases is true. To be sure that the browser exits the block, we add the break statement.

If we get back to the script, we see that thename is not equal to George, so this case is skipped; however, the next comparison returns true because thename is equal to Fred in the script. Thus, the set of statements in this case block will be executed.

You will see that we have two lines of JavaScript code before the break statement here. This shows that we could have any number of lines within a case, as long as we remember to end with the break statement.

Finally, we see the keyword default. This is used in the event that none of the case statements return true. If this happens, the default section of code will be executed. Notice that we don't need the break statement after the default section of code. This is because it is at the end of the switch block anyway, so the browser will exit the block afterward, eliminating the need for the break statement.

Keep in mind that the switch statement was added in JavaScript 1.2, so when using it you might want to add the condition to your opening <SCRIPT> tag to keep it from trying to run in older browsers. Recall that we do this by using an opening <SCRIPT> tag, such as the following:

```
<SCRIPT language="JavaScript1.2">
```

This would keep the script from running in browsers that don't support it.

The conditional statements will allow us to do much more with our scripts now that we know how to use them. We will be learning about these extensively in later modules, because they can help us code more complex scripts that perform more tasks than we could without them.

Ask the Expert

Question: Do I need to use curly brackets on every if/else block? I have seen them used in code on the Web without the brackets. Why?

Answer: There is a shortcut that allows you to omit the curly brackets if you are only going to execute a single JavaScript statement in the if block and the else block. If you are going to execute more than one statement, the curly brackets should be used. For example, look at the following code:

```
if (x==2)
{
 window.alert("Hi");
}
else
{
 window.alert("Bye");
}
```

Since only one JavaScript statement is used inside the code blocks, we can use a shortcut that allows us to omit the brackets:

```
if (x==2)
  window.alert("Hi");
else
  window.alert("Bye");
```

As you can see, it can save you some typing (which is why you see this technique often in scripts on the Web). Keep in mind, however, that if you decide to add more statements within one of the blocks, you will need to add the brackets back around the code in that block.

Question: Why are we bothering with conditional statements if all we can do is assign the variable a value and then test it? If we already know what the value of the variable is, why use a conditional?

Answer: In later modules, we will get to the point where we are getting information from the viewer. This information can vary depending on the viewer (for example, if the viewer needs to enter his/her name into a text box or a prompt), thus making the conditional blocks more useful since you will be able to perform one action for one viewer, and another task for a different user. With user input, we won't know the value of the variable beforehand, and we will need to handle the possibilities using conditional blocks.

Question: The switch statement doesn't seem to work for me. Why is that?

Answer: The switch statement was an addition to the JavaScript language. If you are using an older browser, the switch statement may not work because it was not part of the language at that time. The switch statement was added in JavaScript 1.2 for Netscape Navigator 4.

6

Question: I don't like the idea of nesting one block inside of another. Can I just forget about it and never nest anything?

Answer: You could do that, but it will severely limit the scripts you code later because you won't be able to use one comparison statement within another (which is sometimes necessary in more complex scripts). Nesting allows you to perform more complex tasks, as we will see in later scripts. It is best to learn it so you can make use of it when you need to.

pr6_1.html

Project 6-1: Construct an if/else block

This project will help you learn how to construct an if/else block of your own. You will be given some variables to test, but you will need to write the if/else block.

Step-by-Step

1. Create an HTML page, leaving some space between the <HEAD> and </HEAD> tags on the page.

2. Add the <SCRIPT> and </SCRIPT> tags to the page inside of the <HEAD> and </HEAD> tags. You will place your code in this area.

3. Create a variable named "thesport" and assign it the following string value:

   Golf

4. Create a variable named "myfood" and assign it the following string value:

   Pizza

5. Based on the thesport variable, create a block of code that will send an alert saying "Cool Sport!" if the variable is equal to Football"; otherwise, it will send an alert that says "That sport might be cool."

6. Based on the myfood variable, create a block of code that will send an alert saying "My favorite food!" if the variable is equal to Pizza; otherwise, it will send an alert that says "That food sounds OK I guess."

7. Save the file as pr6_1.html and view the page in your browser.

8. You should get an alert saying "That sport might be cool." When you press OK, you should then get another alert saying "My favorite food!"

Defining Loops

To begin using loops, we will want to know what loops are, what they can do, and why they can be useful to us in our scripts.

What Is a Loop?

A loop is a block of code that allows us to repeat a section of code a certain number of times, perhaps changing certain variable values each time the code is executed. By doing this, we are often able to shorten certain tasks into a few lines of code, rather than writing the same line over and over again within the script and tiring our fingers.

Why Loops Are Useful

Loops are useful because they allow us to repeat lines of code that would otherwise require us to type it repeatedly, or use cut and paste in our text editors more than we would like. We are also able to change one or more variable values each time through, which again saves us the trouble of typing a line that is only slightly different than the previous line.

As a simple example, suppose we wanted to write a sentence onto a Web page ten times in a row using JavaScript. To do this normally, we might have to write something like the following:

```
document.write("All this typing gets tiring after a while!<BR>");
document.write("All this typing gets tiring after a while!<BR>");
document.write("All this typing gets tiring after a while!<BR>");
document.write("All this typing gets tiring after a while!<BR>");
document.write("All this typing gets tiring after a while!<BR>");
document.write("All this typing gets tiring after a while!<BR>");
document.write("All this typing gets tiring after a while!<BR>");
document.write("All this typing gets tiring after a while!<BR>");
document.write("All this typing gets tiring after a while!<BR>");
document.write("All this typing gets tiring after a while!<BR>");
```

6

Ouch! Cut and paste can make it easier, but it would still be a bit tedious, especially if we decide to write the sentence 50 times instead. With a loop, we could write that document.write statement just one time and adjust the amount of times we wish to see it written.

It would be something like the following example (which is not actual code), but we will see the actual code needed to repeat a statement multiple times when we look at the loop structures in more detail in the next section, "Loops":

```
Do this block 10 times
{
 document.write("I only had to type this once!<BR");
}
```

Of course, we will replace the "Do this block 10 times text" with an actual statement that JavaScript will understand. We will see what statements we can use to form loops after the following 1-Minute Drill.

1-Minute Drill

- **What is a loop?**
- **Why are loops useful in our scripts?**
- **Why is using a loop better than writing out the code repeatedly?**

Loops

In order to see how loops can really be helpful to us, we will need to take a look at the different loop structures we can use in JavaScript. The loop structures we will cover are the *for, while,* and *do while* loops. To begin, let's take a look at how to use a for loop in our scripts.

- A loop is a block of code that allows us to repeat a section of code a certain number of times
- Loops are useful because they allow us to repeat lines of code that would otherwise require us to type it repeatedly
- You can change the number of times the code is written more easily with a loop, rather than needing to cut and paste repeatedly to adjust the code

for

To use a for loop in JavaScript, we will need to know how to code the basic structure of the loop and to take a look at how a for loop can be nested within another for loop. To begin, let's get to the basic structure of a for loop.

Structure of a for Loop

The structure of a for loop is very similar to that of the conditional blocks. The only major differences are that a loop serves a different purpose and, as a result, the first line is different. After that, we use the familiar curly brackets to enclose the contents of the loop.

The first line of a for loop would look similar to the following line:

```
for (varname=1;varname<11;varname+=1)
```

6

The first thing we see is the for keyword. This is followed by a set of parentheses with three statements inside. These three statements tell the loop how many times it should repeat by giving it special information. The text "varname" will be replaced with a variable name that we will be able to use within the loop if we need it.

The first statement (varname=1) creates a variable named "varname" (if the variable has not been created already in the script) and assigns it an initial value of 1. This initial value can be any number. This number is used as a starting point for the number of times the loop will repeat. Using the number 1 will help us see the number of times the loop will repeat more easily. In the preceding code, we began the loop with varname having a value of 1.

The next statement tells the loop when to stop running. The loop will stop running based on this conditional statement. The condition here is to stop only when the variable varname is no longer less than 11. This means that if we add 1 to the value of varname each time through the loop, the loop's last run-through will be when varname is equal to 10. When one is added to 10, it becomes 11; and that doesn't pass the conditional test, so the loop stops running.

The last statement in the set determines the rate at which the variable is changed and whether it gets larger or smaller each time. In the preceding code, we add 1 to the variable each time we go back through the loop.

Remember, the first time through, the variable has been set to 1. Since we add 1 each time, the variable will have a value of 2 the second time through, 3 the third time through, and so on, until the variable is no longer less than 11.

To finish the structure, we insert in the curly brackets to enclose the code we wish to use within the loop. An example of the full structure of a for loop is shown in the following code:

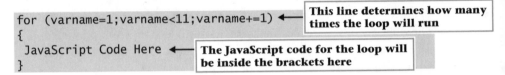

```
for (varname=1;varname<11;varname+=1)   ◄── This line determines how many
{                                            times the loop will run
  JavaScript Code Here  ◄── The JavaScript code for the loop will
}                           be inside the brackets here
```

Now, we just need to add a real variable and some JavaScript code to be executed, and we will have a full for loop put together.

To do this, let's begin with a script to write a sentence to the page ten times. Now that we can use a loop, we will only need to write the sentence itself once, rather than ten times in a row. The following example code shows how this can be done using a for loop:

```
for (count=1;count<11;count+=1)
{                                              This line of code is looped
  document.write("I am part of a loop!<BR>"); ◄── through ten times
}
```

The count variable is going to begin counting at 1, since it is assigned an initial value of 1. We are adding 1 to it each time through the loop. When the count variable has a value that is no longer less than 11, the loop will stop. In this case, the count will run from 1 to 10, thus running the loop ten times.

When 1 is added the next time the for statement is hit, the value of the count variable is 11, which is no longer less than 11; thus, the browser will skip over the loop and continue to the next line of code after the closing curly bracket for the loop. The <BR> tag is used in the document write command to be sure that each sentence will have a line break after it and will not write the next sentence on the same line.

To see this work on a page, we can add the SCRIPT tags and insert the code into the BODY section of a Hypertext Markup Language

(HTML) page. The following example adds the code to a Web page so that we can see the loop do its work in the browser:

```
<HTML>
<HEAD>
<TITLE>Looping</TITLE>
</HEAD>
<BODY>
Get ready for some repeated text.
<P>
<SCRIPT language="JavaScript">
<!--
for (count=1;count<11;count+=1)
{
  document.write("I am part of a loop!<BR>");
}
//-->
</SCRIPT>
<P>
Now we are back to the plain HTML code.
</BODY>
</HTML>
```

> This code will now run in an HTML document

6

The page represented by the preceding code has a short line of text that is followed by our repeating line of text. The page ends with a note that we are back to the plain HTML code. Figure 6-1 shows how this will appear in the browser window when viewed. Notice that the sentence "I am part of a loop!" is repeated ten times.

Now that we can do a basic loop, let's add something to it that will make the loop even more useful. Within the loop, we can use the value of the count variable (or whatever variable is used) to do various things.

One thing we can do (this will become more apparent when we get to arrays later) is to make use of the fact that the variable is changing each time. With the variable going up by 1 each time through, we could use a loop to number the sentences from 1 to 10 and make the lines more readable. The following code does this:

```
<HTML>
<HEAD>
<TITLE>More Looping</TITLE>
```

```
</HEAD>
<BODY>
Get ready for some repeated text.
<P>
<SCRIPT language="JavaScript">
<!--
for (count=1;count<11;count+=1)
{
  document.write(count+". I am part of a loop!<BR>");
}
//-->
</SCRIPT>
<P>
Now we are back to the plain HTML code.
</BODY>
</HTML>
```

> Now the variable is used to add line numbers each time the code is repeated

In the preceding code, we just added the value of the count variable to our string at the beginning. The period before the sentence will make the line of text appear with a period after the number, a space, and our sentence on each line. Figure 6-2 shows how the script would look in the browser with this addition.

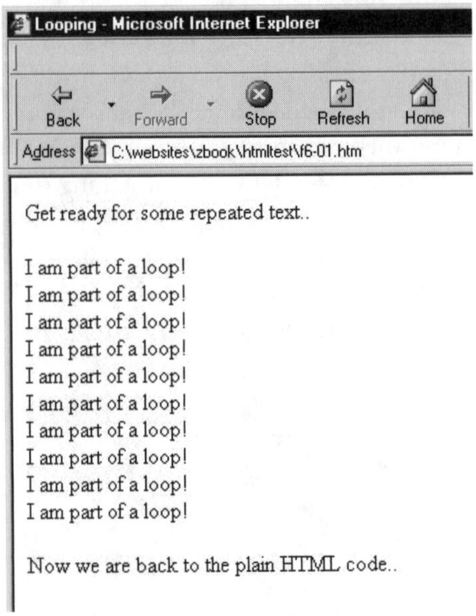

Figure 6-1   The loop displays the line of text ten times

More Looping - Microsoft Internet Explorer

| ⇐ Back | ⇒ Forward | ⊗ Stop | 🔄 Refresh | 🏠 Home |

Address 📄 C:\websites\zbook\htmltest\f6-02.htm

Get ready for some repeated text..

1. I am part of a loop!
2. I am part of a loop!
3. I am part of a loop!
4. I am part of a loop!
5. I am part of a loop!
6. I am part of a loop!
7. I am part of a loop!
8. I am part of a loop!
9. I am part of a loop!
10. I am part of a loop!

Now we are back to the plain HTML code..

6

Figure 6-2 Now the repeated lines are numbered from 1 to 10

We need to cover one more thing about the for loop before we continue. Just as with the if/else blocks, a for loop can be nested within another for loop.

Block Nesting

Yes, we now have to deal with nested loops. As with if/else blocks, we can nest as many levels deep as we can handle. For now, we will just nest one loop within another. The following example shows a for loop within a for loop:

```
for (count=1;count<11;count+=1)
{
 document.write(count+". I am part of a loop!<BR>");
  for (nestcount=1;nestcount<3;nestcount+=1)
  {
   document.write("I keep interrupting in pairs!<BR>");
  }
}
```

This nested loop interrupts the outside loop

Hint

Be careful when you nest loops to be sure that each nested loop has its own counter on its first line, such as for(count=1;count<11;count+=1). A counter will need to be unique to its own loop, in most cases. Also, many errors may occur if the curly brackets are not included or paired correctly.

Now we get a loop that interrupts our outer loop text with text of its own. Each time we go through the outer loop, we write out the "I am part of a loop!" line. Then, we encounter another loop that writes out "I keep interrupting in pairs!" to the screen.

The inner loop is set up to repeat twice; so each time we have one sentence from the outside loop, it is immediately followed by two sentences from the inside loop. In order to see this more clearly, let's insert the script inside an HTML page and then look at the result:

```
<HTML>
<HEAD>
<TITLE>Nesting & Looping</TITLE>
</HEAD>
<BODY>
Get ready for some repeated text.
<P>
<SCRIPT language="JavaScript">
<!--
for (count=1;count<11;count+=1)
{
 document.write(count+". I am part of a loop!<BR>");
  for (nestcount=1;nestcount<3;nestcount+=1)
   {
    document.write("I keep interrupting in pairs!<BR>");
   }
}
//-->
</SCRIPT>
<P>
Now we are back to the plain HTML code.
</BODY>
</HTML>
```

Figure 6-3 illustrates how this nested loop affects the appearance of the page in the browser. We can now see how nested loops are useful to add even more information along the way if we need to do so.

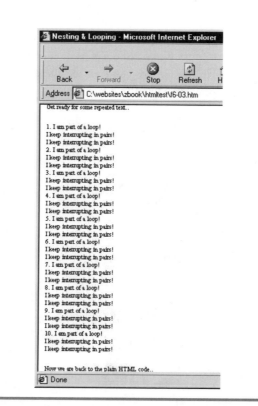

| **Figure 6-3** | **The nested loop inserts text within the outside loop's text** |

To further complicate matters, we can also nest different types of blocks inside one another. For example, we can put an if/else statement block inside a loop, or a loop inside the if block or the else block of an if/else statement. The following example creates an if/else block within a for loop:

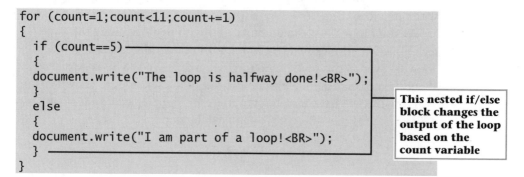

```
for (count=1;count<11;count+=1)
{
  if (count==5)
  {
  document.write("The loop is halfway done!<BR>");
  }
  else
  {
  document.write("I am part of a loop!<BR>");
  }
}
```

This nested if/else block changes the output of the loop based on the count variable

In this case, we will check whether or not the count variable has a value of 5. If it does, we will print a different message to the screen than we would otherwise. Again, we can best see the effects of this by adding the preceding script to an HTML document:

```
<HTML>
<HEAD>
<TITLE>More Nesting & Looping</TITLE>
</HEAD>
<BODY>
Get ready for some repeated text.
<P>
<SCRIPT language="JavaScript">
<!--
for (count=1;count<11;count+=1)
{
  if (count==5)
  {
  document.write("The loop is halfway done!<BR>");
  }
  else
  {
  document.write("I am part of a loop!<BR>");
  }
}
//-->
</SCRIPT>
<P>
Now we are back to the plain HTML code.
</BODY>
</HTML>
```

Figure 6-4 shows the result of this code when run in the browser. Notice how the fifth line is different based on our conditional statement within the loop.

As you can see, we can do quite a bit with nesting. Using the same techniques we just learned, we can nest all of the other statement blocks we will cover in this book; therefore, we won't need to be as detailed about the nesting techniques with the rest of the statements we will cover.

Now that we have seen how to use a for loop, let's take a look at how we can loop a little differently using a while loop.

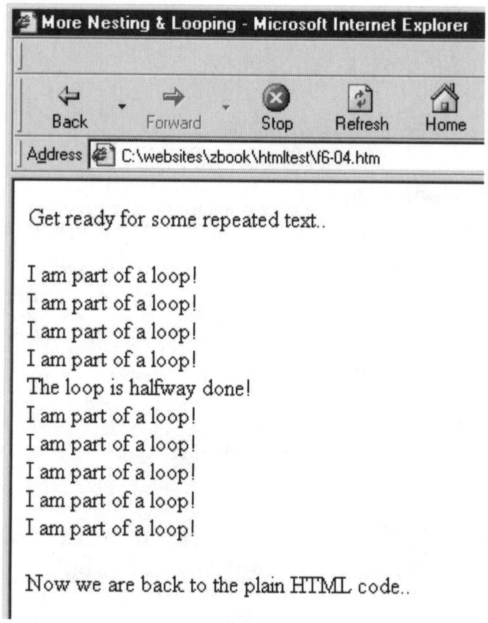

```
More Nesting & Looping - Microsoft Internet Explorer

    ⇐        ⇒         ⊗         ⊡         ⌂
   Back    Forward     Stop    Refresh    Home

Address  C:\websites\zbook\htmltest\f6-04.htm

Get ready for some repeated text..

I am part of a loop!
I am part of a loop!
I am part of a loop!
I am part of a loop!
The loop is halfway done!
I am part of a loop!
I am part of a loop!
I am part of a loop!
I am part of a loop!
I am part of a loop!

Now we are back to the plain HTML code..
```

Figure 6-4   **The nested if/else block causes the fifth line to be different from the other lines**

while

A while loop just looks at a short comparison and repeats until the comparison is no longer true. To begin, let's take a look at the general syntax for the first line of a while loop:

```
while (varname<11)
```

We replace *varname* with the name of a real variable; however, the while statement does not create a variable the way a for statement can. When using a while loop, we must remember to declare the variable we wish to use and assign it a value before we insert it into the while loop.

While the less-than comparison is probably the most common, we can use any other type of comparison we wish. This includes the complex comparisons with the logical operators. So, we could have a first line like the one in the following example:

```
while ((varname>4)&&(varname<11))
```

This time, the loop runs only while the variable is greater than 4 and less than 11. For the loop to run at all, the initial value of the variable would need to be within that range; otherwise, the loop would be skipped entirely.

Now, let's put together an entire while loop structure to see how it looks. The following code shows the general structure of a full while loop:

```
var count=1;          ◄——————  A variable is assigned a value to count the loop
while (count<6) ◄————  The while statement begins with a comparison
{
   JavaScript Code Here
   count+=1; ◄————  The count variable is adjusted so we do not
}                    have an endless loop
```

First, notice that we assigned the value of 1 to the variable count before we began the loop. This is important to do so that the loop will run the way we expect it to run. This loop is set up to repeat 5 times, given the initial value of the variable and the increase in the value of the variable by 1 each time through (count+=1).

In a while loop, we must also remember to change the value of the variable we use so that we do not get stuck in a permanent loop. If we had not put in the count+=1 code in the previous sample loop, the loop would have repeated indefinitely, and we do not want that. So, the main things we must remember with a while loop are to give the variable an initial value before the loop and to adjust the value of the variable within the loop itself.

For an example of the while loop in action, we can recode our sentence repeat script to work with a while loop:

```
<HTML>
<HEAD>
<TITLE>Looping</TITLE>
</HEAD>
<BODY>
Get ready for some repeated text.
```

```
<P>
<SCRIPT language="JavaScript">
<!--
var count=1;
while (count<11)
{
 document.write(count+". I am part of a loop!<BR>");
 count+=1;
}
//-->
</SCRIPT>
<P>
Now we are back to the plain HTML code.
</BODY>
</HTML>
```

> This line is written on the page ten times, just as with the for loop

The preceding code will produce the same result as our for loop did, just with a different look, as seen in Figure 6-5. In many cases, we can choose to use a for loop or a while loop based on personal preference, since they can perform many of the same tasks.

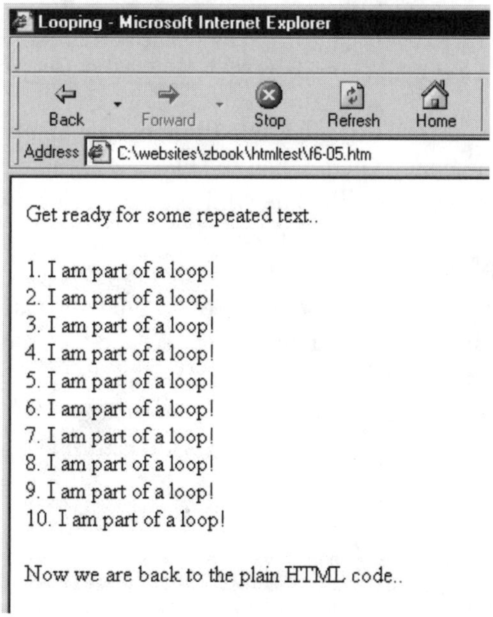

6

Figure 6-5   A line of text is repeated ten times using a while loop

As far as nesting with while loops, it works the same as with the for loops. We can insert another while loop, a for loop, or an if/else block within a while loop. We can also insert a while loop within the other statement blocks if we wish.

Now that we know how while loops work, let's look at a loop that has a special feature added to it.

do while

The do while loop is special because the code within the loop is performed at least once, even if the comparison used would return false the first time. A comparison that returns false in other loops on the first attempt would cause them never to be executed. In the case of a do while loop, the loop is executed once, and then the comparison is used each time afterward to determine whether or not it should repeat.

The following is an example of a do while loop that will run five times:

```
var count=1;
do  ◄───────────────── The do keyword begins the do while loop
{
  document.write("Hi!");
  count+=1;                    The while statement runs the comparison
} while (count<6);  ◄───────  each time after the first run-through
```

Notice the keyword do is the only thing on the first line of the block in the preceding code. Then, when the block is complete, we see the while statement and comparison. The while statement is how we ensure the code block is executed at least once.

After that, it checks to see that the comparison returns true before repeating. In this case, it repeats five times since the variable count starts at 1 and is increased by 1 each time through. When the value of count reaches 6, the loop is skipped and no longer executed.

To see an example of a do while loop that gets executed at least once even though the initial comparison would return false, look at the following example code:

```
var count=11;
do
{                                       This is only written to the page
  document.write("Hi!");  ◄─────────    once, since the comparison will
  count+=1;                             return false
} while (count<10);
```

Since the count variable has an initial value of 11, the loop in the preceding code will only run the first time through. When the comparison is checked (count will be 12 by this time, since 1 is added to it in the execution of the loop), it returns false and the loop is no longer run.

A do while loop is most useful when you have some code you need executed at least once, but only need repeated if certain conditions are met; otherwise, one of the other two loops would be sufficient for the task.

?-Ask the Expert

Question: **Are loops useful for anything other than writing a line of text to the page repeatedly?**

Answer: Yes, we will see their usefulness more as we progress through the modules. We will see that they can be useful when dealing with arrays and for repeating various actions that, in turn, create certain effects on the page.

Question: **Is it really okay to use the variable we have counting the loop inside the loop? Couldn't that lead to problems?**

Answer: It is okay to use that variable within the loop, as long as you do not somehow assign it a new value when using it. If you are worried that you might do this, assign its value to another variable and use that one in the code instead. For example, take a look at the following code:

```
for (count=1;count<11;count+=1)
{
 var thenum=count;
 document.write(thenum+". I am part of a loop!<BR>");
}
```

Here, we assign the value of the count variable to a variable named "thenum." We then use the thenum variable in the code instead of the count variable.

Question: **Should I use a for loop or a while loop when I want to use a loop? Which one is better?**

Answer: Use the type of loop you personally prefer. Often, the type of loop used depends upon the situation at hand. One type of loop might seem to make more sense than the other type under different circumstances. For the most part, though, you can use either loop you feel comfortable coding.

Question: **Will the do while loop ever be useful to us?**

Answer: While the do while loop does have its usefulness, it is unlikely we will use it often in this book since we won't use scripts that will need to have a loop run at least once before it is checked. However, the knowledge you gained about the do while loop in this module will help you if you should encounter a script that uses it on the Web or elsewhere.

`pr6_2.html, pr6_2_2.html`

Project 6-2: Work with for loops and while loops

This project will allow you to work with for loops and while loops in order to see how they can perform similar tasks.

Step-by-Step

1. Create an HTML page, leaving room between the <BODY> and </BODY> tags to insert your code.

2. Insert the <SCRIPT> and </SCRIPT> tags inside the <BODY> and </BODY> tags, and then insert your script code.

3. Using a for loop, create some code that will write the and sentence following to the page 15 times. Be sure to number each line from 1–15:

    This is getting way too repetitive.

4. Save the file as pr6_2.html and view the results in the browser. You should see the sentence 15 times, numbered from 1 to 15.

5. Repeat steps 1 and 2, creating a new HTML page.

6. Write some code that will do the same thing as in step 3, but use a while loop instead.

7. Save the file as pr6_2_2.html and view the results in the browser. It should appear the same way as the other page.

☑ *Mastery Check*

1. Which of the following would be valid as the first line of an if/else statement?

    A. if (*x*=2)

    B. if (*y*<7)

    C. else

    D. if ((*x*==2 &&)

2. What do we use to enclose the blocks of code in conditionals and loops?

    A. Parentheses

    B. Square brackets

    C. Curly brackets

    D. Less-than and greater-than characters

3. Which of these would be valid as the first line of a for loop?

    A. for (*x*=1;*x*<6;*x*+=1)

    B. for (*x*==1;*x*<6;*x*+=1)

    C. for (*x*=1;x=6;*x*+=1)

    D. for (*x*+=1;*x*<6;*x*=1)

4. Which of these would not be valid as the first line of a while loop?

    A. while (*x*<=7)

    B. while (*x*=7)

    C. while (*x*<7)

    D. while (*x*!=7)

5. How many times can you nest a code block within another?

    A. None

    B. Once

    C. Three times, but no more

    D. As many times as you like

6

Module 7

Event Handlers

The Goals of This Module

- Learn about event handlers
- Determine how events are useful in JavaScript
- Discover where event handlers can be placed on a page
- Find out what the events are in JavaScript
- Determine the event handlers that are used for each event
- Be able to code scripts that make use of event handlers

As we mentioned in Module 2, there is a way to have JavaScript code outside of the <SCRIPT> and </SCRIPT> tags. The way we are able to do this is through the use of event handlers.

To learn how the event handlers work, we need to learn what they are and why they are useful to us. We will then learn where event handlers are placed in a document and how to make use of them. Finally, we will see the various events in JavaScript and the event handlers that take care of each event. Let's get started with a general overview of event handlers.

What Is an Event Handler?

An event handler is a predefined JavaScript keyword that is used to handle an event on a Web page. Often, an event is something that happens when the viewer of the page performs some sort of action. This action may be a mouse click, the clicking of a button on the page, changing the contents of a form element, or moving the mouse over a link on the page.

When events like these occur, we are able to use JavaScript event handlers to identify them and then perform a specific task or set of tasks. JavaScript enables us to react to an action by the viewer and to make scripts that are interactive, and more useful to us and to the viewer.

Why Event Handlers Are Useful

Event handlers are useful because they enable us to gain access to the events that may occur on the page. For instance, if we wanted to send an alert to the viewer when he or she moves the mouse over a link, we could use the event handler to invoke the JavaScript alert we have coded to react to the event. We are now making things happen based on the actions of the viewer, which enables us to make more interactive Web pages.

Creating this interactivity is where many of us find that JavaScript starts to become a little more fun to code and to use. With event handlers, we can create some surprises for the viewer or make some scripts that will simply add more functionality to the page. JavaScript can make a number of things happen on a Web page that will make the page more interesting than a static HTML document.

1-Minute Drill

- **What is an event handler?**
- **Is moving the mouse over a link considered an event in JavaScript?**
- **Why are event handlers useful?**

Event Handler Locations and Uses

To see how event handlers work, we need to know where we can place them in a document and how to use them to add JavaScript code for an event. To begin, let's look at the possible locations for event handlers in an HTML document.

Event Handler Locations

Event handlers can be used in a number of locations. They are most often used in form elements, link tags, and the opening body tag; however, we will see that in newer browsers they can also be used in other areas as well. For now, we will concentrate on the three main areas listed in the previous sentence because they are supported by a majority of the browsers out there.

To understand the location of an event handler better, we will need to learn how to add them to the HTML code. So, let's take a look at how to use event handlers to add JavaScript to an HTML page.

- An event handler is a predefined JavaScript keyword that is used to handle an event on a Web page
- Yes
- They enable us to gain access to the events that may occur on the page

Using Event Handlers

To use an event handler, we need to know the keyword for the event handler and where to place the event handler within the HTML code. To get an example, we will introduce the onClick event handler. The onClick event handler is used to make something happen when the viewer clicks a specific area of the document.

One of the valid places to be clicked is a form button. So, let's say we want to alert something to the viewer when he/she clicks a form button. We would write something similar to the following code:

```
<INPUT type="button" onClick="JavaScript Code Here">
```

To use an event handler, we add it as an additional attribute to an HTML tag. The only difference between an event handler "attribute" and an HTML attribute is that we can add JavaScript code inside an event handler attribute rather than just an attribute value. In the previous code, we would replace the JavaScript Code Here text with some actual JavaScript code.

So, to make an alert pop up when the user clicks the button, we can add the necessary JavaScript code right inside our onClick attribute, as shown in the following example:

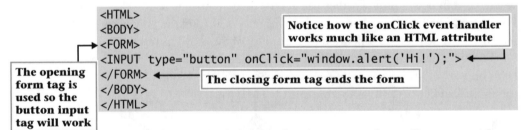

```
<HTML>
<BODY>
<FORM>
<INPUT type="button" onClick="window.alert('Hi!');">
</FORM>
</BODY>
</HTML>
```

Notice how the onClick event handler works much like an HTML attribute

The closing form tag ends the form

The opening form tag is used so the button input tag will work

When the viewer clicks this plain button, an alert will pop up with a greeting. Notice that the rules on the quote marks apply here. Using the onClick event handler as an attribute requires us to use double quotes around all of our JavaScript code, so when we need quote marks for the alert, we use single quotes in order to avoid possible errors.

Also notice that our alert command ends with a semicolon. This enables us to add additional JavaScript code after the alert, which enables us to perform multiple actions on the click event rather than just a single JavaScript statement.

We could code in two alerts if we wanted to do so. All we have to do is remember the semicolons to separate the alert commands. This will be a little different because all of the code will be on one line rather than separate lines, as we normally see:

```
<HTML>
<BODY>
<FORM>
<INPUT type="button"
onClick="window.alert('Hi!');window.alert('Bye!');">
</FORM>
</BODY>
</HTML>
```

> **Note how the semicolons separate the JavaScript statements**

We were able to perform two JavaScript statements on the same event by using semicolons to separate them. When using event handlers, we can execute multiple commands this way. It is important, however, to keep everything between the event handler keyword (in this case, onClick) and the ending set of quotes (in this case, after the last semicolon in the code) on one line in your text editor; otherwise, a line break in the code could cause it not to run properly or to give a JavaScript error.

If the code you want to use becomes really long, you may wish to put the code in a function instead. The event handler can be used for any JavaScript code, so you can use it to call a function you have defined earlier in the page. For example, we could place our two alerts within a function inside the head section of the HTML document, and call the function from an event handler in the BODY section. The following code shows how this is done:

```
<HTML>
<HEAD>
<TITLE>Events & Functions</TITLE>
```

7

```
<SCRIPT language="JavaScript">
<!--
function hi_and_bye()
{
 window.alert('Hi!');
 window.alert('Bye!');
}
//-->
</SCRIPT>
</HEAD>
<BODY>
<FORM>
<INPUT type="button" onClick="hi_and_bye();">
</FORM>
</BODY>
</HTML>
```

> **This function sends two alerts to the screen**

> **Notice how the function is called using the event handler**

Notice how the function is called using the event handler just like a normal function call within a script. This enables us to shorten the code within the event handler, plus we can reuse the function on another button click or event later in the page instead of writing the two alerts out again. The use of a function can help us quite a bit, especially when the code we want to use becomes extremely long.

As you can see, using event handlers isn't as bad as it may have seemed before we looked at it. The tough part is to know when to use which event handler and where each event handler can be used in a document. We will cover those topics in this module, after a short break for questions and a project.

Ask the Expert

Question: Is there a JavaScript event for everything a viewer could do on a Web page?

Answer: No, but many of the actions a viewer may take are covered by one of the events in JavaScript. It would be difficult to cover every possibility. For example, there isn't yet an event for when a viewer scrolls up and down a Web page.

Question: You said some of the newer browsers could have event handlers in more locations than older browsers. Will this be a problem when I go through the book?

Answer: You will probably be okay, because we don't need to place event handlers in those locations until we start writing Dynamic HTML (DHTML) scripts. The newer event handlers could give you a problem with an older browser, but they won't be used much except in an advanced module.

Question: You mean I can just write some JavaScript by using an event handler like an HTML attribute?

Answer: Yes, but keep in mind there are limitations as to which event handlers can be used in what tags. We will see this in more detail when we go through each event handler individually later in the module.

Question: How do I decide when to use a function and when to just add the code directly into the event handler?

Answer: If your JavaScript code is short and you won't be repeating it multiple times with other tags and/or events, then you'll probably want to add the code straight into the event handler as an attribute. If your code is really long or you will be repeating it numerous times, you'll probably want to use a function instead to make things easier to read and the code reusable.

7

pr7_1.html

Project 7-1: Create a Button

This project will create a button that will send the viewer three alerts when it is clicked. It will help you master the use of a function call in an event handler.

Step-by-Step

1. Create an HTML page, and leave space for a script in the HEAD section and a form button in the BODY section.

2. In the HEAD section, write a function named "send_alerts()" that will send three alerts to the viewer. The following are the three alerts:

Alert 1: Hi there, and welcome to my page!

Alert 2: Please sign the guest book before you leave!

Alert 3: Are these alerts annoying you yet? Ha, Ha!

3. In the BODY section, create a button that uses the onClick event handler to call the send_alerts() function when the user clicks it. Add a value="Click Me" attribute to the button tag so that it has a label.

4. Save the file as pr7_1.html, and load the page in your browser. You should have a button that says "Click Me" on it. Click the button, and you should get the three alerts—one after another.

The Event Handlers

Now that we know what event handlers are and how to use them, we need to see which event handlers are used for various events on a page. We will begin by looking at Table 7-1, which lists the events, their event handlers, and samples of what actions might trigger each event. We will follow the table with a more detailed description of each event and its event handler.

Now that we have a general idea about event handlers, let's take a look at each one in more detail to see how they work.

The Click Event (onClick)

The click event occurs when a viewer clicks certain areas of a Web page. These areas are found in form elements and links. With some later browsers, the click event may also work for more general areas, such as within a table cell or within a set of <DIV> and </DIV> tags. We will concentrate on the form elements and links in this module, as they are the most widely supported.

The easiest way to see the click event in action is to use a form button. When the button is clicked, we want an event to occur. To make this

Event	Event Handler	Event Trigger
Click	onClick	Viewer clicks an area (such as a button or form input area)
Mouseover	onMouseOver	Viewer moves the mouse over a link
Mouseout	onMouseOut	Viewer moves the mouse away from a link
Load	onLoad	Web page finishes loading
Unload	onUnload	Viewer leaves the current page
Focus	onFocus	Viewer gives focus to something
Blur	onBlur	Viewer removes focus from something
Change	onChange	Viewer changes the contents of a form element
Submit	onSubmit	Viewer submits a form on the page
Abort	onAbort	Viewer stops the loading of an image
Dragdrop	onDragDrop	Viewer uses the drag-and-drop feature of an operating system and drops something into the window
Error	onError	An error occurs in the loading of a page or image
Keydown	onKeyDown	Viewer presses a key down on the keyboard
Keypress	onKeyPress	Viewer presses a key on the keyboard, and releases or holds the key down
Keyup	onKeyUp	Viewer releases a key on the keyboard
Mousedown	onMouseDown	Viewer presses the mouse button
Mouseup	onMouseUp	Viewer releases the mouse button
Mousemove	onMouseMove	Viewer moves the mouse (moves the cursor)
Move	onMove	A window is moved
Reset	onReset	Viewer resets a form on the page
Resize	onResize	A window is resized
Select	onSelect	User makes a selection in a form field

Table 7-1   The Events and Event Handlers

happen, we will need to place the onClick event handler inside the button input tag, as shown in the following example:

```
<HTML>
<HEAD>
<TITLE>onClick</TITLE>
```

```
</HEAD>
<BODY>
<FORM>
<INPUT TYPE="button" value="Do not Click Here"
 onClick="window.alert('I told you not to click me!');">  ◄
</FORM>
</BODY>
</HTML>
```

The onClick event handler
is used on a button

This will send the viewer an alert once the button has been clicked. Figure
7-1 shows the result of this code when the viewer clicks the button.

To use this event handler to do the same thing with a link, we might
be tempted to do something similar to the following:

Oh no! This will give us problems because
the browser will try to follow the link

```
<HTML>
<BODY>
<A HREF="http://none" onClick="window.alert('Hey! You clicked me!');">
Don't Click Me</A>
</BODY>
</HTML>
```

The problem with this code is that the alert will work, but the browser
will try to continue the original action of the link tag and attempt to go to

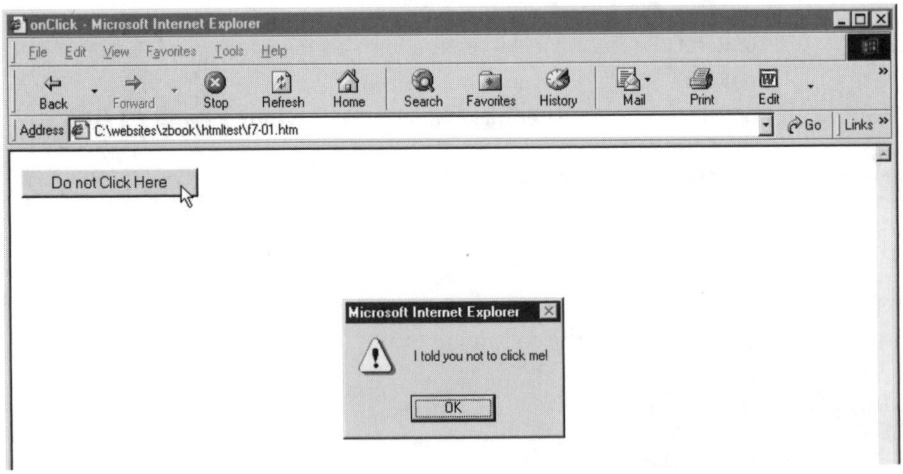

Figure 7-1 This alert pops up when the viewer clicks the button

http://none. This would probably cause a "Server not found" error in the browser.

One way we can avoid a "Server not found" error is to link to an actual page; however, if the alert shows up and the user remains on the same page, then that does not help. To keep the link from being followed, we need to add an extra statement to the JavaScript in the click event. We need to tell the browser not to continue after we have shown the viewer our alert. To do this, we will add a return statement.

Recall from Module 4 on functions that we used a return statement to return a needed value to a script. Here, we are going to do essentially the same thing. We are going to return the Boolean value of false, which tells the browser that the event has been handled and no further action is required for the event. This will keep the browser from following the link after the alert has been shown. The following code shows how to add in the return statement:

```
<HTML>
<BODY>
<A HREF="http://none"
 onClick="window.alert('Hey! You clicked me!');return false;">
Don't Click Me</A>
</BODY>
</HTML>
```

The return false statement keeps the browser from trying to follow the link

7

With this code in place, the click event will be taken care of by the onClick event handler, and the browser will not need to worry about attempting to follow the link in the hypertext reference (HREF) attribute.

In Module 15, we will see another way to perform JavaScript tasks when a link is clicked.

The Mouseover Event (onMouseOver)

A mouseover event occurs when a viewer moves the mouse cursor over a text link, linked image, or linked portion of an image map. In some later browsers, the mouseover event will also work in other areas such as table cells and <DIV></DIV> tags. The mouseover event is handled with the onMouseOver event handler.

The quickest way to use an onMouseOver event handler is to set up a text link. When we add the onMouseOver event handler to the link, we have the option to perform JavaScript commands when the viewer passes the cursor over the link. Thus, if we want an alert to pop up when the viewer moves the mouse over a link, we could code something like the following:

```
<A HREF="http://www.pageresource.com"
 onMouseOver="window.alert('I told you not to try to click me!');">
Don't Try Clicking Me!</A>
```

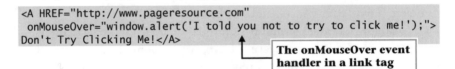

The onMouseOver event handler in a link tag

This time we don't even get to click the link before we are greeted with an alert. Keep in mind that a script like this could could annoy your visitors if it is overused. Figure 7-2 shows the result of this script in a browser. The alert pops up as soon as the mouse cursor moves over the link.

Since there is no need to click the link for something to happen, the browser won't try to follow the link afterward. In fact, with this script in place, it makes it quite difficult to click the link at all because the alert keeps popping up when you move your mouse over to click it!

Figure 7-2   This alert pops up when the mouse cursor moves over the link

The mouseover event will become much more useful to us in later modules when we learn more things about what we can do with the various parts of a page.

The Mouseout Event (onMouseout)

The mouseout event occurs when a viewer moves the mouse cursor away from a link, linked image, or linked area of an image map. As with the mouseover event, some of the later browsers will support the mouseout event in other areas. We take care of a mouseout event by using the onMouseOut event handler.

Again, we can see the mouseout event most easily by setting up a link and adding the onMouseOut event handler to the link. This time, we can make an alert pop up once the user moves the mouse away from the link after passing over it (assuming it has not been clicked). To do this, we could use the following code:

```
<A HREF="http://www.pageresource.com"
  onMouseOut="window.alert('What, you didn\'t like my link?');">
Click Me!</A>
```

The onMouseOut event handler in a link tag

This time the alert pops up when the viewer moves the mouse off the link and asks the viewer a question. Notice also the escaped quote mark (\') used in the word *didn't,* which keeps us from getting a string error. Figure 7-3 shows this script in action.

The mouseout event will become more useful for us later (see Module 17), especially when used in tandem with the mouseover event.

The Load Event (onLoad)

The load event occurs when a Web page finishes loading. To handle this event, we use the onLoad event handler and place it in the opening <BODY> tag on a Web page.

Keep in mind the load event occurs at a slightly different time than the alert scripts we placed in the head section of our pages in earlier modules. Those started our tasks before the remainder of the page began loading.

7

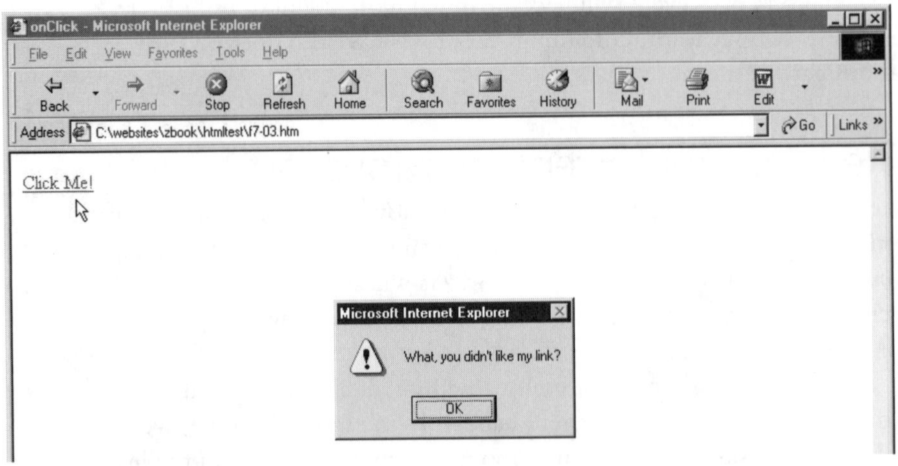

Figure 7-3 This alert pops up when the mouse is moved off the link

With the load event, however, our tasks will be executed as soon as the page finishes the loading process.

If we want an alert to be shown when the page has finished loading, we could use the following code:

> **Notice that the onLoad event handler is added to the \<BODY> tag**

```
<BODY onLoad="window.alert('I\'m done loading now!');">
<B>Text for the body of the page</B>
</BODY>
```

When the page has finished loading, we will get an alert that tells us it is finished. It will be hard to distinguish the timing of the load event from the preceding code from the timing of the instant alerts in earlier scripts because the page will load very quickly, since it is all text. Figure 7-4 shows how the preceding code example would appear in the browser.

In order to see the difference in timing between an alert in the head section and one in the onLoad event handler, you may want to add some images to the body of the page and then put the page and images on the Web. This way, the page will take some time to load, and you will see that

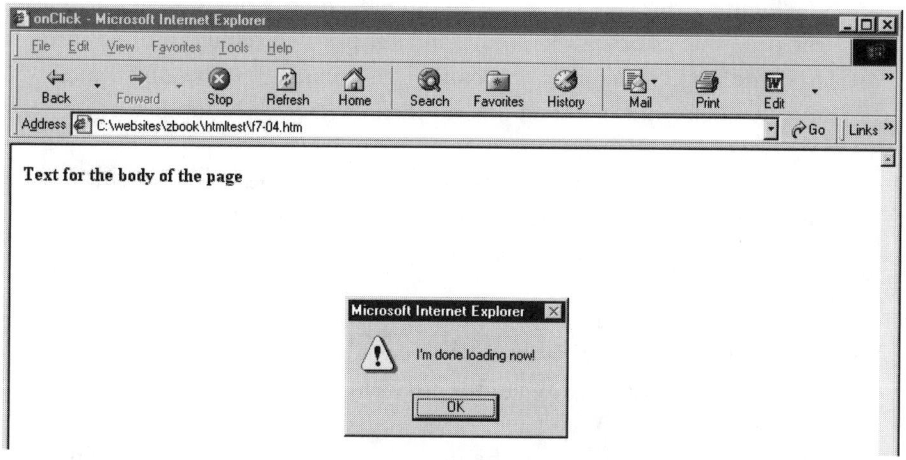

![onClick - Microsoft Internet Explorer window showing "Text for the body of the page" with a Microsoft Internet Explorer alert dialog reading "I'm done loading now!" and an OK button]

Figure 7-4   This is displayed in the browser window after the page has finished loading

7

the alert pops up when the page has finished loading instead of showing up instantly.

The Unload Event (onUnload)

The unload event occurs when a viewer leaves the current Web page. The viewer could leave by clicking a link, typing another address in the browser, or closing the window. The event handler used for the unload event is onUnload, and it is placed in the opening <BODY> tag on a Web page.

This event is known to annoy viewers quite often, because it enables the site owner to do something while visitors are trying to move on to another page or another Web site (forcing them to wait). To have an alert pop up when the user leaves the page, we could write the following code:

> **The onUnload event handler is also added to the <BODY> tag**

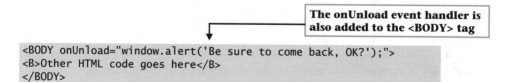

```
<BODY onUnload="window.alert('Be sure to come back, OK?');">
<B>Other HTML code goes here</B>
</BODY>
```

Figure 7-5 shows the result of the preceding script. As we try to leave the page that contains this script, an alert pops up telling us to be sure to come back. Of course, this could cause a viewer to become quite inconvenienced if it is used on an index page or on a number of pages within a Web site.

Overall, be sure to think twice before using the unload event on a live page. There can be good uses for it, but be careful because it does annoy some Web users.

The Focus Event (onFocus)

The focus event occurs when the viewer gives focus to a window or a form element on a Web page. A viewer gives focus to something by clicking somewhere within the item. For instance, a viewer clicking a text input box (before entering anything) gives that text box the focus. Also, clicking an inactive window and making it the active window will give the window the focus.

The event handler used with this event is onFocus, and it can be used in a form element or in the opening <BODY> tag on a Web page (for

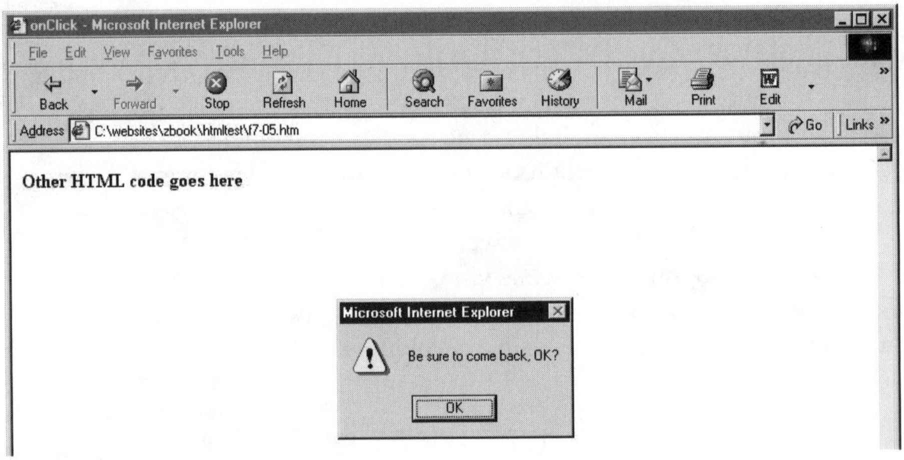

Figure 7-5 This alert pops up when the viewer tries to leave the page

focus on a window). The onFocus event handler also has a related method called focus(), which we will cover in Module 14.

To see the focus event in action, we can create a text input box, which is one of the form elements that will enable us to give it focus. We will code a reminder alert to pop up when the viewer gives focus to the text box. We can do this by using the code shown in the following example:

The onFocus event will work with a text box

```
<FORM>
Enter Your Name:
<INPUT type="text" onFocus="window.alert('Don\'t forget to capitalize!');">
</FORM>
```

This code will give the viewer an alert before he or she can begin typing. The alert would serve as a reminder to capitalize the name. Figure 7-6 shows the result of the preceding code in the browser when the viewer gives focus to the text box.

We will examine better uses for the focus event in later modules, but this gives you an idea of how it works.

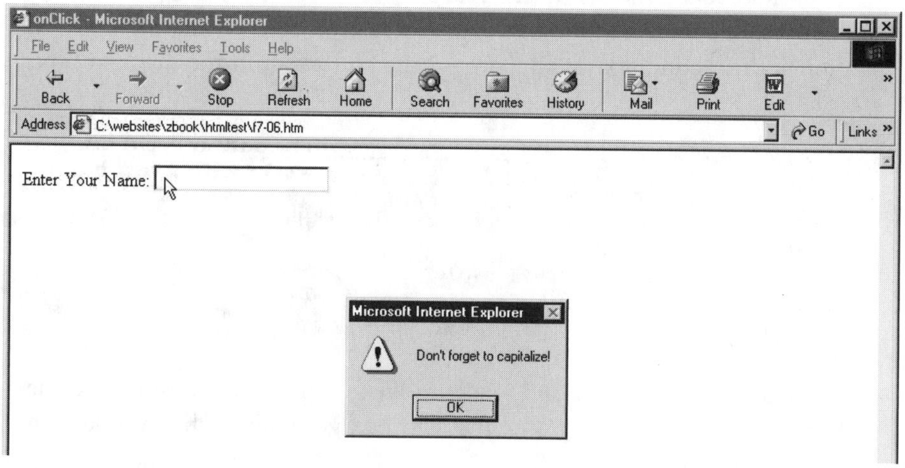

7

Figure 7-6 This alert is pops up when the text box receives focus from the viewer

The Blur Event (onBlur)

The blur event is the opposite of the onFocus event, and it occurs when the viewer takes the focus away from a form element or a window. To take the focus off something, the viewer usually gives focus to something else. For instance, the viewer could move from one form element to another, or from one window to another.

The onBlur event handler is used to handle this event, and it can be used in a form element's tag or in the opening <BODY>tag (for windows). The onBlur event handler also has a related method called blur(), which we will cover in Module 14.

Hint

The blur event is triggered only when you give focus to another area, which is the only way the browser will know you released the focus from the first area. For example, when you press the ENTER key in an input field, the focus goes from the input field to the document window.

To see the blur event in action, we can also use a text box for the onBlur event handler. In the following example, we will use two text boxes. We will click the first text box to give it focus, and then we will click the second text box to invoke the blur event in the first text box:

> **The onBlur event also works with a text box**

```
<FORM>
Give this box focus:<BR>
<INPUT type="text" onBlur="window.alert('Hey! Come back!');">
<BR>
Then give this box focus to blur the first one:<BR>
<INPUT type="text">
</FORM>
```

When we click the second text box, we get the alert from the first one telling us to come back. The first text box got lonely when we gave the focus to something else!

Figure 7-7 shows the result of the preceding code when run in the browser. Notice that the focus is in the second text box when the alert pops up. By clicking the second text box we invoked the blur event in the first text box.

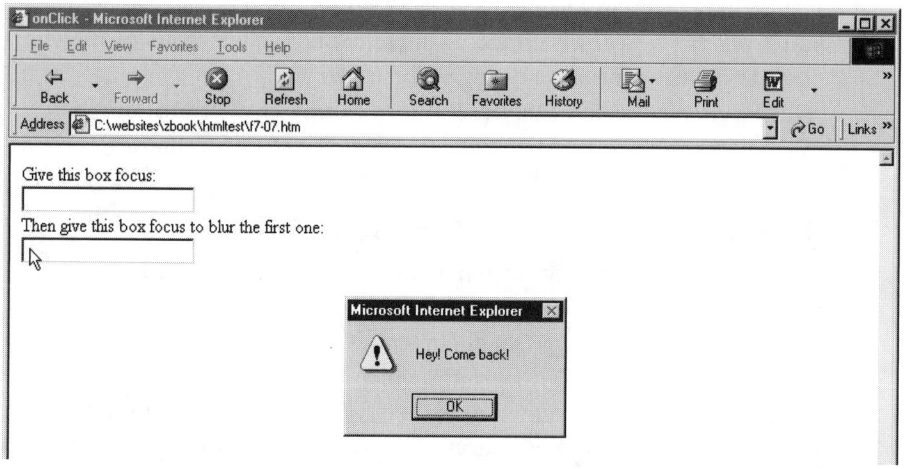

Figure 7-7 This alert pops up when the viewer takes the focus off a text box

The Change Event (onChange)

The change event occurs when a viewer changes something within a form
element. For instance, the viewer might change the text in a text box or
make a selection from a select box. We handle this event with the
onChange event handler.

We can see how this works by setting up a select box. We can give the
viewer some choices within the select box. If the user changes the default
option by choosing a new one, we send an alert to ask why it was
changed, as shown in the following example:

```
<HTML>
<BODY>
<FORM>
Are you cool?<BR>
<SELECT onChange="window.alert('Why did you change that?');">
<OPTION selected>Yes</OPTION>
<OPTION>No</OPTION>
<OPTION>Undecided</OPTION>
</SELECT>
</FORM>
</BODY>
</HTML>
```

> **Making a new selection
> from the list will invoke the
> onChange event handler here**

If the viewer tries to change the default answer of Yes, an alert pops up and gives the viewer a message. If the select box is left alone or the viewer chooses the first option, nothing will happen

The change event is very useful for creating navigational text boxes. We will see how to build navigational text boxes in Module 14.

The Submit Event (onSubmit)

The submit event only occurs when the viewer submits a form on a Web page. This event uses the onSubmit event handler, which can be called from an opening <FORM>tag in a document. The onSubmit event handler also has a related method called submit(), which we will cover in Module 14.

To see the submit event at work, we will have to create a form that can be submitted with a submit button. We will then need to add the onSubmit event handler to the opening <FORM>tag. The following code will give a "Thank You" alert to the viewer once the submit button is clicked:

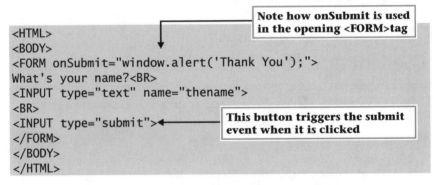

Note how onSubmit is used in the opening <FORM>tag

```
<HTML>
<BODY>
<FORM onSubmit="window.alert('Thank You');">
What's your name?<BR>
<INPUT type="text" name="thename">
<BR>
<INPUT type="submit">
</FORM>
</BODY>
</HTML>
```

This button triggers the submit event when it is clicked

The submit event doesn't do us much good now (especially with the contents of the form not really going anywhere), but this event will become more useful when we get to form validation in Module 14.

1-Minute Drill

● **What action(s) might trigger a mouseover event?**

● **How might a user give focus to a form text box?**

● **What event handler is used to handle the submit event?**

● A mouseover event would be triggered by the viewer moving the mouse cursor over a link, linked image, or linked portion of an image map
● The focus is given to a form text box by clicking inside the text box
● The onSubmit event handler is used to handle the submit event

pr7_2.html

Project 7-2: Use Events to Send Out Alerts

This project will enable you to practice using a few of the event handlers we have learned so far in this module. You will be creating a page with various links and form elements that will use events to send out alerts.

Step-by-Step

1. Create an HTML page, leaving room in the BODY section for the code we will be adding to it.

2. Add a link to the page that links to the URL http://www.yahoo.com. Add an event handler to the link tag so that when the viewer moves the mouse cursor over the link, an alert pops up that says, "Sorry, I'm not in the mood for you to leave yet!"

3. Add a <P> tag after the link.

4. Add the <FORM> and </FORM> tags to the page below the <P> tag, and then add the form elements in the following steps between these tags.

5. Add a text box that asks the viewer for a phone number. Set it up so that when the viewer gives the text box focus, an alert pops up that says, "Format is xxx-xxxx."

6. Add a second text box that will ask for the viewer's name. Set it up so that when a blur event occurs, an alert will pop up that says, "Thanks, if that is your real name!"

7. Add a third text box that asks for the viewer's e-mail address. Don't set it to react to any events.

8. Add a button that says, "Click Here." When the viewer clicks it, have an alert pop up that says, "Hey! I'm just a button. Leave me alone!"

9. Save the file as pr7_2.html, and open it in your browser.

10. Move your mouse over the first link. You should get the first alert.

11. Click inside the text box that asks for a phone number. You should get an alert.

12. Click the text box that asks for your name, and type in a name if you'd like.

7

13. Click the text box that asks for an e-mail address. You should get an alert about your name since you gave focus to this new text box, taking it away from the previous one. Note that if you have not clicked the text box for the name, you won't be removing focus from it; so be sure to give the name box focus, and then give this box focus right afterward.

14. Click the button so that it gives you an alert letting you know it doesn't want any company.

More Events

So far, we have seen the events that will work in the majority of browsers and thus that are used more often. The next set of events we will look at may not work in some older browsers, but they will be more commonly used as more Web surfers are able to get newer browsers.

To keep this from getting tedious by having example code for each of these events, we will just note that they work the same way as the other events. The event handler is placed within certain tags on the page and will perform an action when the event occurs. We will just give a brief description of each event, its event handler, and where it is used in a document.

The Abort Event (onAbort)

The abort event occurs when a viewer stops (aborts) the loading of an image. The event handler used for this is onAbort, which can be placed in an image tag in an HTML document.

The Dragdrop Event (onDragDrop)

The dragdrop event occurs when the viewer uses the drag-and-drop feature of an operating system to drop a file into the browser window. We use the onDragDrop event handler for this event, which is placed in the opening <BODY>tag of the document.

One thing to remember when using the onDragDrop event handler is that you need to return false after your code or the window will open the file that was dropped in (if it can). The following is a sample <BODY>tag using the onDragDrop event handler:

> **Note the return false statement here that prevents the browser from trying to open the dropped-in file**

```
<BODY onDragDrop="window.alert('Hi!');return false;">
```

The return false statement keeps the browser from trying to open the file that was dropped into the window, and, therefore, we get the alert.

The Error Event (onError)
The error event occurs when an error happens during the loading of a page or an image. The event handler for this is onError, and it can be used in an image tag or in the opening <BODY>tag on a page.

The Keydown Event (onKeyDown)
The keydown event occurs when the viewer presses a key down on the keyboard. To handle this event, we use onKeyDown. We can place this event handler in a text area tag or the opening <BODY>tag on a page.

The Keypress Event (onKeyPress)
The keypress event occurs when a viewer holds down a key on the keyboard. To take care of this event we use the onKeyPress event handler, which can be placed in a text area tag or in the opening <BODY>tag on a page.

The Keyup Event (onKeyUp)
The keyup event occurs when the viewer lets go of a key on the keyboard, releasing the key. The event handler for this is onKeyUp, and it can be placed in a text area tag or the opening <BODY>tag on a page.

The Mousedown Event (onMouseDown)

The mousedown event occurs when a viewer presses the mouse button down but before the click is complete (doesn't need to be released). To handle this event, we use the onMouseDown event handler, which can be placed within a link (anchor) tag on a Web page or in other areas (such as DIV tags) with some newer browsers.

The Mouseup Event (onMouseUp)

The mouseup event occurs when the viewer releases the mouse button after pressing it down. The onMouseUp event handler is used for this event, and it can be placed in a link (anchor) tag on a page or in other areas (such as <DIV>tags) with some newer browsers.

The Mousemove Event (onMouseMove)

The mousemove event occurs when the viewer moves the mouse cursor. The event handler for this is onMouseMove, which is often used in the opening <BODY>tag of the page. It can also be used in a number of other tags on a page (such as a <DIV> tag).

The Move Event (onMove)

The move event occurs when the viewer moves the browser window or when the window is moved through the use of a script. The event handler we use for this is onMove, which is placed in the opening <BODY> tag on a page.

The Reset Event (onReset)

This event occurs when a viewer uses a form Reset button to reset the form fields in a form. To take care of this event, we use the onReset event handler, which is added to the opening <FORM>tag in a form. The onReset event handler also has a related method called reset(), which we will cover in a later module.

The Resize Event (onResize)

This event occurs when a viewer resizes a window or when the window is resized through the use of a script. The event handler we use for this is onResize, and it is used in the opening <BODY>tag of a document.

The Select Event (onSelect)

The select event occurs when the user selects (highlights with the mouse) some text inside a text box or a text area on a page. To handle this event, we use the onSelect event handler, which can be placed inside a text input tag or a text area tag in an HTML document.

Scripts for Event Handlers

Now that we have the long list of event handlers tackled, it's time to have a little fun. In this section, we are going to learn two new properties that will do things other than writing to the page and sending an alert.

7

Ask the Expert

Question: Why are we learning these newer events if they only work in later browsers?

Answer: More and more Web surfers are beginning to use the latest browsers, so these will be helpful to know in the long run. Also, there are already numerous scripts out on the Web that use these events, so it is quite possible to see one or more of them. Knowing what they do will help you understand the script better.

Question: Why are there so many events?

Answer: There are so many things that a viewer (or the browser itself) can do while on a Web page that we end up with a bunch of events. It's possible that more events could be added to the list as the JavaScript language expands.

Question: Do I need to memorize all of these?

Answer: You probably only need to memorize them if you have a test, are doing this for a job and need to know things quickly, or if you just like knowing the events off the top of your head; otherwise, you can just refer back to Table 7-1 in this module, if you are not sure which event needs to be used.

Question: Will we be using every single event in this book?

Answer: Since this book is a beginner's guide, we will not get to the point where we use every single event.

After seeing all of those examples with alerts, the alert is probably a little stale now. Thus, we are going to try two new scripts. One will change the text inside the status bar of the browser window and the other will make a form button into a button that acts like a link. To begin, let's try changing the text in the status bar.

The Status Bar Change

The status bar is at the bottom of the browser window. It is the area where you normally see things such as Opening page or Document:Done. Also, when you move your mouse over a link, the status bar displays the URL address of the link for you (unless we use a script to change it).

If we want to change the text in the status bar of the browser, we will need to learn a new window property. This property is window.status, and it can be used to place a new text string at the bottom of the browser. The following is the basic syntax for the window.status command:

```
window.status="Your text here";
```

We replace the "Your text here" part with the string we wish to place inside the status bar. This is similar to giving a value to a variable, but we are instead giving a new value to a window property.

To see this in action, let's try to change the text in the status bar when the viewer moves the mouse cursor over a link. Rather than displaying the link's URL in the status bar, suppose we want to describe where the link will go with our own text instead. An example of this is shown in the following code:

This may not work; we need one more statement here to make the code complete

```
<A HREF="pr7_2.html" onMouseOver="window.status='My last project';">
Events</A>
```

Note how the single quotes are used to set the window.status string here, since we are already within double quotes from the onMouseOver event handler. Even so, this code still may not work. The problem is that we need to have a return true statement after the status bar change.

We need to return true so that our new text will override the original link URL text the browser will display. Basically, we want to override the default text and not stop the text in the status bar entirely. In order for our new text to be set in the status bar, we need to return true. The following example will work since we have added the return statement:

The return true statement makes sure that the text in the status bar is reset

```
<A HREF="pr7_2.html"
 onMouseOver="window.status='My last project'; return true;">
Events</A>
```

Figure 7-8 shows the result of this code in the browser once the viewer moves the mouse over the link. Look at the bottom-left corner of the browser window to see the new status bar text.

The thing you may notice here is that if you test this code out, you will see that after the text in the status bar has changed on the mouseover event, it does not change back or clear once we move the mouse away. The text just sits there in the status bar until we make another change.

| **Figure 7-8** | The status bar text is changed when the mouse moves over the link |

If we want to make sure the status bar clears when we move the mouse cursor away from the link, we will need to add an onMouseOut event handler to the link tag as well. The following example shows how this is done:

```
<A HREF="pr7_2.html"
 onMouseOver="window.status='My last project'; return true;"
 onMouseOut="window.status=''; return true;">
Events</A>
```

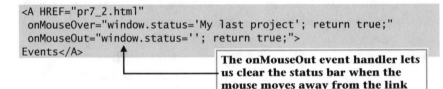

The onMouseOut event handler lets us clear the status bar when the mouse moves away from the link

Notice how we used a blank string for the status bar value on the mouseout event. This is what clears the status bar when the mouse moves away.

Hint

Even though the code has line breaks in the examples in this module, it is best to keep the entire contents of the opening link (anchor) tag on one line.

Using the window.status property, we will be able to make use of more events, as well as be able to use more than one event at a time as we just did. It will also give us another technique to use in examples. Now that we know how to change the status bar text in the browser, let's see how we can create a button that acts like a link.

The Button Link

Using JavaScript, we can turn a plain form button into a link. To do this, we will need to use another new property: the window.location property. This property enables us to change the URL address of the window in which we use it. The following is the general syntax for the command:

```
window.location="http://someplace.com";
```

We replace the URL http://someplace.*com* with the address we wish to use in its place, such as http://www.yahoo.com or some other Web address.

Now, to make a button work like a link, all we need to do is use the location property with the onClick event handler inside a button input tag. The following is an example of this:

```
<FORM>
<INPUT TYPE="button" value="Go Searching!"
 onClick="window.location='http://www.yahoo.com';">
</FORM>
```

Notice the single quotes around the URL here

Again, we need to use the single quotes inside because there are already double quotes outside the command. Clicking this button would take you to a popular Web directory, thus acting like a regular link.

Of course, we can do this for any number of buttons. If we want three buttons to link to three places, we could use the following code:

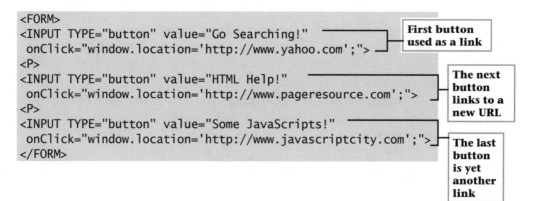

```
<FORM>
<INPUT TYPE="button" value="Go Searching!"
 onClick="window.location='http://www.yahoo.com';">
<P>
<INPUT TYPE="button" value="HTML Help!"
 onClick="window.location='http://www.pageresource.com';">
<P>
<INPUT TYPE="button" value="Some JavaScripts!"
 onClick="window.location='http://www.javascriptcity.com';">
</FORM>
```

First button used as a link

The next button links to a new URL

The last button is yet another link

7

This code creates three buttons that link to three different sites. Of course, if you decide to use a large number of these, it might be easier to call a function with the URL sent as a parameter, as shown in the following code:

```
<HTML>
<HEAD>
<TITLE>Button Links</TITLE>
<SCRIPT language="JavaScript">
<!--
function go_to(place)          The function takes in a parameter
{
  window.location=place;       The location of the window changes
}                              to the value of the variable
//-->
</SCRIPT>
</HEAD>
<BODY>
<FORM>
<INPUT TYPE="button" value="Go Searching!"
 onClick="go_to('http://www.yahoo.com');">
<P>
<INPUT TYPE="button" value="HTML Help!"
 onClick="go_to('http://www.pageresource.com');">
<P>
<INPUT TYPE="button" value="Some JavaScripts!"
 onClick="go_to('http://www.javascriptcity.com');">
</FORM>
</BODY>
</HTML>
```

Each button sends one URL as a parameter to the function

By using the function in the preceding code, you can save yourself having to write out window.location on every button. Also, you are able to use the function elsewhere on the page if you decide you want to change the window location through another event.

Now we can do a few more things and have a little more fun with our examples. The window.location property will become quite useful to us as we move through the later modules.

pr7_3.html

Project 7-3: Practicing with Window Status and Location Properties

This project will help you continue to practice the use of the window.status and window.location properties. You will make a button that changes the window status, and you will make a text link that changes the document location without the need to click it.

Step-by-Step

1. Create an HTML document, leaving some space in the BODY section to add the code that will be used.

2. Create a form button that changes the text in the status bar of the browser to "Hey there!" when clicked by the viewer. Use a value="Change Status!" attribute in the button input tag to give it a label.

3. Add a <P> tag after the button code.

4. Create a second button that will clear the status bar when the viewer clicks it. Use a value="Clear Status!" attribute in the button input tag to give it a label.

5. Add a <P> tag after the button code.

6. Create a text link that changes the window location when the viewer moves the mouse over it but before the viewer clicks it. Make the text for the link read "No need to click this link." Make the new window location the URL http://www.yahoo.com so the viewer will go there on a mouseover event.

7. Save the file as pr7_3.html, and open it in your Web browser.

8. Click the first button, and you should see the status bar text change. Click the second button, and the status bar should clear.

9. If you are online, move your mouse over the link and watch as you are taken away without clicking the link!

7

☑ Mastery Check

1. Event handlers are useful because they enable us to gain _____ to the _____ that may occur on the page.

2. Which of the following correctly codes an alert on the click event?

    A. <INPUT type="button" onClick="window.alert("Hey there!");">

    B. <INPUT type="button" onclick="window.alert('Hey there!');">

    C. <INPUT type="button" onClick="window.alert('Hey there!');">

    D. <INPUT type="button" onChange="window.alert("Hey there!");">

3. The onLoad event handler is placed inside the opening _____ tag.

4. A mouseover event occurs when

    A. The viewer clicks the mouse while the cursor is over a button.

    B. The viewer moves the mouse cursor away from a link.

    C. The viewer clicks a link, linked image, or linked area of an image map.

    D. The viewer moves the mouse cursor over a link, linked image, or linked area of an image map.

5. Which of the following calls a function named "major_alert()" inside the onFocus event handler correctly?

    A. <INPUT type="text" onFocus= "major_alert();">

    B. <INPUT type= "text" onFocus= "major alert();">

    C. <INPUT type= "text" onfocus= "major_alert();">

    D. <INPUT type= "text" onFocus= "major_alert()">

Module 8

Objects

The Goals of This Module

- Learn what objects are
- Find out why objects are useful
- Learn how to name objects
- Create your own object
- Learn about predefined JavaScript objects
- Discover how to use the JavaScript history object

Since JavaScript is an object-based language, we need to look at objects to understand what they are and how we can use them. The predefined objects in JavaScript are the ones that we will probably find most useful; however, to use them effectively, it is a good idea to learn how objects work in general and how to create your own objects if you need them.

We will begin by defining what objects are and how objects can be useful to us in our scripts. We will then look at how to create and name our own objects that we can use in our code. Finally, we will take a look at a number of predefined JavaScript objects and cover properties and methods of the predefined history object.

Defining Objects

To begin using JavaScript objects, we will need to find out what they are and how they can be useful to us in our scripts. Let's take a look at what JavaScript objects are.

What Is an Object?

An object is a way of modeling something real, even though the object is an abstract entity. When you think of an object, you'll probably want to visualize something general, such as a car. When you see a car, you will notice it has certain features, which we could call "properties". You might see that the car has a radio with a CD player, leather seats, and a V–8 engine. All these things are parts of the car, or if we think about it in terms of objects, these things would all be properties of the car object.

We could break this down further by making the radio have properties, or we could go the other way and make the car part of a larger object. For instance, we could say the CD radio has certain features, such as touch volume control, radio station presets, and a digital interface. If we go the other way, we could say a car is part of an automobile object that could include cars, vans, trucks, and various other motor vehicles.

By doing this, we could create a visualization that could be followed down from the top. If we have an automobile that is a car, which has a CD radio with a digital interface, we would see a pattern like the following:

```
Automobile -> Car -> CD Radio -> Digital Interface
```

We could instead have a truck, but leave the other features the same. Then we would have the following pattern:

```
Automobile -> Truck -> CD Radio -> Digital Interface
```

The preceding example works a little bit like a family tree, with the top level starting everything. Each level after the top level may have brothers and sisters (objects on the same level). Then it can continue expanding.

The visualization can get confusing, but the confusion won't be a problem for us when we work with the actual JavaScript objects. Many objects go just one level deep, so we probably won't need to worry about the "family tree" very much. The main thing we want to learn is that an object can hold a number of properties inside it that we can access from the outside in order to use them in our scripts.

Why Objects Are Useful

8

Objects are useful because they give us another way to organize things within a script. Rather than having a bunch of similar variables that are out there on their own, we can group them together under an object.

If we take our car object and make the features of the car "variables," we can begin to see how this type of grouping works. We could make the variables "seats," "engine," and "theradio," and for now we will assume them to be properties of the car object. In order for this to be the actual case, we would need to create the car object.

We will do that later in the module, but for now we will assume the car object exists and has the properties of seats, engine, and theradio. Since these properties are variables, they can have values. The question is, how do we access these properties to get their values?

In JavaScript, we access object properties through the use of the dot operator, which is just a dot or period. For instance, if we wanted the value of the seats property of the car, we could access it with the following line:

```
var chtype= car.seats;
```

Don't let the assigning of the value of the seats property to a variable (chtype) be confusing. What we want to see here is the car.seats part of the code. The name of the object is written first, then the property we want to access is connected to it on the right using the dot operator.

The seats property doesn't currently have a value (since we haven't created the car object). We will see how to give it and other properties values when we begin creating objects in the near future in the next section.

1-Minute Drill

● **When you think about objects, should you think of something general or something specific?**

● **Why are objects useful?**

● **What operator is used to access a property of an object?**

Creating Objects

Now that we understand what objects are and their usefulness, we can begin creating our own JavaScript objects. To do this, we will learn about naming conventions, the structure of an object, and how to include methods in our objects.

Naming

As with variables and functions, there are certain rules we have to follow when naming our objects in JavaScript. They are essentially the same rules

---

● You'll want to visualize something general
● They give us another way to organize things within a script
● The dot (.) operator

we follow for naming variables and functions, so we will just discuss them briefly here since we have been through this twice already.

Case Sensitivity

As with previous naming, object names are case sensitive. Thus, an object named "car" would be different than Car, CAR, or caR. In order to access the right object, we have to be sure to use the proper case when we use it in the script; otherwise, we will receive an error such as "Car is not an object" when we try to run the script.

Avoiding Reserved Words/Objects

The other thing to remember when naming our own objects is that we cannot use a JavaScript reserved word (see Module 2, Table 2-1); thus, trying to make an object named "switch" could give us problems because that word is used for the JavaScript switch statement.

Object Structure

There are two ways to create objects in JavaScript. We can create objects either by using a constructor function or by using an object initializer. Note that the object initializer option was added in JavaScript 1.2 and, thus, will not work with older browsers. We will discuss how to make use of constructor functions when we create objects, and we will also discuss the object initializer briefly in this section.

Constructor Functions

A constructor function allows us to build an object using the same basic syntax as a regular function. The only difference is the code we place inside of the function and how we access its contents.

For example, to create our car object, we would create a constructor function named "car" and then add our properties within the function. The following example shows an outline of the car function:

```
function car()  ◄————— The constructor function is defined
{
  Properties Go Here. ◄————— The properties will be listed here
}                                for the object we are creating
```

To complete the preceding function, we will need to add our properties to the function. Recall that we want to create an object named "car" with the properties of seats, engine, and theradio. The following code shows how this is done:

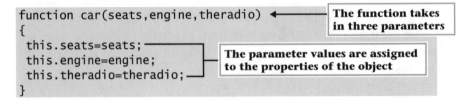

```
function car(seats,engine,theradio)          The function takes
{                                            in three parameters
  this.seats=seats;
  this.engine=engine;                        The parameter values are assigned
  this.theradio=theradio;                    to the properties of the object
}
```

In this code, on the first line, you will see that the function takes three parameters. These just happen to match the number of properties we want the car object to have. The next thing we see is that the values of the parameters are assigned to the properties we want the car object to have; however, there is a new keyword there named "this." The keyword "this" in JavaScript is a keyword used to represent the current object being used, or "this object," so to speak.

Once we have the object's properties set with the constructor function, we will need to create what is called an "instance" of the object in order to make use of it. This is because a constructor function only creates the structure of an object, not a usable instance of an object. To create an instance of an object, we use another JavaScript keyword: new.

The use of the new keyword to create an instance of our car object is shown in the following code:

```
var work_car= new car("cloth","V-6","Tape Deck");
```

The first thing we see is that we are creating a new variable named "work_car." This variable will be a new instance of the car object due to the value we are assigning to it.

We see that we assigned the work_car variable the result of the car constructor function, with a twist. In front of the call to the car function, we have the new keyword. The new keyword makes sure we are creating a new instance of the constructor function object.

Next, we see that the car function is called with values sent as parameters. These are the values we want to use for this instance of the car object. Given the order, we are saying we want the seats to be cloth, the engine to be V-6, and theradio to be Tape Deck.

We can now access the work_car instance of the car object. If we want to know what type of engine the work_car has, we can access it with the dot operator:

```
var engine_type= work_car.engine;
```

This assigns the value of the engine property of the work_car instance of the car object to the variable engine_type. Since we sent V-6 as the engine parameter to the constructor function, the engine_type variable is assigned a value of V-6.

Putting the Pieces Together   To help us visualize this process, let's put all these parts together so we can see how it works. The following code below combines all of the separate codes of our previous examples to make things easier to see:

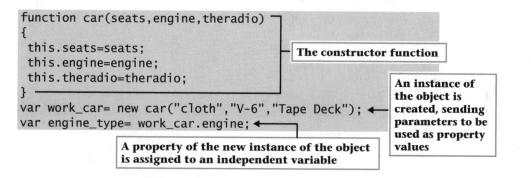

```
function car(seats,engine,theradio)
{
  this.seats=seats;
  this.engine=engine;                      ─── The constructor function
  this.theradio=theradio;
}
var work_car= new car("cloth","V-6","Tape Deck");   ◄──  An instance of
var engine_type= work_car.engine;  ◄──                     the object is
                                                           created, sending
                A property of the new instance of the object   parameters to be
                is assigned to an independent variable          used as property
                                                                values
```

8

Now we can see the constructor function, the creation of an instance of the car object, and the assignment of one of the properties of the object to a variable. When the work_car instance of the car object is set, it gets the values of cloth for the property work_car.seats, V-6 for the property work_car.engine, and Tape Deck for the property work_car.theradio.

In order to see how an instance of an object works, let's add another instance of the car object to our code. The following code uses two instances of the car object, one named "work_car" and a new one named "fun_car":

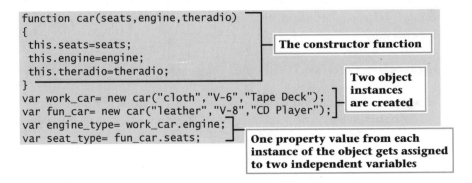

```
function car(seats,engine,theradio)
{
  this.seats=seats;
  this.engine=engine;
  this.theradio=theradio;
}
var work_car= new car("cloth","V-6","Tape Deck");
var fun_car= new car("leather","V-8","CD Player");
var engine_type= work_car.engine;
var seat_type= fun_car.seats;
```

The constructor function

Two object instances are created

One property value from each instance of the object gets assigned to two independent variables

Notice how the new instance of the object uses the same constructor function, but with different values. We also have a new variable named "seat_type," which is given the value of the seats property of the fun_car instance of the car object.

By doing this, we could now write out the features we would like to have in a custom car that combines features from each type of car. For example, take a look at the following code, which writes out the features we might like in a custom car:

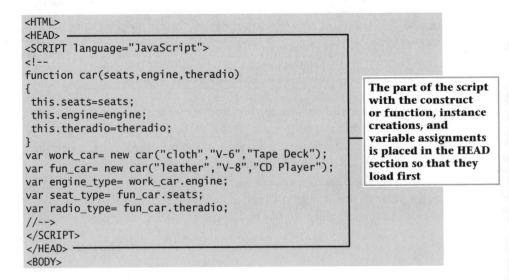

```
<HTML>
<HEAD>
<SCRIPT language="JavaScript">
<!--
function car(seats,engine,theradio)
{
  this.seats=seats;
  this.engine=engine;
  this.theradio=theradio;
}
var work_car= new car("cloth","V-6","Tape Deck");
var fun_car= new car("leather","V-8","CD Player");
var engine_type= work_car.engine;
var seat_type= fun_car.seats;
var radio_type= fun_car.theradio;
//-->
</SCRIPT>
</HEAD>
<BODY>
```

The part of the script with the construct or function, instance creations, and variable assignments is placed in the HEAD section so that they load first

```
<SCRIPT language="JavaScript">
<!--
document.write("I want a car with "+seat_type+" seats.<BR>");
document.write("It also needs a "+engine_type+" engine.<BR>");
document.write("Oh, and I would like a "+radio_type+" also.");
//-->
</SCRIPT>
</BODY>
</HTML>
```

The document.write() commands are used in the BODY section so that they display in the browser

Using the variable values that grab what we want from each instance of the car object, we are able to print the description of the car we would like to have to the screen. The results of this script are shown in Figure 8-1.

We could also do what we did in the preceding example by creating a new instance of the car object with our choices and then printing those to the screen. If we create an instance named "custom_car," we could use the following code:

```
<HTML>
<HEAD>
<SCRIPT language="JavaScript">
<!--
function car(seats,engine,theradio)
{
 this.seats=seats;
 this.engine=engine;
 this.theradio=theradio;
}
var work_car= new car("cloth","V-6","Tape Deck");
var fun_car= new car("leather","V-8","CD Player");
var custom_car= new
car(fun_car.seats,work_car.engine,fun_car.theradio);
//-->
</SCRIPT>
</HEAD>
<BODY>
<SCRIPT language="JavaScript">
<!--
document.write("I want a car with "+custom_car.seats+" seats.<BR>");
document.write("It also needs a "+custom_car.engine+" engine.<BR>");
document.write("Oh, and I would like a "+custom_car.theradio+" also.");
//-->
</SCRIPT>
</BODY>
</HTML>
```

A new instance of the object is created, sending the values of the properties of other object instances as parameters

The properties of the new instance of the object are used like variables in the document.write() statements

8

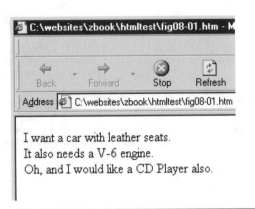

I want a car with leather seats.
It also needs a V-6 engine.
Oh, and I would like a CD Player also.

Figure 8-1 The features we like from each type of car are printed in the browser

Notice how the creation of the custom_car instance of the car object sends parameters that happen to be the properties of the other instances of the car object. We are able to use object properties like variables in many cases, so this cuts the amount of code we need to write. Also, we changed the document.write() commands to use the properties of the custom_car instead of the old variables. The output of the script is the same, as shown in Figure 8-2.

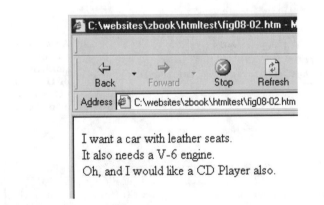

I want a car with leather seats.
It also needs a V-6 engine.
Oh, and I would like a CD Player also.

Figure 8-2 Although coded differently, the output is the same as that of Figure 8-1

Property Values   While this isn't real estate, we can alter our
property values. In our scripts, we can change the value of an object
property on the fly by assigning it a new value, just like a variable. For
example, if we wanted to change the value of the work_car.engine
property from our previous examples, we could just assign it a new value
of our choice. The following example shows the assignment of a new
value to the work_car.engine property:

```
work_car.engine= "V-4";
```

While perhaps not a good change, it could save us money on insurance!

It is important to note that the preceding assignment will change the
value of the work_car.engine property for any calls made to it after the
change. Anything we do with its value before the change would not be
affected. So, to have an effect on the outcome of our script, we would
have to change the value of the work_car.engine property before we
create our custom_car instance of the car object, which uses this property.

The following code gives a new assignment to the property before we
create the new instance of the object:

8

```
<HTML>
<HEAD>
<SCRIPT language="JavaScript">
<!--
function car(seats,engine,theradio)
{
  this.seats=seats;
  this.engine=engine;
  this.theradio=theradio;
}
var work_car= new car("cloth","V-6","Tape Deck");
var fun_car= new car("leather","V-8","CD Player");

work_car.engine="V-4";  ◄─────────────

var custom_car= new car(fun_car.seats,work_car.engine,fun_car.theradio);
//-->
</SCRIPT>
</HEAD>
<BODY>
<SCRIPT language="JavaScript">
<!--
document.write("I want a car with "+custom_car.seats+" seats.<BR>");
document.write("It also needs a "+custom_car.engine+" engine.<BR>");
document.write("Oh, and I would like a "+custom_car.theradio+" also.");
//-->
```

> **One of the properties of an object is changed, which alters that property for anything using it afterward**

```
</SCRIPT>
</BODY>
</HTML>
```

The work_car.engine property is originally set to V–6, but we changed it to V–4 just before we created our custom_car instance of the car object. This means that when we use the work_car.engine property while creating our custom_car instance, it will use the changed value of V–4 since it is used after the change was made. Figure 8-3 shows the results of this changed code.

To drive home the point, we could use the property both before and after it is changed to see how it affects the script. The following code shows this.

```
<HTML>
<HEAD>
<SCRIPT language="JavaScript">
<!--
function car(seats,engine,theradio)
{
 this.seats=seats;
 this.engine=engine;
 this.theradio=theradio;
}
var work_car= new car("cloth","V-6","Tape Deck");
var fun_car= new car("leather","V-8","CD Player");

var first_engine=work_car.engine;   ◄───  The original value of the
                                          property is assigned to an
                                          independent variable
work_car.engine="V-4";   ◄───

var custom_car= new car(fun_car.seats,work_car.engine,fun_car.theradio);
//-->
</SCRIPT>                          The property is changed, changing
</HEAD>                            the value of it when used afterward
<BODY>
<SCRIPT language="JavaScript">
<!--
document.write("At first, I wanted a "+first_engine+" engine.<BR>");
document.write("But after thinking about it a bit:<BR>");
document.write("I want a car with "+custom_car.seats+" seats.<BR>");
document.write("It also needs a "+custom_car.engine+" engine.<BR>");
document.write("Oh, and I would like a "+custom_car.theradio+" also.");
//-->
</SCRIPT>
</BODY>
</HTML>
```

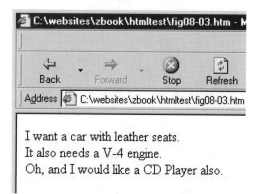

Figure 8-3   One of the property values is changed, changing the output of the script

Notice how the work_car.engine value is assigned to the first_engine variable. It is then changed before we create our custom_car instance of the car object. When we write the value of the first_engine variable to the browser, it has the old value of the work_car.engine property since it was assigned before the change was made.

When we write the values of our custom_car properties, we can see that the change was made sometime before we created the custom_car instance of the car object. Figure 8-4 shows the results of this script in a browser.

Now that we know how to make use of constructor functions, let's take a look at the new object initializer method in JavaScript 1.2.

Object Initializers

An object initializer is a little bit shorter than a constructor function, but it is only supported in JavaScript 1.2 and higher. Thus, if you decide to use this method, you might wish to add the language="JavaScript1.2" attribute to your opening <SCRIPT> tag so that your visitors with older browsers won't receive errors.

The following is the syntax of an object initializer:

object_name= {property:value}

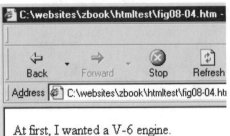

At first, I wanted a V-6 engine.
But after thinking about it a bit:
I want a car with leather seats.
It also needs a V-4 engine.
Oh, and I would like a CD Player also.

Figure 8-4   The change in the property value affects the statements that use it after the change, but not those that use it before the change

In the preceding code, we would replace *object_name* with the name we want to give our object. We would replace *property* with the name we want to use for a property of the object. Then would we replace *value* with the value of the property that precedes it. We can add more properties and values by separating each with a comma.

An object created with the initializer function is already an instance of the object, so we can just use the properties without the need to create a new instance of the object.

Let's create a work_car object using the initializer method. We want the object name to be "work_car," and we will have three sets of properties and values. The following code shows how to create the object we want using the object initializer method:

```
work_car= {seats:"cloth",engine:"V-6",theradio:"Tape Deck"}
```

Since there is no need to create an instance of the object, we can use its properties just as we did before, and assign them to variables or write them to the page. For instance, the property of work_car.seats would be cloth.

If we want the fun_car object back as well, we can use another initializer, as shown in the following example code:

```
work_car= {seats:"cloth",engine:"V-6",theradio:"Tape Deck"}
fun_car= {seats:"leather",engine:"V-8",theradio:"CD Player"}
```

We can then write out what we want to have in a car using those properties, as shown in the following code:

```
<HTML>
<HEAD>
<SCRIPT language="JavaScript">
<!--
work_car= {seats:"cloth",engine:"V-6",theradio:"Tape Deck"}
fun_car= {seats:"leather",engine:"V-8",theradio:"CD Player"}
//-->
</SCRIPT>
</HEAD>
<BODY>
<SCRIPT language="JavaScript">
<!--
document.write("I want a car with "+fun_car.seats+" seats.<BR>");
document.write("It also needs a "+work_car.engine+" engine.<BR>");
document.write("Oh, and I would like a "+fun_car.theradio+" also.");
//-->
</SCRIPT>
</BODY>
</HTML>
```

Objects are created using object initializers

Properties of the objects are used in document.write() statements

8

This prints what we like from each type of car to the browser screen. Figure 8-5 shows the results of this script in a browser.

This method can cut the coding a bit, at least if you only want to use one or two instances of the same type of object.

Adding Methods

A method is a function call that is part of an object. The function called can perform various tasks that we might want to execute with the properties of the object.

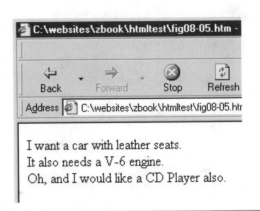

Figure 8-5 **The properties we like from each type of car are shown in the browser**

Consider the car object that we created with a constructor function earlier in the module. If we wanted to add a function for that object that would calculate the monthly payments on the various types (instances) of cars that we sent to it, we could create a function like the following:

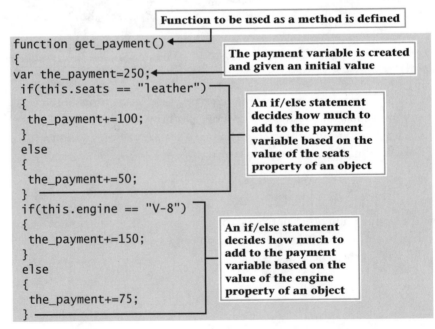

Function to be used as a method is defined

```
function get_payment()
{
var the_payment=250;
  if(this.seats == "leather")
  {
   the_payment+=100;
  }
  else
  {
   the_payment+=50;
  }
  if(this.engine == "V-8")
  {
   the_payment+=150;
  }
  else
  {
   the_payment+=75;
  }
```

The payment variable is created and given an initial value

An if/else statement decides how much to add to the payment variable based on the value of the seats property of an object

An if/else statement decides how much to add to the payment variable based on the value of the engine property of an object

```
if(this.theradio == "CD Player")
{
  the_payment+=35;
}
else
{
  the_payment+=10;
}
return the_payment;
}
```

> An if/else statement decides how much to add to the payment variable based on the value of the theradio property of an object

Well, the previous function is really long. It can be shortened by eliminating the brackets on the if/else blocks as along as we do not have more than one statement in any of them. We could make it shorter:

```
function get_payment()
{
var the_payment=250;
  if(this.seats == "leather")
    the_payment+=100;
  else
    the_payment+=50;
  if(this.engine == "V-8")
    the_payment+=150;
  else
    the_payment+=75;
  if(this.theradio == "CD Player")
    the_payment+=35;
  else
    the_payment+=10;
return the_payment;
}
```

> The brackets are removed from the if/else statements to make the code shorter, since each block has only one statement

8

──┼Caution──

Remember to exercise caution when removing brackets to reduce code listings because you will need to add the brackets back in any block you decide to expand on later.

After we have the function defined, we need to make a call to it within our object constructor function. Using our trusty car object constructor function, we would add the call to it as shown in the following code:

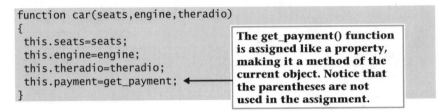

```
function car(seats,engine,theradio)
{
  this.seats=seats;
  this.engine=engine;
  this.theradio=theradio;
  this.payment=get_payment;
}
```

The get_payment() function is assigned like a property, making it a method of the current object. Notice that the parentheses are not used in the assignment.

Notice that we define a method named "payment" that calls the get_payment() function from outside the constructor function. Also notice that when we call the function here, we do not use the parentheses on the end of the function call. This is how our outside function becomes a method of the object.

In order to call the payment() method of the object, we need an instance of the car object. If we add the three instances we made earlier, we will be able to do some things with our new method. So, let's add those to the code we already have:

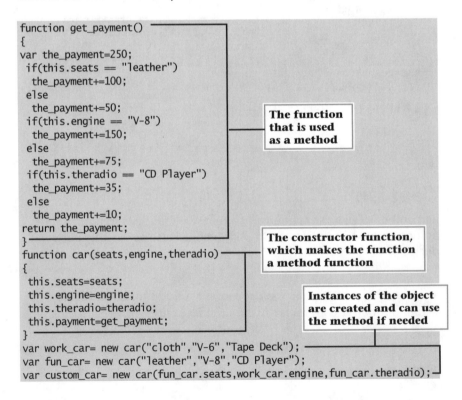

```
function get_payment()
{
var the_payment=250;
  if(this.seats == "leather")
    the_payment+=100;
  else
    the_payment+=50;
  if(this.engine == "V-8")
    the_payment+=150;
  else
    the_payment+=75;
  if(this.theradio == "CD Player")
    the_payment+=35;
  else
    the_payment+=10;
  return the_payment;
}
function car(seats,engine,theradio)
{
  this.seats=seats;
  this.engine=engine;
  this.theradio=theradio;
  this.payment=get_payment;
}
var work_car= new car("cloth","V-6","Tape Deck");
var fun_car= new car("leather","V-8","CD Player");
var custom_car= new car(fun_car.seats,work_car.engine,fun_car.theradio);
```

The function that is used as a method

The constructor function, which makes the function a method function

Instances of the object are created and can use the method if needed

Now we have the function that is used to create the payment()
method of the car object, the creation of the payment() method within the
car object constructor function, and three instances of the car object.

To find the monthly payments for work_car, we would call the
payment() method using the following syntax:

```
var work_car_payments= work_car.payment();
```

The value of the work_car_payments variable will be the value returned
from the payment() method, which is what is returned from the
get_payment() function when run with the values used for the
work_car instance of the car object.

Since the seats are cloth, the_payment is increased by 50 (if they were
leather it would have been 100). Since the engine is a V-6, the_payment
is increased by 75. Finally, since the theradio property has a value of Tape
Deck, the the_payment variable is increased by 10. This gives us a
payment of 250 (initial value) + 50 (nonleather seats) + 75 (non-V-8
engine) +10 (radio without CD player), which turns out to be 385.

Using the payment() method, we could now write a script to display
the payment amount for each type of car in the browser so the viewer can
decide what type of car to buy. We would just expand on our previous
code to include some document.write() commands in the body of the
page that use the values returned from the payment() method.

The following code gives an example of the payment() method when
used for each instance of the car object:

```html
<HTML>
<HEAD>
<SCRIPT language="JavaScript">
<!--
function get_payment()
{
var the_payment=250;
 if(this.seats == "leather")
  the_payment+=100;
 else
  the_payment+=50;
 if(this.engine == "V-8")
  the_payment+=150;
 else
  the_payment+=75;
 if(this.theradio == "CD Player")
  the_payment+=35;
 else
```

8

```
  the_payment+=10;
return the_payment;
}

function car(seats,engine,theradio)
{
 this.seats=seats;
 this.engine=engine;
 this.theradio=theradio;
 this.payment=get_payment;
}

var work_car= new car("cloth","V-6","Tape Deck");
var fun_car= new car("leather","V-8","CD Player");
var custom_car= new car(fun_car.seats,work_car.engine,fun_car.theradio);

var work_car_payment= work_car.payment();
var fun_car_payment= fun_car.payment();
var custom_car_payment= custom_car.payment();
//-->
</SCRIPT>
</HEAD>
<BODY>
<SCRIPT language="JavaScript">
<!--
document.write("<H2>The information on the cars you requested:</H2>");
document.write("<B>Work Car: </B>");
document.write(work_car.seats+","+work_car.engine+","+work_car.theradio);
document.write("<BR>");
document.write("<B>Payments:</B> $"+work_car_payment);
document.write("<P>");
document.write("<B>Fun Car: </B>");
document.write(fun_car.seats+","+fun_car.engine+","+fun_car.theradio);
document.write("<BR>");
document.write("<B>Payments:</B> $"+fun_car_payment);
document.write("<P>");
document.write("<B>Custom Car: </B>");
document.write(custom_car.seats+","+custom_car.engine+",");
document.write(custom_car.theradio);
document.write("<BR>");
document.write("<B>Payments:</B> $"+custom_car_payment);
//-->
</SCRIPT>
</BODY>
</HTML>
```

> The returned value of the method function for each of three instances of the object is assigned to three independent variables

> Various object properties and variables are used in the document.write() statements to create a listing of the cars, their features, and the payment amounts

The script is quite long compared to most of the scripts we have done up to this point. The result of the preceding script is a listing of each type of car, its features, and the payment amount for the car.

Some of the document.write() statements in the previous code are being used to continue the statement preceding them. This is due to the space available to show the code, so we could put as much code in one document.write() command as we like in out text editor. Figure 8-6 shows the results of the code when run in a browser. We are starting to make some scripts that are more useful!

Now that we have seen how to create objects, properties, and methods of our own, we can better understand how some of the predefined JavaScript objects work. We will be discussing a number of predefined JavaScript objects as we move through the rest of this module and through several of the modules to follow.

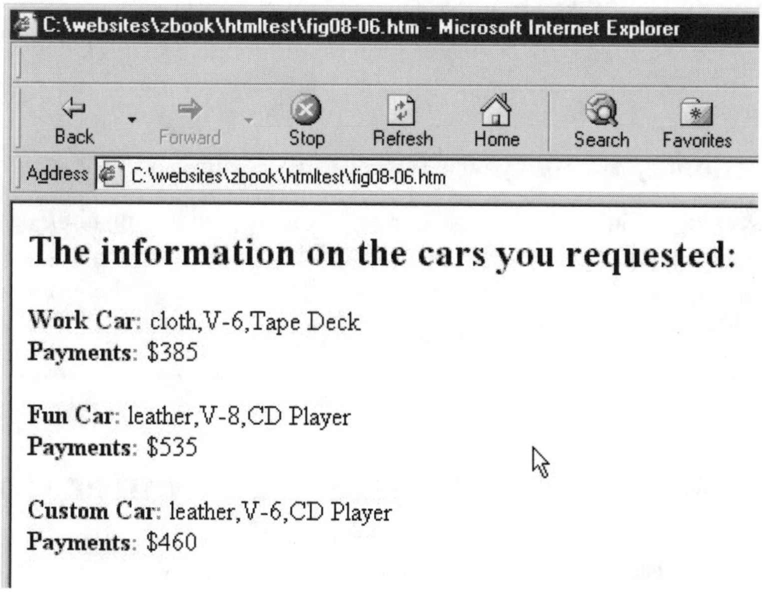

Figure 8-6   A listing of the types of cars, their features, and their calculated monthly payments

Ask the Expert

Question: Do I really have to create an instance of an object every time I want one when I use a constructor function?

Answer: Yes. The constructor function only gives the browser the structure of an object. To make use of that structure, we need to create an instance of the object. We will see in Module 12 that we need to create instances with some of the predefined JavaScript objects as well.

Question: So what about object initializers? We don't have to create instances with them?

Answer: Object initializers create an object rather than just giving it a structure like a constructor function. So, the object created doesn't need to have instances created.

Question: Will we need to use self-written objects a lot?

Answer: Probably not, but it depends on your script and what you want to do. Many of our scripts will use predefined JavaScript objects; however, we may use a self-written object if it helps us with our scripts later.

Question: Can an object have more than one method?

Answer: You can include as many methods as you like in an object by repeating what we did with our method earlier in the module. For instance, we could have added another method to calculate the insurance costs of each type of car based on the properties we had for the car types.

pr8_1.html

Project 8-1: Create a Computer Object

This project will allow you to create objects on your own and develop the skills involved in object creation. The script will create a computer object and then make use of properties, methods, and instances of the object to create feature lists and price lists for the different types of computers.

Step-by-Step

1. Create an HTML page, and leave space in both the HEAD and BODY sections of the page for the parts of the script.

2. Create an object named "computer" that has three properties named "speed," "hdspace," and "ram."

3. Create an instance of the computer object and name it "work_computer." Send the string values of 500MHz for the speed parameter, 15GB for the hdspace parameter, and 128MB for the ram parameter.

4. Create an instance of the computer object and name it "home_computer." Send the string values of 450MHz for the speed parameter, 10GB for the hdspace parameter, and 64MB for the ram parameter.

5. Create an instance of the computer object and name it "laptop_computer." Send the string values of 350MHz for the speed parameter, 7GB for the hdspace parameter, and 32MB for the ram parameter.

6. Create a function named "get_price()" that will calculate the price of a computer. The base price of a computer is 1000 and should be assigned to a variable named "the_price." If the speed property of an object is equal to 500MHz, add 200 to the value of the_price; otherwise, add 100 to the_price. If the hdspace property of an object is 15GB, add 50 to the value of the_price; otherwise, add 25 to the_price. If the ram property of an object is 128MB, add 150 to the value of the_price; otherwise, add 75 to the_price. End the function with a return statement that returns the value of the variable the_price.

7. Add a call to the function created in step 6 to the car object. Give the method the name "price."

8. Assign the value returned by the price method when used with the work_computer instance of the object to a variable named "work_computer_price."

9. Assign the value returned by the price method when used with the home_computer instance of the object to a variable named "home_computer_price."

8

10. Assign the value returned by the price method when used with the laptop_computer instance of the object to a variable named "laptop_computer_price."

11. Write the features and price for each type of computer to the browser screen in the same format we used in our car example earlier in the module.

12. Save the file as pr8_1.html, and view the file in your browser. You should have a list of features and the price for each computer written on the screen.

Predefined JavaScript Objects

In JavaScript, there are many predefined objects we can use to gain access to certain properties or methods we may need. We can make our scripts even more interactive once we learn the various objects and what we can do with them.

In this book, we will be covering a number of the major predefined objects. Some of them will be the basis for an entire module, while others are smaller and may only need a portion of a module. To get started in this module, we are going to look at the navigator object and what we can do with it.

The Navigator Object

The navigator object gives us access to various properties of the viewer's browser, such as its name, version number, and more. First, we will take a look at the properties of the navigator object.

Properties

The properties of the navigator object let us find out various things about the browser the viewer is using. The properties of the navigator object cannot be changed, because they are set as read-only. This is so we don't try to change the user's browser version from 3.0 to 4.0 or something similar. Instead, we can just find out what the value of the property is and use it to allow our scripts to do different things for different browsers.

Table 8-1 shows the properties of the navigator object and the values returned by each property.

Now that we know the properties of the navigator object, we can begin to make use of them in our scripts. Let's take a look at each property in more detail.

The appCodeName Property

This property holds the value of the application code name of the browser, which is often something like Mozilla. Other than writing it to the screen or sending an alert to the viewer, we don't have much use for it at this time. The following code shows how to send an alert to the viewer to tell him or her the appCodeName of the browser being used to view the page:

```
window.alert("You are using "+navigator.appCodeName);
```

Notice how we used the object name followed by the dot operator and then the property name, just like we did when we created our own objects. This is how we are able to access the properties of the navigator object.

The appName Property

This property allows us to find out which type of browser the viewer is using to browse the page. If the browser is Netscape, the value of this property will be Netscape. If the browser is Internet Explorer, then the value of this property will be Microsoft Internet Explorer. Other browsers will have corresponding values.

Property	Value
appCodeName	The code name of the browser (such as Mozilla)
appName	The name of the browser (such as Microsoft Internet Explorer)
appVersion	The version of the browser and some other information
language	The language of the browser being used
mimeTypes	An array of mime types supported by the browser
platform	The machine type for which the browser was created
plugins	An array of the plugins the browser has installed on it
userAgent	The user agent header for the browser

Table 8-1 Properties of the Navigator Object

If you need to know the value for a particular browser, you can create a script to alert the value of this property, place the script inside SCRIPT tags on a Web page, and then view the page in that browser. You will then be alerted to the value of the property for that browser. The following code shows how the alert can be coded:

```
window.alert("You have "+navigator.appName);
```

Since we can find out the type of browser being used this way, we are able to create a simple browser detection script.

Suppose we want to send the viewer an alert based on our opinion of the browser being used. We could use the navigator.appName property to create an if/else block and send the appropriate comment to the viewer based on the browser type.

The following code shows an example of how we could perform this task:

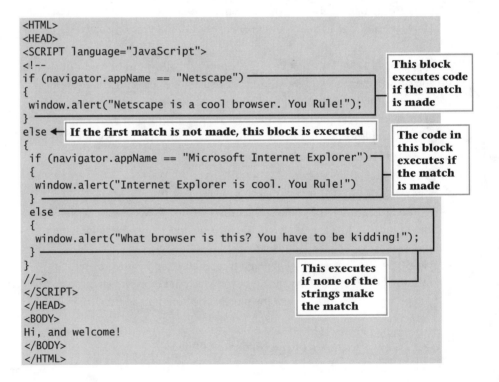

```
<HTML>
<HEAD>
<SCRIPT language="JavaScript">
<!--
if (navigator.appName == "Netscape")
{
 window.alert("Netscape is a cool browser. You Rule!");
}
else
{
 if (navigator.appName == "Microsoft Internet Explorer")
 {
  window.alert("Internet Explorer is cool. You Rule!")
 }
 else
 {
  window.alert("What browser is this? You have to be kidding!");
 }
}
//-->
</SCRIPT>
</HEAD>
<BODY>
Hi, and welcome!
</BODY>
</HTML>
```

This block executes code if the match is made

If the first match is not made, this block is executed

The code in this block executes if the match is made

This executes if none of the strings make the match

As you can see, the viewer can now find out just what you think of the
browser being used. Figure 8-7 shows the alert we would get using
Internet Explorer to view the page. In a later module, the appName
property will be more useful, as we see how to redirect the viewer to
different pages made for different browsers using this property.

The appVersion Property   This property has a value of the version
number of the browser and some additional information. For example, in
Netscape Navigator 4.7 for Windows 98, you might see the following text
as the value of this property:

```
4.7 [en] (Win98; I)
```

In a later module, we will see that the version number portion of this
will be helpful if we decide we need to redirect viewers to different pages
based on how old or new their browsers are. This can be beneficial when
we use techniques that should only be executed in browser versions above
a certain level.

The language Property   This property has a value of a two-letter
string representing a language, or a five-character string that allows for
the representation of a sublanguage. This value represents the type of
language to which the browser has been translated. A browser that used
the English language for its interface will return the two-letter string "en,"
for instance.

As of this writing, this property only seemed to be supported by
Netscape Navigator. So, if we use this, we may need to employ the
navigator.appName property to see if we can get the value of this property

Figure 8-7   The alert we get when entering the page with Internet Explorer

or not before we execute any code. So, if we want to alert the language code of the viewer's browser, we could use the following code:

```
if (navigator.appName == "Netscape")
 window.alert("Hi! Your language code is "+navigator.language);
else
 window.alert("Hi there!");
```

In this way, we don't get an error or a value of "undefined" displayed to the viewer if the browser is not Netscape.

Tip

The language property would probably best be used if you had several translations of your site and wanted to send the viewer to the right one automatically.

The mimeTypes Property   This is an array of the Multipurpose Internet Mail Extensions (MIME) types supported by the browser. At the time of this writing, this property seemed to be supported only by the Netscape Web browser.

The platform Property   This property holds the value of the type of machine for which the browser was created. For example, on a Windows 95 machine, the value would probably be Win32. There are different values for various types of machines. If you want to let the viewer know the machine type being used, you could send an alert with this property:

```
window.alert("Your machine is a "+navigator.platform+" machine.");
```

While not very useful here, the property could be used to redirect viewers to an appropriate page based on their machine type.

The plugins Property   This array holds the values of all the plugins installed in the viewer's browser. We will see more on arrays in Module 12.

The userAgent Property   This property gives us another long string of information about the browser. This string is the user agent header for the browser. For instance, in Netscape 4.7 for Windows 98, you might see the following string:

```
Mozilla/4.7 [en] (Win98; I)
```

It is pretty similar to the text we saw for the navigator.appVersion property, but with a little more information.

Now that we know about the properties of the navigator object, we can look at the methods of the object.

Methods

The navigator object also has a number of methods we can use to perform various tasks. Table 8-2 shows the methods available in the navigator object.

Now we will look at all of these methods in more detail to see what they do.

The javaEnabled() Method   This method returns a Boolean value of true if the viewer has Java enabled in the browser; otherwise, it returns false. The javaEnabled() method could be useful if you want to display a Java Applet to the viewer, but only if the viewer has Java enabled in the browser.

For now, we will just send the viewer an alert as an example. This way we don't need to mess with any Java syntax yet. The following code sends one alert if the viewer has Java enabled and sends another if it is not:

```
var hasJava= navigator.javaEnabled()
if (hasJava==true)
 window.alert("Cool, you have Java!");
else
 window.alert("Java disabled? You cannot see my Java Applet!");
```

Method	Purpose
javaEnabled	Used to test whether or not Java is enabled in the browser
plugins.refresh	If new plugins have been installed in the browser, this makes them available for use
preference	Allows certain browser preferences to be set (requires signed script)
savePreferences	Allows the browser preferences to be saved to a local file (requires signed script)

Table 8-2   Methods of the Navigator Object

This tests the value returned by the navigator.javaEnabled() method and gives the user the correct alert. Again, this is more useful if we have a Java applet that we want to use someplace on the page.

The plugins.refresh() Method   This method can be used to refresh the plugins the browser has available to use while on the page. For instance, if the viewer needed to download a plugin to view something on the page, we would want to refresh this information so that the plugin can be used.

We can call it with a parameter of a Boolean value of true or false. If we call it with true as the parameter, the plugins information and the current Web page will be reloaded. The following code shows a call with the true parameter:

```
navigator.plugins.refresh(true);
```

If we call it with the parameter value set to false, the plugin information is refreshed but the Web page is not reloaded. The following is an example of a call with a parameter of false:

```
navigator.plugins.refresh(false);
```

Now the plugin information is reloaded, but the page itself is not.

The preference() Method   This method allows us to set certain preferences in the viewer's browser. It requires the use of a signed script, which deals with JavaScript security. We will cover JavaScript security in a later module.

The savePreferences() Method   This allows us to save the preferences to a local file. It also requires the use of a signed script, so we will have to pass on making use of this method for now as well.

Project 8-2: Practicing with the Predefined Navigator Object

pr8_2.html

This project will allow you to practice using some of the properties and methods of the predefined navigator object. A page will be created that alerts the viewer to various types of information, based on the browser being used.

Step-by-Step

1. Create an HTML page, and leave space in the HEAD section of the page to add the script code.

2. Code an alert that pops up when the viewer enters the page. The alert should say "Hi! You are viewing my page with . . ." followed by the name of the browser being used by the viewer.

3. If the user has Java enabled, send a new alert that says "You have Java enabled, that is cool!" to the viewer. If the viewer does not have Java enabled, send an alert that says "No Java? Well, no fun stuff here then."

4. Send a new alert that tells the viewer what type of machine is being used. The alert should say "You are using . . ." followed by the type of machine the viewer is using to view the page.

5. Save the file as pr8_2.html and view it in one or more browsers (or other computers if you can). See how the results vary based on what is being used while viewing the Web page.

8

☑ *Mastery Check*

1. In JavaScript, we access object properties through the use of the

  A. Addition operator

  B. Dot operator

  C. Multiplication operator

  D. We can't access the properties of an object

2. What could we say about the following code:
```
var x=myhouse.kitchen;
```

  A. It assigns the string myhouse.kitchen to the variable *x*.

  B. It adds the values of myhouse and kitchen and assigns them to an object named *x*.

☑ Mastery Check

    C. Assuming the myhouse object exists, it assigns the value of the kitchen property of the myhouse object to the variable *x*.

    D. Assuming the kitchen object exists, it assigns the value of the myhouse property of the kitchen object to the variable *x*.

3. Which of the following lines correctly creates a method named "cost" from a function named "get_cost()," if this line is within a constructor function?

    A. this.cost=get_cost();

    B. cost=get_cost;

    C. get_cost=this.cost();

    D. this.cost=get_cost;

4. Which of the following would send an alert to the viewer that tells the name of the browser being used?

    A. window.alert("You are using "+navigator.appVersion);

    B. window.alert("You are using "+navigator.appName);

    C. window.alert("You are using "+navigator.javaEnabled());

    D. window.alert("You are using navigator.appName");

5. What could we say about the following code:
`myhouse.kitchen="big";`?

    A. Assuming the kitchen object exists, the myhouse property is assigned a new string value.

    B. Assuming the myhouse object exists, the value of the variable kitchen is added to the string big.

    C. Assuming the myhouse object exists, the kitchen property is assigned a new string value.

    D. This wouldn't do anything.

Module 9

The Document Object

The Goals of This Module

- Learn what the document object is
- Learn how to use the properties of the document object
- Learn how to use the methods of the document object
- Discover how to use these properties and methods together for different purposes

Now that we know how objects work and how to use predefined JavaScript objects, it is time to look at some of the major predefined objects in JavaScript.

In this chapter, we will cover the document object. This object will help us gather information about the page that is being viewed in the browser. Some of the properties will be used to display information to the viewer, while others will be changed on the fly and used to make the document react to user events. Also, the methods of the document object will allow us to perform some new JavaScript tricks.

An Introduction to the Document Object

The document object is an object that is created by the browser for each new HTML page (document) that is viewed. By doing this, JavaScript gives us access to a number of properties and methods that can affect the document in a number of ways.

As you know, we have been using the write() method of the document object for quite some time in this book. This method allows us to write a string of text into an HTML document.

To begin our journey through the document object, let's take a look at the various properties we can access with this object. Many of these properties will turn out to be quite useful when writing scripts. First though, we will do a 1-Minute Drill.

1-Minute Drill

● **What creates a document object?**

● **What does the document object give us access to?**

● **Which method of the document object should you know already?**

● A document object is created when an HTML page is viewed (loaded in the browser)
● We gain access to properties and methods that can affect the document in a number of ways
● The write() method

Properties

Table 9-1 lists the properties of the document object with a short description of each. Following the table, we will discuss each property in more detail and see sample scripts for the properties.

Property	Description
alinkColor	Returns the hexadecimal value of the active link color of the document
anchors	An array of all the named anchors in the document
applets	An array of all of the Java applets in a document
bgColor	Returns the hexadecimal value of the background color of the document
cookie	Used to set JavaScript cookies in a document
domain	Returns the domain name of the server for the document.
embeds	An array of all the EMBED tags in the document
fgColor	Returns the hexadecimal value of the default text color of the document
formName	Not a property itself, but creates a new property with each named form placed in the document
forms	An array of all the form tags in a document
images	An array of all the image tags in the document
lastModified	Returns the date of the last modification of the document
layers	An array of all the layer tags on the page (Netscape Navigator only)
all	Property that intends to allow access to all the objects on a page (Internet Explorer only)
linkColor	Returns the hexadecimal value of the default link color for the document
links	An array of all the link tags in the document
plugins	An array of all the plugins used in the document
referrer	Returns the Web address (URL) of the document that referred the viewer to the current document
title	Returns the text used inside the TITLE tags of the document
URL	Returns the URL of the current document
vlinkColor	Returns the hexadecimal value of the visited link color for the document

9

Table 9-1   The Properties of the Document Object

As you can see in Table 9-1, the list of properties is fairly long. There are a number of different types of values returned from the properties as well. Now let's discuss each property in detail.

The alinkColor Property

The alinkColor property holds the value of the active link color for the HTML document. The active link color is set in the opening <BODY> tag of the document in the alink attribute. If it is not set, the browser uses its own default color, and that color will be the value of the alinkColor property.

Using JavaScript, we can set this value with a script in the HEAD section of a document. All we need to do is place the correct color name string or the hexadecimal red-green-blue (RGB) value in as a string, as shown in the following code:

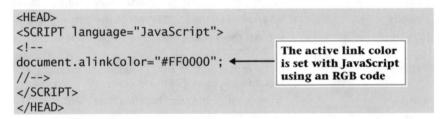

```
<HEAD>
<SCRIPT language="JavaScript">
<!--
document.alinkColor="#FF0000";   ◄────   The active link color
//-->                                     is set with JavaScript
</SCRIPT>                                 using an RGB code
</HEAD>
```

The #FF0000 code is the hexadecimal RGB code for the color red. The RGB codes for the various colors can be found in many HTML references, so we will not dwell on how these are created.

Another way to set the active link color would be to use the right text string for the color you want. For instance, if you want to use the color light blue, you could use the text string "lightblue" instead of the #ADD8E6 RGB code. An example of this follows:

```
<HEAD>
<SCRIPT language="JavaScript">
<!--
document.alinkColor="lightblue";   ◄────   The active link color
//-->                                       is set with JavaScript
</SCRIPT>                                    using a color name
</HEAD>
```

Most of the text strings like this will be the color name itself, such as
red, green, blue, black, and so on. If the name has more than one word,
the two are usually put into one long string, such as lightblue, darkblue,
steelblue, and other similar strings. If you need to use one of these, an
HTML reference will usually have a number of these listed for you;
however, it is best to use the RGB codes since the color names only
work on certain platforms.

Unfortunately, this property doesn't seem to be able to be changed
on the fly. In other words, we can't use an event handler later in the
document to change the color of an active link on the page. With this
property, you may not have a real interest in doing that anyway; but we
will see some properties like this later that we will want to be able to
change in this way.

The only other use we may have for the alinkColor is for informational
purposes. We can write the value of it out to the browser if we want to
show the viewer what we have set as the active link color on the page.
When we access the value of the property, we will get back the RGB
code as a string rather than a text string of a color name (even though we
may set the active link color with a color name). For example, take a look
at the following code:

```
<BODY alink="red">          ◄────    The active link color is set in the
<H1>My Super Duper Web Page</H1>      opening <BODY> tag
<SCRIPT language="JavaScript">
<!--
document.write("The active link color here is "+document.alinkColor); ◄─┐
//-->
</SCRIPT>
<P>                                  The RGB code for the color is displayed
<A HREF="#">Try a Link</A>           with the document.write() command
</BODY>
```

The page that would be displayed using this code is shown in Figure 9-1.
Notice how the value of the document.alinkColor property is displayed
as its RGB code #ff0000, even though we defined the color with the
color name red in the opening <BODY> tag. When we set the value
of the property, we can use either method we like (name or RGB);
however, when we take the value of the property, it will return the
RGB code.

If you like, you can test the color of the active link by clicking the link
on the page. When you press the mouse button down on the link, hold it

9

Figure 9-1 **The RGB code for the active link color is displayed in the browser window**

down for a moment to see the active link color. The link tag is linked to an address of #, which should keep you from going anywhere when you click the link.

The anchors Property (Array)

The anchors property is actually an array set by the browser for all of the named anchors in a document (such as <A NAME="top">). Since we haven't gotten into arrays yet, this won't be very helpful to us for now; however, we will see more on how arrays like this one can be useful when we get to Module 11 on arrays.

JavaScript gives us the length property to allow us to find out the number of named anchors on the page. We can use the length property to write how many named anchors are on a page to the browser:

```
<BODY>
<A NAME="Sec1"></A>        ◄——  The first named anchor is
<H2>Section 1</H2>               set with the anchor tag
This section is all about section 1 stuff...
<P>
<A NAME="Sec2"></A>        ◄——  The second named anchor is set with
<H2>Section 2</H2>               the anchor tag
This section talks about all the section 2 issues and ...
<P>
```

```
<SCRIPT language="JavaScript">
<!--
document.write("There are "+document.anchors.length+" named anchors");
//-->
</SCRIPT>
</BODY>
```
↑

The number of named anchors is displayed on the page

Notice that we create two named anchors on the page, and then we write the number of anchors on the page to the screen afterward. Figure 9-2 shows the result of this script in the browser window.

Again, this is more of an informational property for now. Once we learn arrays, we can make more use of the length property.

The applets Property (Array)

The applets property is another array. It has an entry for each Java applet using the APPLET tags on the page (note these tags are being phased out in favor of the OBJECT tags). As with the anchors property, we can use

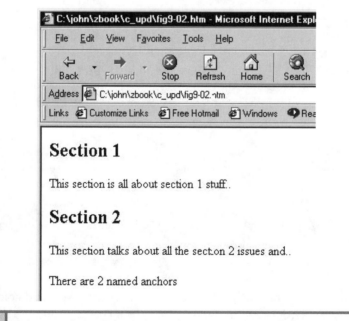

Figure 9-2 | The number of named anchors on the page is displayed in the browser window

the document.applets.length property to find out the number of APPLET tags on the page. For now, this property is mainly useful for informational purposes.

The bgColor Property

The bgColor property holds the value of the background color of a Web page. The background color is set in the bgColor attribute of the opening <BODY> tag, or set using the browser defaults. It can also be set with a script in the HEAD section of a page by using the bgColor property of the document object, much like we did with the alinkColor property.

To set this value with a script in the head section, we again use either the color name text string or an RGB value as a string. The following example code shows the setting of this property using a color name:

```
<HEAD>
<SCRIPT language="JavaScript">
<!--
document.bgColor="lightblue";
//-->
</SCRIPT>
</HEAD>
```

This would set the background color of the page to light blue.

As with the alinkColor property, we can use the bgColor property for informational purposes and let the viewer know the RGB code for the background color on the page. The following code shows one way to do this:

```
<BODY bgColor="red" text="white">
<H1>My Super Duper Web Page</H1>
<SCRIPT language="JavaScript">
<!--
document.write("The background color here is "+document.bgColor);
//-->
</SCRIPT>
</BODY>
```

This just tells the viewer the RGB code for the background color being used. We set it to red in the opening <BODY> tag using the bgColor attribute. Figure 9-3 shows how this would look in a browser.

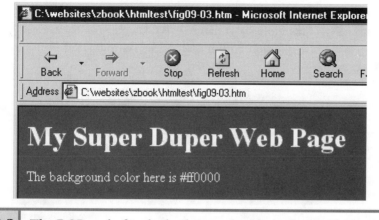

Figure 9-3 The RGB code for the background color is displayed in the browser

While identifying the RGB color is nice, there is something more fun that we are able to do with this property. Unlike the alinkColor property, we can change the bgColor property on the fly when the viewer does something. This makes this property a little bit more useful for us, as we can alter it to fit our needs or the needs of the viewer.

Suppose we would like to allow the viewer to be able to change the background color by clicking a button. Using the following code, the viewer could change the background color to light blue by clicking the button:

```
<BODY bgColor="yellow">  ◄━━  The background color is set in the opening BODY tag
<B>Want a new background color, change it to light blue by clicking the
button below!</B>
<P>
<FORM>
<INPUT TYPE="button" value="Click" onClick="document.bgColor='lightblue';">
</FORM>                                                                    ▲
</BODY>
        Clicking this button changes the background color to light blue
```

As the original background color is yellow, the viewer will probably want to change it. By setting the button up with the onClick event handler, we are able to change the background color by giving the document.bgColor property a new value.

If we want to give the viewer multiple options, we could code a function that will take in a color name or RGB code as a parameter. Then we can just call the function within each of the buttons, as shown in the following example:

```
<HTML>
<HEAD>
<TITLE>Background Colors</TITLE>
<SCRIPT language="JavaScript">
<!--
function newbg(thecolor)
{
  document.bgColor=thecolor;
}
//-->
</SCRIPT>
</HEAD>
<BODY bgColor="yellow">
<B>Want a new background color, change the color by clicking a button
below!</B>
<P>
<FORM>
<INPUT TYPE="button" value="Light Blue" onClick="newbg('lightblue');">
  
<INPUT TYPE="button" value="Orange" onClick="newbg('orange');">
  
<INPUT TYPE="button" value="Beige" onClick="newbg('beige');">
  
<INPUT TYPE="button" value="Yellow" onClick="newbg('yellow');">
</FORM>
</BODY>
</HTML>
```

This function changes the background color based on the parameter it is sent

The original background color is set

Clicking one of these buttons changes the background color

The original background is yellow. The buttons allow the viewer to change the color from yellow to light blue, orange, or beige, and back to yellow again. Figure 9-4 shows the result of clicking the orange button on the page.

Of course, we can use this property with a number of events. If we want to offer this feature when the viewer moves the mouse over a link, we can use our function in an onMouseover event handler in a link tag instead. The example code for this follows. Notice the similarities to the preceding script, but also notice the change of events and tags used on the page:

```
<HTML>
<HEAD>
<TITLE>Background Colors Again!</TITLE>
<SCRIPT language="JavaScript">
<!--
function newbg(thecolor)
{
 document.bgColor=thecolor;
}
//-->
</SCRIPT>
</HEAD>
<BODY bgColor="yellow">
<B>Want a new background color, change it by placing your mouse over one of
the links below!</B>
<P>
<A HREF= "#"  onMouseover="newbg('lightblue');">Light Blue</A>
  
<A HREF= "#"  onMouseover="newbg('orange');">Orange</A>
  
<A HREF= "#"  onMouseover="newbg('beige');">Beige</A>
  
<A HREF= "#"  onMouseover="newbg('yellow');">Yellow</A>
</BODY>
</HTML>
```

> **This time, the background color is changed when the mouse moves over one of these links**

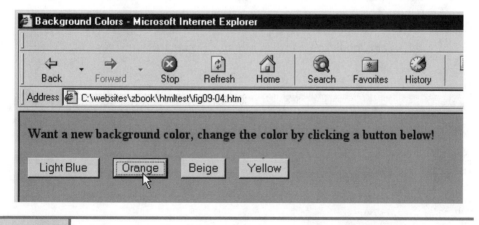

Figure 9-4   When the orange button is clicked, the background color is changed to orange

This time, moving the mouse over the link with the color you like will change the background color. Figure 9-5 shows the result of moving the mouse over the light blue link.

As you can see, being able to change the color on the fly gives us more options. We can offer the viewer a selection of background colors or change the background color by surprise when the mouse is moved over a link. This allows us to make some fun scripts if we want to play with the background color of the page.

The cookie Property

The cookie property is used to set a JavaScript cookie to store information for the viewer. To set a cookie, we would set the value of the document. cookie property to a string that contains the information we want to store for the viewer. The following is the syntax:

```
document.cookie=string;
```

We would replace *string* with a text string that contains the information we want to use. Usually, this is in a format like the one shown in the following example setting of a cookie:

```
document.cookie="site=homepage:food=cheeseburgers";
```

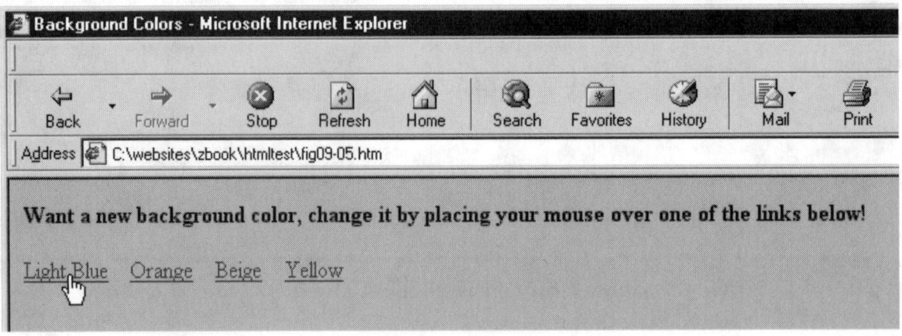

Figure 9-5   When the mouse is moved over the light blue link, the background color is changed to light blue

You can see that there are two things that are set by the cookie. The site is homepage and the food is cheeseburgers. In between the two there is a colon (actually, this could be any character of your choice) that is used to help separate things when the cookie is read.

We will need to get a handle on more advanced string-handling techniques before we try to deal with cookies any further. We will see how to use the advanced string-handling techniques, and how to set and read cookies in more detail in later chapters. For now, we just need to know that the document.cookie property is used to set cookies.

The domain Property

The domain property holds the value of the domain name that served the page to the viewer. This value is whatever comes after http:// at the beginning of a Web address and before any forward slashes. So, if you were looking at a page from http://www.pageresource.com, the document.domain value would be www.pageresource.com.

To use the domain property, we will send an alert to the viewer that tells the domain. Placing the following code in the HEAD section of a document would pop up an alert with the value of the domain property:

```
<SCRIPT language="JavaScript">
<!--
window.alert("You have reached the "+document.domain+" domain!");
//-->
</SCRIPT>
```

9

If this code were placed on any page at http://javascriptcity.com, an alert saying "You have reached the javascriptcity.com domain!" would be sent to the viewer.

The embeds Property (Array)

The embeds property is an array that has an entry for each set of EMBED tags used on the page. Like the other arrays, we don't have much use for it just yet; however, we can use the document.embeds.length property to get the number of EMBED tags on the page as we did with the anchors array earlier.

The fgColor Property

The fgColor property is the equivalent of the regular text color on a Web page. The "fg" in this property stands for foreground. This color is set with the text attribute in the opening <BODY> tag, by the browser's default, or through JavaScript as we have done with other similar properties.

For instance, we can set this property with a script in the HEAD section of a page, as shown in the following example code:

```
<HEAD>
<SCRIPT language="JavaScript">
<!--
document.fgColor="#000000";
//-->
</SCRIPT>
</HEAD>
```

Again, this is similar to the alinkColor and bgColor properties because we can set them in the HEAD section.

As with similar properties, we can use the fgColor property to show the information it holds by adding it to a script. The following code will write out the text color for the page by using the document.fgColor property:

```
<BODY text="black">
<H1>My Super Duper Text Color</H1>
<SCRIPT language="JavaScript">
<!--
document.write("The text color here is "+document.fgColor);
//-->
</SCRIPT>
</BODY>
```

This will show us the RGB code of the text color in the browser window. Notice that here the color is set in the opening <BODY> tag with the text attribute. Figure 9-6 shows how this page looks when it is viewed in a browser.

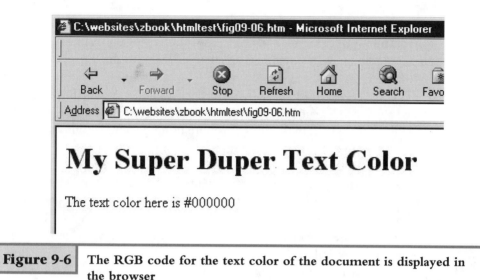

Figure 9-6 The RGB code for the text color of the document is displayed in the browser

The formName Property

The formName property isn't actually a property itself. Any time you name a form, you create a formName property, but the property is actually the name of the form and not formName.

In order to see the meaning of this, let's look at a page with a form on it. The following code will give us an HTML page that includes a form:

```
<HTML>
<HEAD>
<TITLE>Forms and Names</TITLE>
</HEAD>
<BODY>
<FORM name="funform">   ◄──────  The form is given a name to create a property
<INPUT TYPE= "button" name="funb" value="You can click me I suppose">
</FORM>
</BODY>
</HTML>
```

9

What this code does is create a document.funform property from the name="funform" attribute in the opening <FORM> tag. While this doesn't do much on it's own, it does allow us access to the form elements within the form.

The funform property actually has properties under it, which are named after the elements of the form. We could access the button we used in the form from its name="funb" attribute using document.funform.funb to get to it; however, even this doesn't let us do much by itself.

We will need to dig down one more level. The value property allows us to set or change the value of the contents of a form element. These contents are usually set in the value attribute of the form element's tag. In our form here, we could change the value of the text on the button by accessing its value property using document.funform.funb.value and assigning it a new value.

The following example shows how we could use the onClick event handler to make the button text change when the button is clicked:

```
<HTML>
<HEAD>
<TITLE>Forms and Names</TITLE>
</HEAD>
<BODY>
<FORM name="funform">
<INPUT TYPE= "button" name="funb" value="You can click me I suppose"
  onClick= "document.funform.funb.value='Thanks, you clicked me!';">
</FORM>                                                    ↑
</BODY>        The button text is changed by giving it a new value
</HTML>
```

Figure 9-7 shows how the page and the button will look before the button is clicked. Notice that the button shows the text that was set in the value attribute of its <INPUT> tag.

Now take a look at the button in Figure 9-8, after it has been clicked. The text on the button has been changed! The button lets you know that you clicked it, and it is displaying manners by saying "Thanks" to you for the click.

This can be fun if you want to change the value of text boxes, text areas, and other things as well. We will get into more detail on the things we can do with forms in Module 14, and these properties will play a large role in the scripts that we create in that module.

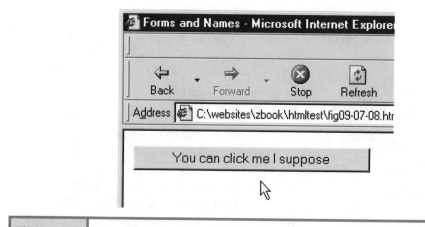

Figure 9-7 | The browser display before the button is clicked

The forms Property (Array)

The forms property is yet another array that has an entry for each form on a Web page. The array gives us an alternative to using the formName property; however, we still need to study arrays before we look into this array in more detail.

9

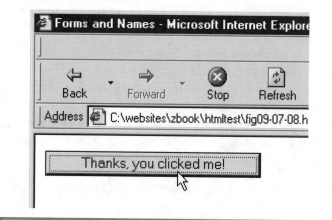

Figure 9-8 | The browser display after the button is clicked

As with the other similar properties, you can use the length property in the form of document.forms.length to find out how many forms are on the page.

The images Property (Array)

The images property is yet another array. This one has an entry for each image on a Web page. As with the other similar properties, we can use the length property in the form of document.images.length to find out the number of images that are in an HTML document.

Another thing this property can be used for is to detect what browsers support the Image object in JavaScript. This is helpful if you wish to preload an image. Preloading an image is a good idea when using image rollover scripts (which we will create in Module 17) and can also be useful if you want to place an image that will be used on another page within your Web site in the viewer's cache file to make that page load more quickly for the viewer.

To check whether a browser supports the image object, we can place any code that needs the Image object within an if block. The if block will test for the existence of the document.images property, as shown in the following example code:

```
if (document.images)
{
    JavaScript Statements  ←  This is where we place code that needs
                                the document.images property to work
}
```

Notice that all we need inside the parentheses is document.images. If this property exists, it returns true, and the statements inside the block are executed. If the property does not exist, the block is ignored, and the older browsers are happy that they don't have to try any of that code.

To preload an image, we first need to create a new instance of the JavaScript Image object. The following code shows the syntax used for creating a new instance of the Image object:

```
var varname= new Image(width,height);
```

We replace *varname* with the name we want to give to this instance of the Image object. We replace *width* with the width in pixels of the image we wish to use, and then we replace *height* with the height in pixels of the image.

So, if we want to create an instance of the Image object named "myimage" where the image would have a width of 100 pixels and a height of 75 pixels, we could use the following code:

```
var myimage= new Image(100,75);
```

Once we have this, we need a way to define what image will be used (like the source (SRC) attribute in an image tag). The image object comes with an src property that allows us to do this. We just have to set it by giving it a value. The following code shows how this is done:

```
var myimage= new Image(100,75);
myimage.src= "smile.gif";
```

Now the browser will try to load the image at the local address of smile.gif. We can also use a full URL if we need to do so here. Since the image tries to load here without the need to be displayed, it is being preloaded.

─Hint─

Preloading is usually done in the HEAD section of a document so that the image starts loading as soon as possible.

To put all of this together, we need to place this code inside our if block so that it does not get run by browsers that don't support the Image object.

The following code puts both pieces together and places the script inside the HEAD section of a document. This will preload the image for later use:

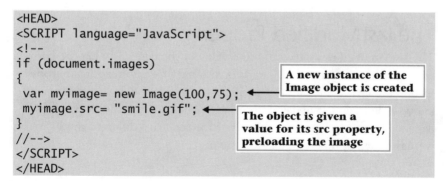

```
<HEAD>
<SCRIPT language="JavaScript">
<!--
if (document.images)
{
  var myimage= new Image(100,75);    ◄── A new instance of the
  myimage.src= "smile.gif";    ◄──       Image object is created
}
//-->                               The object is given a
</SCRIPT>                           value for its src property,
</HEAD>                             preloading the image
```

9

This does the job of preloading our image so we can make use of it later.

To preload more than one image, we need to create an instance of the image object for each image we want to preload. So, if we want to preload three images, we could use the following code:

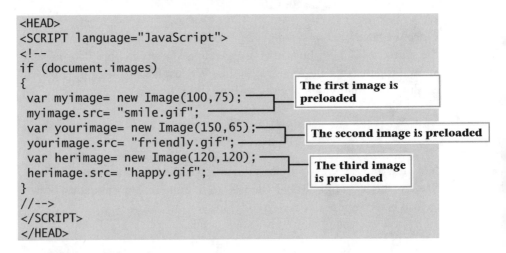

```
<HEAD>
<SCRIPT language="JavaScript">
<!--
if (document.images)
{
  var myimage= new Image(100,75);            The first image is
  myimage.src= "smile.gif";                  preloaded
  var yourimage= new Image(150,65);          The second image is preloaded
  yourimage.src= "friendly.gif";
  var herimage= new Image(120,120);          The third image
  herimage.src= "happy.gif";                 is preloaded
}
//-->
</SCRIPT>
</HEAD>
```

This preloads three images for us. The new instance yourimage preloads an image at the address of friendly.gif with a width of 150 and a height of 65. The instance herimage preloads an image at the address of happy.gif with a width of 120 and a height of 120. We can still add more, using the same technique, if we'd like.

The document.images property gives us a handy way of checking for the JavaScript Image object. We will see more on the Image object in Module 17.

The lastModified Property

The lastModified property holds the value of the date and time the current document was last modified. This is used mostly for informational purposes, such as displaying the date the document was last modified so the viewer knows when you last updated your page. The value of this property depends on your browser, as different browsers have different results if we write the last modified date on the page.

To see the difference between Internet Explorer and Netscape Navigator on this, let's write the value of the document.lastModified property into a Web page and then look at the results in the two browsers. The following code will display the last modified date and time:

```
<BODY>
<H1>My Always Updated Web Page!</H1>
<SCRIPT language="JavaScript">
<!--
document.write("Last Updated: "+document.lastModified);
//-->
</SCRIPT>
</BODY>
```

Figure 9-9 shows the result of this when viewed in Internet Explorer 5.5. Notice the format of the date and time.

Now, take a look at Figure 9-10, which shows what the same script displays in Netscape Navigator 4.7. Notice the addition of the day of the week and the expanded format of the date.

When writing the date of the last modification on the page, the differences only matter in terms of space on the page. Some layouts may need to have extra space arranged for the longer version of the property.

Figure 9-9   The last modified date when viewed in Internet Explorer

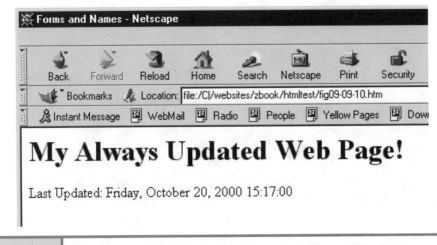

| **Figure 9-10** | **The last modified date when viewed in Netscape Navigator** |

The layers Property (Array)

The layers property is yet another array, but this one has its use in detecting what browser is being used. This array has an entry for each <LAYER> tag on the page, and we can use the length property in the form of document.layers.length to find the number of layers on a page.

Since this property is only available in version 4 or higher of Netscape Navigator, we could use it as a shortcut to detecting the browser with the navigator.appName property. By testing for the document.layers property, we can see whether the browser being used is Netscape Navigator 4 or higher without having to pick apart the navigator.appVersion property.

We can test for the document.layers property in the same way we tested for the document.images property, which is nice and short:

```
if (document.layers)
{
 window.alert("You have Netscape Navigator 4 or better!");
}
```

This is a little bit shorter than using the properties of the navigator object, which would require us to use two properties and get the information from them. Keep in mind that Netscape Navigator 6 may or may not have this property, so this may only end up being useful for detecting version 4 of Netscape Navigator.

The all Property

While the layers property helped us detect Netscape Navigator 4 or higher, the all property can help us detect Internet Explorer 4 or higher. The all property was created to give JavaScript access to all of the objects on a page. We will discuss this more in Module 17 when we deal with Dynamic HTML (DHTML). For now, we will just use it as we did the layers property to detect a browser.

So, to see if the viewer is using Internet Explorer 4 or higher, we could use the following code:

```
if (document.all)
{
 window.alert("You have Internet Explorer 4 or better!");
}
```

If we like, we could combine this with our code to detect Netscape Navigator 4 or higher. We can even add something for the remaining browsers to see, as in the following code:

```
<SCRIPT language="JavaScript">
<!--
if (document.layers)
{
 window.alert("You have Netscape Navigator 4 or better!");
}
else
{
 if (document.all)
 {
  window.alert("You have Internet Explorer 4 or better!");
 }
 else
 {
  window.alert("Your browser is something, but I am not sure what!");
 }
}
//-->
</SCRIPT>
```

This checks for Netscape Navigator 4 or higher

This checks for Internet Explorer 4 or higher

This displays something for any other browser

9

This time it tests for the document.layers property. If it exists, the viewer gets an alert saying the browser is Netscape Navigator 4 or higher. If not, it checks for the document.all property. If it exists, the viewer gets an alert that says Internet Explorer 4 or higher is being used. If not, the viewer gets a general-purpose alert.

One thing to keep in mind is that Netscape Navigator 6 may support the document.all property and, thus, eliminate the shortcut for finding which browser is being used based on the use of the all and layers properties. However, the detection of the all property could still be useful if we use DHTML scripts that only work when the document.all property is available.

The linkColor Property

The linkColor property holds the value of the link color of the document. The link color is set in the link attribute of the opening <BODY> tag, in the browser's default, or through a script.

As with other similar properties, we can set it with JavaScript in the HEAD section if we like, as shown in the following code:

```
<HEAD>
<SCRIPT language="JavaScript">
<!--
document.linkColor="#0000FF";
//-->
</SCRIPT>
</HEAD>
```

This sets the link color in the document to blue.

We can use this property to display information, such as the RGB code for the link color, to the viewer.

```
<BODY link="blue">
<H1>My Super Duper Link Color</H1>
<SCRIPT language="JavaScript">
<!--
document.write("The link color here is "+document.linkColor);
//-->
</SCRIPT>
</BODY>
```

Notice that the color was defined in the opening <BODY> tag with the link attribute. Figure 9-11 shows the result of the preceding code when viewed in a browser.

This cannot be changed on the fly, so we can't have any more fun with it.

The links Property (Array)

The links property is another array that holds a value for each link (such as <A HREF="url">) and linked area of an image map (such as <AREA HREF="url">) on a page. We can find out how many links are on the page using the document.links.length property.

The plugins Property (Array)

The plugins property is an array that holds a value for each plugin object on the page. As with other similar properties, we can find out the number of plugin objects on a page using the length property in the form of document.plugins.length and use it for informational purposes.

9

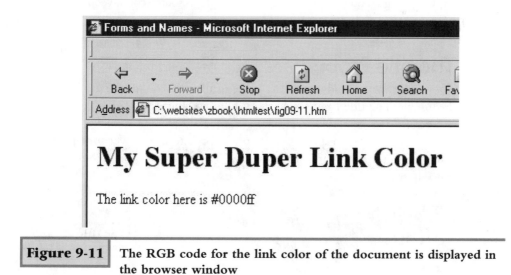

Figure 9-11   The RGB code for the link color of the document is displayed in the browser window

The referrer Property

The referrer property is used for informational purposes and holds the value of the URL of the page that the viewer was on before arriving at your page (the referring page). While this can be useful, the viewer doesn't always come in with a referring URL (such as using a bookmark or typing in the address), so the value could be nothing. Also, the value of this property isn't always correct because different browsers may consider different types of things as referring the viewer to the new page, rather than just links.

To use this, we could send an alert to the viewers of a page telling them where they were before they got to our page. Placing the code in the following example into the HEAD section of a document would do the trick:

```
<SCRIPT language="JavaScript">
<!--
document.write("You came from "+document.referrer+"!");
//-->
</SCRIPT>
```

So, if the referring page were http://www.pageresource.com/webdes.htm, an alert saying "You came from http://www.pageresource.com/webdes.htm!" would be sent to the viewer.

The title Property

The title property holds the string value of the title of the HTML document. The title is set inside the <TITLE> and </TITLE> tags of a page.

We can use it to display the title of the page to the viewer someplace other than in the top bar of the window. The following code would allow us to do this:

```
<HTML>
<HEAD>
<TITLE>Lions, Tigers and Bears!</TITLE>  ◄────  The title of the
</HEAD>                                         document is set here
<BODY>
<SCRIPT language="JavaScript">
```

```
<!--
document.write("<H1>"+document.title+"</H1>");
//-->
</SCRIPT>
Lions and tigers and bears were what I saw when I went to ...
</BODY>
</HTML>
```

> The title is displayed in a heading in the body of the page

This displays our title as a heading on the page. Figure 9-12 shows the result of this when viewed in a browser.

The URL Property

The URL property holds the value of the full URL of the current document. This information can be useful if you print it at the bottom of your HTML page, because it will show the page URL for anyone who prints out your page.

While you could just type the URL at the bottom on your own, this could become tedious when it needs to be done on numerous pages. This is where this property can be handy, as you can cut and paste a little script to each page rather than typing the various URL addresses each time. An

Figure 9-12   The title of the document is shown as a heading on the page

example of writing the URL address on the page is shown in the following code:

```
<HTML>
<HEAD>
<TITLE>Buy!</TITLE>
</HEAD>
<BODY>
<H1>Buy Something!</H1>
If you don't buy something I will be really upset so you had better...
<P>
<SCRIPT language="JavaScript">
<!--
document.write("You are at: "+document.URL);
//-->
</SCRIPT>
</BODY>
</HTML>
```

Figure 9-13 shows the result of the preceding code in a browser. The last line of the page tells the viewer the current location. The figure shows a local file address, but it would show a regular URL if the page were online.

Figure 9-13 | The URL of the document is shown at the end of the page contents

The vlinkColor Property

The vlinkColor property holds the RGB code for the visited link color on a Web page. This color is set using the vlink attribute in the opening <BODY> tag, in the browser's default, or through a script.

As we have done with other properties like it, we can set this property with JavaScript inside the <HEAD> and </HEAD> tags on the page, as shown in the following code:

```
<HEAD>
<SCRIPT language="JavaScript">
<!--
document.vlinkColor="#00FF00";
//-->
</SCRIPT>
</HEAD>
```

This sets the visited link color of the document to green.

To display the RGB code information to the viewer, we could use the following code:

```
<BODY vlink="green">
<H1>My Super Duper Visited Link Color</H1>
<SCRIPT language="JavaScript">
<!--
document.write("The visited link color here is "+document.vlinkColor);
//-->
</SCRIPT>
</BODY>
```

Notice that the color is set in the opening <BODY> tag using the vlink attribute. Figure 9-14 shows the results of this code when viewed in a browser.

Again, as with most properties like this, it cannot be changed on the fly, so we don't have much else we can do with it for now.

Finally, we have finished the last property on the list, and we can move on to other things in the module. After a break for some practice, we will look at the methods of the document object.

9

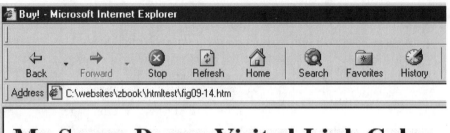

Figure 9-14 The RGB code for the visited link color is displayed in the browser window

Ask the Expert

Question: So many of these properties were arrays that we couldn't really use yet. Will we ever use them for anything?

Answer: The reason we didn't look at the arrays in more detail is because we haven't yet discussed how arrays work When we do, we will be able to make better use of the properties that create arrays because we will know how to access the array and what we can do with the elements of the array when we access them.

Question: The layers and all properties are interesting, but you said that I may not be able to detect the browsers using these properties soon. Why is this?

Answer: Netscape 6 is likely moving toward the all property and away from the layers property. This could mean that to detect a specific browser, we would need to use the naviagator.appName and navigator.appVersion properties. However, detecting the all and layers properties can still be useful if we just need to know whether or not the browser supports the property we need to run our script.

Question: The referrer property is cool! Is there any way I can write that information to a file each time a visitor drops in so I know where my visitors are coming from?

Answer: Unfortunately, client-side JavaScript cannot save information in a file (other than cookies, which are only useful to an individual viewer); thus, we can't make use of this property to track the URL addresses of referring pages in a personal file. To do this, we would need to use a server-side language to get the information and save it in a file on the server.

Question: The creation of a formName property through naming a form was a little confusing. Then, trying to change the value of a form element by using its name and a value property made it more confusing. Can I see another example, perhaps with a text box or something other than a button?

Answer: We will be using this again when we discuss the open() and close() methods in the next section. When we do, we will be using a text box instead, so it should help to clear up confusion a little bit. If it is still confusing afterward, do not fear. We have an entire module on the use of JavaScript with forms later in the book.

9

pr9_1.html

Project 9-1: Using Properties to Create a Page

This project will allow you to practice seeing how some of the properties we have discussed work. A page will be created that will display the document title, the color codes used to build the page, the date the page was last modified, and the URL of the document.

Step-by-Step

1. Create an HTML document, leaving room inside the BODY section for our script.

2. Give the page a title of "This is Project 9-1" by placing that text inside the <TITLE> and </TITLE> tags in the HEAD section.

3. In the opening <BODY> tag, set the following attributes:

bgColor="beige"
text="black"
link="darkblue"
vlink="honeydew"

4. Add a set of SCRIPT tags to the page, and then begin creating a page with the information in the following steps.

5. Begin the page with a heading 1 that displays the title of the document.

6. After that, display a list of the colors used on the page so that the list will look something like this:

The background color is [RGB code]
The text color is [RGB code]
The link color is [RGB code]
The visited link color is [RGB code]
The active link color is [RGB code]

Note that the active link color will end up being the browser's default for that color, since we did not assign it a value.

7. At the end of the page, display the date the document was last modified and the URL of the document.

8. Save the file as pr9_1.html, and view the page in your browser. Notice the various RGB codes that come up and the information at the bottom of the page.

Methods

The methods of the document object will allow us to do some new things we haven't been able to do yet. Table 9-2 lists the methods with a short description of each. Following the table, we will discuss each method in more detail.

The open() and close() Methods

The open() method allows you to open a new document and create its contents entirely with document.write() or document.writlen() statements.

Method	Description
open()	Opens a new document that allows you to write its contents using write() or writeln() statements
close()	Closes a new document that has been opened with the open() method
write()	Allows you to write a string of text into an HTML document
writeln()	Allows you to write a string of text into an HTML document, but ends the line with a JavaScript new line character

Table 9-2   The Methods of the Document Object

When the open() method is called, the browser looks for these statements so it can write the new page. Once the write() and/or writeln() statements are completed, we need to use document.close() to finish the new page.

To get an example of the use of the open() method, let's say we want to write a new page based on the name of the viewer. In order to do this, we are not only going to need the open() and close() methods, but we will also need to create a formName property to use so we can grab the name entered by the viewer in a text box.

Let's start with the code for the BODY section of the initial page. What we need here is a form with a text box and a way to invoke a function that will create the new document. The following code shows a way that we can do this:

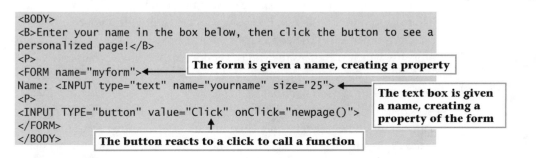

```
<BODY>
<B>Enter your name in the box below, then click the button to see a
personalized page!</B>
<P>
<FORM name="myform">          The form is given a name, creating a property
Name: <INPUT type="text" name="yourname" size="25">
                                              The text box is given
<P>                                           a name, creating a
<INPUT TYPE="button" value="Click" onClick="newpage()">   property of the form
</FORM>
</BODY>             The button reacts to a click to call a function
```

Notice how we named the form in the opening <FORM> tag, and then named the text box in its INPUT tag. We will need these in our function to get the text the viewer entered. In the button input tag, we call a function named "newpage()" with the onClick event handler. We now need to create the newpage() function in the HEAD section of the document so that this form will work.

The newpage() function will need to grab the contents of the text box and assign it to a variable. It will then need to open our new customized page in the browser window. The following code shows how this can be done:

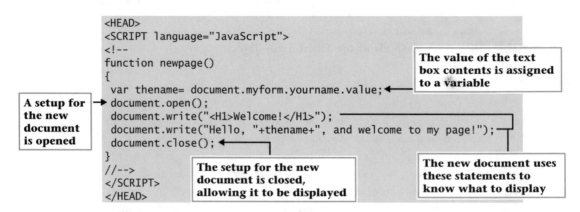

The first thing the function does is to grab the contents of the text box. Recall from our discussion of the formName property in the previous section that when we name a form, we are able to use that name as a property of the document object. Since the name of our form is myform, we are able to use document.myform to access the form.

To gain access to the text box, we need to use its name, which is "yourname." Thus, we can get to the text box using document.myform.yourname for access. In order to get the contents of the text box, we need to use the value property, which we add to the end to get document.myform.yourname.value. This value is then assigned to the thename variable for easy use within our document.write() commands.

Once we have that value, we are ready to open the new page. To do this, we use the document.open() command, which allows us to use a series of document.write() statements until the document.close() command is used. We use the document.write() statements to write a greeting to the viewer on the page.

Now, we just need to put the two parts together so that we have a viewable example. The following code combines the HEAD and BODY sections of code into one HTML page:

```
<HTML>
<HEAD>
<TITLE>New Page Maker</TITLE>
<SCRIPT language="JavaScript">
<!--
function newpage()
{
 var thename= document.myform.yourname.value;
 document.open();
 document.write("<H1>Welcome!</H1>");
 document.write("Hello, "+thename+", and welcome to my page!");
 document.close();
}
//-->
</SCRIPT>
</HEAD>
<BODY>
<B>Enter your name in the box below, then click the button to see a
personalized page!</B>
<P>
<FORM name="myform">
Name: <INPUT type="text" name="yourname" size="25">
<P>
<INPUT TYPE="button" value="Click" onClick="newpage()">
</FORM>
</BODY>
</HTML>
```

Figure 9-15 shows the initial page with the form (the page before the form button is clicked). This is where the viewer can enter a name and click the button.

Figure 9-16 shows the result of entering the name "John" in the text box and clicking the button. The new page appears with a greeting!

Note that this script doesn't check to see if nothing has been entered. If nothing is entered into the text box, you will see a blank space or null in place of the name. If you want to add a check for this, you could place the following code right after the creation of the thename variable and before the document.open() command:

```
if ((thename=="") || (thename==null))
 window.alert("Enter something, then try again!");
```

This will be sure that something is entered into the text box, but the viewer could still enter one or more blank spaces into the text box and make nothing show up anyway. However, at least something will need to be entered when the preceding code is used.

9

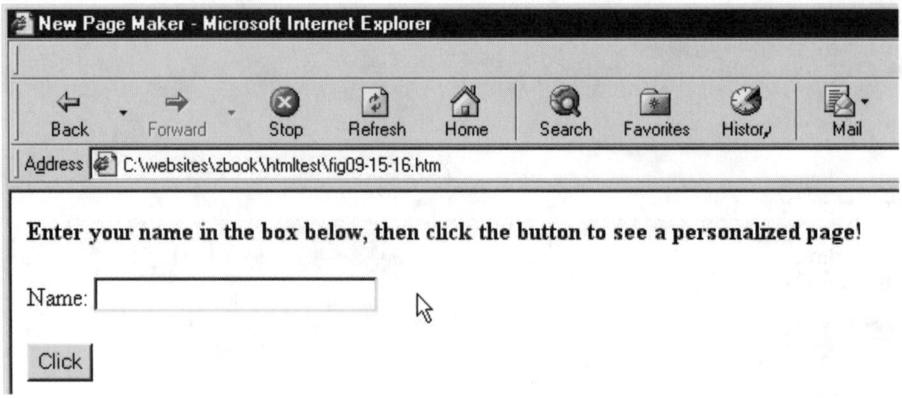

Figure 9-15 | This is the page that allows the viewer to enter information

Hint

The open() and close() methods can be useful to make pages on the fly based on variables like names, favorite foods, or other things for which you may want to customize a new page.

Figure 9-16 | Once the button is clicked, the viewer will get a new page similar to this one

The write() Method

We started using the write() method early in the book, and so we know quite a bit about how it works already; but let's look at a brief description of this method.

The document.write() method is used to write a string value to the page. The following code would write the "hi there" in the body of an HTML document:

```
<BODY>
<SCRIPT language="JavaScript">
<!--
document.write("hi there");
//-->
</SCRIPT>
</BODY>
```

The writeln() Method

The writeln() method works the same way as the document.write() method, but adds a JavaScript newline character (\n) at the end of the statement. Recall that in Module 3 we discussed how the JavaScript newline character works—it only places a new line in the page source code to make it easier to read.

The appearance of the page itself is not affected by the JavaScript newline character. Recall our example from Module 3 in which we split the code into two different lines with the newline character:

```
<SCRIPT language="JavaScript">
<!--
document.write("<B>JavaScript Rules!</B>\n This is fun.");
//-->
</SCRIPT>
```

Since the document.writeln() method adds a newline character at the end of the statement, we could rewrite the preceding code using the following document.writeln() statements:

```
<SCRIPT language="JavaScript">
<!--
document.writeln("<B>JavaScript Rules!</B>");
```

9

```
document.writeln(" This is fun.");
//-->
</SCRIPT>
```

This would put the lines of code on two different lines in the page source, but would not affect the appearance of the page in the browser.

Well, that does it for the methods of the document object. As you can see, some of these may be quite useful to us in future scripts.

pr9_2.html

Project 9-2: Extending the Basic Script

This project will allow you to practice using the new methods we have learned in this module. This will be a basic extension of the script we used when we used the open() and close() methods, but should help you with the form naming and element naming we used earlier.

Step-by-Step

1. Create an HTML page, leaving space in both the HEAD and BODY sections of the document.

2. In the BODY section, create a form named "myform." Create two text boxes. Name the first one "yourname" and the second "yourfood." Be sure to ask for the viewer's name for the first text box and the viewer's favorite food in the second text box. Create a button that calls a function named "newpage()" when it is clicked. Label the button with the text "Click Here for a New Page."

3. Go to the HEAD section and set up a set of SCRIPT tags so we can create our function.

4. Create the newpage() function. Be sure it assigns the value of the first text box to a variable named "thename," and that it assigns the value of the second text box to a variable named "thefood." Then have a new document open in the browser window that displays a page with the viewer's name and favorite food. It should look something like this:

    Your name is [name]!
    Your favorite food is [food]!

5. Save the file as pr9_2.html, and open it in your browser. Enter the requested information, and click the button. You should get a new page customized to what you have entered.

☑ *Mastery Check*

1. Which of the color properties allows us to change its value on the fly?

   A. fgColor

   B. bgColor

   C. linkColor

   D. alinkColor

2. Which property returns the complete URL of the current document?

   A. domain

   B. referrer

   C. URL

   D. title

3. How does the writeln() method differ from the write() method?

   A. It adds the equivalent of an HTML <BR> tag at the end of the line.

   B. It adds the equivalent of an HTML <P> tag at the end of the line.

   C. It adds a JavaScript newline character at the end of the line.

   D. It is exactly the same as the write() method.

4. How is a formName type property created in JavaScript?

   A. When a form is given a name, the name of the form becomes the property name.

   B. When a form is given a name, the string formName is used as the property name.

   C. The forms aren't given names; instead, formName is used as the property name.

   D. When the form is given a name, an "f" is added to the beginning and is used as the property name.

9

☑ *Mastery Check*

5. What statements are allowed between a document.open() and a document.close() statement?

A. HTML commands

B. document.write() and document.writeln() statements

C. Only document.writeln() statements

D. Only window.alert() statements

Module 10

Window Object

The Goals of This Module

- Learn what the window object is
- Use the properties of the window object
- Use the methods of the window object
- Discover how to prompt viewers for information
- Open new windows with JavaScript
- Learn how to use various properties and methods together

Now we move on to the use of the JavaScript window object. This object gives us access to an even larger list of properties and methods than we had with the document object. We will be able to do a number of new things, such as prompt the user for information, open new windows, confirm an action by a viewer, and more. This object will be one we will use quite often due to the properties and methods it provides for us to interact with the viewer.

An Introduction to the Window Object

The window object is created for each window that appears on the screen. A window can be the main window, a frame set or individual frame, or even a new window created with JavaScript. This object opens up a number of new properties and methods for us to use in our scripts, and some of these will enable us to have more viewer interaction than in previous modules.

In previous modules, we have used both the alert() method and the status() property of the window object within our scripts. The alert() method enabled us to pop up a message for the viewer, while the status() property enabled us to change the value of the text string in the status bar at the bottom of the browser. We will now see a number of new methods of this object that will do things such as confirm a viewer's action or prompt the viewer for information, and this will enable us to add more interactivity to our scripts.

The first thing we will look at will be the properties of the window object. In the next section, we will introduce and explain the properties we can use with this object. But, first, we will do a 1–Minute Drill.

1-Minute Drill

- **What type of documents might create a window object?**
- **Which window object properties and methods have we used in previous modules?**
- **What is the advantage of confirming a viewer's action or prompting the viewer for information?**

- The main window, a frameset or frame, or a new window could all create a window object
- We have used the alert() method and status property previously
- It enables us to have more interactivity with the viewer

Properties

To begin our study of the window object, we will want to take a look at the properties that we can use. Table 10-1 lists a number of the properties of the window object with a description of each. Following the table, we will discuss each property in more detail.

Now that we have seen a list of properties we can use with the window object, let's take a closer look at each property individually.

The closed Property

The closed property is used to check whether a not a window has been closed by the viewer. The way it is normally used is with the name of a window, followed by the closed property, such as in the following example:

```
if (windowname.closed)
```

The *windowname* part would be replaced with the name of the window that we wish to check. This is often a new window we opened with JavaScript, and we will see how to name a new window later in the module when we get to the open() method.

Property	Description
closed	Holds the value based on whether or not a window has been closed
defaultStatus	Defines the default message displayed in the status bar
frames	An array that represents all of the frames in a given window
length	Holds a value equal to the number of frames in a window
location	The value is the current URL of the window
name	Enables a window to be named
opener	Refers to the window that opened another window
parent	Refers to the frame set that contains the current frame
self	Another way to reference the current window
status	Enables a message to be placed in the status bar; overrides defaultStatus
top	A reference to the top window containing a frame, frame set, or nested frame set

Table 10-1   **The Properties of the Window Object**

10

It can also be used inside a new window to check whether the window that opened it has been closed. To do that, we would use it after the opener property (which we will get to soon), as in the following example:

```
if (window.opener.closed)
```

This use of the property is really handy if you choose to create a new window that enables the viewer to navigate the main window through links in the new window.

The defaultStatus Property

The defaultStatus property is like the window.status property we have used in previous modules, but it has one difference: the defaultStatus property sets the text string for the status bar that shows when nothing else has been assigned there (which window.status does not do), meaning that it changes what is shown in the status bar by default. A change of the window.status property overrides this setting, as it is only showing as the default.

The defaultStatus property is often set in the onLoad event handler in the opening <BODY> tag:

```
<BODY onLoad="window.defaultStatus='Welcome!';">
```

This is used mainly for a custom message to appear by default when the viewer is not performing an action that would change the text in the status bar. It can be set at any time though, so you could set this using other events besides the onLoad event.

The frames Property (Array)

The frames property is an array that holds a value for each frame within a frame set. It is often used to gain access to the properties of the various frames on a page. Since we have not studied arrays yet, we don't have much we can do with it now. We will be learning arrays in Module 12, however.

We can find the number of frames in a window by using the window.frames.length property. This is handy if we decide to use the array later to perform tasks on the frames of a page in sequence.

The length Property

The length property tells us how many frames are in a window, just like the window.frames.length property. This just shortens it to window.length.

The location Property

The location property holds the current URL of the window, and this URL can be changed on the fly to direct a viewer to a new page just like any link would. This is handy if we wish to make a button link or to have the viewer go to another page based on a certain action.

To create a button link, we would change the value of this property using the onClick event handler:

```
<FORM>
<INPUT type="button" value="Click to Search the Web"
 onClick="window.location='http://www.yahoo.com';">
</FORM>
```

This is similar to the way we changed the window.status property in previous modules. We give it a new string value; and with this command, we tell the browser to go to the new URL. This code would take the viewer to http://www.yahoo.com when the button is clicked.

We can also change this at any time in a script. We could change the previous code to enable the viewer to enter a name inside a text box, and then take the viewer to a site based on the name using a function to do the work. The following is an example of this:

10

```
<HTML>
<HEAD>
<SCRIPT language="JavaScript">
<!--
function gothere()
{
 var thename=document.myform.yourname.value;
 if (thename=="John")
  window.location="http://www.pageresource.com";
 else
  window.location="http://www.yahoo.com";
}
//-->
</SCRIPT>
```

> This tests the value of the variable and then sends the viewer to one page or the other based on that value

```
</HEAD>
<BODY>
<FORM name="myform">
Your Name:
<BR>
<INPUT type="text" name="yourname" size="25">
<P>
<INPUT type="button" value= "Click for Your Page"
 onClick="gothere();">  ◄─────
</FORM>
</BODY>
</HTML>
```

> The function is called to start things when the button is clicked

This time the page to which the viewer is taken on the button click is different based on the name entered. Recall from a previous module that we can get the contents of the text box by accessing its name property through the document object, the form name, and the name of the text box. Of course, this is limited in that only those who type in the string *John* exactly will be taken to the first option. We could expand this with logical OR operators if we wish to make it more inclusive.

We can also use this for an instant redirection of the browser to a new page (if your page has moved to a new location, for instance). The thing to watch here is that you don't use this on a page that is listed with search engines that do not allow quick redirection, because they may drop the page from the listings.

If a page has been moved and you want to redirect the viewer without a wait, you could just give the location property a new value with a script in the HEAD section of the page, as shown in the following code:

```
<HTML>
<HEAD>
<TITLE>Page has moved</TITLE>
<SCRIPT language="JavaScript">
<!--
window.location="page2.html";  ◄─────
//-->
</SCRIPT>
</HEAD>
<BODY>
Lacking JavaScript? Click the link below for the new page then!
<BR>
<A HREF="page2.html">New Page</A>
</BODY>
</HTML>
```

> This sends the viewer away instantly, since no action needs to take place to set this in motion

Hint

Instant redirection is best used for testing purposes on pages not indexed by a search engine, since the rules on redirection vary from one search engine to the next.

This would just take the viewer to the local URL page2.html. An option was included in the BODY section for browsers without JavaScript. Otherwise, the preceding code would load a blank page for those viewers and nothing would happen.

This property will become quite useful to us when we build scripts for navigation in Module 14.

The name Property

The name property holds the name of the current window and also enables you to give a window a name. If you want to give the main window a name, you could assign the name in the HEAD section of the page. If you want to test to see that it worked, you could write the value of the property to the page in the BODY section.

The following code shows an example of assigning a name to a window and then writing the name into the body of the page:

```
<HTML>
<HEAD>
<SCRIPT language="JavaScript">
<!--
window.name="cool_window";     ◄——— The window is given its own name
//-->
</SCRIPT>
</HEAD>
<BODY>
<SCRIPT language="JavaScript">
<!--
document.write("This window is named "+window.name);◄—
//-->
</SCRIPT>          The name of the window is written to the screen
</BODY>
</HTML>
```

10

The script in the HEAD section gives the window a name, and then the script in the BODY section writes that name into the document. Figure 10-1 shows the result of this script in a browser. Notice how the name "cool_window" is written on the screen.

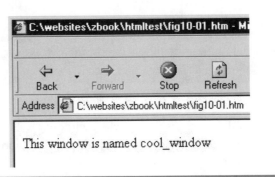

This window is named cool_window

Figure 10-1   **The name of the window is written on the screen**

The opener Property

The opener property is used to reference the window that opened the current window. This is often used in new windows opened using the open() method, which we will see later in the module. By using the opener property in a new window, we could detect whether the main window has been closed using the closed property we learned earlier. The following example shows how we could perform this test:

```
if (window.opener.closed)
```

This adds the closed property after the opener property to check whether the window that opened the current window has been closed. This is helpful if we want to perform an action in the main window through the new one, because we could check to see that it still exists before doing anything.

The parent Property

The parent property is only used when there are frames on a page. It enables us to access the parent frame set of the current frame. This is helpful when we wish to change a property in one frame from another frame. We will discus this in more detail when we cover JavaScript and frames in Module 15.

The self Property

The self property is another way of saying "the current window" in JavaScript. It is used like the window object and can access the properties of the current window just like the window object. So, we could also change the location of the current window using self.location rather than window.location, if we wish, as shown in the following example:

```
<FORM>
<INPUT type="button" value="Click to Search the Web"
 onClick="self.location='http://www.yahoo.com';">
</FORM>
```

This does the same thing as our first window.location example in the module. When the button is clicked, the new URL is opened in the current window.

The self property is useful if you have a lot of windows with names and want to be sure you are using a property of the current window and not one in another named window.

The status Property

The status property contains the value of the text set in the status bar of the window. Changing this property overrides the content of the status bar set with the defaultStatus property. Since we have used this property already, we can keep this example brief. To change the content in the status bar, we assign it a new value, as shown in the following example code:

```
<FORM>
<INPUT type="button" value="Click for Status Message"
 onClick="window.status='Hello!';">
</FORM>
```

This changes the contents of the status bar on the click of a button.

Also, recall that when we changed this property using the onMouseOver and onMouseOut events, we needed to use a return true statement afterward to ensure that it worked. This leads us to a new script.

Since the status command overrides the defaultStatus property, we could use an onMouseOver event to change the contents of the status bar to something else. Moving the mouse away automatically returns the status

10

bar to the value of our defaultStatus property, unless we use an onMouseOut event and change it.

The following code shows an example of changing the status after setting the default status value:

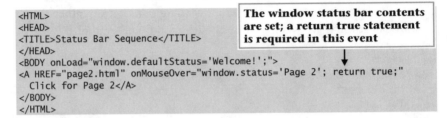

```
<HTML>
<HEAD>
<TITLE>Status Bar Sequence</TITLE>
</HEAD>
<BODY onLoad="window.defaultStatus='Welcome!';">
<A HREF="page2.html" onMouseOver="window.status='Page 2'; return true;"
   Click for Page 2</A>
</BODY>
</HTML>
```

> The window status bar contents are set; a return true statement is required in this event

First, we set the default status with the onLoad event in the opening <BODY> tag. In the onMouseOver event, we change the contents of the status bar to "Page 2" to let the viewer know where the link is headed. When the mouse moves away, the browser restores the default status message for us.

The top Property

The top property is used to access the top window out of all the frame sets (which could be nested) that contains the current frame. This is a little different from the parent property, which only goes to the top of the frame set that contains the current frame. The top property instead goes all the way to the top window, even if the window contains nested frame sets.

We will see more on the use of this property when we get to Module 15 on JavaScript and frames, later in the book.

1-Minute Drill

● **What can we do with the closed property?**

● **What does the name property enable us to do?**

● **What is the difference between the parent and top properties?**

● The closed property enables us to test to see whether a window has been closed
● The name property enables us to give a window a name
● The parent property goes to the top of the current frame set, while the top property goes to the top window of all frame sets on a page

pr10_1.html

Project 10-1: Using the Location Property of the Window Object

This project will enable you to practice using the location property of the window object. A page will be created with button navigation.

Step-by-Step

1. Create a Hypertext Markup Language (HTML) page, leaving space in the BODY section to put in some code.

2. Create a form on the page with five buttons.

3. Place each of the five buttons on separate lines using the <P> tag.

4. Make each button link to one of these URL addresses:

http://www.pageresource.com
http://www.javascriptcity.com
http://www.yahoo.com
http://www.netscape.com
http://www.microsoft.com

5. Give the buttons the following labels with the value attribute:

Page Resource
JavaScript City
Yahoo! Web Site
Netscape Web Site
Microsoft Web Site

6. Save the file as pr10_1.html, and open it in your browser. Try out some of the buttons while online to see if they take you to the new URL.

10

Methods

Now that we know how to use the properties of the window object, we can move on to using window methods. Table 5-2 lists a number of the methods of the window object with a description of each. Following the table, we will discuss each method in more detail.

Method	Description
alert()	Pops up an alert to the viewer, and viewer must click an OK button to proceed
confirm()	Displays a confirmation box to the viewer, and viewer must click an OK or Cancel button to proceed
find()	Enables the viewer to launch the Find utility in the browser to find text on a page
print()	Prints the contents of a window
prompt()	Pops up a prompt box asking the viewer to input information
open()	Opens a new browser window
close()	Closes a browser window
blur()	Removes the focus from a window
focus()	Gives the focus to a window
moveBy()	Moves a window by certain pixel values that are sent as parameters
moveTo()	Moves the top-left corner of the window to the coordinates sent as parameters
resizeBy()	Resizes a window by moving the bottom-right corner by certain pixel numbers that are sent as parameters
resizeTo()	Resizes an entire window to the height and width that are sent as parameters
scrollBy()	Scrolls the viewing area of a window by certain pixel values sent as parameters
scrollTo()	Scrolls the viewing area of the window to the specified coordinates that are sent as parameters
setInterval()	Calls a function each time a certain amount of time passes
clearInterval()	Cancels the action of a setInterval() method call
setTimeout()	Calls a function once after a certain amount of time has passed
clearTimeout()	Cancels the action of a setTimeout() method call

Table 10-2   The Methods of the Window Object

The alert() Method

The alert() method is a method we have used extensively in earlier modules in our example scripts. This pops up a message to the viewer, and the viewer has to click an OK button to continue. Recall that the syntax was like the following alert:

```
window.alert("Hi there!");
```

This would just give the viewer the "Hi there!" message we provided as an alert on the screen.

When the alert() method was first introduced, we noted that this method was often shortened in scripts using a syntax like the following:

```
alert("Hi there!"):
```

How can we get away with that? Remember that JavaScript is fairly lenient, so we are allowed to take shortcuts like this is some instances. In this case, it is because the browser assumes the window object exists already.

Since it is assumed to be there, we don't need to make the call to it. Instead, we can just call the method, and JavaScript will know it is a window method.

This will work for all the window properties and methods in most cases. In fact, the document object we studied in the last module is under the window object in the object hierarchy. We are able to leave the window part off of the document object calls because the window is assumed to exist.

The cases in which we may need to be more specific are often with new windows and with the location property. For the time being, we won't use this type of shortcut.

The confirm() Method

The confirm() method can be used to give the viewer a chance to confirm or cancel an action. This method returns a Boolean value of true or false, so its result is often assigned to a variable when it is used.

The following is the syntax for assigning the value to a variable:

```
var varname=window.confirm("Your Message");
```

We would replace *varname* with a variable name we wish to use. We would then replace the "Your Message" text with the text we wish to have in the box that pops up. So, if we wanted to assign the result to a

10

variable named is_sure and ask the question "Are you sure?," we could use the following code:

```
var is_sure=window.confirm("Are you sure?");
```

Figure 10-2 shows a sample of a confirm box that will be displayed by the preceding code. Notice the two buttons the viewer can choose to click: OK and Cancel. Depending on the browser, this may look slightly different. If the viewer clicks the OK button, the method returns true. If the user clicks the Cancel button, the method returns false. The bad news is we can't change the value of the text in the buttons. We are stuck with OK and Cancel, at least while using the confirm method.

As a real example of this method, let's say we want to create a button that links to another page, but we want to be sure the viewer wants to leave before being sent away. We could use the confirm box to find out whether or not the viewer wishes to leave the page. The following code shows how we can get a confirmation from the viewer using the confirm method and an if block:

```
<HTML>
<HEAD>
<SCRIPT language="JavaScript">
<!--
function gothere()
{
 var is_sure=window.confirm("Are you sure you want to leave?");
 if (is_sure==true)
 {
  window.location="http://www.yahoo.com";
 }
}
//-->
</SCRIPT>
</HEAD>
<BODY>
<FORM>
<INPUT type="button" value="Click to Search the Web"
 onClick="gothere();">
</FORM>
</BODY>
</HTML>
```

The function confirms whether or not the viewer wants to leave

The function call starts the process to confirm

Figure 10-2   An example of a confirm box

First, look at the BODY section and see that we call the gothere()
function when the button is clicked. Inside the gothere() function, we
begin by assigning the value returned a confirm box to a variable name
is_sure. If the value of is_sure is true (viewer clicked OK), the viewer goes
to the new site. If the value of is_sure is false (viewer clicked Cancel),
nothing happens (since we left out the else block, nothing will happen
unless the value of is_sure is true) and the viewer stays on our page.

Figure 10-3 shows the browser window when the button is clicked on
the page. The confirm box with our "Are you sure?" message pops up on
the screen.

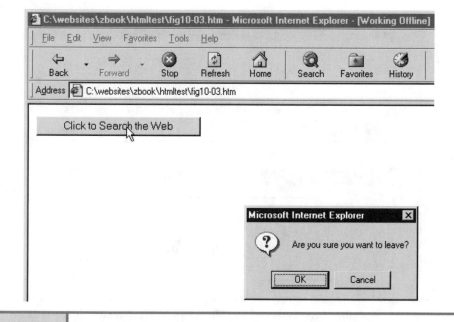

10

Figure 10-3   A confirm box pops up when the button is clicked

The find() Method

The find() method can be used to let the viewer find a certain bit of text on your page. It tells the browser to use its built-in Find utility and enables the viewer to type in what to look for on the page. (It seems to work only in Netscape Navigator 4 or higher, however.)

For example, if we wanted to create a button for viewers to click when they want to find something on our page, we could use the following code:

```
<FORM>
<INPUT type="button" value="Click to Find Text"
 onClick="window.find();">
</FORM>
```

This pops up the Find dialog box in the browser and enables the viewer to search for text within the page. Figure 10-4 shows the result of this script when it is added to the BODY section of an HTML document.

This is useful if you have a really long page and want the viewer to be able to find things more quickly by using search. Remember also that this method was introduced in JavaScript 1.2 and may not work in older browsers.

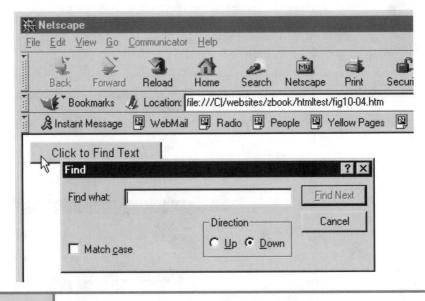

Figure 10-4 A dialog box pops up, enabling the viewer to search for text on the page

The print() Method

The print() method enables the viewer to print the current window.
When this method is called, it should bring up the viewer's print dialog
box so the printer settings can be set by the viewer to print the document.

To use it, we could create a button that enables the viewer to print the
page being viewed. The following code creates the button:

```
<FORM>
<INPUT type="button" value="Click to Print Page"
 onClick="window.print();">
</FORM>
```

This code should bring up the user's print options box. Figure 10-5 shows
the result of running this script in a browser. This screen may appear
differently, depending on the browser and printer being used.

A print button can be a useful feature to have on informational sites.
Remember, though, that this method was introduced in JavaScript 1.2 and
may not work in older browsers.

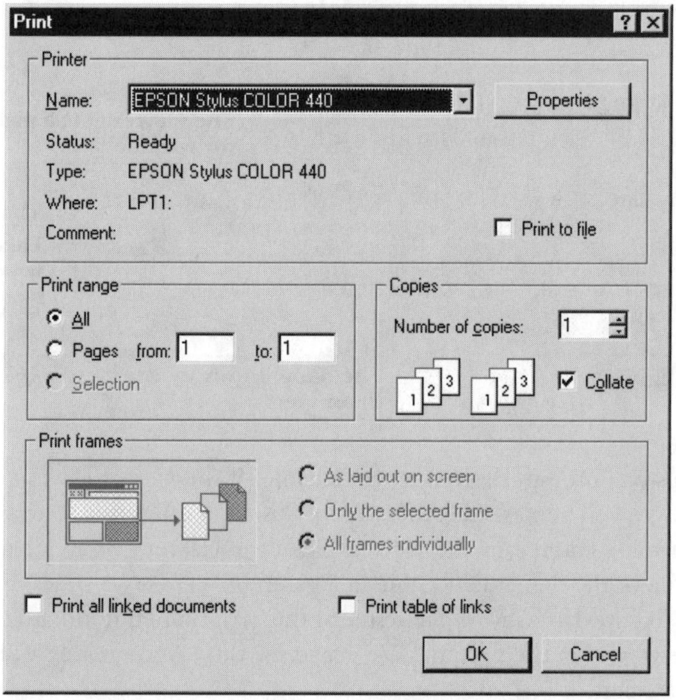

10

Figure 10-5 The viewer's print options pop up when the button is clicked

The prompt() Method

The prompt() method is used to prompt the viewer to enter information. Using this method, we can do things based on what the viewer enters into the text box at the prompt. This enables us to add more interactivity to a page or even to customize a page with the viewer's name.

First, we need to see the syntax for this method. As with the confirm() method, the result (what the viewer enters) is assigned to a variable for later use. The following is an example of the syntax:

```
var varname=window.prompt("Your Text","Default Entry");
```

We replace *varname* with a variable name, and we replace "Your Text" with the message we want to send the viewer (usually a question). The second parameter, Default Entry, enables us to enter a default entry for the viewer. Often this is left as "", which is nothing. However, it could be set to something else if you would like to have a default answer ready for the viewer to use.

We could use this to get the viewer's name and send an alert while the page is loading. The following code gets the viewer's name from a prompt and then alerts it to the viewer:

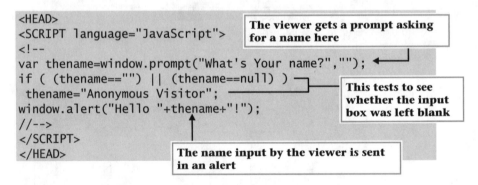

```
<HEAD>
<SCRIPT language="JavaScript">
<!--
var thename=window.prompt("What's Your name?","");
if ( (thename=="") || (thename==null) )
  thename="Anonymous Visitor";
window.alert("Hello "+thename+"!");
//-->
</SCRIPT>
</HEAD>
```

The viewer gets a prompt asking for a name here

This tests to see whether the input box was left blank

The name input by the viewer is sent in an alert

This will prompt the viewer for a name. If the viewer leaves it blank, the viewer will be named "Anonymous Visitor"; otherwise, thename keeps the value entered by the viewer. Then the viewer gets an alert with the value of the thename variable in a greeting.

Figure 10-6 shows the result of this script when nothing is entered by the viewer in the prompt. We get to see the "Anonymous Visitor" name in an alert.

| **Figure 10-6** | **An alert shows up greeting the viewer** |

Instead of placing the name into an alert, we could write it on the page for the viewer instead. In this way, the viewer isn't bothered with an alert, and the name appears as though it is part of the page. The following code shows how this can be done:

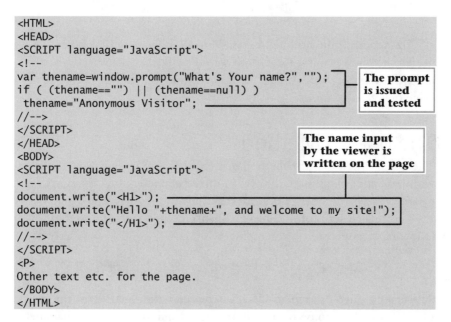

```
<HTML>
<HEAD>
<SCRIPT language="JavaScript">
<!--
var thename=window.prompt("What's Your name?","");      ⎤ The prompt
if ( (thename=="") || (thename==null) )                  │ is issued
  thename="Anonymous Visitor";                           ⎦ and tested
//-->
</SCRIPT>
</HEAD>                         ⎡ The name input
<BODY>                          │ by the viewer is
<SCRIPT language="JavaScript">  ⎣ written on the page
<!--
document.write("<H1>");
document.write("Hello "+thename+", and welcome to my site!");
document.write("</H1>");
//-->
</SCRIPT>
<P>
Other text etc. for the page.
</BODY>
</HTML>
```

This script sets the variable thename in the same way using the prompt and the if block. In the BODY section, we write the variable in with a document.write command as part of the heading. Figure 10-7 shows the result of this in the browser if the viewer enters the name "John" at the prompt.

10

Figure 10-7 The viewer's name is written on the page after the viewer has entered it at a prompt

The prompt() method will be useful to us in future scripts when we need to get viewer input for various purposes. Rather than needing to make the variable values on our own, we can let the viewer decide the value of a variable for us.

The open() Method

The open() method is the method that enables us to open a new window with JavaScript. This method takes in three parameters, and the third parameter sets a number of options that the window may need.

The general syntax for using the open() method is shown in the following example:

```
window.open("URL","name","attribute1=value,attribute2=value");
```

The first parameter shown as URL is replaced with the URL of the HTML document to be opened in the new window. The name parameter is replaced with the name we wish to give to the window. The last parameter enables us to add attributes for the new window.

These are set using "yes" or "no" on the right side of the equal sign. Notice that each time an attribute is set with a value, there is a comma before the next one and no spaces in between.

If we want to open a window with the features of the current window, we could do this by leaving off the last parameter with the attributes. The following example would open a new window with a local URL of "newpage.htm" and a name of "my_window":

```
window.open("newpage.htm","my_window");
```

This would open a window with the contents of the HTML document newpage.htm and name the window my_window; it will have the same features as the window that opened it.

Standard Attributes

If we want to include window features, we will need to learn some of the attributes we can use with the windows. Table 10-3 lists the standard attributes we can use as part of the last parameter in the open() method.

Attribute Name	Possible Values	Function
width	number	Defines the width of the new window in pixels
height	number	Defines the height of the new window in pixels
directories	yes, no, 1, 0	Defines whether or not the new window has directory buttons (like the What's New or Link buttons near the top of the browser)
location	yes, no, 1, 0	Defines whether or not the new window has a location box to type in a new URL
menubar	yes, no, 1, 0	Defines whether or not the window has a menu bar (File menu, Edit menu, and so on)
resizable	yes, no, 1, 0	Defines whether or not the viewer is allowed to resize the new window
scrollbars	yes, no, 1, 0	Defines whether or not the new window will have scroll bars if the contents of the window are more than the window's size

10

Table 10-3 The Standard Attributes for a New Window

Attribute Name	Possible Values	Function
status	yes, no, 1, 0	Defines whether or not the new window will have a status bar at the bottom
toolbar	yes, no, 1, 0	Defines whether or not the new window has a toolbar (Forward and Back buttons, Stop button, and so on)

Table 10-3 The Standard Attributes for a New Window *(continued)*

If we begin to use the attribute parameter, we should note that once we place something in the attribute parameter, any attribute not defined will now default to "no" instead of copying the main window. So, if we want to open a basic new window with a width of 400 and a height of 300, we could use the following code:

```
window.open("newpage.html","my_window","width=400,height=300");
```

This window will be 400×300 pixels, and the only feature it will have is a title bar that shows the title of the document and the buttons on the top right for the viewer to close or minimize it.

To set the other attributes (which are all Boolean), we can assign them a value of "yes" or "no" depending on whether or not we want each feature. You may also use 1 for yes and 0 for no if you prefer, as they will have the same effect. So, if we wanted to have a 300×200 window with just a menu bar added (this adds the Forward, Back, Stop and other similar buttons), we could use the following code:

```
window.open("newpage.html","cool","width=300,height=200,menubar=yes");
```

This gives us a new window with the contents of newpage.html, a name of "cool," dimensions of 300×200, and a menu bar.

We can add as many of the attributes as we want inside the quote marks of the third parameter by separating each one with a comma. Remember that there are no spaces between anything here and the entire command should be on one line in your text editor.

Hint

Due to space limitations, a new window command may occasionally be on more than one line in the code in this book. Be sure that when you use the code you put everything from window.open to the ending semicolon (;) on one line to avoid JavaScript errors.

The following example will open a window with all the features mentioned in Table 10-3 (note that this will take up more than one line here, but when used in real life, the code should go on a single line):

```
window.open("newpage.html","cool","width=300,height=200,directories=yes,
location=yes,menubar=yes,resizable=yes,scrollbars=yes,status=yes,
toolbar=yes");
```

This will open a 300×200 window with all of the standard features. If we want a viewable example, we will need to make a page named "newpage. html" with code, and create the code for the main page to include a window.open() command.

First, let's create the code for newpage.html. We will make this a short page that just has some text in it. The following is the code for this page:

```
<HTML>
<BODY>
I am a new window! I am newer than that old window that opened me, so I am
special. Ha, ha!
</BODY>
</HTML>
```

Now, let's create the main page. The following is the code for the main window:

```
<HTML>
<HEAD>
<TITLE>I'm a Window Warrior</TITLE>          The new window is opened
<SCRIPT language="JavaScript">               when this function is called
<!--
function launchwin()
{
window.open("newpage.html","cool","width=400,height=300,status=yes");
}
//-->
</SCRIPT>
</HEAD>
<BODY>
```

10

```
Click the button below to open an arrogant new window ...
<P>
<FORM>
<INPUT type="button" value="New Window" onClick="launchwin();">
</FORM>
</BODY>
</HTML>
```

The button calls the function when it is clicked

This page uses a form button to call the function launchwin() when the button is clicked. The launchwin() function then launches the new window, including the contents of our newpage.html document. This window is 400×300 and has only a status bar at the bottom as an added feature.

Figure 10-8 shows the result of opening the main page in the browser and clicking the button to open the new window. A new window appears and has some special words for us and for its opener.

Just when you thought there could be no more features to digest, we come to a point at which newer browsers give us additional options.

Figure 10-8 A new window is opened when a button is clicked

Extended Attributes

With JavaScript 1.2, we are able to use a number of new attributes for our new windows. The only trouble is that they only work in version 4+ browsers; and each one only works in either Internet Explorer or Netscape, but not both. With that in mind, Table 10-4 lists the extended attributes for new windows in JavaScript 1.2 and which browsers can use which attributes.

Attribute	Possible Values	Browser	Function
alwaysLowered	yes, no, 1, 0	Netscape Navigator 4+	Allows new window to be opened below all other windows; requires signed script
alwaysRaised	yes, no, 1, 0	Netscape Navigator 4+	Allows new window to be opened above all other windows; requires signed script
dependent	yes, no, 1, 0	Netscape Navigator 4+	Allows new window to be dependent on its opener (if the opening window is closed, the new window is also closed)
hotkeys	yes, no, 1, 0	Netscape Navigator 4+	Defines whether or not hotkeys are enabled in the new window
innerHeight	number	Netscape Navigator 4+	Defines the height of the content area of the new window; may replace the height attribute in the future
innerWidth	number	Netscape Navigator 4+	Defines the width of the content area of the new window; may replace the width attribute in the future
outerHeight	number	Netscape Navigator 4+	Defines the vertical height of the outside edge of the new window

10

Table 10-4   The Extended New Window Attributes in JavaScript 1.2

Attribute	Possible Values	Browser	Function
personalbar	Yes, no, 1, 0	Netscape Navigator 4+	Defines whether or not the new window has a personal toolbar
titlebar	yes, no, 1, 0	Netscape Navigator 4+	Defines whether or not the new window has a title bar; requires a signed script to set to no
z-lock	yes, no, 1, 0	Netscape Navigator 4+	Enables a new window to be set so that it doesn't rise above other windows when focused; requires signed script
screenX	number	Netscape Navigator 4+	Defines the distance from the left of the screen for the new window
screenY	number	Netscape Navigator 4+	Defines the distance from the top of the screen for the new window
left	number	Internet Explorer 4+	Defines the distance from the left of the screen for the new window
top	number	Internet Explorer 4+	Defines the distance from the top of the screen for the new window
fullscreen	yes, no, 1, 0	Internet Explorer 4+	Allows the new window to be set to the full screen view allowed by Internet Explorer

Table 10-4   The Extended New Window Attributes in JavaScript 1.2 *(continued)*

The problem with the atributes in Table 10-4 is that they are all browser specific, and a number of them require signed scripts. We will only deal with the four attributes we can use to set the position of the window—screenX, screenY, left, and top, because they work in both browsers.

To make the screen position work with both Internet Explorer and Netscape Navigator, we need to add all four of the attributes to the last parameter of the open() method. Each browser will just ignore the attributes it does not recognize. The following example opens our

newpage.html document in a new 300×200 window at the top-left
corner of the screen (0 pixels from the left, 0 pixels from the top) when
the button is clicked:

```
<HTML>
<HEAD>
<TITLE>I'm a Window Warrior</TITLE>
<SCRIPT language="JavaScript">
<!--
function launchwin()
{
window.open("newpage.html","cool","width=400,height=300,status=yes,
screenX=0,left=0,screenY=0,top=0");
}
//-->
</SCRIPT>
</HEAD>
<BODY>
Click the button below to open an arrogant new window ...
<P>
<FORM>
<INPUT type="button" value="New Window" onClick="launchwin();">
</FORM>
</BODY>
</HTML>
```

> **The new window is given some standard attributes
> and then a position on the screen by using all four
> attributes (two for each browser)**

Again, note that the window.open() contents should all be on one line in
actual use, as the line breaks here due to space constraints. In this version,
we added the new attributes to set the new window at the coordinates
(0,0) on the screen.

Figure 10-9 shows the result of this in a browser after the button
is clicked. Notice how the new window now opens at the top left of
the screen.

The other attributes are not as useful at this point; but as the browsers
develop further, some of the attributes may begin to be supported in both
browsers in one form or another.

Now back to examining the methods.

The close() Method

The close() method is used to close a window; however, unless you use
signed scripts, this can only be used to close a window that has been
opened by you with JavaScript.

10

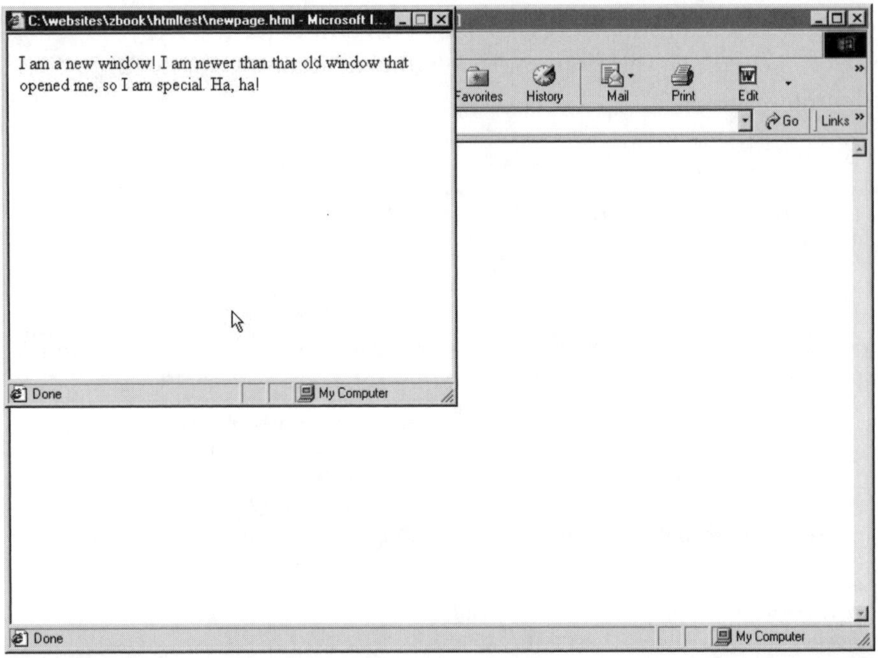

Figure 10-9 The new window opens where we want it to on the screen, at the top left

To use the close() method, we could modify our newpage.html code to provide a button at the end of the text that enables the viewer to close the window by clicking it. So, we could change the code of newpage.html to look like the following code:

```
<HTML>
<BODY>
I am a new window! I am newer than that old window that opened me, so I am
special. Ha, ha!
<FORM>
<INPUT type="button" value="Close Window" onClick="window.close();">
</BODY>
</HTML>
```

> The window is closed when the button is clicked

When the button is clicked now, the window.close() method is invoked and closes the window just like the standard close button at the top right of a window. If you want to try it out, use the main page we used in the previous section and click the button to open the new window. It should offer the new button with the option to close the window, and it will close the window if you click the button.

The blur() Method

The blur() method enables us to put the window in the background behind the main window. A good use for this might be to create a button that enables the viewer to move the window out of the way, but not close it, so that it can be used again later.

To do this, we would again need to modify our newpage.html code. The following is the new code for the page:

```
<HTML>
<BODY>
I am a new window! I am newer than that old window that opened me, so I am
special. Ha, ha!
<FORM>
<INPUT type="button" value="Hide Window" onClick="window.blur();">
<P>
<INPUT type="button" value="Close Window" onClick="window.close();">
</BODY>
</HTML>
```

The window loses focus and moves behind the main window when the button is clicked

Now when this window is opened, there are options to either hide it or close it. Clicking the Hide Window button makes the new window lose focus and move behind the main window. It can be brought back by the viewer using the operating system, or we could bring it back from the main window by calling its name with the focus() method, discussed next.

10

The focus() Method

The focus() method enables us to bring a window into focus (on top of the other windows). Suppose we want to allow the viewer to bring our newpage.html window back after the Hide Window button has been clicked. We would need to bring it back into focus in some way.

We could decide that we want to keep the new window on top even if the viewer clicks the Hide Window button. To do this, we would again modify the newpage.html code:

> **The added event forces the window to remain in focus even when the viewer tries to remove focus from it**

```
<HTML>
<BODY onBlur="window.focus();">  ◄─
I am a new window! I am newer than that old window that opened me, so I am
special. Ha, ha!
<FORM>
<INPUT type="button" value="Hide Window" onClick="window.blur();">
<P>
<INPUT type="button" value="Close Window" onClick="window.close();">
</BODY>
</HTML>
```

Notice the addition of the onBlur event handler to the opening <BODY> tag. Now, when the focus moves off the window, the focus is forced back onto the window! This renders our Hide Window button useless; however, the Close Window button will still work to get rid of the window.

The moveBy() Method

The moveBy() method can be used to move a new window to a new location on the screen. This moves a window by the number of pixels given as parameters in the method call. The following is the syntax for using this method:

```
window.moveBy(x-pixels,y-pixels);
```

We replace *x-pixels* with the number of pixels we want to move the window from left to right. So, if we want the window to move to the right, we enter a positive number. If we want it to move to the left, we enter a negative number.

We replace *y-pixels* with the number of pixels we want to move the window from top to bottom, with positive numbers pushing the window down and negative numbers pulling the window up.

For example, our newpage.html window is set at (0,0) when it is opened. If we want to give the viewer the option to move the window to a new location of our choice, we could add a button to do it when clicked by the viewer. The following code gives us a new version of newpage.html (the focus and blur bits have been removed):

```
<HTML>
<BODY>
I am a new window! I am newer than that old window that opened me, so I am
special. Ha, ha!
<FORM>
<INPUT type="button" value="Move Window" onClick="window.moveBy(50,50);">
<P>
<INPUT type="button" value="Close Window" onClick="window.close();">
</BODY>
</HTML>
```

> **The window will move 50 pixels to the right and 50 pixels downward**

This moves the window 50 pixels to the right and 50 pixels down when the button is clicked. If we open this from the main window we coded earlier in the module, we can see this in action. Figure 10-10 shows the initial position of the new window when it is opened from a button on the main page.

Figure 10-11 shows the window after the Move Window button is clicked in the new window. Notice it has moved to the right and downward by 50 pixels in each direction.

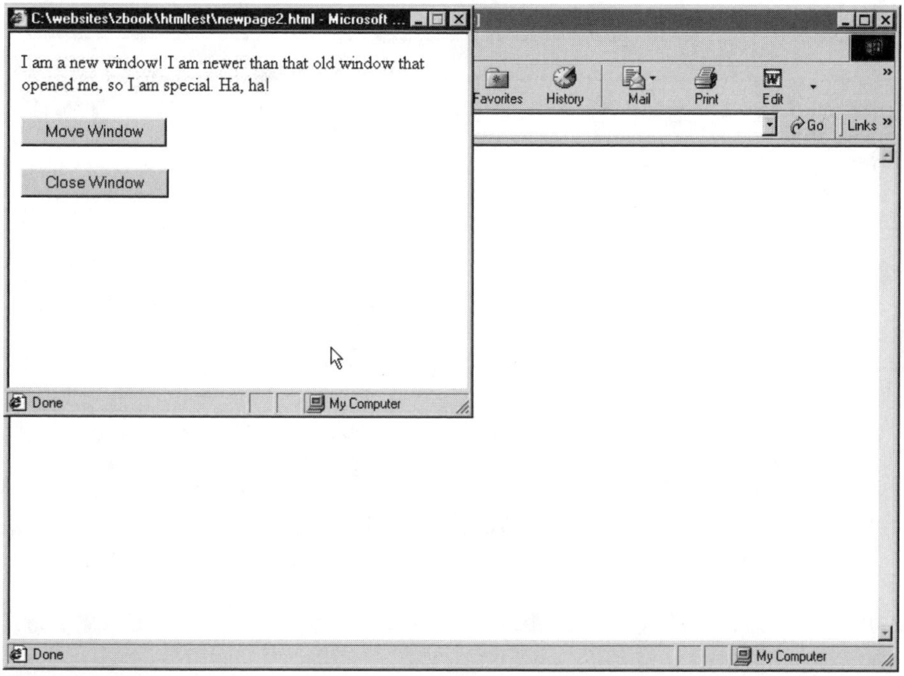

Figure 10-10   The new window in its initial position when it is opened

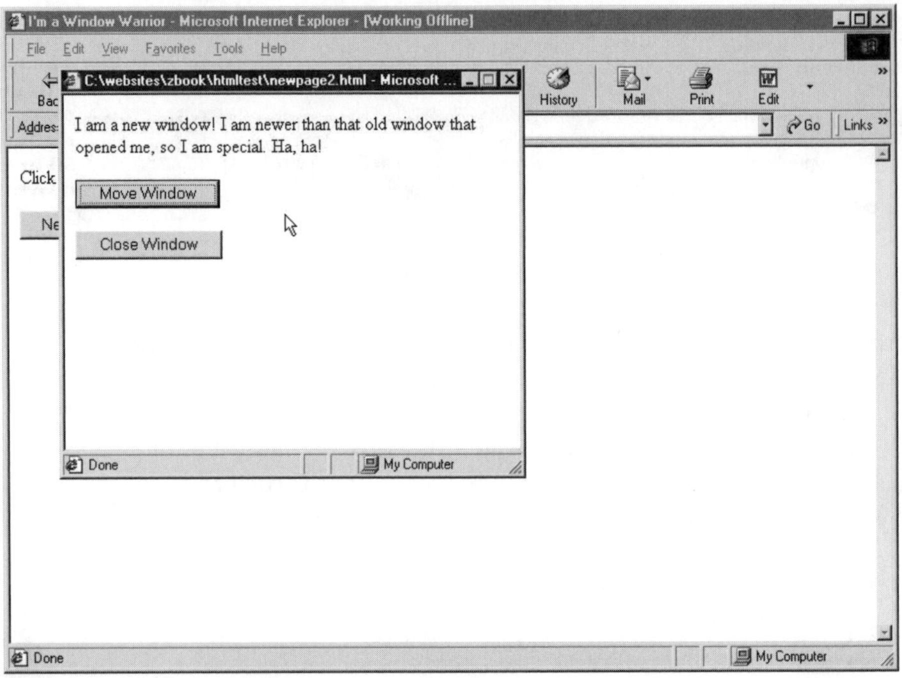

Figure 10-11 The window in its new position after being moved

The way this works, the viewer could continue clicking the button and moving the window by another 50 pixels in both directions as long as the button is viewable. The window just continues to move by the number of pixels it has been set to move by in the script. Our next method will move the window to a particular location, so it will not continue to move on successive clicks like this one did.

The moveTo() Method

The moveTo() method is used to move a window to a specific destination on the screen based on the parameters given in the method call. The following is the general syntax for using this method:

```
window.moveTo(x-value,y-value);
```

Here we replace *x-value* with the number of pixels from the left of the screen where we want the window to be moved. For example, if we input **300**, the window would be moved 300 pixels from the left of the screen.

We then replace *y-value* with the number of pixels from the top of the screen that we want the window to be moved.

As an example, we could recode our Move Window button in our newpage.html page to use moveTo() instead of moveBy(). The following is the example code:

```
<HTML>
<BODY>
I am a new window! I am newer than that old window that opened me, so I am
special. Ha, ha!
<FORM>
<INPUT type="button" value="Move Window" onClick="window.moveTo(50,50);"> ◄—
<P>
<INPUT type="button" value="Close Window" onClick="window.close();">
</BODY>
</HTML>
```

The window will move to the coordinates (50,50) on the screen, which is 50 pixels from the left and 50 pixels from the top

This time the window would be moved to the coordinates (50,50) on the screen when the button is clicked. By using our main page code, we can open the window again to test this out. Figure 10-12 shows the initial position of the window when it is opened.

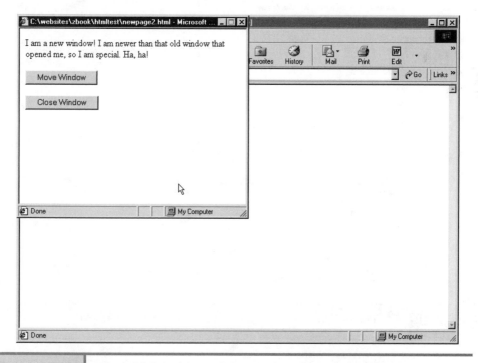

Figure 10-12   The initial position of the window when it is opened

After clicking the button, the window moves to the position (50,50) on the screen. Figure 10-13 shows the new window position after the button is clicked.

To see that this works differently than the moveBy() method, try clicking the button again. Rather than making another move, it stays in the same place because it has already made it to its destination.

The resizeBy() Method

The resizeBy() method is used to resize a window by the number of pixels given in the parameters sent in the method call. The syntax and usage are just like the moveBy() method; it just performs a resize instead. To make the window larger, use positive numbers. To make it smaller, use negative numbers.

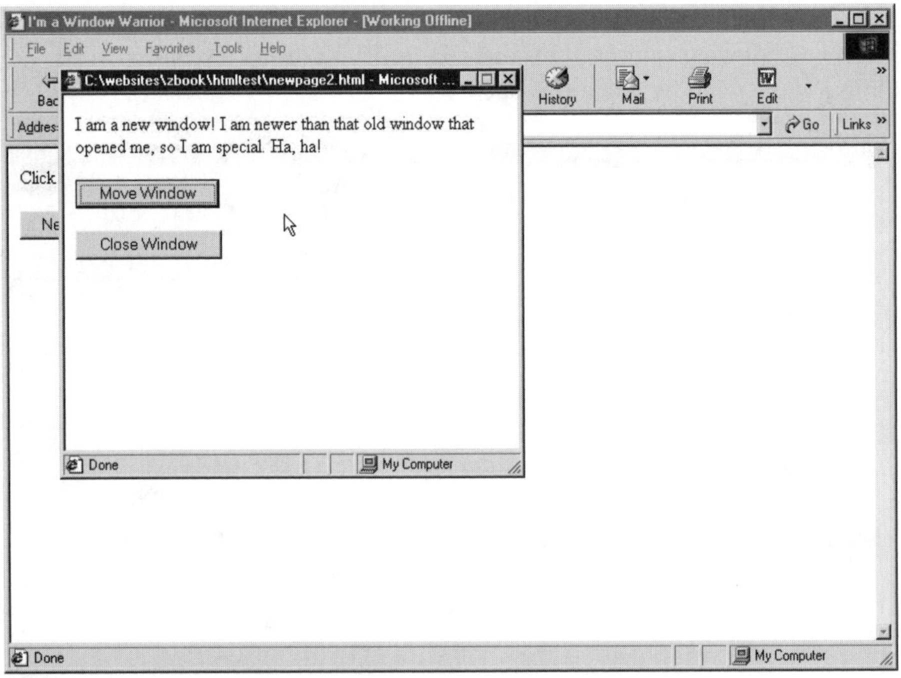

Figure 10-13   The new position of the window after being moved

The resizeTo() Method

The resizeTo() method is used to resize a window to a specific dimension in pixels based on the parameters sent in the method call. The syntax and usage are just like the moveTo() method; it just performs a resize instead. You input the new width and height in place of the coordinates used in the moveTo() method.

The scrollBy() Method

The scrollBy() method is used to scroll a window by the number of pixels given in the parameters sent in the method call. The syntax and usage are just like the moveBy() method; it just performs a scroll instead. To make the window larger, use positive numbers. To make it smaller, use negative numbers.

The scrollTo() Method

The scrollTo() method is used to scroll a window to a specific destination in pixels based on the parameters sent in the method call. The syntax and usage are just like the moveTo() method; it just performs a scroll to the specified point instead.

The setInterval() Method

The setInterval() method is used to execute a JavaScript function repeatedly at a set interval. The following is the general syntax for using this method:

```
window.setInterval("function()",time);
```

We replace *function()* with the name of the function we wish to repeat. We then replace *time* with the time (in milliseconds) we want to wait before each repetition of the function.

So, if we really wanted to annoy our viewers, we could use this method to pop up an alert every 10 seconds (10,000 milliseconds) once

10

```
<HEAD>
<SCRIPT language="JavaScript">
<!--
function annoy_alert()
{
 window.alert("Am I bothering you yet?");
}
window.setInterval("annoy_alert()",10000);
//-->
</SCRIPT>
</HEAD>
```

An interval is set; note the use of quote marks around the function call

Notice that this is a special case in which the function must be called inside quote marks. Normally, in which a function must be called outside quote marks. The reason for it here is to keep the function from executing immediately rather than at the set interval. The function name is being sent as a string parameter to the setInterval() method, where it is then called after the correct time lapse.

This, of course, could become quite annoying. The less time set in the interval, the more annoying it would become. Luckily, the ten-second interval gives us enough time to leave the page before another alert pops up.

The clearInterval() Method

To end the barrage of alerts from the previous script, we could use the clearInterval() method. The following is the general syntax for using this method:

```
window.clearInterval(name);
```

We must replace *name* with a variable name that has been assigned to the setInterval() method call we want to clear. The problem is, we didn't set our setInterval() call to a variable name in our previous example.

In order to clear it, we will need to adjust our code. The following code is updated and assigns the setInterval() call to a variable name:

```
<HEAD>
<SCRIPT language="JavaScript">
<!--
```

```
function annoy_alert()
{
 window.alert("Am I bothering you yet?");
}
var madness=window.setInterval("annoy_alert()",10000);
//-->
</SCRIPT>
</HEAD>
```

> The method call is set to a variable for later reference

We now have a way to use the clearInterval() method by calling it with the madness variable as the parameter. So, let's offer the visitor a button that enables him or her to stop the madness. As long as it is clicked between intervals, it will stop the interval from running any further. The following code gives us a full page with the button for the viewer to click:

```
<HTML>
<HEAD>
<SCRIPT language="JavaScript">
<!--
function annoy_alert()
{
 window.alert("Am I bothering you yet?");
}
var madness=window.setInterval("annoy_alert()",10000);
//-->
</SCRIPT>
</HEAD>
<BODY>
Click the button below to end the endless barrage of alerts.
<P>
<FORM>
<INPUT type= "button" value= "Stop the Madness!"
 onClick="window.clearInterval(madness);">
</FORM>
</BODY>
</HTML>
```

> The method call is set to a variable for later reference

> This method refers to the first method through the variable name to cancel its action

10

Now the viewer can stop the alerts by clicking the Stop the Madness button.

Of course, there are better uses for this method. We will see in later modules that it can be handy for clocks and other things that need to be updated at regular intervals on the page.

The setTimeout() Method

The setTimeout() method enables us to execute a JavaScript function after a certain amount of time has passed. It differs from the setInterval() method because it is only executed once (unless it is put inside a loop of some sort). The general syntax is the same as that of the setInterval() method.

If we want to have only a single alert pop up after ten seconds and not repeat, we could use the following code in the HEAD section of a page:

```
<HEAD>
<SCRIPT language="JavaScript">
<!--
function annoy_alert()
{
 window.alert("Sign my guest book NOW!");
}
var theguest=window.setTimeout("annoy_alert()",10000);
//-->
</SCRIPT>
</HEAD>
```

> **The timeout is set, and also set to a variable**

This would send the viewer an alert after ten seconds demanding that the guest book be signed immediately.

We set the method to a variable so that we could use the next method in line, the clearTimeout() method.

The clearTimeout() Method

The clearTimeout() method enables us to cancel a setTimeout() call if we somehow call the clearTimeout() method before the time expires from the setTimeout() call. The general syntax is the same as that of the clearInterval() method: we use a variable name as a parameter so that it knows which setTimeout() call to cancel.

So, if we want to give viewers a chance to avoid getting an alert, we could add a button for them to click within ten seconds. If it is clicked in time, the setTimeout() call is canceled and no alert pops up. The following is the example code:

```
<HTML>
<HEAD>
<SCRIPT language="JavaScript">
```

```
<!--
function annoy_alert()
{
 window.alert("Sign my guest book NOW!");
}
var theguest=window.setTimeout("annoy_alert()",10000);
//-->
</SCRIPT>
</HEAD>
<BODY>
Click the button below within 10 seconds to avoid an alert message.
<P>
<FORM>
<INPUT type= "button" value= "No Alert for Me!"
 onClick="window.clearTimeout(theguest);">
</FORM>
</BODY>
</HTML>
```

◄— **The timeout is set, and set to a variable for later reference**

◄— **This method refers to the first method through the variable name to cancel its action**

If the button is clicked in time, the viewer avoids receiving an alert about signing the guest book.

For now, we have finally finished with the window object methods. In the modules that follow, we will have uses for a number of these methods in various scripts.

Ask the Expert

Question: There are way too many properties and methods here! How am I ever going to remember all of these?

Answer: As you begin using them with more frequency, they will be easier to remember. I remember the ones I use more often better than those I don't use much. If you do a lot of coding, it is good to keep a reference handy in case you need to check the details of a property or method now and then. I keep a bunch of books and bookmarks to reference Web sites on hand.

Question: Will we be making window remote controls any time soon?

Answer: A new window that changes properties (like the location property) in the main window is a "remote control." There are scripts for these at free script sites on the Web. For now, we want to be sure to master the coding we need to create and manipulate a regular new window.

10

Question: Why do so many of those extended new window attributes require signed scripts? Why would that be needed just to change some features?

Answer: Some of these attributes would enable you to create a window that can't be seen or does not have basic controls (minimize, close). This could be a security risk, and, thus, signed scripts are required. Also, opening a window that is less than 100×100 pixels is a security risk (based on the window possibly becoming too small to be seen) and also requires a signed script. We will touch a little bit on signed scripts when we talk about security in Module 17.

Question: Will we be using the timed methods like setTimeout() and setInterval() often?

Answer: They may not come up very often, but we will have a use for them when we need to build time-dependent scripts such as clocks, slide shows, or Dynamic HTML (DHTML) animations.

pr10_2.html, pr10_2_1.html

Project 10-2: Create a New Window

This project will enable you to practice using some of the window methods. It will create a new window and add some features to it.

Step-by-Step

1. Create an HTML page, leaving space in the HEAD and BODY sections for code.

2. In this page, create a function in the HEAD section named "new_win()" that opens a new window with the URL pr10_2_1.html. Give it dimensions of 400x300, and give it an initial position on the screen of (50,50). Also, give it a status bar and a menu bar.

3. In the body of the page, create a button that calls the new_win() function when clicked to open a new window. Using the value attribute, give the button a label of "Open New Window."

4. Save the file as pr10_2.html, but don't open in your browser just yet. First, we need to create the HTML code for the pr10_2_1.html page that opens in the new window.

5. In the pr_10_2_1.html page, first create a heading 2 that says "Welcome to the New Window!"; then move on to the next step.

6. Create a button that enables the viewer to move the window 10 pixels to the right and 10 pixels down from its current position. Using the value attribute, label the button "Move Window."

7. Create a button that enables the viewer to move the window to a position of (240,200) on the screen. Label the button "Set a Position."

8. Create a button that lets the viewer close the window. Label it "Close Window."

9. Save this file as pr10_2_1.html.

10. Open the pr10_2.html file in your browser, and click the button to open the new window. Try clicking the various buttons in the new window to see what they do to the window.

☑ *Mastery Check*

1. The calls to properties and methods of the window object can often be shortened because

A. The browser typically assumes the window object exists.

B. The window properties and methods are assumed to be part of the navigator object.

C. There really is no window object.

D. The browser assumes the window object is part of the document object.

2. Why would this code not work:

```
onMouseOver="window.status='Page 2';" ?
```

A. It should work without a problem.

10

☑ Mastery Check

B. The quote marks are not set correctly.

C. A change in the status property in an onMouseOver event must return true afterward.

D. A change in the status property in an onMouseOver event must return false afterward.

3. What value is returned by the confirm() method if the viewer clicks the OK button?

   A. true

   B. false

   C. OK

   D. 25

4. When setting the toolbar attribute as part of the third parameter in the open() method, what values may the attribute have?

   A. yes and no only

   B. 1 and 0 only

   C. yes, no, true, and untrue

   D. yes, no, 1, and 0

5. What is the difference between the setInterval() method and the setTimeout() method?

   A. The setTimeout() method is used when the viewer needs to take a break from reading, while setInterval() is used when the viewer needs no breaks.

   B. The setInterval() method is used to repeat a function at a set time interval, while setTimeout() executes a function only once after a set time delay.

   C. The setInterval() method flashes an advertisement across the screen at a set interval by default, while setTimeout() is ad free.

   D. They both perform the same function.

Module 11

JavaScript Arrays

The Goals of This Module

- Learn what arrays are
- Find out why arrays are useful
- Define and access arrays
- Learn the properties and methods of the Array object
- Discover how to use arrays with loops
- Learn how to use associative arrays

In previous modules, we have discussed object properties for which, in order to use them, we need knowledge of arrays. In this module, we are going to learn about those JavaScript arrays and what they can do to help us improve our scripts.

We will begin with a basic overview of what arrays are and why they are useful to us. Then we will learn how to define and access arrays in JavaScript. After that, we will learn about how to use loops in order to gain access to all the elements of an array during the course of a script. Finally, we will take a look at associative arrays and how to use them.

What Is an Array?

An array is a way of storing data of similar types for easy access later in a script. In JavaScript, an array is basically a user-defined object that is typically accessed in a different way than other objects. In a regular array, access to an element is usually through the use of an index number. An associative array allows access using a string in place of the number. We will see how to use both of these later in the module.

To get an idea of how a regular array works, let's say we have a class full of students, and, with a script, we want to be able to quickly print out the name of every student. We could use regular variables to hold the names of each student, but this would make it take a long time (a lot of typing!) to write each variable name into a document.write() statement. Instead, we could store each student's name in an array, which will allow us to access it more easily with a few lines of code using a loop.

The array would allow us to put together a number and a name, such as in the following example:

- Student 0: Thomas

- Student 1: Roger

- Student 2: Amber

- Student 3: Jennifer

By storing it in a manner like this, we could use the numbers to get the name of each student. This is where arrays become useful as a way to store information and access it later.

Hint

You will notice we made the first student Student 0 rather than Student 1. The reason is that arrays begin with 0 rather than 1. This manner of numbering is only to avoid confusion, as we will want the student at index number 1 in the array to match up with Student 1 rather than Student 0.

Why Arrays Are Useful

Why would the use of numbers make it easier for us to access the stored information? Because, with the use of numbers, we are able to use a loop to cycle through the information, rather than writing out each entry by hand. If the list of students in our example becomes long, the loop would save us quite a bit of typing when we want to have all of the names printed onto the browser screen.

For instance, if we assigned the name of each student in our example list to a variable and then wrote the names to the screen, we would need to rewrite each variable name in the document.write() statements. The following code shows an example of this:

```
<HTML>
<HEAD>
<SCRIPT language= "JavaScript">
<!--
var student0="Thomas";
var student1="Roger";        The variables are given values
var student2="Amber";
var student3="Jennifer";
//-->
</SCRIPT>
</HEAD>
<BODY>
document.write(student0+"<BR>");
document.write(student1+"<BR>");   Each variable is individually
document.write(student2+"<BR>");   written into the page
document.write(student3+"<BR>");
</BODY>
</HTML>
```

11

If we were able to use a loop to repeat a single document.write() statement for each student, we could avoid writing four separate document.write() statements. An array will be a handy way to store the values (student names), as we will be able to cycle through the values with a loop instead of writing out each one with a separate document.write() statement.

An array is basically a quick way to create an object (since it already has a constructor function) with a list of properties. A regular object (like the objects we created in Module 8) can be accessed like an array; but it is often easier to create an array, rather than an object, since you do not need to deal with the constructor function.

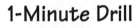

1-Minute Drill

● **What would we want to store in an array?**

● **What is used to access an array element?**

● **Why would the use of numbers make it easier for us to access stored information?**

Defining and Accessing Arrays

Now that we know what arrays are, we need to see how to define and access arrays in JavaScript. To begin, let's look at the naming conventions for an array in JavaScript.

● We would store the data of similar types
● An index number (or a string for associative arrays) is used to access an array element
● A loop can be used to cycle through the information rather than writing out each entry by hand

Naming

We can name an array using the same rules we learned in earlier modules on naming variables, functions, and objects. Basically, avoid numbers in the first character, avoid spaces, and avoid using reserved words.

Defining an Array

Defining an array is similar to creating an instance of an object. In fact, one method of defining an array looks and acts just like the creation of an instance of an object. That's what we are actually doing—creating an instance of the JavaScript Array object.

Since the creation of an instance of an object is already familiar to us, we will use that method first. The following example shows the general syntax of an array definition in JavaScript:

```
var arrayname= new Array(element0,element1);
```

We replace *arrayname* with the name we wish to give to the array, and we replace *element0* and *element1* with the values that each element will have. We can use as many elements as we like.

To see a real example, let's take the student names from the first section of this module and use them as array elements. This array will have four elements, and each one will be the value of a student's name. The following example shows the definition of the array, with the names as string values:

```
var s_list= new Array("Thomas","Roger","Amber","Jennifer");
```

Now we have the values stored inside a four-element array named "s_list." Notice that since the values are strings, quote marks are used (as with a regular object). The question is, how do we begin to access the values now that they are in an array?

11

Accessing an Array

To access the elements of an array, we use what is often called an "index number" that will allow us access to each element of the array by its position in the array. For instance, the syntax to assign the first element of an array to a variable is shown in the following example:

```
var varname= arrayname[0];
```

We would replace *varname* with a variable name and *arrayname* with the name of the array we wish to access. Notice that there is a 0 in brackets after *arrayname*. That 0 is the index number for the first element of an array.

The index number is 0 because arrays begin counting at 0 instead of 1; thus, we need to be careful that we do not get confused about the index number of an element in an array. The first element has an index number of 0, the second has an index number of 1, the third has an index number of 2, and so on.

Inside the square brackets immediately following the array name is where we place the index number of the element we wish to access in the array. To see this in action, let's go back to our four wonderful students. The array for the name of each student was defined as in the following code:

```
var s_list= new Array("Thomas","Roger","Amber","Jennifer");
```

Now, suppose we want to assign the value of the first element in the array (Thomas, in this case, since that is the first element in the list) to a variable named "tall_student." Remember that the first element has an index number of 0; so, to get the value of the first element assigned to the variable, we would use the following code:

```
var tall_student= s_list[0];
```

To see that the value of the tall_student variable comes out as we planned, we could write a short script to write it on the page. The following example writes the value on the page as part of a sentence:

```
<HTML>
<HEAD>
<SCRIPT language="JavaScript">
```

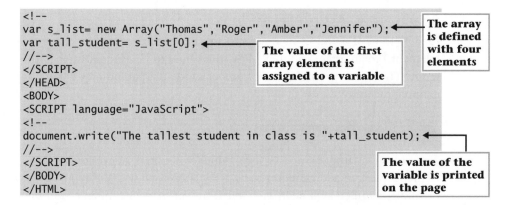

```
<!--
var s_list= new Array("Thomas","Roger","Amber","Jennifer");
var tall_student= s_list[0];
//-->
</SCRIPT>
</HEAD>
<BODY>
<SCRIPT language="JavaScript">
<!--
document.write("The tallest student in class is "+tall_student);
//-->
</SCRIPT>
</BODY>
</HTML>
```

The array is defined with four elements

The value of the first array element is assigned to a variable

The value of the variable is printed on the page

We don't really need to assign the array element to a variable in this case (it just makes us type more). We could just write the array element into the docment.write() statement to save the extra line of code:

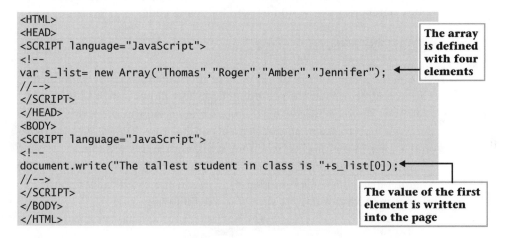

```
<HTML>
<HEAD>
<SCRIPT language="JavaScript">
<!--
var s_list= new Array("Thomas","Roger","Amber","Jennifer");
//-->
</SCRIPT>
</HEAD>
<BODY>
<SCRIPT language="JavaScript">
<!--
document.write("The tallest student in class is "+s_list[0]);
//-->
</SCRIPT>
</BODY>
</HTML>
```

The array is defined with four elements

The value of the first element is written into the page

Now we are accessing the array element directly, and we save a little typing in the process.

Other Ways to Define Arrays

We have seen the quickest way to define an array, but there are other methods (though longer) of doing so that will come in handy later in the module. This will allow you to use the method best suited for various situations.

Space Now, Assign Later

One method of defining an array is to assign a certain amount of space (elements) to an array, and then allow the values to be assigned later in the script. This is done using a single number inside the parentheses when defining the array:

```
var s_list= new Array(4);
```

This creates an array named "s_list," which will initially have four elements (we can add elements to an array later if we wish). Keep in mind the index numbers will be 0, 1, 2, and 3, rather than 1, 2, 3, and 4. In this case, we will give the four elements of the array values later in the script.

To give an element a value, we just assign a value to it using the array name and the index number to which we want the value assigned. So, if we want to assign a value of Amber to the third position in the array (index number 2), we would use the following code:

```
s_list[2]="Amber";
```

We can use a line such as this anywhere after the array has been defined. The technique used in the preceding code also allows us to add elements to an array if we decide we need more elements later in the script. We can also use a loop to assign all the elements of the array, but we will see more on that later in the module when we work with arrays and loops.

So, suppose we would like to add a fifth element to our s_list array. By assigning it a value (index number 4), a new name can be added to the array in the fifth position, as shown in the following code:

```
s_list[4]="Pat";
```

This now adds a fifth element to our s_list array with a value of Pat.

Space Now, Assign Numerically Now

Another way we can define an array is very similar to the one we just covered. The only difference is that some or all of the elements of the array are assigned right after the new array is created.

To see an example, let's use our s_list array again. The following code shows how we can assign the elements of an array if we want to do so right after the line that creates the array space:

```
var s_list= new Array(4)
s_list[0]="Thomas";
s_list[1]="Roger";
s_list[2]="Amber";
s_list[3]="Jennifer";
```

This time all four elements are assigned as the array is created. This is done by leaving off the semicolon at the end of the line that creates the new array. This method is advantageous if you want to assign each element but do not wish to use one long list of parameters on the same line. It is also easier to look back and see what value is assigned to which element more quickly, as there isn't a need to count across. This can be quite advantageous in a long list of elements.

As with the other methods, we can still add more elements later in the script by using the next index number in the sequence.

Array Name, No Parameters

Another option we have for defining an array is to define it with no parameters. This will create an array with no elements, but we are able to add elements later as we did with the other options for defining arrays.

To create an array with no elements, we create an array with no parameters, as shown in the following example code:

```
var s_list= new Array();
```

This creates an array named "s_list" with no elements. We can still add more elements later in the script by using the next index number in the sequence. So, if we decide later that we want the array to contain one element, we could use the following code:

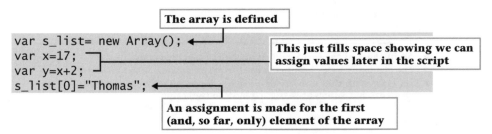

The array is defined

```
var s_list= new Array();
var x=17;
var y=x+2;
s_list[0]="Thomas";
```

This just fills space showing we can assign values later in the script

An assignment is made for the first (and, so far, only) element of the array

This puts the single element in the array.

If we assign a value to an element that has a higher index number, the array expands to have a slot for any elements that come before it. For instance, take a look at the following code:

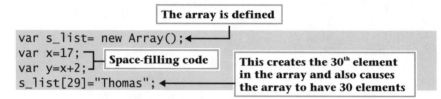

```
var s_list= new Array();
var x=17;
var y=x+2;
s_list[29]="Thomas";
```

The array is defined

Space-filling code

This creates the 30th element in the array and also causes the array to have 30 elements

The last line of this code assigns the string "Thomas" to the 30th element (index number 29) in the array. This means that the array went from having 0 elements to having 30. By assigning a value to this element, the array expands to have enough slots to compensate, and values for those slots can be assigned later if we wish.

Now that we know how to define arrays in various ways, we will need to look at some of the properties and methods of an Array object in JavaScript.

1-Minute Drill

- **When we create a new array, what is actually being created?**
- **What is used to access an element of an array?**
- **What happens if we use one number as a parameter when creating a new array?**

Array Object Properties and Methods

As with other objects, an instance of the JavaScript Array object is able to use various properties and methods of the Array object. We will see that

- An instance of the JavaScript Array object is being created
- The element's index number is used to access an element of an array
- An array with that number of elements is created with space for each of the elements, but values are assigned later in the script

we access the properties by using the array name followed by the property or method name we wish to use. This will be explained as we move through the properties and methods; but, first, let's look at the properties of the Array object.

Properties

Table 11-1 lists the properties of the Array object with a short description of each. Following the table, we will discuss each property in more detail.

The constructor Property

The constructor property contains the value of the function code that constructed an array:

```
function Array() { [native code] }
```

It is mainly useful for informational purposes or for comparisons. To access the property, we use the array name followed by the dot operator and the constructor keyword. The following is the general syntax for using an Array object property:

```
arrayname.property
```

We replace *arrayname* with the name of the array we need to have use the property, and we replace *property* with the property we wish to use.

So, to use the constructor property, we need to create an array so that we have an instance of the Array object to use. We can go back to our

Property	Description
constructor	Refers to the constructor function used to create an instance of an object
index	Property used when an array is created by a regular expression match
input	Another property used when an array is created by a regular expression match
length	Contains a numeric value equal to the number of elements in an array
prototype	Allows the addition of properties and methods to objects such as the JavaScript Array object

Table 11-1   **Properties of the Array Object**

s_list array from earlier to give us an array we can use. This would allow us to use the following code:

```
var s_list= new Array(4);
window.alert(s_list.constructor);
```

This would send an alert with the text function Array() { [native code] } (it would be the same text we saw the property return earlier in this section).

The index and input Properties

The index and input properties deal with regular expressions (a method of matching text strings), so we won't deal with them in detail here as regular expressions will require a lengthy explanation. We will touch on regular expressions in Module 16.

The length Property

The length property returns a number that tells us how many elements are in an array.

Note

The length property is useful later when we begin using loops to cycle through arrays. We may need to know the length of the array (in case we add elements after the array is defined) in order to make the loop go through each element of the array.

To use the length property, we use the name of the array and then add the length property afterward. The following code shows an example of the length property being used to tell the viewer how many elements are in an array:

```
var s_list= new Array(4)
s_list[0]="Thomas";
s_list[1]="Roger";
s_list[2]="Amber";
s_list[3]="Jennifer";
window.alert("The array has "+s_list.length);
```

This will send an alert that says "The array has 4 elements" to the viewer.

The prototype Property

The prototype property allows us to add properties and methods to an object that already exists, such as the Array object. By using this, we are able to add properties to the object from outside the constructor function. Keep in mind, however, that a change made with the prototype property affects each instance of an object that uses the same constructor function.

For example, if we decide the Array object needs another property for one of our pages, we could use the prototype property to assign a new property using the following syntax:

```
Array.prototype.new_property=default_value;
```

We would replace *new_property* with the name we wish to use for our new property and then replace *default_value* with a default value for that property.

So, if we want to add a new property named "attitude" to the Array constructor function on our page and give it a default value of "cool," we could use code such as the following:

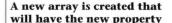

A new array is created that will have the new property

A new property is given to the Array object for this page

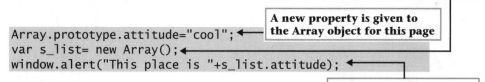

```
Array.prototype.attitude="cool";
var s_list= new Array();
window.alert("This place is "+s_list.attitude);
```

The value of the property is alerted to the screen

11

This will cause an alert to the viewer of the value of the new property. In this case, we are using the default value since we didn't change it (more on that soon).

Now, we need to remember that the addition of a property like this affects every array in the document afterward. So, by adding the property this way, every array on the page will now have this new property we can access.

The following code shows the use of the prototype property with two arrays on the page. The first array will alert the default value of our new property, while we change the value of the new property for the other array to alert the new value. The following example shows how we can utilize the prototype property using our new attitude property:

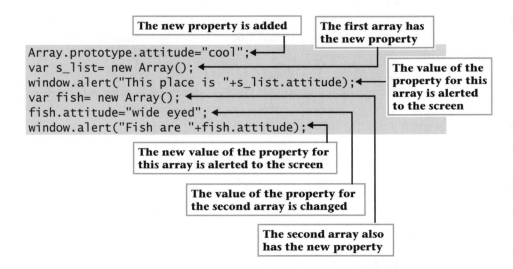

The first array and alert are the same as in the previous example. The second array is named "fish." The second array also has the new attitude property; but, rather than keep the default value, we changed it using the array name followed by the property and the new value.

We then alerted the value of the changed property to the viewer; thus, the viewer gets an alert saying "Fish are wide eyed" after clicking the OK button on the first alert.

Methods

Now that we know the properties of the Array object, we need to look at the methods we can use to do different things with our arrays. Table 11-2 lists the methods with a description of what each method does. Following the table, we will discuss each method in more detail.

Method	Description
concat()	Combines the elements of two or more arrays into one new array
join()	Combines the elements of an array into a single string with a separator character
pop()	Removes the last element from an array and then returns the removed element if needed
push()	Adds elements to the end of an array and then returns the numeric value of the new length of the array if needed
reverse()	Reverses the direction of the elements in an array: the first element is moved to the last slot and the last element is moved to the first slot, and so on
shift()	Removes the first element from an array and then returns that element if needed
unshift()	Adds elements to the beginning of an array and returns the numeric value of the length of the new array if needed
slice()	Pulls out a specified section of an array and returns the section as a new array
splice()	Removes elements from an array or replaces elements in an array
sort()	Sorts the elements of an array into an alphabetical order based on the string values of the elements

Table 11-2   Methods of the Array Object

The concat() Method

The concat() method is used to combine (or concatenate) the elements of two or more arrays and return a new array containing all of the elements. We use array names as parameters, and we set them in the order in which we want the array elements to be combined.

In our first example, let's combine two arrays. To do this, we will only need to use one parameter. The parameter will be the name of the array to add to the end of the array we use to call the method. The following example code combines the elements of two arrays:

```
var fruits= new Array("oranges","apples");
var veggies= new Array("corn","peas");
var fruits_n_veggies=fruits.concat(veggies);
```

11

The code creates an array named "fruit" with two elements, and an array named "veggies" with two elements. Next, we define a new array based on the combination of the previous two arrays. The name of the new array will be "fruits_n_veggies." We assign the value returned by the concat() method to this array name, creating the new combined array.

The reason we use the fruits array to call the concat() method and send the veggies array name as a parameter is so that we get the elements of the fruits array at the beginning of the new array, while the elements of the veggies array are added to the end of the new array. The previous code creates the new array fruits_n_veggies with the following elements:

```
oranges, apples, corn, peas
```

If we wanted to have the elements of the veggies array listed first, we would call the method using the veggies array name and send the fruits array name as the parameter. The following example shows how we can do this:

```
var fruits= new Array("oranges","apples");
var veggies= new Array("corn","peas");
var fruits_n_veggies=veggies.concat(fruits);
```

Now the elements of the veggies array are listed first, and the new fruits_n_veggies array has the following elements:

```
corn, peas, oranges, apples
```

When using this method, we want to be sure to set the order the way we want it by using the techniques just described.

If we combine three arrays, the elements of the array with which we call the concat() method will come first, and then the elements of each array name sent as a parameter will be added in the order in which they are sent:

```
var fruits= new Array("oranges","apples");
var veggies= new Array("corn","peas");
var meats= new Array("fish","chicken");
var three_groups=fruit.concat(veggies,meat);
```

Now we are combining three arrays, and the following are the elements of the new three_groups array:

```
oranges, apples, corn, peas, fish, chicken
```

If we code it in the following way instead, we will get an array with the same elements, but in a new order:

```
var fruits= new Array("oranges","apples");
var veggies= new Array("corn","peas");
var meats= new Array("fish","chicken");
var three_groups=meat.concat(veggies,fruit);
```

The following is the order of the elements in the new three_groups array when using this code:

```
fish, chicken, corn, peas, oranges, apples
```

The join() Method

The join() method is used to combine the elements of an array into a single string, with each element separated by a character sent as a parameter to the method. If no parameter is sent, a comma is used as the default separator character when the method is called.

To see how this method works, let's look at a little bit of code. We need to define an array and then we will call the join() method using the array name. The following is the example code:

```
var fruits= new Array("oranges","apples","pears");
var fruit_string=fruits.join();
```

This code assigns the result of the join() method when called with the fruits array to the variable fruit_string. Since we did not send a parameter, the elements of the array will be separated by commas in the new string. The fruit_string variable will have the following string value:

```
oranges, apples, pears
```

11

We can see this result by writing the string variable into a Web page. The following code will do this for us:

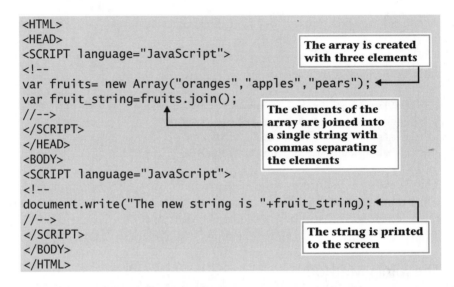

```
<HTML>
<HEAD>
<SCRIPT language="JavaScript">
<!--
var fruits= new Array("oranges","apples","pears");
var fruit_string=fruits.join();
//-->
</SCRIPT>
</HEAD>
<BODY>
<SCRIPT language="JavaScript">
<!--
document.write("The new string is "+fruit_string);
//-->
</SCRIPT>
</BODY>
</HTML>
```

> The array is created with three elements

> The elements of the array are joined into a single string with commas separating the elements

> The string is printed to the screen

Now we can see the string that is returned from the join() method. Figure 11-1 shows what this code produces when run in a browser.

If we want to separate the elements in the new string with something other than a comma, we can send the character we want to use as a

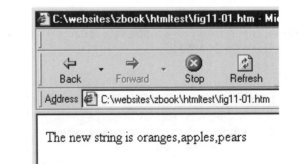

Figure 11-1 The new string is written on the page

parameter. The following code sends a colon as a string parameter to the join() method:

```
<HTML>
<HEAD>
<SCRIPT language="JavaScript">
<!--
var fruits= new Array("oranges","apples","pears");
var fruit_string=fruits.join(":");
//-->
</SCRIPT>
</HEAD>
<BODY>
<SCRIPT language="JavaScript">
<!--
document.write("The new string is "+fruit_string);
//-->
</SCRIPT>
</BODY>
</HTML>
```

> The array is created with three elements

> The elements of the array are joined into a single string with colons separating the elements

> The string is printed to the screen

This time the string will be a little different than the previous one, as there will be colons in place of the commas we had in the previous example. Figure 11-2 shows how this string would print in the browser window.

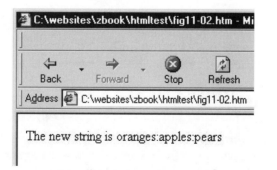

Figure 11-2   The new string is written on the page with colons as separators

11

The pop() Method

The pop() method is used to remove the last element from an array. If we assign the result of the method to a variable, the popped element will be returned and assigned to the variable.

To use the pop() method, let's take a look at some code that creates an array and then removes the last element from the array using the pop() method:

```
var fruits= new Array("oranges","apples","pears");
fruits.pop();
```

This creates an array named "fruits" with three elements (oranges, apples, pears). Then the last element is removed using the pop() method, shortening the array to have only the first two elements (oranges, apples).

If we want to remove an element but still use it in some way later, we can assign the result of the method to a variable. The variable will be assigned the value of the element that was removed. The following example removes the last element of an array and then sends the removed element as an alert to the viewer:

```
var fruits= new Array("oranges","apples","pears");
var picked_fruit=fruits.pop();
window.alert("You picked my "+picked_fruit);
```

This will pop up an alert that says "You picked my pears" to the viewer.

The push() Method

The push() method is used to add elements to the end of an array. The parameters sent to the method are the new element or elements we wish to add to the array.

Caution

The value returned by the push() method depends on the version of JavaScript being used by the browser. In JavaScript 1.2, the value returned is the last element that has been added to the array. In later versions, it returns the numeric value of the new length of the array.

As an example, let's look at some code that adds one element to the end of an array:

```
var fruits= new Array("oranges","apples");
fruits.push("pears");
```

This code creates an array named "fruits" with two elements (oranges, apples) and then uses the push() method to add a third element, pears. The array now contains three elements (oranges, apples, pears) with pears being the last element in the array.

We can add more than one by sending more than one parameter. The elements will be added in the order in which they are sent in the parameter list. The following code adds two elements to the fruits array:

```
var fruits= new Array("oranges","apples");
fruits.push("pears","grapes");
```

This code takes an array with two elements (oranges, apples) and adds two more elements to it. In the end, the array contains four elements (oranges, apples, pears, grapes).

If we want the value that is returned by the method, we can assign the result to a variable. The following code does this and then alerts the viewer to the returned value :

```
var fruits= new Array("oranges","apples");
var who_knows=fruits.push("pears","grapes");
window.alert("The method returned "+who_knows);
```

The value of the who_knows variable will be different depending on your browser. If the browser has JavaScript 1.2, the value should be the string grapes (the last element added to the array). If the browser has JavaScript 1.3 or better, the value of the variable should be the numeric value of 4 (the new length of the array).

The reverse() Method

The reverse() method is used to reverse the order of the elements in an array. Since that is all it does, there is no need to send any parameters or return a value.

11

To use this method, let's create an example. The following code will create an array and then reverse the order of the elements in the array:

```
var fruits= new Array("oranges","apples","pears");
fruits.reverse();
```

The initial order of the array is oranges, apples, pears. When the reverse() method is called for this array, the order of the elements is reversed, and the array now is in the order pears, apples, oranges.

The shift() Method

The shift () method is used to remove the first element of an array. It returns the value of the element that was removed in case we need to use it later in the script.

So, if we want to remove the first element in an array, we could use something similar to the following code:

```
var fruits= new Array("oranges","apples","pears");
fruits.shift();
```

This code creates an array with three elements (oranges, apples, pears), and removes the first element with the shift() method. This causes the array to have only two elements remaining (apples, pears).

To use the value of the element that was removed, we can assign the result of the method to a variable. The following code assigns the removed element to a variable and then alerts the viewer about what was removed:

```
var fruits= new Array("oranges","apples","pears");
var picked_fruit=fruits.shift();
window.alert("You picked my "+picked_fruit);
```

This code displays the alert "You picked my oranges" in the browser window.

The unshift() Method

The unshift() method is used to add elements to the beginning of an array. The elements we wish to add to the array are sent as parameters to the method. The value returned by the method is the numeric value of the new length of the array.

For our example, we will add one new element to the beginning of an array:

```
var fruits= new Array("apples","pears");
fruits.unshift("oranges");
```

This creates an array named "fruits" with two elements (apples, pears), and then adds an element to the beginning of the array using the unshift() method. The array then contains three elements (oranges, apples, pears).

If we want to add more than one element at a time, we send them all as parameters in the order in which we wish to add them. The following example adds two elements to the beginning of the array:

```
var fruits= new Array("apples","pears");
fruits.unshift("oranges","grapes");
```

This takes the initial array of two elements (apples, pears), and adds two elements to the beginning of the array. The array ends up containing four elements (oranges, grapes, apples, pears) after the unshift() method is called.

The slice() Method

The slice() method is used to remove a specified section of an array and then to create a new array using the elements from the sliced section of the old array.

The following is the general syntax for using this method:

```
arrayname.slice(start,stop)
```

We would replace *arrayname* with the name of the array from which we want to remove a certain set of elements for a new array. We would replace *start* with the index number from which to start the slice. We would replace *stop* with the index number that comes after the last element we wish to slice.

For an example, the following code will slice two elements from an array and create a new array with those elements:

```
var fruits= new Array("oranges","apples","pears","grapes");
var somefruits=fruits.slice(1,3);
```

11

This removes the second element (index number 1) through the third element (index number 2) of the array. It does not pull out the fourth element (index number 3) because 3 is the index number after 2, which was the index number of the last element we wish to remove. The new array named "somefruits" contains the elements we removed (apples, pears).

The splice() Method

The splice() method allows us to remove or replace elements within an array. The parameters that can be sent include the index number at which to begin the splice, the number of elements to remove, and the option to add new elements to the array as well.

If we want to remove a single element from an array, we could use code such as the following:

```
var fruits= new Array("oranges","apples","pears","grapes");
var somefruits=fruits.splice(2,1);
```

This will begin removing elements at index number 2. The next parameter is 1, so only one element will be removed; thus, we only remove the element at index number 2 here, which is pears. The array after the splice contains only three elements (oranges, apples, grapes).

To remove more than one element, we increase the value of the second parameter. The following code removes two elements, starting at index number 2:

```
var fruits= new Array("oranges","apples","pears","grapes");
var somefruits=fruits.splice(2,2);
```

This time the array is cut down to two elements (oranges, apples), as the last two elements are removed by the splice() method.

We can also use the method to replace spliced elements in an array or to add elements to an array. The following code replaces the spliced element at index number 2 with a new element by sending an additional parameter:

```
var fruits= new Array("oranges","apples","pears","grapes");
var somefruits=fruits.splice(2,1,"watermelons");
```

This time, the element at index number 2 is removed. Since the second parameter is 1, only one element is removed. The next parameter tells the browser to add this value at the index number specified in the first parameter (index number 2).

This value replaces the value that was removed (pears). The array will still have four elements, just different elements (oranges, apples, watermelons, grapes).

If we want to use the method to add one or more elements to an array but not remove anything, we can set the second parameter to 0 (thus removing zero elements). We set the first parameter to the index number at which we wish to begin adding elements. For example, take a look at the following code:

```
var fruits= new Array("oranges","apples","pears","grapes");
var somefruits=fruits.splice(2,0,"watermelons","plums");
```

This time we begin at index number 2 as specified in the first parameter. We then see that nothing is removed, but two elements are added beginning at index number 2. When this is done, the array will have six elements (oranges, apples, watermelons, plums, pears, grapes).

The sort() Method

The sort() method sorts an array in alphabetical order (like a directory listing). This is not in numerical order, however. As an example, let's go to our fruit array once again. If we want to change the order of the elements so that they are in alphabetical order, we could use the following code:

```
var fruits= new Array("oranges","apples","pears","grapes");
fruits.sort();
```

11

This will reorder the array so that the elements will be in alphabetical order, changed from oranges, apples, pears, grapes to apples, grapes, oranges, pears.

We may find this useful when we want to display the contents of an array on a page. We will see how to use loops to make the display of array contents easy for us right after "Ask the Expert."

Ask the Expert

Question: Among all the properties, are there any that are specifically useful?

Answer: The length property will come in handy in a number of cases. The other properties are not likely to be used much here, but you may find some of them useful in your own scripts as you progress.

Question: Is there an easy way to remember all of these methods?

Answer: As with other lists, how well you remember them depends on how often you use the methods. One helpful thing is to look for the pairs that complement each other, like pop() and push(), or shift() and unshift().

Question: So the reverse method just turns everything around backward? Why would I want to do that?

Answer: You probably won't want to do it that often, but it can be helpful after using the sort() method for placing a list of strings in reverse alphabetical order. It can be helpful in a few other ways as well; it just depends on the data in the array.

Question: So the sort method sorts the data in alphabetical order, but why does 70 come before 9 when this is sorted?

Answer: When the sort method is used, it sorts using alphabetical order by default, meaning it converts all values to string values and then compares them. In that case, anything that begins with 7 comes before anything that begins with 9, even if the numeric value of the former is higher.

Arrays and Loops

Loops allow us to move through array elements without the need to deal with each element one at a time with new lines of code. Instead, we can use a loop to cycle through each element of an array and cut down the number of lines we would need to write for a large array.

To begin, let's take a look at how we can create the elements of an array using a loop instead of a straight assignment of values.

Creating Array Elements

A loop can be useful in the creation of the elements of an array. This is especially useful if we need the viewer to enter the contents of the array for some reason, or if we wish to perform a similar calculation in creating each element.

Suppose we want the viewer to be able to input the names of the four students from our old s_list array of student names. Using a for loop, we could use the following code to allow the viewer to enter each name:

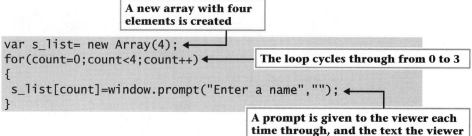

A new array with four elements is created

```
var s_list= new Array(4);
for(count=0;count<4;count++)
{
  s_list[count]=window.prompt("Enter a name","");
}
```

The loop cycles through from 0 to 3

A prompt is given to the viewer each time through, and the text the viewer types in is assigned to the element

This code creates a new array with four elements. We then use a for loop to assign each value. The loop begins by setting the loop's count variable to 0 and will run until the expression count<4 is no longer true.

Since we add one to the value of count each time through (count++), this means that the count variable will have the value of 0 the first time through, 1 the second time, 2 the third time, and 3 the fourth time. It doesn't go through another time because count would be equal to 4, which is no longer less than 4.

11

Hint

Starting the count variable at 0 gives us an advantage in that we will less likely confuse ourselves when we use the loop. The count variable will represent the index number of each array element, so we won't need to subtract 1 from its value as we would if we had started count at 1 instead.

Inside the loop, we assign a value to the element at the index number represented by the count variable each time through. The value assigned is the result of what the viewer types in when prompted for a name. The viewer will get four prompts in this case and will assign all four of the element's values.

Another use for assigning element values with a loop would be to perform a similar calculation that would affect each element. For instance, if we wanted an array of ten even numbers, we could use the following code:

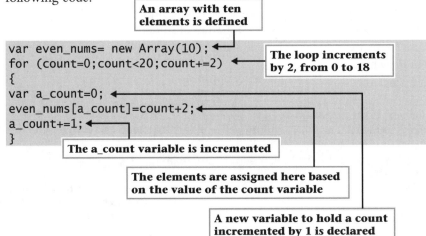

```
var even_nums= new Array(10);
for (count=0;count<20;count+=2)
{
var a_count=0;
even_nums[a_count]=count+2;
a_count+=1;
}
```

An array with ten elements is defined

The loop increments by 2, from 0 to 18

The a_count variable is incremented

The elements are assigned here based on the value of the count variable

A new variable to hold a count incremented by 1 is declared

By increasing count by two each time through, we ensure that an even number is used for our calculation. We then assign the value of the count value plus 2 to each array element while going through the loop. The use of the a_count variable allows us to keep the array from missing elements based on our count variable being incremented by 2. The a_count variable is incremented by 1 to keep the array index numbers increasing by only one (instead of assigning even_nums[0] and then even_nums[2], and skipping over even_nums[1]—which is what would have happened if we had used the count variable for the index number slot, rather than a_count, which increases by only one each time).

The first time through, count is 0, so even_nums[0] is assigned a value of 0+2, or 2. The next time through count is equal to 2, so even_nums[1] is given a value of 2+2, or 4. This happens until we have ten array elements (index numbers 0–9) that are all even numbers.

Moving Through Arrays

We can also cycle through an array that has been created in order to change it, gain information from it, or list its contents in a way we like. This is quite useful and can save us some time with larger arrays.

If we go back to our old s_list array listing the names of students in a class, we can see that a loop would save us a little typing when we decide to print the list of students on the screen. We can also set the loop so that it will adjust itself if we decide to add to the array later. First, let's see how to print the list of names to the browser screen using a loop:

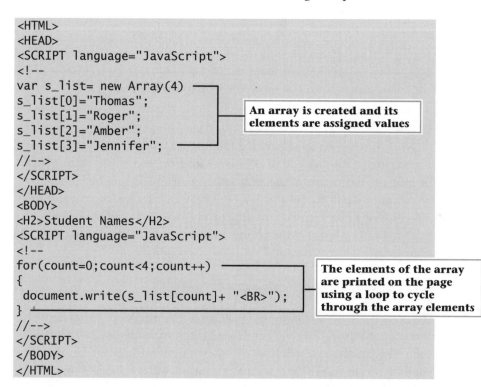

```
<HTML>
<HEAD>
<SCRIPT language="JavaScript">
<!--
var s_list= new Array(4)
s_list[0]="Thomas";
s_list[1]="Roger";
s_list[2]="Amber";
s_list[3]="Jennifer";
//-->
</SCRIPT>
</HEAD>
<BODY>
<H2>Student Names</H2>
<SCRIPT language="JavaScript">
<!--
for(count=0;count<4;count++)
{
  document.write(s_list[count]+ "<BR>");
}
//-->
</SCRIPT>
</BODY>
</HTML>
```

An array is created and its elements are assigned values

The elements of the array are printed on the page using a loop to cycle through the array elements

We are basically using the same method in the loop as we did while creating an array. This time, however, we use the loop to print the contents of the array to the screen. Figure 11-3 shows how this script looks when run in a browser.

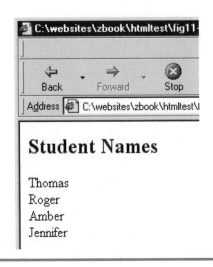

⇐ Back   ⇒ Forward   ⊗ Stop

Address C:\websites\zbook\htmltest\l

Student Names

Thomas
Roger
Amber
Jennifer

Figure 11-3	**The names from the array are written on the page**

Now, if we want to be sure the loop adjusts itself to show every element just in case we add or take away students, we will need to have the loop use the length of the array rather than a plain number to find out when to stop itself. Recall that JavaScript can use the length property to find out how many elements are in an array. So, instead of using the number 4 in our loop for the comparison, let's use the length property of the array:

```
for(count=0;count<s_list.length;count++)
```

The array can have any number of elements, and the loop will cycle through until the full array is used (until count<s_list.length is no longer true). The last element will have an index number that is one less than the length of the array, which is what we want since arrays begin count at 0 instead of 1.

To put this all together, let's make a few changes to our array and then print the array elements in the browser window. The following code shows the adjustments and our new loop code:

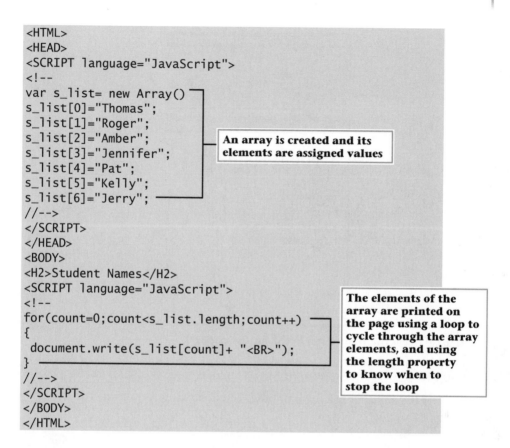

```
<HTML>
<HEAD>
<SCRIPT language="JavaScript">
<!--
var s_list= new Array()
s_list[0]="Thomas";
s_list[1]="Roger";
s_list[2]="Amber";
s_list[3]="Jennifer";
s_list[4]="Pat";
s_list[5]="Kelly";
s_list[6]="Jerry";
//-->
</SCRIPT>
</HEAD>
<BODY>
<H2>Student Names</H2>
<SCRIPT language="JavaScript">
<!--
for(count=0;count<s_list.length;count++)
{
  document.write(s_list[count]+ "<BR>");
}
//-->
</SCRIPT>
</BODY>
</HTML>
```

An array is created and its elements are assigned values

The elements of the array are printed on the page using a loop to cycle through the array elements, and using the length property to know when to stop the loop

We have now adjusted the array so that it initially has no direct number of elements, but we define them as we go by assigning values to each element. This array has added three names to the list, giving us an array with seven elements (index numbers 0–6). The list is then written to the page. Figure 11-4 shows the result of this script when run in a browser. Notice that the list now has all the new names.

We could take this one step further and use the sort() method to put the names of the students in alphabetical order. To do this, we only need to add a single line calling the sort() method for the s_list array before we print the elements to the screen. The order of the elements is adjusted,

11

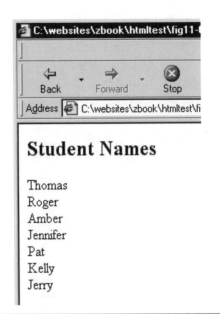

Figure 11-4 **All the names are listed on the page**

and the alphabetized list is printed. The following is the code for
alphabetizing:

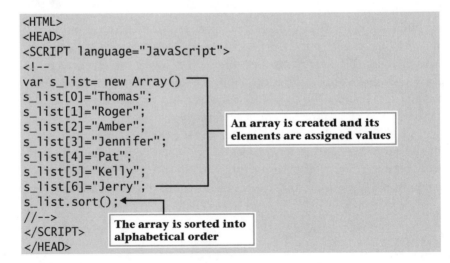

```
<HTML>
<HEAD>
<SCRIPT language="JavaScript">
<!--
var s_list= new Array()
s_list[0]="Thomas";
s_list[1]="Roger";
s_list[2]="Amber";
s_list[3]="Jennifer";
s_list[4]="Pat";
s_list[5]="Kelly";
s_list[6]="Jerry";
s_list.sort();
//-->
</SCRIPT>
</HEAD>
```

An array is created and its elements are assigned values

The array is sorted into alphabetical order

```
<BODY>
<H2>Student Names</H2>
<SCRIPT language="JavaScript">
<!--
for(count=0;count<s_list.length;count++)
{
 document.write(s_list[count]+ "<BR>");
}
//-->
</SCRIPT>
</BODY>
</HTML>
```

> **The sorted elements of the array are printed on the page using a loop to cycle through the array elements, and using the length property to know when to stop the loop**

Notice the addition of the s_list.sort() call. This sorts the array for us to give us our alphabetized output. Figure 11-5 shows the result of this script when it is run in a browser.

We can begin to use loops that become much more involved with the arrays, and use more of the properties and methods as well. For now, this

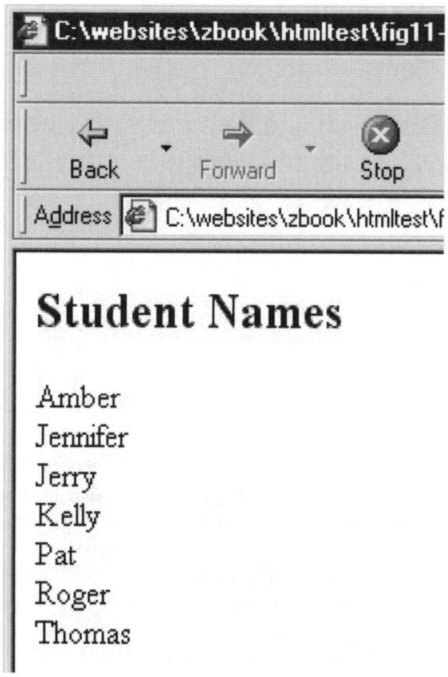

Figure 11-5   The names are listed in alphabetical order

11

will get us started and build a foundation from which we can build the more complex loops for our JavaScript arrays.

1-Minute Drill

● **What are two possible uses for assigning the elements of an array with a loop?**

● **Why would the use of a loop to print the elements of an array help us?**

● **How does the length property help us with our loops?**

pr11_1.html, pr11_1_2.html

Project 11-1: Using Loops with Arrays

This project will allow you to practice using loops with arrays and to practice using some of the properties of arrays. It will create a list of computer parts that we want to print to the screen.

Step-by-Step

1. Create an HTML page with space in the HEAD and BODY sections for our JavaScript code.

2. In the HEAD section, create a new array and assign the following list of parts as values for the elements in the array:

monitor

motherboard

chip

hard drive

● The two possible uses for assigning the elements of an array with a loop are when we need the viewer to enter the contents of the array or if we wish to perform a similar calculation when creating each element

● The use of a loop to print the elements of an array will help us if the array is long, because it saves us the trouble of typing out each element by cycling through the array and writing each element

● The length property helps us with our loops if we use it in the comparison for the loop cycle, because we are able to change the number of elements in the array and still have the loop cycle through each element without needing to change the loop code

3. In the BODY section, create a heading 2 that says "Computer Parts Needed" to give the list a title.

4. After that heading, print out each computer part on its own line in the browser window (use a loop).

5. Save the file as pr11_1.html, and look at the results in your browser.

6. Reopen the file in your text editor, and make the changes described in the next steps.

7. If you didn't before, use the length property in the comparison instead of a number.

8. Add some elements to the array by coding them into the HEAD section. Add the following items after the first four we already had:

> disk drive
>
> power supply

9. Have the array sort itself so that it is in alphabetical order.

10. Save this version of the file as pr11_1_2.html, and view it in your browser. The new elements should show up in an alphabetical listing of the array elements.

Associative Arrays

Associative arrays allow us to use strings in place of index numbers. The use of an associative array is quite similar to using a property name with a regular object, we just do it in an array format. Since numbers are not used, their use is more limited, but they can still be useful to store information and make the elements easier to remember when we want to access them. To begin, let's look at how to define an associative array.

Defining Associative Arrays

We can do this in much the same way as a normal array, but we will want to use the methods that allow us to assign each element individually. Here, we will create a blank array and give it values by assigning values to elements.

11

To assign a value to an element, we need to give the element a string in place of its index number. The value we use for the string would be something we could associate with the value we are going to assign to the element. For instance, if we wanted to change our old s_list array into an associative array based on a trait of each student, we could use the following code:

```
var s_list= new Array()
s_list["tall"]="Thomas";
s_list["cool"]="Roger";
s_list["clever"]="Amber";
s_list["attentive"]="Jennifer";
```

The assignments here give an index string of a trait, and then a student's name is assigned to the element that has his or her trait.

This will make it easier to remember when we want to access an element of the array later, since we can remember a trait instead of a number when we need an element. This makes array declarations semantically richer, which can also be useful if we wish to query or otherwise reference a certain element.

Accessing Associative Arrays

Accessing an associative array is done in the same way we access a normal array, except we use an index string rather than an index number.

If we wanted to access the element that had the name of the tall student, for instance, we could access it using the following syntax:

```
s_list["tall"]
```

Thus, we could print out a listing of the students by their traits by using the following example code:

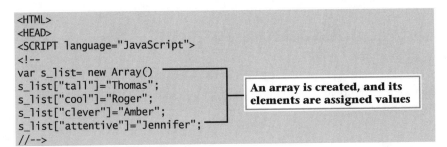

```
<HTML>
<HEAD>
<SCRIPT language="JavaScript">
<!--
var s_list= new Array()
s_list["tall"]="Thomas";
s_list["cool"]="Roger";
s_list["clever"]="Amber";
s_list["attentive"]="Jennifer";
//-->
```

An array is created, and its elements are assigned values

```
</SCRIPT>
</HEAD>
<BODY>
<H2>Student Names</H2>
<SCRIPT language="JavaScript">
<!--
document.write("The tall one is " +s_list["tall"]+ "<BR>");
document.write("The cool one is " +s_list["cool"]+ "<BR>");
document.write("The clever one is " +s_list["clever"]+ "<BR>");
document.write("The attentive one is " +s_list["attentive"]+ "<BR>");
//-->
</SCRIPT>
</BODY>
</HTML>
```

> **The elements of the array are printed on the page**

This will print out the list based on the traits. Figure 11-6 shows the results of this script when run in a browser.

We will be using arrays in the next module in order to help us create scripts that use random numbers.

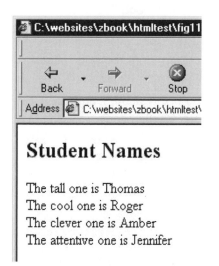

Figure 11-6   The names are listed based on the traits of each student

11

Project 11-2: Using Associative Arrays

This project will allow you to practice using associative arrays. It will have you create an array of elements based on the qualities of various cars.

Step-by-Step

1. Create an HTML page, leaving room in the HEAD and BODY sections for our code.

2. In the HEAD section, create an associative array with the following index strings:

   cool

   small

   long

3. Assign a value of "Mustang" to the element with the index string of "cool." Assign a value of "Bug" to the element with the index string of "small." Assign a value of "Station Wagon" to the element with the index string of "long."

4. In the BODY section, create a heading 2 that says "List of Cars."

5. After the heading, print the value of each element to the browser window.

6. Save the file as pr11_2.html, and open it in your browser. You should see the list of cars!

✓ Mastery Check

1. Which of the following does not correctly create an array?

   A. var myarray= new Array();

   B. var myarray= new Array(5);

   C. var myarray= new Array("hello","hi","greetings");

   D. var if= new Array[10];

2. Which of the following will correctly access the fifth element of an array named "cool"?

   A. cool[5];

   B. cool(5);

   C. cool[4];

   D. cool.array[4];

3. What property of the Array object will return the numeric value of the length of an array?

   A. The length property

   B. The getlength property

   C. The constructor property

   D. The lengthOf property

4. By default, how does the sort() method sort the contents of an array?

   A. It reverses the contents of the array.

   B. It sorts the contents numerically.

   C. It sorts the contents alphabetically.

   D. It removes the last element from an array.

11

☑ Mastery Check

5. What is used in place of an index number in an associative array?

A. A floating point value

B. A Boolean value

C. A negative number

D. A string value

Module 12

Math and Date Objects

The Goals of This Module

- Introduce the Math object
- Find out how the Math object can be useful
- Learn the properties and methods of the Math object
- Introduce the Date object
- Find out how the Date object can be useful
- Learn the properties and methods of the Date object

In the previous module, we looked at JavaScript arrays and the Array object. In this module, we will learn about the JavaScript Math and Date objects.

We will begin with a short introduction to the Math object and see why it can be useful to us. We will then take a look at the various properties and methods we can use from the Math object. Next, we will introduce the Date object and see how it can be useful to us. We will then look into the properties and methods of the Date object to see what we can do with it.

The Math Object

The Math object can be useful to us when we need to perform various calculations in our scripts. To begin, let's take a look at what the Math object is.

What Is the Math Object?

The Math object is a predefined JavaScript object. It gives us properties and methods to use just like the other predefined objects we have studied in this book. The Math object is used for mathematical purposes to give us the values of certain mathematical constants or to perform certain operations when we use a method function.

How the Math Object Is Useful

As we have mentioned, the Math object is useful when we need to make mathematical calculations in our scripts. For instance, if we need the value of pi for a calculation, the Math object gives us a property to use so we can get that value.

Also, if we need to find the square root of a number, a method of the Math object enables us to do this. Another thing this object provides us with is a way to generate random numbers in JavaScript, which we will find useful in certain scripts.

1-Minute Drill

- **What is the Math object?**
- **Is the value of pi given to us as a property or as a method of the Math object?**
- **When is the Math object useful?**

Properties

The Math object gives us a number of properties that can help us if we need to perform certain mathematical calculations. Table 21-1 lists the properties of the Math object, with the values of each. Following the table, we will discuss each property in more detail.

Property	Value
E	Value of Euler's constant (E), which is about 2.71828. . .
LN10	Value of the natural logarithm of 10, which is about 2.302585 . . .
LN2	Value of the natural logarithm of 2, which is about 0.693147 . . .
LOG10E	Value of the base 10 logarithm of E, which is about 0.43429 . . .
LOG2E	Value of the base 2 logarithm of E, which is about 1.442695 . . .
PI	Value of pi, often used with circles, which is about 3.14159 . . .
SQRT2	Value of the square root of 2, which is about 1.4142 . . .
SQRT1_2	Value of the square root of one half, which is about 0.7071 . . .

Table 12-1	Properties of the Math Object

12

- The Math object is another predefined JavaScript object. It gives us properties and methods to use for mathematical calculations.
- It is given as a property.
- The Math object is useful when we need to make mathematical calculations in our scripts.

As you can see in Table 12-1, all of the properties simply hold numeric values that can be useful in mathematical calculations.

The E Property

The E property holds the value of Euler's constant, which is about 2.71828 . . . (this is just an approximation, the actual value is nonterminating since it is an irrational number).

To see the value of the E property, we can use it in an alert. The following code alerts the value of the E property to the viewer:

```
window.alert(Math.E);
```

This would display the alert box found in Figure 12-1.

The LN10 Property

The LN10 property holds the value of the natural logarithm of 10, which is about 2.302585 . . . (again, this is only an approximation).

To see the value of this property, we can use it in an alert. The following code pops up an alert with this property's value:

```
window.alert(Math.LN10);
```

This would display an alert box similar to the one found in Figure 12-2.

Figure 12-1 An alert box showing the value of the E property

An alert box showing the value of the LN10 property

The LN2 Property

The LN2 property holds the value of the natural logarithm of 2, which is about 0.693147 . . .

To see the value of this property, we could again use an alert. The following code shows an alert with this property's value:

```
window.alert(Math.LN2);
```

This would display an alert box similar to the one found in Figure 12-3.

The LOG10E Property

The LOG10E property holds the value of the base 10 logarithm of E, which is about 0.43429 . . .

Figure 12-3 **An alert box showing the value of the LN2 property**

12

As we have been doing, we can see the value of this property by using an alert. The following code shows an alert with this property's values:

```
window.alert(Math.LOG10E);
```

This would display an alert box similar to the one found in Figure 12-4.

The LOG2E Property

The LOG2E property holds the value of the base 2 logarithm of E, which is about 1.442695 . . .

Again, we can use an alert to see the value of the property. The following code shows an alert with this property's values:

```
window.alert(Math.LOG2E);
```

This would display an alert box similar to the one found in Figure 12-5.

The PI Property

The PI property holds the numerical value of pi, which is about 3.14159 . . .

We can see the value of the PI property by using an alert. The following shows an alert with this property's values:

```
window.alert(Math.PI);
```

This would display an alert box similar to the one found in Figure 12-6.

Figure 12-4 An alert box showing the value of the LOG10E property

Figure 12-5 An alert box showing the value of the LOG2E property

The SQRT2 Property

The SQRT2 property holds the value of the square root of 2, which is about 1.4142 . . .

To see the value of this property, we could use an alert to show it on the screen. The following code shows an alert with this property's values:

```
window.alert(Math.SQRT2);
```

This would display an alert box similar to the one found in Figure 12-7.

The SQRT1_2 Property

The SQRT1_2 property holds the value of the square root of one half, which is about 0.7071 . . .

12

Figure 12-6 An alert box showing the value of the PI property

Figure 12-7 An alert box showing the value of the SQRT2 property

To see the value of this property, we can use an alert. The following code shows an alert with this property's values:

```
window.alert(Math.SQRT1_2);
```

This would display an alert box similar to the one found in Figure 12–8.

1-Minute Drill

● **Which property gives us the value of pi?**

● **Which property gives us the value of Euler's constant?**

● **What is the code that displays an alert with the value of the square root of one half?**

Figure 12-8 An alert box showing the value of the SQRT1_2 property

---

● The property that gives us the value of pi is the pi property
● The property that gives us the value of Euler's constant is the E property
● window.alert(Math.SQRT1_2);

Methods

The methods of the Math object enable us to perform certain calculations that can be helpful to us in our scripts. Table 12-2 lists various methods of the Math object and their purposes. Following the table, we will discuss each method in more detail.

Method	Purpose
abs()	Returns the absolute value of the number sent as a parameter
acos()	Returns the arccosine of the number sent as a parameter, in radians
asin()	Returns the arcsine of the number sent as a parameter, in radians
atan()	Returns the arctangent of the number sent as a parameter, in radians
ceil()	Returns the smallest integer greater than or equal to the number sent as a parameter
cos()	Returns the cosine of the number sent as a parameter, in radians
exp()	Returns the value of E to the power of the number sent to the method as a parameter
floor()	Returns the largest integer less than or equal to the number sent as a parameter
log()	Returns the natural logarithm of the number sent as a parameter
max()	Returns the larger of the two numbers that are sent as parameters
min()	Returns the smaller of the two numbers that are sent as parameters
pow()	Returns the numeric value of the first parameter raised to the power of the second parameter
random()	Returns a random number between 0 and 1; does not require a parameter
round()	Returns the value of the number sent as a parameter rounded to the nearest integer
sin()	Returns the sine of the number sent as a parameter, in radians
sqrt()	Returns the square root of the number sent as a parameter
tan()	Returns the tangent of the number sent as a parameter, in radians

Table 12-2   The Methods of the Math Object

12

The Basic Methods

For the purpose of this book, we will define the basic methods as the methods that take in a single number, do a simple calculation with it, and return a value. This grouping of the methods is just a way for us to make this go more quickly by not having to list each method with the same sort of example—it is not any sort of official organization of the methods.

The following basic methods are the ones that work in generally the same way (take in and return a numeric value):

- abs()
- acos()
- asin()
- atan()
- cos()
- exp()
- log()
- sin()
- sqrt()
- tan()

These basic methods take in a numeric value and send back another value. Since the general usage is the same, we will just take one of these and use it as an example of how the rest could be used to get their various values. If you need to know what type of value is returned from a different method, refer back to Table 12-2 to see what each method does.

We will use the sqrt() method for our examples. The easiest way to use the method is to input a positive number as the parameter to the method, as shown in the following example:

```
window.alert(Math.sqrt(4));
```

This alerts the value of the positive square root of 4, which is 2.

Instead of calculating a static number, we could get the user to input a number and then send an alert to the user with the square root of the number input by the user. We could do this using the following code:

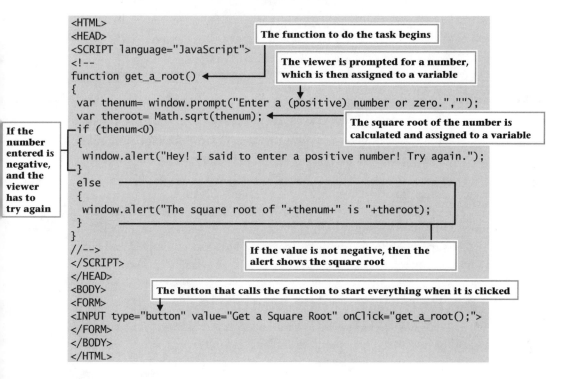

```
<HTML>
<HEAD>
<SCRIPT language="JavaScript">
<!--
function get_a_root()
{
 var thenum= window.prompt("Enter a (positive) number or zero.","");
 var theroot= Math.sqrt(thenum);
 if (thenum<0)
 {
  window.alert("Hey! I said to enter a positive number! Try again.");
 }
 else
 {
  window.alert("The square root of "+thenum+" is "+theroot);
 }
}
//-->
</SCRIPT>
</HEAD>
<BODY>
<FORM>
<INPUT type="button" value="Get a Square Root" onClick="get_a_root();">
</FORM>
</BODY>
</HTML>
```

Annotations in figure:
- The function to do the task begins
- The viewer is prompted for a number, which is then assigned to a variable
- The square root of the number is calculated and assigned to a variable
- If the number entered is negative, and the viewer has to try again
- If the value is not negative, then the alert shows the square root
- The button that calls the function to start everything when it is clicked

The preceding code begins with the get_a_root() function in the HEAD section of the document, which is called when the viewer clicks the button in the BODY section. The function begins by prompting the viewer for a positive number and assigning it to the thenum variable.

Next, the Math.sqrt() method is called using the number entered by the viewer (thenum) as a parameter. This returns the number's square root, which is then assigned to the variable named "theroot." Once this is done, we check to see if the viewer entered a negative number.

If so, an alert appears, telling the viewer to try again; otherwise, an alert appears telling the user the square root information. The result of this script when the viewer enters the number 16 is shown in Figure 12-9.

The only quirk here is if the viewer enters characters such as a, qwerty, #$^, or other things, the alert will tell the viewer the square root of what

12

Figure 12-9   The square root of 16 is alerted to the viewer

was entered is NaN, which JavaScript returns to stand for Not a Number. Of course, regular expressions (see Module 16) can fix this, but those are something we will not get into just yet. The result of this script when the viewer enters **a round tree** is shown in Figure 12-10.

The other methods in this section work in much the same way, they just return different results such as absolute values, tangents, or logarithms.

Let's move on to the methods that are a little more involved and take in two parameters.

The Two-Parameter Methods

We will use this section to discuss the methods that take in two parameters instead of just one. These methods include the following:

- max()
- min()
- pow()

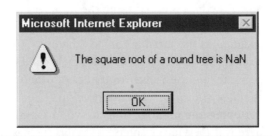

Figure 12-10   The square root of "a round tree" is not a number

The max() and min() methods are very similar, while the pow() method does something a bit different. Let's take a look at these methods in a little more detail.

The max() and min() Methods

The max() method takes two numbers and returns the larger number. The min() method also takes two parameters, but returns the smaller number. We could use these in a script that enables the viewer to enter two numbers and then alerts the user which number is larger.

The following example code uses both of these methods and gives the viewer the results in an alert:

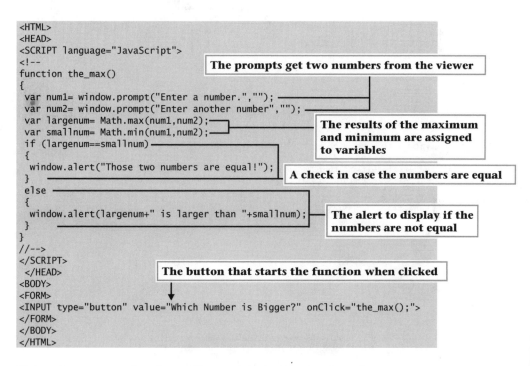

```
<HTML>
<HEAD>
<SCRIPT language="JavaScript">
<!--
function the_max()
{
  var num1= window.prompt("Enter a number.","");
  var num2= window.prompt("Enter another number","");
  var largenum= Math.max(num1,num2);
  var smallnum= Math.min(num1,num2);
  if (largenum==smallnum)
  {
    window.alert("Those two numbers are equal!");
  }
  else
  {
    window.alert(largenum+" is larger than "+smallnum);
  }
}
//-->
</SCRIPT>
</HEAD>
<BODY>
<FORM>
<INPUT type="button" value="Which Number is Bigger?" onClick="the_max();">
</FORM>
</BODY>
</HTML>
```

Annotations:
- The prompts get two numbers from the viewer
- The results of the maximum and minimum are assigned to variables
- A check in case the numbers are equal
- The alert to display if the numbers are not equal
- The button that starts the function when clicked

This script prompts the viewer for two numbers and assigns them to variables. It then takes the maximum and minimum from both numbers and assigns the values returned to variables. Those variables are then used to check whether they are equal. If so, an alert comes up saying they are; otherwise, an alert pops up with the results.

12

Figure 12-11 shows the results of this script in a browser if we enter **2** as the first number and **54** as the second number.

The pow() Method

The pow() method takes two parameters and calculates the value of the first parameter to the power of the second parameter. For instance, the following code would return the value of 2 to the 3rd power:

```
Math.pow(2,3);
```

Other than its difference in calculations, we can use it in the same general way we used the other two-parameter methods by assigning the result to a variable and then using the variable in a script. As an example, we could use the following script:

```
<HTML>
<HEAD>
<SCRIPT language="JavaScript">
<!--
function the_pow()
{
 var num1= window.prompt("Enter a base number.","");
 var num2= window.prompt("What power should we set it to (a number)?","");
 var theresult= Math.pow(num1,num2);
 window.alert(num1+" to the power of "+num2+" is "+theresult);
}
//-->
</SCRIPT>
</HEAD>
<BODY>
<FORM>
<INPUT type="button" value="Find a Power" onClick="the_pow();">
</FORM>
</BODY>
</HTML>
```

```
Microsoft Internet Explorer  [X]

   /!\    54 is larger than 2

          [    OK    ]
```

Figure 12-11 The alert gives us the verdict on which number is bigger

Using this, if we enter **2** as the first number and **3** when it asks for a power, the script will compute the result of 2 to the 3rd power. We then are given an alert showing us the answer. The button in the BODY section is how the viewer starts the function. The result of this script when we input the numbers **2** and **3** is shown in Figure 12-12.

Now that we know about these two-parameter methods, let's take a look at some other methods we haven't covered yet.

The Other Methods

These methods are methods that take in single parameters, but what they do warrants a closer look at each of them. The individual methods include the following:

- ceil()

- floor()

- random()

- round()

We will look at the first three, and then we will examine the random() method afterward on it's own since it enables us to write a few new scripts.

The ceil() Method

The ceil() method stands for *ceiling* and returns the smallest integer that is greater than or equal to the number sent as the parameter. This is used mainly when there are likely to be numbers after the decimal point in a

Figure 12-12   The result of 2 to the 3rd power is shown as an alert

number. This rounds the number up to the next highest integer, unless the number is an integer already. In that case, the same number is returned (because it can be equal). For instance, Math.ceil(12.23); would return 13, but Math.ceil(12); would return 12.

As an example, we will use the following script to see what different values will return to us:

```
<HTML>
<HEAD>
<SCRIPT language="JavaScript">
<!--
function get_ceil()
{
  var num1= window.prompt("Enter a number.","");
  var theceil= Math.ceil(num1);
  window.alert("The ceiling of "+num1+ " is "+theceil);
}
//-->
</SCRIPT>
</HEAD>
<BODY>
<FORM>
<INPUT type="button" value="Find the ceiling!" onClick="get_ceil();">
</FORM>
</BODY>
</HTML>
```

The prompt gets a number from the viewer

The result of the ceil of the number is assigned to a variable

The alert tells the viewer the result

The button that starts the function

This script alerts the ceiling of the number entered by the viewer on the screen. Figure 12-13 shows the result of this in the browser when the viewer enters **4.55** into the prompt.

The floor() Method

The floor() method is like the ceil() method, but it goes the opposite way. The floor() method returns the largest integer less than or equal to the parameter sent to the method. This rounds down to the next lowest integer, unless the parameter is an integer already. In that case, it returns the same integer since it is already equal to an integer. Basically, this method just takes the decimal part out of a number and leaves the integer as the result.

For instance, Math.floor(12.23); will return 12 and Math.floor(12); will also return 12. We can use the floor() method like we used the ceil() method earlier—by assigning the result to a variable.

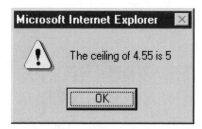

Figure 12-13   **The viewer is alerted to the ceiling of the number 4.55**

The round() Method

The round() method works like the previous two methods, but instead rounds the number entered as the parameter to the nearest integer whether it is greater or less than the number. Any number having the decimal portion's value at .5 or greater will be rounded up, while any decimal portion with a value less than .5 is rounded down.

The .5 cutoff is strict, so Math.round(12.49999999); would return 12 even though our tendency would be to go ahead and round it up.

The random() Method

The random() method is one that is very useful for creating scripts that require random integers. It returns a random number between 0 and 1. This means that we get a number with a decimal that can be quite long and not useful on its own. For instance, it might return something like 0.36511165498095293.

To get a random integer we can use, we need to do some things to get the type of value we want to use.

Random Integers

To get a random integer, the first thing we will want to do is to make the result have a greater range of values so that we are not stuck between 0 and 1. To get a greater range of values, we can multiply the result of the random() method by an integer to create a larger range. Like an array, the range would begin counting from 0; so to get a range of 5 possible

12

integers, we would multiply the result by 5. The following code shows how we can do this:

```
var rand_num= Math.random()*5;
```

This gets the result between 0 and 4, but does not give us an integer yet. The number could still come out as a long decimal number.

To get an integer between 0 and 4, we need to find a way to make all these decimal numbers convert to integers. Recall that we ran through three methods (floor(), ceil() and round()) earlier that converted numbers to integers in various ways. The floor() method is the one we will choose here because it simply removes the decimal places after the integer and gives us the integer portion of the number.

To use the floor() method, we could write the following code:

```
var rand_num= Math.random()*5;
var rand_int= Math.floor(rand_num);
```

The floor method takes in the value of the rand_num variable as a parameter and then gives us an integer from it. If we want to save a line of code, we could get a little fancy. We could just insert the random() method and calculation as the parameter to the floor() method.

We can do this because the result of the calculation, Math.random*5, is a number, and the floor() method can take a number as a parameter. The following code shows how we can code this on a single line:

```
var rand_int= Math.floor(Math.random()*5);
```

Now the variable rand_int will have the value of a random integer between 0 and 4. As you might have noticed, this sort of number range could be quite useful with arrays. This is how we can begin to code some fun scripts with random numbers.

Random Numbers for Scripts

Now we can have a little fun with the Math object by making use of the random() method. By setting up some arrays, we can create a script that can give random quotes or can show a random image each time the page is loaded.

Random Quotes for Fun   If you have thought about adding a quote to your page but don't want to deal with changing the quote all the time to have something different, a random quotes script could be just the thing.

To make such a script, we first need some quotes to use. Let's say we wish to set up ten different quotes that will show randomly each time the page is loaded. Since we have a number of values that are similar (and so we can make use of them with the random integer later), an array would be in order so we can store all of these and retrieve them easily.

So, let's set up an array with ten elements. Each element will be a (not so) famous quote that I throw into the mix for us. We could use the array with the quotes shown in the following example code:

```
var quotes= new Array(10)
quotes[0]="I like JavaScript (for now)!";
quotes[1]="It is time for a rhyme, I guess.";
quotes[2]="Where is my JavaScript book?";
quotes[3]="If I had a buck for every dollar I spent--Oops, never mind.";
quotes[4]="I suppose you were expecting a real quote here.";
quotes[5]="Quotes are great, but don't quote me on that.";
quotes[6]="What should I write here?";
quotes[7]="Wut hapns iff eye miss spel ohn purpas?";
quotes[8]="Mark my words, I will mark my words.";
quotes[9]="This spot reserved for a better quote.";
```

Now that we have this odd list of quotes in an array, we can make use of them by generating a random integer.

We will need a random integer between 0 and 9 (ten numbers), so we can use the following code to assign a random integer between 0 and 9 to a variable:

```
var rand_int= Math.floor(Math.random()*10);
```

Now the value of the variable rand_int will be a random integer between 0 and 9. We can now use it to access the element of the array whose index number matches the random integer in the rand_int variable. We just need to access the array element using the variable as the index number, as in the following example:

```
quotes[rand_int]
```

12

We will want to write this value in the body of the page in a document.write() statement. To do this, we will now look at the full page of code for our random quotes script:

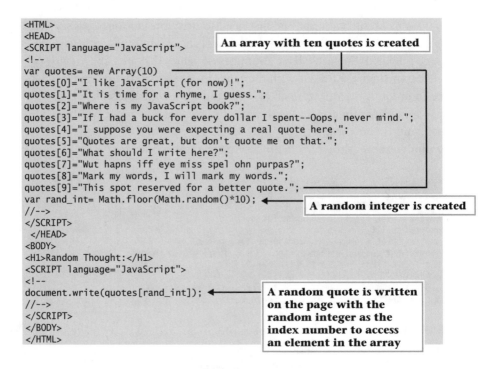

```
<HTML>
<HEAD>
<SCRIPT language="JavaScript">
<!--
var quotes= new Array(10)
quotes[0]="I like JavaScript (for now)!";
quotes[1]="It is time for a rhyme, I guess.";
quotes[2]="Where is my JavaScript book?";
quotes[3]="If I had a buck for every dollar I spent--Oops, never mind.";
quotes[4]="I suppose you were expecting a real quote here.";
quotes[5]="Quotes are great, but don't quote me on that.";
quotes[6]="What should I write here?";
quotes[7]="Wut hapns iff eye miss spel ohn purpas?";
quotes[8]="Mark my words, I will mark my words.";
quotes[9]="This spot reserved for a better quote.";
var rand_int= Math.floor(Math.random()*10);
//-->
</SCRIPT>
 </HEAD>
<BODY>
<H1>Random Thought:</H1>
<SCRIPT language="JavaScript">
<!--
document.write(quotes[rand_int]);
//-->
</SCRIPT>
</BODY>
</HTML>
```

An array with ten quotes is created

A random integer is created

A random quote is written on the page with the random integer as the index number to access an element in the array

The full code just adds a BODY section that writes one of the random quotes on the page based on the random integer value in the rand_int variable. Reloading the page will enable the random number to be reset and will probably (though not necessarily, because it is random) show a different quote.

Figure 12-14 shows one of the possible results of this script when run in a browser.

Figure 12-15 shows another one of the possible results of this script when run in a browser. We can keep getting different (or sometimes the same) results by refreshing the page.

Now that we can write random quotes into a page, how about a random image? It is very similar to the last script; we just need to make some small adjustments.

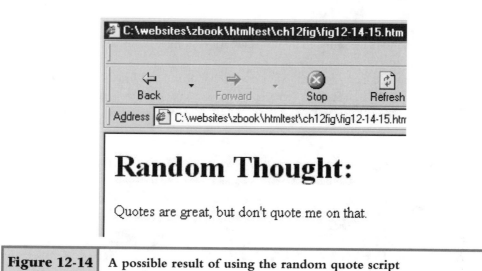

| **Figure 12-14** | A possible result of using the random quote script |

Random Images for the Updated Look   A random image script can give your page the feel of being updated without the need to run in and change an image all the time. Of course, the images would all need to

12

| **Figure 12-15** | Another possible result of using the random quote script |

fit the content where we decide to place the randomly chosen image. A random image script could be useful, for example, for an art gallery to display its collection.

The first thing we will want is an array of image Universal Resource Locator (URL) addresses (which can be local or absolute—we will use local addresses here). The array we will use for this script is shown in the following example code:

```
var r_image= new Array(10)
r_image[0]="image0.gif";
r_image[1]="image1.gif";
r_image[2]="image2.gif";
r_image[3]="image3.gif";
r_image[4]="image4.gif";
r_image[5]="image5.gif";
r_image[6]="image6.gif";
r_image[7]="image7.gif";
r_image[8]="image8.gif";
r_image[9]="image9.gif";
```

This array sets up the addresses of images that can be displayed at random each time the page is loaded.

Next, we need a way to get a random integer between 0 and 9. This is the same as in our previous script:

```
var rand_int= Math.floor(Math.random()*10);
```

Now that we have that, the next step is to access the array in the BODY section of the document to show a random image from the array when the page is loaded in the browser.

The following code is the full page, with the addition of the BODY section, which enables us to display the random image using a document. write() statement to print the image tag:

```
<HTML>
<HEAD>
<SCRIPT language="JavaScript">
<!--
```

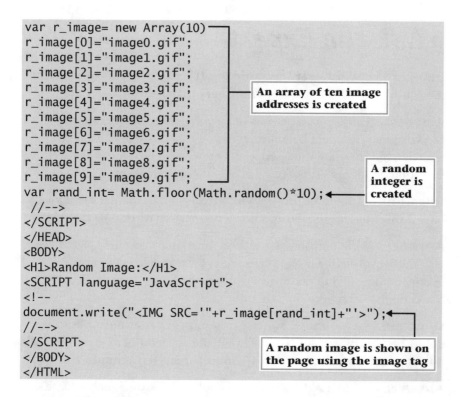

```
var r_image= new Array(10)
r_image[0]="image0.gif";
r_image[1]="image1.gif";
r_image[2]="image2.gif";
r_image[3]="image3.gif";
r_image[4]="image4.gif";
r_image[5]="image5.gif";
r_image[6]="image6.gif";
r_image[7]="image7.gif";
r_image[8]="image8.gif";
r_image[9]="image9.gif";
var rand_int= Math.floor(Math.random()*10);
 //-->
</SCRIPT>
</HEAD>
<BODY>
<H1>Random Image:</H1>
<SCRIPT language="JavaScript">
<!--
document.write("<IMG SRC='"+r_image[rand_int]+"'>");
//-->
</SCRIPT>
</BODY>
</HTML>
```

An array of ten image addresses is created

A random integer is created

A random image is shown on the page using the image tag

As you can see, this is quite similar to the quote script. We just needed to change the contents of the array and of the document.write() statement to make the script display an image rather than a quote.

With the random() method, we could go on for some time because there are numerous things we could randomize. For now though, we will go through our "Ask the Expert" section and then learn about the Date object.

─Hint─

For this example, we will just pretend we saved our images as image0.gif, image1.gif, and so on; however, they could be saved under any name you like.

12

Ask the Expert

Question: Will I ever have any use for any of the properties of the Math object? They are all numbers that I don't even use!

Answer: This depends on how often you perform different types of calculations. It would be unlikely for you to use any of them as a beginner, but there are some scripts out there that make use of them for various advanced purposes, such as JavaScript calculators.

Question: I have no interest in writing a calculator. Do I really have to bother memorizing all the properties of the Math object?

Answer: Well, probably not, since a situation to use them probably won't come up all that often. It is good to have a reference on hand just in case, though, and to know generally what they are since they appear in scripts on the Web from time to time.

Question: You know, some of these properties and methods could be handy if I don't have a calculator around. I could write a little script to calculate some things for myself, couldn't I?

Answer: Of course! Just be sure to double check the numbers with something you know the answer to first to be sure that there are no mistakes in your code.

Question: The random() method is fun so far, but I can't think of anything else I could use it for. Could you give me some ideas for using it to do other things?

Answer: There are a number of other things you could use it for. You can randomize pretty much anything that can be displayed with a Hypertext Markup Language (HTML) tag or plain text, so try out some ideas and see if they work for you. Here are some thoughts off the top of my head for you, though: random links, random linked images, random tasks for a JavaScript game of some sort (like rolling dice or drawing a card), random background music, random page greetings, random alerts, and I'm sure there are plenty more.

Project 12-1: Displaying a Random Link on a Page

This script will enable you to work with the random() method a little more by enabling you to create a script to display a random link on a page.

Step-by-Step

1. Create an HTML page, leaving room in the HEAD and BODY sections for our code.

2. Create a set of five Web addresses in an array. Use the following addresses:

http://www.pageresource.com
http://www.javascriptcity.com
http://www.ad-help.com
http://www.yahoo.com
http://www.excite.com

3. Use the random() method to create a random integer you can use to access the array with the integer as an index number.

4. Display a random link on the page in the format shown next by using a document.write() statement in the BODY section:

```
<A HREF="random address here">Random Site!</A>
```

5. Save the file as pr12_1.html, and open it in your Web browser. Try reloading a few times to see how the random addresses show up for the link.

The Date Object

The Date object is another predefined JavaScript object. It enables us to deal with time and to get certain time values that we can use in our scripts. In order to use this object, we need to create an instance of the object to which we can refer.

To create an instance of the Date object, we use the new keyword as we have with a number of other objects, as shown in the following example:

12

```
var instance_name= new Date();
```

We would replace *instance_name* with a name we wish to use for the instance of the Date object. So, if we wanted an instance named "rightnow," we could use the code shown in the following example:

```
var rightnow= new Date();
```

Now we have an instance of the object named "rightnow."

Once we have an instance of the object, we are able to use the properties and methods of the Date object to perform various tasks (such as creating JavaScript clocks). So, let's look into these, beginning with the properties.

Properties

The Date object has only two properties. Table 12-3 lists the properties and their purposes. Following the table, we will discuss each property in more detail (these may look familiar, as the Array object has these same properties).

The constructor Property

The constructor property holds the value of the constructor function of the object, much like the use of this property in the Array object. To see what the value is, we could write it to the page, as shown in the following code:

```
<BODY>
<SCRIPT language="JavaScript">
<!--
var rightnow= new Date();
document.write(rightnow.constructor);
//-->
</SCRIPT>
</BODY>
```

Property	Purpose
constructor	Holds the value of the constructor function that created the object
prototype	Enables us to add properties to the object if we wish

Table 12-3   Properties of the Date Object

If you run the code, you will probably see something similar to the following line written on the page:

```
function Date() { [native code] }
```

This is pretty much what we got using this with the Array object: we get the name of the constructor function and any public code in the function. Since the function code is private, we get the [native code] text in place of the actual function code.

The prototype Property

The prototype property enables us to add a property or method to the Date object, much like we did with the Array object in Module 11.

For instance, if we want to add a new property named "attitude" for each instance of the Date object, we could use the following code:

```
Date.prototype.attitude="cool";
var rightnow= new Date();
window.alert("This date is "+rightnow.attitude);
```

This code creates the new property, creates an instance of the Date object, and then alerts the value of the new property to the screen.

Now that we know the properties of the Date object, let's take a look at the methods we can use.

Methods

The Date object didn't give us many properties, but it does have quite a large number of methods we can use. Table 12-4 lists various methods of the Date object and the purpose of each method. Following the table, we will discuss each method in more detail.

Now that we have the long list of methods, let's look at them in a little more detail, beginning with the methods used to get date values in an instance of the Date object.

12

Method	Purpose
getDate()	Returns the day of the month based on the viewer's local time
getDay()	Returns the number of days into the week based on the viewer's local time (0–6)
getHours()	Returns the number of hours into the day based on the viewer's local time (0–23)
getMinutes()	Returns the number of minutes into the hour based on the viewer's local time (0–59)
getMonth()	Returns the number of months into the year based on the viewer's local time (0–11)
getSeconds()	Returns the seconds into the minute based on the viewer's local time (0–59)
getTime()	Returns a numeric value of the time based on the viewer's local time
getTimezoneOffset()	Returns the time-zone offset in minutes based on the viewer's local time
getYear()	Returns the year based on the viewer's local time (two digits)
getFullYear()	Returns the full year based on the viewer's local time (four digits)
parse()	Returns the number of milliseconds since January 1, 1970, at midnight of a date sent as a parameter based on the viewer's local time
setDate()	Sets the day of the month for an instance of the Date object
setHours()	Sets the hours for an instance of the Date object
setMinutes()	Sets the minutes for an instance of the Date object
setMonth()	Sets the month for an instance of the Date object
setSeconds()	Sets the seconds for an instance of the Date object
setTime()	Sets the time (in milliseconds since January 1, 1970, at midnight) for an instance of the Date object
setYear()	Sets the year as an instance of the Date object (two digits)
setFullYear()	Sets the full year as an instance of the Date object (four digits)
toGMTString()	Returns a string that is the date in Greenwich Mean Time (GMT) format
toLocaleString()	Returns a string that is the date in a format based on the locale

Table 12-4   Methods of the Date Object

Methods That Get Values

Methods that get values enable us to get various time and date values that we can use in our scripts. The methods that enable us to get values for an instance of the Date object include the following:

- getDate()
- getDay()
- getHours()
- getMinutes()
- getMonth()
- getSeconds()
- getTime()
- getTimezoneOffset()
- getYear()
- getFullYear()

To use the methods, we need an instance of the Date object. Once we have that, we can call any of the methods by using the instance name. The following is the syntax for doing this:

```
instance_name.method();
```

We would replace *instance_name* with the name of our instance of the Date object, and we would replace method with the method function we wish to use.

So, if we wanted to use the getDate() method with an instance of the Date object named "rightnow," we could use the following code:

```
var rightnow= new Date();
var theday= rightnow.getDate();
```

This assigns the value returned from the getDate() method to a variable named "theday."

12

The values returned form the Date methods are often numeric and need to be explained a bit, so let's take a look at these methods more closely.

The getDate() Method

The getDate() method enables us to get the day of the month for use in a script. The value returned is a number that represents the day of the month. So, if it is the 5th of the month, the getDate() method would return 5. If it is the 22nd, the getDate() method would return 22. This method is nice because it is fairly straightforward.

The getDay() Method

The getDay() method enables us to get the day of the week; however, rather than returning a name such as Monday or Friday, it returns a number. The number represents the number of days *into* the week (0–6) rather than the day *of* the week we would commonly have in mind (1–7). So, if it is Sunday, the method returns 0; and if it is Wednesday, the method returns 3. We have to remember that it counts from 0 when we begin using it in our scripts. Many of the methods that follow will count beginning at zero.

The getHours() Method

The getHours() method enables us to get the number of hours into the day (0–23). The count begins at 0. So, when it is midnight, the method returns 0; and when it is 2:00 P.M., it returns 14.

The getMinutes() Method

The getMinutes() method enables us to get the number of minutes into the current hour (0–59). Again, the counting begins at 0. So, if it is 2:00 (either A.M. or P.M., or any hour) on the dot, the method returns 0; and if it is 2:23, the method returns 23.

The getMonth() Method

The getMonth() method enables us to get the number of months into the current year (0–11). This one also begins counting at 0, which makes the result a little tricky. For instance, if it is January (the month we tend to think of as 1), the method returns 0; and if it is October (the month we tend to think of as 10), the method returns 9. This is one we have to watch a little more closely when we use it in scripts, as we will need to remember to make an adjustment if we want to use numeric dates (like 10/24/2000).

The getSeconds() Method

The getSeconds() method enables us to get the number of seconds into the current minute (0–59). So, if the time is 2:42:23, the method returns 23; and if the time is 2:23:00, the method returns 0.

The getTime() Method

The getTime() method gets the time (in milliseconds since January 1, 1970, at midnight) for an instance of the Date object. So, if we wanted to know the number of milliseconds since that date at our current time, we could use the following code:`

```
var rightnow= new Date();
var theday= rightnow.getTime();
```

This assigns the result of the method to a variable so we can use it later if we need it in our script.

The getTimezoneOffset() Method

The getTimezoneOffset() method gives us the number of minutes that separate the local time from GMT. So, if we are 6 hours apart from GMT, the method would return 360 (6*60); and if we are only 1 hour apart, the method returns 60.

Hint

The getTimezoneOffset () method doesn't show whether our time is ahead or behind (by using a negative value, for instance), it just shows how many minutes the offset is from GMT overall.

The getYear() Method

This method returns the last two digits of the current year (at least if the year is between 1900 and 1999). For instance, if the year is 1988, the method returns 88. Since it is 2000, we need to make an adjustment so that we don't get the year returned as 100. This depends on the browser, however. Some will go ahead and return 2000 instead.

The adjustment we make will keep this working for a while (for the current millennium) and give us a four-digit date. What we need to check

12

is whether or not the browser supports 2000 or returns 100. The
following is the code for the adjustment:

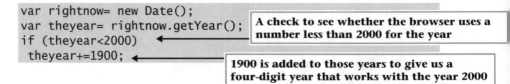

```
var rightnow= new Date();
var theyear= rightnow.getYear();
if (theyear<2000)
  theyear+=1900;
```

> A check to see whether the browser uses a number less than 2000 for the year

> 1900 is added to those years to give us a four-digit year that works with the year 2000

This will give us a four-digit date that works for the old dates as well
as the new ones. The code will work for some time, but the getYear()
method will likely be replaced with a new method in JavaScript 1.3 that
fixes this by giving a full date from the start.

The getFullYear() Method

The getFullYear() method is very similar to the getYear() method, except
it returns a four-digit year consistently to avoid the year 2000 problem.
The downside is that it was implemented in JavaScript 1.3 and, thus,
will only work with newer browsers (the same will be true for the
setFullYear() method mentioned in the next section). Since that is the
case, we will use the old getYear() more often in this book; however,
the getFullYear() method will be used more over time as browsers are
upgraded.

The getFullYear() method works like the getYear() method, but you
do not need to run any extra checks to be sure the year is correct:

```
var rightnow= new Date();
var theyear= rightnow.getFullYear();
```

This assigns the value returned by the method to the rightnow variable.
This time, the value is already four digits and won't need any adjusting.

Now that we have seen the methods that get, let's take a look at the
methods that enable us to set values for an instance of the Date object.

Methods That Set Values

The methods that set values work with the same types of values as the
methods that get values. The methods that enable us to set values for an
instance of the Date object include the following:

- setDate()

- setHours()

- setMinutes()

- setMonth()

- setSeconds()

- setTime()

- setYear()

- setFullYear()

To set these, we send them a numeric parameter based on the time or date we want to use. For instance, if we wanted to set the day of the month for an instance of the Date object, we could use the following code:

```
var rightnow= new Date();
rightnow.setDate(22);
```

This would set the day of the month to the 22nd for the rightnow instance of the Date object.

The others work in the same way. In order to know what value needs to be sent to one of these methods, take a look at what type of value is returned by its counterpart in the methods that get values. The parameter the method will expect will be a value like the one returned by the method.

Other Methods

The three remaining methods perform various tasks that the other methods don't cover in some way. Let's take a look at each of them.

The parse() Method

The parse() method is used to find out the number of milliseconds since January 1, 1970, at midnight for a date string (such as Dec 12, 1999) input as a parameter. This is often used with the setTime() method since it needs a parameter in milliseconds to set the time. We could use the parse method to find the number of milliseconds since January 1, 1970, for the date Dec 12, 1999, as shown in the following code:

12

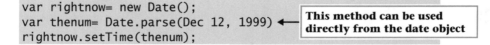

```
var rightnow= new Date();
var thenum= Date.parse(Dec 12, 1999)
rightnow.setTime(thenum);
```

This method can be used directly from the date object

This code parses the date into a number of milliseconds, and then sends it to the setTime() method used with the rightnow instance of the Date object.

The toGMTString() Method

The toGMTString() method returns a date string in GMT format. We can use it to get the GMT format for an instance of the Date object, as shown in the following code:

```
var rightnow= new Date();
var thedate= rightnow.toGMTString();
```

This will assign a value, such as Wed, 21 Dec 1998 11:12:44 GMT, to the variable thedate. It can then be written to the page or used with other methods of the Date object in a script.

The toLocaleString() Method

The toLocaleString() method returns a date string in the format of the viewer's locale. We can use it to get the locale format for an instance of the Date object, as shown in the following code:

```
var rightnow= new Date();
var thedate= rightnow.toLocaleString();
```

This will assign a date string value to the variable thedate. The value of the string depends on what browser the viewer is using to view the page. It can then be written to the page or used with other methods of the Date object in a script.

Now that we have the methods down, let's see if we can have a little fun with the Date object.

How About Some Date Scripts?

With the technical overview out of the way, let's create some scripts that make use of the methods of the Date object. For now, we will write a script to display the date on the page, and then we will create a script for a simple status bar clock.

Write the Date on the Page

To write the date on the page, we will want to use some of the Date object methods to get the values we need. Let's say we want to write a date with the format of Tuesday, 11/21/2000. To do this, we will need to find out the day of the week, the month, the day of the month, and the year. We can do this using the getDay(), getMonth(), getDate(), and getYear() methods.

The following script will write the date to the page:

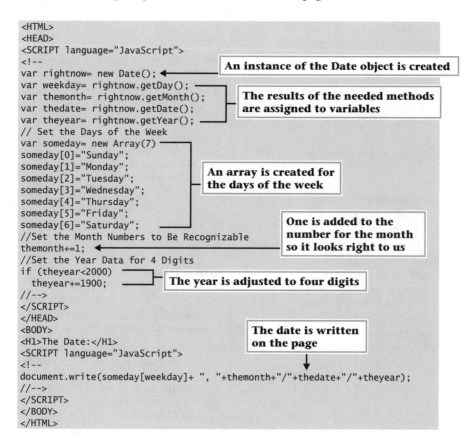

```
<HTML>
<HEAD>
<SCRIPT language="JavaScript">
<!--
var rightnow= new Date();          ◄——— An instance of the Date object is created
var weekday= rightnow.getDay();
var themonth= rightnow.getMonth();      The results of the needed methods
var thedate= rightnow.getDate();        are assigned to variables
var theyear= rightnow.getYear();
// Set the Days of the Week
var someday= new Array(7)
someday[0]="Sunday";
someday[1]="Monday";
someday[2]="Tuesday";              An array is created for
someday[3]="Wednesday";           the days of the week
someday[4]="Thursday";
someday[5]="Friday";
someday[6]="Saturday";                One is added to the
//Set the Month Numbers to Be Recognizable   number for the month
themonth+=1;  ◄————                       so it looks right to us
//Set the Year Data for 4 Digits
if (theyear<2000)
    theyear+=1900;     ——— The year is adjusted to four digits
//-->
</SCRIPT>
</HEAD>
<BODY>
<H1>The Date:</H1>                   The date is written
<SCRIPT language="JavaScript">       on the page
<!--
document.write(someday[weekday]+ ", "+themonth+"/"+thedate+"/"+theyear);
//-->
</SCRIPT>
</BODY>
</HTML>
```

12

This script sets the results of the methods to variables. It then creates an array to hold the days of the week, which we later access using the number returned from the getDay() method as the index number. We then make an adjustment so that the month will show up the way we

would expect it by adding 1 to the number returned by the getMonth()
method (recall that it counts months starting at 0 instead of 1).

After that, we adjust the year to give us a four-digit year. In the BODY
section, we write the formatted output onto the page for the viewer to
see. The result of this script when run in a browser is shown in Figure
12-16, which will show you the date I wrote this part of the module!

Create a Simple Status Bar Clock

To create a simple clock, we will need the hours, minutes, and seconds of
the current time. To get these, we can use the getHours(), getMinutes(),
and getSeconds() methods.

The following code will create a clock in the status bar of a document:

```
<HTML>
<HEAD>
<SCRIPT language="JavaScript">
<!--
function theclock()
{
var rightnow= new Date();          An instance of the
                                   Date object is created
var thehours= rightnow.getHours();
var themins= rightnow.getMinutes();   The results of the needed
var theseconds= rightnow.getSeconds();  methods are assigned to variables
//format the hours, minutes, and seconds with leading zeros
if (thehours<10)
  thehours="0"+thehours;        Leading 0s added for the hours for formatting
if (themins<10)
  themins="0"+themins;        Leading 0s added for the minutes for formatting
if (theseconds<10)
  theseconds="0"+theseconds;     Leading 0s added for the seconds for formattin
//write the time to the status bar
window.status=thehours+":"+themins+":"+theseconds;   The time
}                                                    is written
setInterval("theclock()",1000);    An interval is set  in the
//-->                              to start the clock   status bar
</SCRIPT>                          and keep it
</HEAD>                            running
<BODY>
<H1>The Time Is in the Status Bar at the Bottom!</H1>
</BODY>
</HTML>
```

C:\websites\zbook\htmltest\ch12

Back   Forward

Address   C:\websites\zbook\htmltest\

The Date:

Wednesday, 1/3/2001

Figure 12-16   The date is shown on the page

The script creates a function that sets the results of the methods to variables. We then adjust the values of the variables that show the hours, minutes, and seconds by adding a leading 0 when the number is less than 10. This way the clock will show 12:02:34 for 12:02:34, instead of leaving out the 0 and displaying 12:2:34.

At the end, the function displays the output in the status bar. The function is initially called using a setInterval() command from the window object. The function is repeated at intervals of 1000 milliseconds, or one second. This enables the clock to stay current. The results of this script when run in a browser are shown in Figure 12-17.

Project 12-2: Creating a JavaScript Clock

12

`pr12_2.html` This project will enable you to work with the methods of the Date object more, as well as help you learn how to adjust the values that are returned

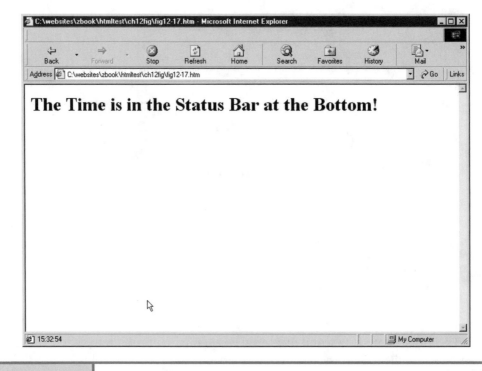

Figure 12-17 A clock is shown in the status bar of the window

so they can be used in various ways. This creates a JavaScript clock with a few more options than our simple clock in the previous section.

Step-by-Step

1. Create an HTML page, leaving room in the HEAD section of the document for our JavaScript code.

2. Write some code that will create a status bar clock. In this clock, include the following information:

   The date in the form mm/dd/yyyy
   The time with hours, minutes, and seconds
   Whether it is A.M. or P.M.

3. This will be a 12-hour clock instead of our previous 24-hour clock, so be sure to adjust the value of the hours so that they stay between 1 and 12.

4. Begin the clock with a setInterval() statement, and have it update every second.

5. Save the file as pr12_2.html, and open it in your browser. The date and time should appear in the status bar.

☑ *Mastery Check*

1. What do the properties and methods of the Math object enable us to do?

    A. Take the square roots and other such values of strings and return a number

    B. Perform mathematical calculations

    C. Go to math class to learn new theorems

    D. Nothing, they are useless

2. Which of the following would correctly write the value of pi on a Web page?

    A. document.write(Math.Pi);

    B. document.write(Math.pi);

    C. document.write(Math.PI);

    D. document.write(Date.PI);

3. Which of the following would correctly generate a random number between 0 and 7?

    A. var rand_int= Math.floor(Math.random()*7);

    B. var rand_int= Math.floor(Math.random()*6);

    C. var rand_int= Math.floor(Math.random()*8);

    D. var rand_int= Math.sqrt(Math.random());

12

☑ *Mastery Check*

4. What must be created in most cases before the Date object's properties and methods can be used?

   A. The viewer must have a date on Friday night

   B. A number for reference to the date

   C. A time for the date to be set

   D. An instance of the Date object

5. Which of the following correctly assigns the day of the week for an instance of the Date object named "rightnow" to a variable named "weekday"?

   A. var weekday= rightnow.getDate();

   B. var weekday= rightnow.getDay();

   C. var weekday= right now.getDay();

   D. var weekly= rightlater.getMinutes();

Module 13

Handling Strings

The Goals of This Module

- Learn what the string object is
- Find out how to create an instance of the string object
- Discover how to create a string literal
- Learn how to use the string object's properties
- Learn how to use the string object's methods
- Create scripts that use the string object's properties and methods

To work with strings in JavaScript, you need to learn about the various methods that handle them. The methods come from the JavaScript string object.

This module explains what the string object is and how to create strings that use its properties and methods. Then the string object's properties and methods are discussed in more detail so you can see how they work. Finally, you'll code a script that uses some of the properties and methods you've learned. But first, take a look at the introduction to the string object.

Introduction to the string Object

The string object provides properties and methods to get information about strings or to modify strings. You create a string object either by using the new keyword with the constructor function, or JavaScript will create one temporarily when one of the methods is called from a string literal. What makes a string object and what makes a string literal? Let's find out by looking at how to create a string object in JavaScript.

The string Object

As just explained, one way to create a string object is by using the new keyword, as you've done with other objects previously. The syntax is shown here:

```
var instance_name= new String("string value here");
```

You replace instance_name with the name you want to use for the instance of the string object. You then replace string value here with the string of characters to use as the new string object.

So, if you want to create an instance of the *string* object named "guitar_string", you could use the following code:

```
var guitar_string= new String("G");
```

This script creates an instance of the string object for the string "G".

Although creating a string object with the new keyword can be useful in some ways, string literals are used more often.

The String Literal

You can create a string literal just by assigning a string value to a variable. This technique is a bit shorter than creating a string object using the new keyword and still allows you to use all the methods of the string object (as well as one of the properties).

A string literal is created in the code that follows. Notice that the code assigns a string value to a variable.

```
var guitar_string="G";
```

This makes the string "G" a string literal, which you know as a regular text string. With text strings, you're also allowed to use the properties and methods of the string object.

What's the Difference?

The difference between a string object and a string literal is that a regular text string has the value of the string itself, and it can be compared against another string easily, as in the following code:

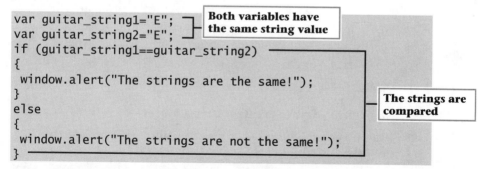

```
var guitar_string1="E";          Both variables have
var guitar_string2="E";          the same string value
if (guitar_string1==guitar_string2)
{
 window.alert("The strings are the same!");
}                                          The strings are
else                                       compared
{
 window.alert("The strings are not the same!");
}
```

Because this code uses regular string literals, the result is what you'd expect. An alert says that the strings are the same.

13

However, if you used string objects to run through the same if block, you would see something unexpected. The code that follows uses string objects instead:

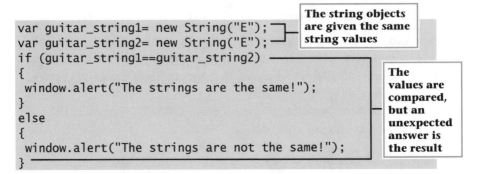

```
var guitar_string1= new String("E");
var guitar_string2= new String("E");
if (guitar_string1==guitar_string2)
{
  window.alert("The strings are the same!");
}
else
{
  window.alert("The strings are not the same!");
}
```

The string objects are given the same string values

The values are compared, but an unexpected answer is the result

This time the alert would tell you that the strings are not the same, even though the string values are both E—because a string object is an object value and not a literal value. Objects aren't going to be equal to one another in the same way regular text strings would be. To find out if two objects are equal, you would have to write extra code to determine that. For most purposes, you wouldn't want to go to all that trouble. Instead, you would probably use string literals and let them use the string object's methods.

A regular text string is able to use the string object's methods because JavaScript takes the string literal and turns it into a temporary string object. Once the method's execution is complete, it returns a string literal. This allows you to use the short string literals rather than forcing you to create string objects to use the methods of the string object you may need.

1-Minute Drill

- **Name two ways to create a string object.**
- **Which type of string were you familiar with before this module, a string object or a string literal?**
- **Why can a string literal use the methods of the string object?**

- Use the new keyword with the constructor function, or create a *string* object temporarily when one of the methods is called from a string literal
- You've used some string literals in your scripts as regular text strings
- A string literal can use the methods of the string object because JavaScript turns the string literal into a temporary string object

Properties of the string Object

The string object doesn't have many properties, so this section will go fairly quickly. See Table 13-1 for a brief description of each property and the sections that follow for more details.

The constructor Property

This property performs the same task as it does in the other objects that have it (like the date and array objects). It sends back the value of the constructor function. To use the constructor property, you have to use a string object rather than a literal.

Hint

You can use a string literal for the length property and all of the methods of the string object, but the constructor and prototype properties require string objects.

The following code writes the value of the constructor property onto a Web page:

```
<HTML>
<HEAD>
<SCRIPT language="JavaScript">
<!--
var guitar_string= new String("G");      A new string
//-->                                     object is
</SCRIPT>                                 created
<BODY>
<SCRIPT language="JavaScript">            The value
<!--                                      of the
document.write(guitar_string.constructor);   constructor
//-->                                     property is
</SCRIPT>                                 printed on
</BODY>                                   the page
</HTML>
```

13

This code produces text similar to the following:

```
function String() { [native code] }
```

Property	Purpose
constructor	Holds the value of the constructor function for an instance of the object
length	Holds the numeric value of the length of the string (its number of characters)
prototype	Allows you to add properties to the object

Table 13-1 Properties of the string Object

The length Property

This property returns the length of the string, which is the number of characters contained in the string. You can use it with both string objects and string literals. You've seen this property with other objects as well, such as the array object. (In that case, the value was the number of elements in an array.)

The following code uses a regular text string. It writes the length of the string variable onto the page.

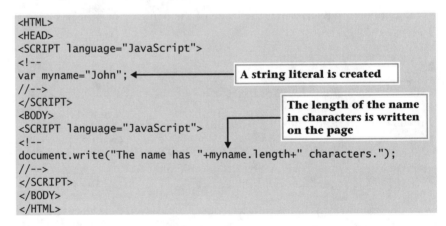

```
<HTML>
<HEAD>
<SCRIPT language="JavaScript">
<!--
var myname="John";          ←————  A string literal is created
//-->
</SCRIPT>
<BODY>
<SCRIPT language="JavaScript">          The length of the name
<!--                                    in characters is written
                                        on the page
document.write("The name has "+myname.length+" characters.");
//-->
</SCRIPT>
</BODY>
</HTML>
```

Notice how the name of the variable is used like an object name here. This is how to get JavaScript to create a temporary string object to use the property. The script writes the result to the page. Because the name has four characters, the length property has a value of 4 here.

The length property will be quite useful later in this book (see Module 14) when you want to break strings apart to get information or make changes to them, especially if the viewer enters the string and you don't know its length beforehand.

The prototype Property

As with the other objects that have the prototype property, you can use it to add properties or methods to string objects on the page. The following code shows an example:

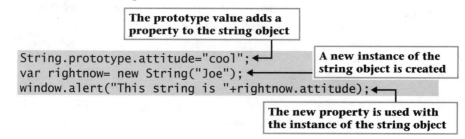

```
String.prototype.attitude="cool";
var rightnow= new String("Joe");
window.alert("This string is "+rightnow.attitude);
```

The prototype value adds a property to the string object

A new instance of the string object is created

The new property is used with the instance of the string object

Now the string object "Joe" has an attitude property of "cool"!

1-Minute Drill

● **Which of the properties just discussed have you seen with other objects you've used?**

● **Which of the properties can you use with string literals?**

● **What value does the length property hold?**

● All of them, in some way
● The length property
● The number of characters in a string

13

Methods of the string Object

The string object has a lot of methods, as shown in Table 13-2.

Method	Purpose
anchor ()	Creates an HTML anchor tag with a target on a page
big()	Adds <BIG> and </BIG> tags around a string value
blink()	Adds <BLINK> and </BLINK> tags around a string value (may work only in Netscape Navigator)
bold()	Adds <B> and </B> tags around a string value
charAt()	Finds out which character is at a given position in a string
charCodeAt()	Finds the character code of a character at a given position in a string
concat()	Adds two or more strings together and returns the new combined string value
fixed()	Adds <TT> and </TT> tags around a string value
fontcolor()	Adds <FONT color="*color*"> and </FONT> tags around a string value, which change the color of the string to a specified color
fontsize()	Adds <FONT size="*number*"> and </FONT> tags around a string value, which change the size of the string to a specified size given as a number
fromCharCode()	Uses character codes sent as parameters to create a new string
indexOf()	Searches for a character sent as a parameter in a string. If it's found, the position of the first instance of the character is returned; otherwise, it returns -1
italics()	Adds <I> and </I> tags around a string value
lastIndexOf()	Searches for a character sent as a parameter in a string: if it's found, the position of the last instance of the character is returned; otherwise, it returns -1
link()	Creates HTML links using the string as the link text and linking to the URL sent as a parameter
match()	Compares a regular expression and a string to see if they match
replace()	Finds out if a regular expression matches a string and then replaces a matched string with a new string
search()	Executes the search for a match between a regular expression and a specified string
slice()	Pulls out a specified section of a string value and returns a new string
small()	Adds <SMALL> and </SMALL> tags around a string value

Table 13-2   Methods of the string Object

Method	Purpose
split()	Separates a string into an array of strings based on a character sent as a parameter to the method
strike()	Adds <STRIKE> and </STRIKE> tags around a string value
sub()	Adds _{and} tags around a string value
substr()	Allows a portion of the string specified with a starting position and ending after a certain number of characters to be returned
substring()	Allows a portion of the string specified with a starting position and an ending position to be returned
sup()	Adds ^{and} tags around a string value
toString()	Returns the string literal value of a string object
toLowerCase()	Converts a string to all lowercase letters and returns the result
toUpperCase()	Converts a string to all uppercase letters and returns the result

Table 13-2   Methods of the string Object *(continued)*

Yes, this list is quite long! Let's take a look at the methods of the string object in the same order they appear in the table.

The anchor() Method

This method places a text string as the text for a named anchor. The anchor() method takes a parameter that will be the name attribute for the named anchor. Basically, it creates an HTML tag set with the following syntax:

```
<A NAME="parameter_string">text_string</A>
```

The parameter_string is a string you send as a parameter in the method call. The text_string is the value of the string from which you call the method.

For example, take a look at this code:

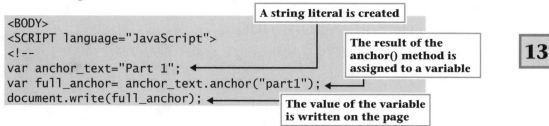

```
<BODY>
<SCRIPT language="JavaScript">
<!--
var anchor_text="Part 1";
var full_anchor= anchor_text.anchor("part1");
document.write(full_anchor);
```

A string literal is created

The result of the anchor() method is assigned to a variable

The value of the variable is written on the page

13

```
//-->
</SCRIPT>
</BODY>
```

Here, you assign a string literal to the variable link_text. You then call the anchor() method with a parameter of part1 from the string literal. The result is assigned to the full_link variable. The value of the full_link variable is then written on the page. The code writes the following link into the code for the page:

```
<A NAME= "part1">Part 1</A>
```

Figure 13-1 shows what this code looks like when viewed in the browser. Notice that the viewer sees only the anchor text for the section.

The big() Method

The big() method creates <BIG> and </BIG> tags around the text string that calls the method. For example, take a look at this code:

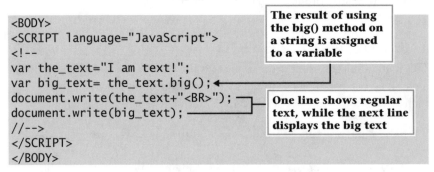

```
<BODY>
<SCRIPT language="JavaScript">
<!--
var the_text="I am text!";
var big_text= the_text.big();
document.write(the_text+"<BR>");
document.write(big_text);
//-->
</SCRIPT>
</BODY>
```

> The result of using the big() method on a string is assigned to a variable

> One line shows regular text, while the next line displays the big text

This code writes the regular text on the page and then writes the big text on the page. Figure 13-2 shows the result of this script in a browser.

The blink() Method

This method adds <BLINK> and </BLINK> tags around the text string that calls the method. Netscape Navigator supports the blink tag, but other browsers may not be able to make this work. If the browser supports the tag, the text within the tags will blink on the screen.

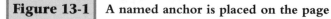

Part 1

Figure 13-1 A named anchor is placed on the page

The code that follows shows this method in action, creating a string variable and then calling the blink() method:

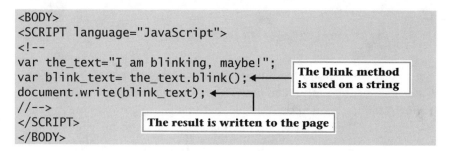

```
<BODY>
<SCRIPT language="JavaScript">
<!--
var the_text="I am blinking, maybe!";
var blink_text= the_text.blink();      The blink method
document.write(blink_text);            is used on a string
//-->
</SCRIPT>                   The result is written to the page
</BODY>
```

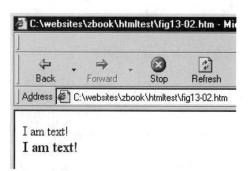

I am text!
I am text!

Figure 13-2 Regular text followed by the big text from the big() method

13

The preceding script writes this code into the page source:

```
<BLINK>I am blinking, maybe!</BLINK>
```

If the browser supports the blink() method and the blink tag, then the text will be blinking when the page is viewed.

The bold() Method

This method adds <B> and </B> tags around the text string that calls it. Here's some code that shows the bold() method in action:

```
<BODY>
<SCRIPT language="JavaScript">
<!--
var the_text="I am making a bold statement now.";
document.write(the_text.bold());
//-->
</SCRIPT>
</BODY>
```

Notice that you can shorten the code a bit by calling the method directly in the document.write() statement. The preceding code works the same way it would if you used the variable, but you get to cut one line from the code this way. This script writes the following code into the page source:

```
<B>I am making a bold statement now.</B>
```

The text will be bold when a viewer sees it in a browser.

The charAt() Method

This method determines which character resides at a particular position in a string. You can find out what the first or last character is, or you can find any character in between. The charAt() method takes in a number representing the position where you want to know the character.

Finding a Character

When you want to find a character, remember that the position count begins at 0 (as with arrays) rather than 1, so the first character is at position 0. The following code shows how to get the first character in a string by using the charAt() method:

```
var the_text="Character";
var first_char= the_text.charAt(0);
window.alert("The first character is "+first_char);
```

> **The charAt() method finds the character at position 0 (the first character) in the string**

This code assigns the result of the charAt() method call to a variable named first_char, which is then used in an alert. The alert will tell the viewer the first character in the text string that called the method. In this case, the alert would say "The first character is C."

Finding the Last Character with the length Property

If you want to find the last character, either you need to know how many characters are in the string before you use the method, or you can use the length property to determine the number of characters in the string. When using the length property, remember that it returns the number of characters, not the position of the last character.

The length property begins count at 1, while you must begin count at 0 using the charAt() method. Thus, the last character in a string will be at a position one less than the number of characters it contains. In other words, if the string has 10 characters (1–10), the last position (0–9) is at 9. If the string has 23 characters (1–23), the last position (0–22) is at 23–1=22.

Let's look at an example of this to see how it works. The code finds the last character in a string:

> **The length property is used. You subtract 1 from it to find the last position available in the string**

> **The charAt() method uses that value to find out which character is in the last position in the string**

```
var the_text="Character";
var position= the_text.length-1;
var last_char= the_text.charAt(position);
window.alert("The last character is "+last_char);
```

13

This code assigns the value of the length of the string minus one to a variable named "position." The position variable now holds the position of the last character in the string. The result of calling the charAt() method with the value of position sent as the parameter is assigned to a variable named last_char. Finally, an alert provides the last character in the string, which is "r." Thus, the viewer gets an alert saying "The last character is r."

The charCodeAt() Method

The charCodeAt() method works the same way as the charAt() method, but it returns the character code for the character at the positions sent as the parameter.

The character code is a numeric code that can be substituted for characters in HTML. In HTML, you can write an angle bracket (<) to show code on a Web page without it converting to HTML itself by using a special character code. In place of a regular angle bracket, for example, you could use &#60. The charCodeAt() method returns the numeric part of that code, the 60.

The charCodeAt() method can be useful if you want to find out the character code for a certain character. This script allows you to do this:

> The charCodeAt() method finds the character code for the character at position 0 (the first character) in the string

```
var the_text="Hello";
var char_code= the_text.charCodeAt(0);
window.alert("The character is &#"+char_code+";");
```

An alert would then tell you the character code at position 0 in the string (H), which is 72. The alert will add the string "&#"on the front and the string ";" to the back end of the character code for you and say "The character code is &#72."

The concat() Method

This method works much like the array object's concat() method. It combines the text string that calls the method with any number of other text strings sent as parameters and returns the combined value. The text string calling the method comes first in the order, while the strings sent as parameters are added in order after it.

The following code shows an example that combines three strings using the concat() method:

```
var string1= "I went to the store";
var string2= "then";
var string3= "I played a video game";
window.alert(string1.concat(string2,string3));
```

> **The three strings are combined in order from left to right**

This code combines the strings in the order string1, string2, and then string3. The result is an alert that says "I went to the store then I played a video game."

If you want it in a different order, you can adjust which string calls the method and the order of the parameters, as this code shows:

```
var string1= "I went to the store";
var string2= "then";
var string3= "I played a video game";
window.alert(string3.concat(string2,string1));
```

> **The three strings are combined in order from left to right (again)**

This time, string3 calls the method, so it comes first in the new string. The values of string2 and string3 are added in order after that. The result in this case is an alert that says "I played a video game then I went to the store."

The fixed() Method

The fixed() method adds <TT> and </TT> tags around the text string that calls it. The code that follows shows how you can use this method:

```
<BODY>
<SCRIPT language="JavaScript">
<!--
var the_text="I am typewriter text, on a computer!";
document.write(the_text.fixed());
//-->
</SCRIPT>
</BODY>
```

13

This script writes the following code into the page source:

```
<TT>I am typewriter text, on a computer!</TT>
```

The fontcolor() Method

The fontcolor() method adds font color to the text string that is used to call it. It takes in a string parameter that indicates what color the text should be. The color can be sent either using the color name or its red-green-blue (RGB) value.

This method formats some code around the text much like the example syntax:

```
<FONT COLOR= "color_value">text_string</FONT>
```

Here, color_value would be replaced with the color name or RGB value sent as a parameter to the method. The text_string part would be replaced with the text string used to call the method.

For an example, this code creates some red text on the page:

```
<BODY>
<SCRIPT language="JavaScript">
<!--
var the_text="I am so mad I am red!";
document.write(the_text.fontcolor("red"));
//-->
</SCRIPT>
</BODY>
```

The text is given a font color based on the color name sent as the parameter

This script places the following code into the page source:

```
<FONT COLOR="red">I am so mad I am red!</FONT>
```

You can also use the RGB value in place of the color name. In this code, the RGB value is used instead:

```
<BODY>
<SCRIPT language="JavaScript">
```

```
<!--
var the_text="I am so mad I am red!";
document.write(the_text.fontcolor("FF0000")); ◄——————
//-->
</SCRIPT>
</BODY>
```

The text is given a font color based on the RGB code sent as the parameter

This time, the code produced would be changed to include the RGB value in place of the color name in the previous example, as shown here:

```
<FONT COLOR= "FF0000">I am so mad I am red!</FONT>
```

The fontsize() Method

The fontsize() method adjusts the font size of the text string that calls the method. It takes in a numeric value to represent the size of the text (between 1 and 7).

The method formats the code so that it uses a syntax like the example here:

```
<FONT SIZE=number>text_string</FONT>
```

The number gets replaced with the number sent as the parameter in the method call, and text_string gets replaced by the text string that is used to call the method.

The example that follows shows this method in action:

```
<BODY>
<SCRIPT language="JavaScript">
<!--
var the_text="I am pretty small!";
document.write(the_text.fontsize(2)); ◄————
//-->
</SCRIPT>
</BODY>
```

The text is given a font size based on the number sent as the parameter

This script provides the code that follows in the page source:

```
<FONT SIZE=2>I am pretty small!</FONT>
```

13

The fromCharCode() Method

The fromCharCode() method creates a string from a series of character codes sent as parameters to the method. The charCodeAt() method returns a numeric code for the character at a given position. This is the type of value you must send to the fromCharCode() method. Also, fromCharCode() is called directly from the string object rather than from an existing string, because it is piecing together a string on the fly and doesn't require one to run. Instead, it uses the parameters sent to it to return a string.

So, if you want to alert the text string "HI," to the viewer, you could use the example code shown here:

```
window.alert(String.fromCharCode(72,73);
```

This code takes in the first parameter (the character code 72) and converts it to an H. It then takes in the second parameter (the character code 73) and converts it to an I. The two are combined in the order they were sent to form the string "HI," which is sent as an alert to the viewer.

The indexOf() Method

The indexOf() method finds out where a certain character or string begins in a string. It returns the position of only the first occurrence of the character or string that is sent as the parameter. If the character or string isn't found in the string value, a value of −1 is returned.

The following code looks for the letter C in the string "Cool":

```
var the_text="Cool";
var position= the_text.indexOf("C");
window.alert("Your character is at position "+position);
```

This code looks for the character C. Remember that the position count begins at 0; so when it finds C as the first character in the string, it returns 0. Thus, the alert will say "Your character is at position 0."

Note that the method is case sensitive, so C and c are two different characters to JavaScript in this case. Thus, the code that follows returns −1 (telling you the character isn't in the string), even though an uppercase C is in the string.

```
var the_text="Cool";
var position= the_text.indexOf("c");
window.alert("Your character is at position "+position);
```

The alert would now say "Your character is at position −1."

If you want to check for that −1 to keep from getting it as a position, you could use this code to send a different alert in case the character you want to find isn't in the string:

```
var the_text="Cool";
var position= the_text.indexOf("c");
if (position == -1)
 window.alert("Your character is not in the string!");
else
 window.alert("Your character is at position "+position);
```

This time, the if statement checks to see whether the method returns −1 to the position variable. If so, the alert says "Your character is not in the string!" Otherwise, the regular alert will tell you the position. In the previous code, the lowercase c isn't in the string, so the "Your character is not in the string!" alert appears.

The indexOf() method returns the position number only for the first occurrence of the character you send as the parameter. So, if you use the code that follows, you will be alerted that your character is at position 1, even though it's also at position 2.

```
var the_text="Cool";
var position= the_text.indexOf("o");
if (position == -1)
 window.alert("Your character is not in the string!");
else
 window.alert("Your character is at position "+position);
```

The lowercase o is in the string twice, but indexOf() locates only the first occurrence of the character.

13

The italics() Method

The italics() method adds <I> and </I> tags around the text string that calls it. This code shows you how to create some italic text on a Web page:

```
<BODY>
<SCRIPT language="JavaScript">
<!--
var the_text="I am leaning for some reason!";
document.write(the_text.italics());
//-->
</SCRIPT>
</BODY>
```

This script places the following code into the page source:

```
<I>I am leaning for some reason</I>
```

The lastIndexOf() Method

The lastIndexOf() method works just like the indexOf() method, but it returns the last occurrence of the parameter you send to the method rather than the first. If the value sent as the parameter isn't in the string, the method returns −1 like the indexOf() method.

Thus, if you use the same code as previously used in the section on the indexOf() method to find the lowercase o in the string "Cool" but replace indexOf() with lastIndexOf(), the value returned will be different:

```
var the_text="Cool";
var position= the_text.lastIndexOf("o");
if (position == -1)
 window.alert("Your character is not in the string!");
else
 window.alert("Your character is at position "+position);
```

This time, the alert says that the character is at position 2, although it is also at position 1 in the string. Because position 2 is the last occurrence of the o, the lastIndexOf() method returns the number 2.

The link() Method

The link() method works like the anchor() method, but instead it creates a
live link on the page. It takes in a string parameter that is the value of the
URL for the link, while the text for the link will be the text string that
called the method.

The method creates a link with the general syntax as shown here:

```
<A HREF="url">text_string</A>
```

The url is replaced with the URL sent as the parameter in the method
call, while text_string is replaced with the text string that made the call.

Look at this example that uses the link() method:

```
<BODY>
<SCRIPT language="JavaScript">
<!--
var link_text="A Web Site";
var full_link= link_text.link("http://www.pageresource.com");
document.write(full_link);
//-->
</SCRIPT>
</BODY>
```

**The link is created based on the URL
sent as the parameter and the string**

This code creates the link shown here in the page source code:

```
<A HREF=http://www.pageresource.com>A Web Site</A>
```

The technique in the preceding code example could also be used as the
other side of the anchor() method to create a link to the named anchor on
the page. For example, take a look at this code:

```
<BODY>
<SCRIPT language="JavaScript">
<!--
var anchor_text="Part 1";
var full_anchor= anchor_text.anchor("part1");
document.write(full_anchor);
//-->
</SCRIPT>
<P>
Part 1 is about this, that and the other thing.
This is irrelevant text in this case used for filler.
```

An anchor is created

13

```
<P>
<SCRIPT language="JavaScript">
<!--
var link_text="Back to Beginning of Part 1";
var full_link= link_text.link("#part1");
document.write(full_link);
//-->
</SCRIPT>
</BODY>
```

A link to the anchor is created

This code creates an anchor that can be referenced elsewhere on the page to get to the Part 1 text by clicking a link. Then you can substitute some text for whatever might be under the Part 1 section of the page. After that, you create a link that points back to the named anchor, offering the viewer a chance to go back to the beginning of the Part 1 section of the page.

Figure 13-3 shows the result of this script when run in a browser. You get the named anchor, the extra text, and the link back to the anchor.

The match() Method

The match() method compares a regular expression and a string to see whether they match. Because it deals with regular expressions, I won't go into detail about this method now.

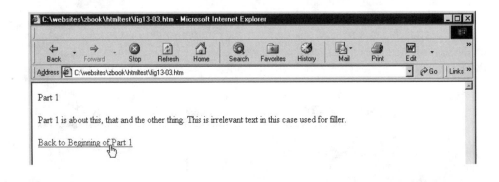

Figure 13-3 A named anchor and a link back to the location of the named anchor

The replace() Method

The replace() method finds out if a regular expression matches a string and then replaces a matched string with a new string. Because it deals with regular expressions, I won't go into detail about this method.

The search() Method

The search() method executes the search for a match between a regular expression and a specified string. Because it deals with regular expressions, I won't go into detail about this method.

The slice() Method

This method pulls out a portion of a string and returns a new string, which is the original text string minus the portion that was sliced. The slice() method takes in two numeric parameters to tell it where to begin and end the portion of the string to be pulled.

This method works much like the slice() method of an array. The first parameter tells it the position at which to start slicing, while the second parameter is one greater than the position where it will stop. For instance, take a look at the code that follows:

```
var the_text="Do not cut this short!";
var shorter_string= the_text.slice(0,7);
window.alert(shorter_string);
```

This code slices the string from position 0 through position 6. Position 7 is where the c is in "cut"; but it isn't sliced because the parameter to end is not included as a position to slice, but is one greater. Thus, the alert will say "Cut this short!"

The small() Method

The small() method places <SMALL> and </SMALL> tags around the text string that calls it. For example, the following code shows this method being used to create some small text on a page:

13

```
<BODY>
<SCRIPT language="JavaScript">
<!--
var the_text="I am feeling small today.";
document.write(the_text.small());
//-->
</SCRIPT>
</BODY>
```

This code creates the following code in the page source:

```
<SMALL>I am feeling small today.</SMALL>
```

The split() Method

The split() method creates an array of string elements based on the string it splits. The string is split based on a character sent as a parameter that acts as a separator.

For instance, the code that follows has a string with a bunch of colons in it:

```
<BODY>
<H2>Fruits to Eat Today:</H2>
<SCRIPT language="JavaScript">
<!--
var the_text="orange:apple:pear:grape";
var split_text= the_text.split(":");
var end_count= split_text.length;
for (count=0; count<end_count; count+=1)
{
  document.write(split_text[count]+"<BR>");
}
//-->
</SCRIPT>
</BODY>
```

First you want to see the string assigned to the the_text variable. It has a bunch of fruits separated by colons (:). The next line creates an array named "split_text" by using the split() method on the text string the_text. The parameter sent is a colon, which is what is used to separate the string into array elements. In this case, the array ends up with four elements.

Hint

The separator character that is sent as a parameter won't end up in the array: it serves only as a divider between the text so the method knows where to begin and end each element.

The next line gets the length of the split_text array and places that value in the variable end_count. This information is then used to loop through the new array and print the elements on the page.

Figure 13-4 shows the result of this script in a browser, which is a listing of fruit names.

Figure 13-4 The array elements created using the split() method are printed on the page

13

The strike() Method

The strike() method adds <STRIKE> and </STRIKE> tags around the text string that calls it to create the strikethrough effect. The code shows this method in action:

```
<BODY>
<SCRIPT language="JavaScript">
<!--
var the_text="I shouldn't wear stripes!";
document.write(the_text.strike());
//-->
</SCRIPT>
</BODY>
```

This code places the following code into the page source:

```
<STRIKE>I shouldn't wear stripes!</STRIKE>
```

The sub() Method

The sub() method adds the _{and} tags around the text string that calls it, creating the subscript effect. This code shows this method used in a script:

```
<BODY>
<SCRIPT language="JavaScript">
<!--
var sub_text="2";
document.write("Water is H"+sub_text.sub()+"O");
//-->
</SCRIPT>
</BODY>
```

This code places the 2 as a subscript between the H and the O, to give the chemical formula for water. This code will be placed in the page source:

```
Water is H<SUB>2</SUB>O
```

The substr() Method

This method pulls out a portion of a string and returns the portion that is removed as a new string. It takes two numeric parameters. The first parameter specifies the beginning of the removal, and the second parameter specifies how many characters to remove.

For instance, the following code removes a portion of a string beginning at position 0 and continues until seven characters are removed:

```
var the_text="Do not cut this short!";
var shorter_string= the_text.substr(0,7);
window.alert(shorter_string);
```

This code removes everything up to the beginning of the word cut in the string. However, the string returned this time is the portion of the string that has been removed. Thus, the alert will say "Do not." Notice that the space character after "not" is included because it was the seventh character removed.

The substring() Method

This method works much like the substr() method, but it allows you to send parameters for the beginning position and the ending position of the portion of the string you want to remove. It then returns the removed portion as a new string.

For example, take a look at the code that follows. Rather that telling the number of characters to remove, you give an ending position. The characters are removed beginning at the starting position and ending at one less than the ending position. (Remember the slice() method.)

```
var the_text="Do not cut this short!";
var shorter_string= the_text.substring(0,7);
window.alert(shorter_string);
```

Again, you remove everything up to the beginning of the word cut. The alert will say "Do not" as it did with the substr() method example.

13

The sup() Method

The sup() method adds the ^{and} tags around the text string that calls it, creating the superscript effect. The following code shows this method being used:

```
<BODY>
<SCRIPT language="JavaScript">
<!--
var sup_text="2";
document.write("I think that 4 is equal to 2"+the_text.sup());
//-->
</SCRIPT>
</BODY>
```

The preceding script creates this code in the page source:

```
I think 4 is equal to 2<SUP>2</SUP>
```

The toString() Method

The toString() method returns a string literal value for a string object that calls it. Here's an example of how you can use this method:

```
var string_obj= new String("Cool");
var string_lit= string_obj.toString();
```

This code takes the string object and uses the toString() method to get its string literal value. It then assigns that value to the string_lit variable.

The toLowerCase() Method

This method returns the value of the string that called it in lowercase letters. Take a look at this code:

```
<BODY>
<SCRIPT language="JavaScript">
<!--
var the_text="I FEEL CALM, REALLY.";
document.write(the_text.toLowerCase());
//-->
</SCRIPT>
</BODY>
```

This code writes the string in all lowercase letters on the page, like this sample text:

```
I feel calm, really.
```

The toUpperCase() Method

This method returns the value of the string that called it in uppercase letters. Here's an example:

```
<BODY>
<SCRIPT language="JavaScript">
<!--
var the_text="I am yelling!";
document.write(the_text.toUpperCase());
//-->
</SCRIPT>
</BODY>
```

This code writes the string in all uppercase letters on the page, like this sample text:

```
I AM YELLING!
```

That's the last of the methods! Now let's test what you've learned.

Ask the Expert

Question: So the length property returns the number of characters in the string, but the string methods start counting at 0. This is a little confusing, just like it is with arrays. Is there an easy way to remember this?

Answer: The easiest way is probably to remember that the length property begins counting at 1, while the methods count positions beginning at 0. Thus, the length property ends up one greater than the last position in a string. So, if the string has a length of 5, that means the last position in the string is position 4.

13

Question: Yes, but it's also confusing because the second parameter in the slice() and substring() methods is a position higher than the point where the methods stop removing characters. Why is this?

Answer: It is confusing in the beginning. You just have to get used to how JavaScript works. The slice() and substring() methods are a bit confusing. But if you use them often enough, then you'll remember which numbers to use in which situations.

Question: Why do I need the split() method? Couldn't I just make my own array and be done with it?

Answer: Yes. However, once you learn about JavaScript cookies, the split() method will be useful because you'll be able to split up the information stored in the cookie to make use of it. Cookies store information in long text strings, usually with some character as a separator. This is one example of when the split() method can be useful to you.

Question: A lot of those methods just add tags around a text string. Couldn't I just write out the HTML for that? It seems easier.

Answer: It should work for you whichever way you feel most comfortable; although with a string object, these methods might be more useful.

pr13_1.html

Project 13-1: Use charAt() to Find a First Letter

In this project, you'll practice using the charAt() method by creating a script that will determine whether the first character in a viewer's entry is valid.

Step-by-Step

1. Create an HTML page, leaving space in the HEAD and BODY sections for scripting.

2. In the HEAD section, write a script that gets the result of a prompt asking for a name, and assign the result of the prompt to a variable named the_name.

3. Use the charAt() method to find out what is entered as the first character of the name in the prompt, and assign the result to a variable named first_char.

4. In the BODY section, add some script so that the page will display the name the viewer entered, but only if it started with an uppercase S. Otherwise, display a message saying the viewer needs a name that starts with an uppercase S to have it displayed.

5. Save the file as pr13_1.html, and try it out in your browser to see what is does.

Putting It All Together

Now that you know how to use the properties and methods individually, let's create a script that uses several of them to see how they can work together. You'll do this by creating a script that will mess with the viewer's name (in good humor, of course).

You want the script to get the viewer's first and last name, change the first letter of each name, and then alert the result to the viewer. The following script does this:

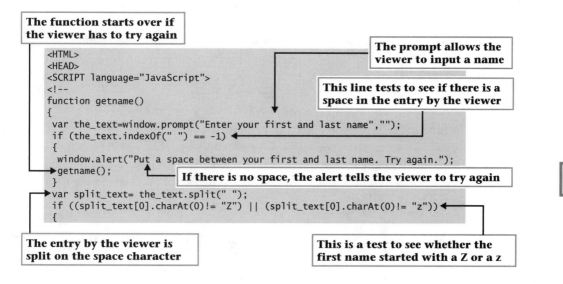

The function starts over if the viewer has to try again

The prompt allows the viewer to input a name

This line tests to see if there is a space in the entry by the viewer

```
<HTML>
<HEAD>
<SCRIPT language="JavaScript">
<!--
function getname()
{
 var the_text=window.prompt("Enter your first and last name","");
 if (the_text.indexOf(" ") == -1)
 {
  window.alert("Put a space between your first and last name. Try again.");
 getname();
 }
var split_text= the_text.split(" ");
 if ((split_text[0].charAt(0)!= "Z") || (split_text[0].charAt(0)!= "z"))
 {
```

If there is no space, the alert tells the viewer to try again

The entry by the viewer is split on the space character

This is a test to see whether the first name started with a Z or a z

13

If the first name doesn't start with Z or z, the first letter is taken out and the remainder of the name is assigned to a variable

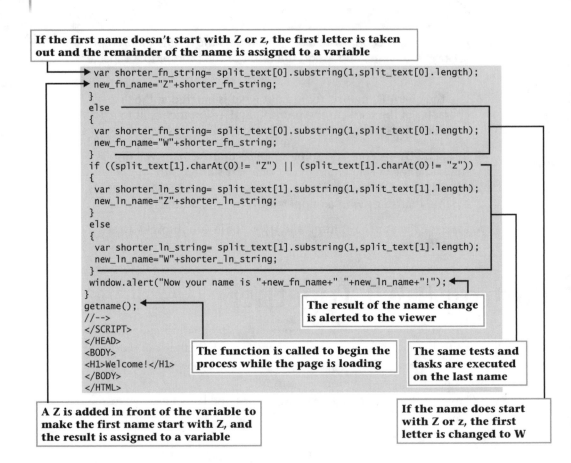

```
    var shorter_fn_string= split_text[0].substring(1,split_text[0].length);
    new_fn_name="Z"+shorter_fn_string;
    }
    else
    {
    var shorter_fn_string= split_text[0].substring(1,split_text[0].length);
    new_fn_name="W"+shorter_fn_string;
    }
    if ((split_text[1].charAt(0)!= "Z") || (split_text[1].charAt(0)!= "z"))
    {
    var shorter_ln_string= split_text[1].substring(1,split_text[1].length);
    new_ln_name="Z"+shorter_ln_string;
    }
    else
    {
    var shorter_ln_string= split_text[1].substring(1,split_text[1].length);
    new_ln_name="W"+shorter_ln_string;
    }
    window.alert("Now your name is "+new_fn_name+" "+new_ln_name+"!");
    }
getname();
//-->
</SCRIPT>
</HEAD>
<BODY>
<H1>Welcome!</H1>
</BODY>
</HTML>
```

The result of the name change is alerted to the viewer

The function is called to begin the process while the page is loading

The same tests and tasks are executed on the last name

A Z is added in front of the variable to make the first name start with Z, and the result is assigned to a variable

If the name does start with Z or z, the first letter is changed to W

This code is placed entirely in the HEAD section of the document and runs as the page loads. Notice that a function named getname() begins. The first task the function performs is to prompt the viewer for a first and last name. The idea is that the viewer will enter a first name, a space, and a last name (although other entries are certainly possible).

Once the name has been obtained, the script uses the indexOf() method to see if the entry has a space in it. If no space exists, there will be only a single name, and that isn't what you want. Thus, if there is no space, the script alerts the viewer to try again and then restarts the function from the beginning. If there is a space, then the script proceeds to the next line after the if block.

The script then uses the split() method to create an array of any data separated by spaces. In theory, a single space should be between the first and last names. If the viewer uses more than one space, then only the first two elements of the resulting array will be used. (They are specifically called later in the script.) So, if the viewer enters **John Doe**, the elements of the resulting array are John and Doe. However, if the viewer enters **John J Doe**, the first two elements are John and J, and the Doe won't be used. (With more advanced validation, this problem could alert the viewer to try again.)

Once the string is split into an array, the script uses charAt() to test the first letter of the first element in the array (the first name). If it isn't Z or z, then the code in the if block is executed. The if block uses the substring() method to get all the letters in the name except the first one, and then assigns that value to the shorter_fn_string variable. Thus, if the first name is John, the variable would have a value of "John." Once that's accomplished, a string value of Z is added to the front of that variable and the result is assigned to a variable name new_fn_name. This basically replaces the first letter in the original name with Z. Thus, John would become Zohn and Mary would become Zary.

If the original name did start with Z or z, the else block is executed instead. Rather than replacing the first letter with Z, it is replaced with W. The next if/else segment performs the same tasks on the second entry in the array, which, if entered correctly, will be the last name. The viewer is then alerted to the result, telling the user the new name. Figure 13-5 shows the result of this script in a browser when the viewer enters **Big Rag**.

| **Figure 13-5** | **The viewer gets a new name in an alert** |

13

pr13_2.html

Project 13-2: Use indexOf() to Test an Address

In this project, you'll practice using the indexOf() method by creating a script that tests an e-mail address that the viewer enters.

Step-by-Step

1. Create an HTML page, leaving space in the HEAD and BODY sections for scripting.

2. In the HEAD section, create a function named "get_add()." In it, assign the results of a prompt asking for an e-mail address to a variable named "email_add."

3. Also in the function, use indexOf() to see if the address has an at (@) character in it. If not, send an alert to the viewer saying that he or she needs one and to try again.

4. Also in the function, use indexOf() to see if the address has a dot (.) character in it. If not, send an alert to the viewer saying that he or she needs one and to try again.

5. Also in the function, if the address has both an at (@) character and a dot (.) character, send an alert thanking the viewer.

6. In the BODY section, create a button the viewer can click to start the function. Label it "Click to enter an e-mail address."

7. Save the file as pr13_2.html and try it out in your browser to see what you can do with it.

☑*Mastery Check*

1. What are the two ways in which we created string objects?

  A. Creating an instance of the string object and creating a string literal

  B. Creating an instance of the array object and creating a string literal

  C. Creating a numeric variable and creating a numeric object

  D. Creating a string and adding numbers

2. Which properties of the string object can you use with both string objects and string literals?

  A. prototype

  B. constructor

  C. length

  D. color

3. Which of the following correctly creates a string literal?

  A. var the_text= "Look at me!;

  B. var the_text= "Look at me!";

  C. var the_text= Look at me!;

  D. var the_text= new String("Look at me!");

4. Which method of the string object can you use to find which character is at a given position in a string?

  A. indexOf()

  B. charAt()

  C. charIsAt()

  D. indexOfThePosition()

13

☑ Mastery Check

5. Which one of the following statements is true?

A. The charAt() method returns a numeric value that is the position of a character sent as a parameter.

B. The split() method creates a new string by removing a portion of the string and returning the string minus the portion removed.

C. The length property allows you to add longer properties and methods to the string object.

D. The indexOf() method returns a numeric value that is the position of a character sent as a parameter, but only the position of the first occurrence of that character.

Module 14

JavaScript and Forms

The Goals of This Module

- Access forms with JavaScript
- Learn the properties and methods of the form object
- Access and use values in various form elements
- Validate the elements of a form
- Use forms for navigation

When you use JavaScript to access forms, you can create new scripts for your Web pages. This module begins by explaining how to access a form with JavaScript. Then you'll learn about the various properties and methods to use with forms and form elements. You'll also learn how to validate form elements. Finally, you'll learn how to use form elements to create navigational devices.

Accessing a Form

Each time you add a set of <FORM> and </FORM> tags to an HTML document, a form object is created. To access one of the forms using JavaScript, you can either use the forms array of the document object, or you can name the form in the opening <FORM> tag and use that name to access the form.

Using the forms Array

The forms array allows you to access a form using an index number in the array. Each set of <FORM> and </FORM> tags on the page will create an additional element in the forms array, in the order in which they appear in the document. Thus, you can reference the first form in a document like this:

```
document.forms[0]
```

As you will recall, arrays begin counting at 0, so the previous example will access the first form in the document. If you want to access the second form, you could use the following:

```
document.forms[1]
```

This will work for the rest of the forms on the page in the same way. Just remember to begin counting at 0 rather than 1 to access the correct form.

Accessing the form doesn't do anything on its own. The form that you access is an object. To make use of it, you will need a property or method of the object. The properties and methods of the form object are listed in a later section, "Properties and Methods of the form Object," in Tables 14–1 and 14–2; but for now, let's look at the length property to see what it does.

A Property Value

The examples in this section use the form object's length property. This property allows you to find out how many elements exist (such as input boxes, select boxes, radio buttons, and others) in an HTML form. For example, take a look at this code:

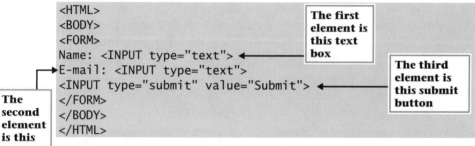

```
<HTML>
<BODY>
<FORM>
Name: <INPUT type="text">
E-mail: <INPUT type="text">
<INPUT type="submit" value="Submit">
</FORM>
</BODY>
</HTML>
```

The first element is this text box

The third element is this submit button

The second element is this text box

The code creates a short form that contains three elements: two text boxes and the submit button. Because it's the only form on the page, it will be the first form, allowing you to access it using document.forms[0]. To use the length property, add it to the end like this:

```
document.forms[0].length
```

Using the preceding code, you can create a short script to tell the viewer how many elements are in the form. (You wouldn't typically use the length property this way, but it's good for an example.) The code that follows will write the information on the page after the form:

```
<HTML>
<BODY>
<FORM>
Name: <INPUT type="text">
E-mail: <INPUT type="text">
<INPUT type="submit" value="Submit">
</FORM>
<P>
<SCRIPT language="JavaScript">
<!--
```

The elements of the form are here

14

```
document.write("The form has "+document.forms[0].length+" elements.");
//-->
</SCRIPT>
</BODY>
</HTML>
```

> **The number of elements in the form is printed on the page**

This code informs the viewer that the form has three elements. Figure 14-1 shows this script's results when run in a browser.

Covering Two length Properties

If you want to try to show the number of elements in the forms on a page when there is more than one form, you can use a more complex script that prints a message for each form on the page. Recall that because forms is an array, you can find the length of the array.

The length of the array is the number of forms on the page (much like the length property of a particular form is the number of elements in the form). To find the number of forms on the page rather than the length of a form, remember not to specify a form by leaving off the brackets and the index number, as in the following example:

```
document.forms.length
```

This syntax finds the number of forms on the page. Thus, you must remember this:

```
Document.forms.length finds the number of forms on the page
Document.forms[x].length finds the number of elements in a specific form on
the page, where x is the index number of the form to be accessed
```

Figure 14-1 The number of elements in the form is displayed to the viewer

This syntax might look a bit confusing, but just remember that one length property is for the array in general, while the other length property is used on a specific form.

Hint

Remember the difference between document.forms.length and document.forms[*x*].length. The former finds the number of forms on the page, while the latter finds the number of elements in a specific form (by replacing *x* with a number).

The following script uses both of the length properties and a loop to cycle through each form. The code displays the number of elements in each form on the page:

```
<HTML>
<BODY>
<B>Form 1</B>
<P>
<FORM>
Name: <INPUT type="text"><BR>
E-mail: <INPUT type="text"><BR>
<INPUT type="submit" value="Submit">
</FORM>
<HR>
<B>Form 2</B>
<P>
<FORM>
Favorite Color: <INPUT type="text"><BR>
Favorite Food: <INPUT type="text"><BR>
<INPUT type="reset" value="Reset"> 
<INPUT type="submit" value="Submit">
</FORM>
<HR>
<P>
<SCRIPT language="JavaScript">
<!--
for(count=0;count<document.forms.length;count+=1)
{
var formnum=count+1;
document.write("Form "+formnum+" has "+document.forms[count].length);
document.write(" elements.<BR>");
}
//-->
</SCRIPT>
</BODY>
</HTML>
```

The elements of the first form

The elements of the second form

The loop to cycle through all the forms on the page begins

The results are written on the page

A variable is created to hold the form number (one more than its index number)

14

The code creates two forms in the HTML document. The script then opens a loop beginning at 0 (where arrays begin counting) and ending before it gets to the value of document.forms.length, which is the number of forms on the page. Because there are two forms (which will make 2 the value of document.forms.length), the count runs from 0 to 1 and then stops. The count allows you to access the forms array at positions 0 and 1, which will turn out to be Form 1 and Form 2 in the HTML code.

The formnum variable has the value of the position number in the array plus one, which is the number of the form as seen in the HTML code. The script then writes the number of elements in each form on the page using the document.write() statements.

The forms array is used with the value of the count variable as the index number, which finds the number of elements in the form that is accessed each time through the loop. Figure 14-2 shows the results of this code when run in a browser.

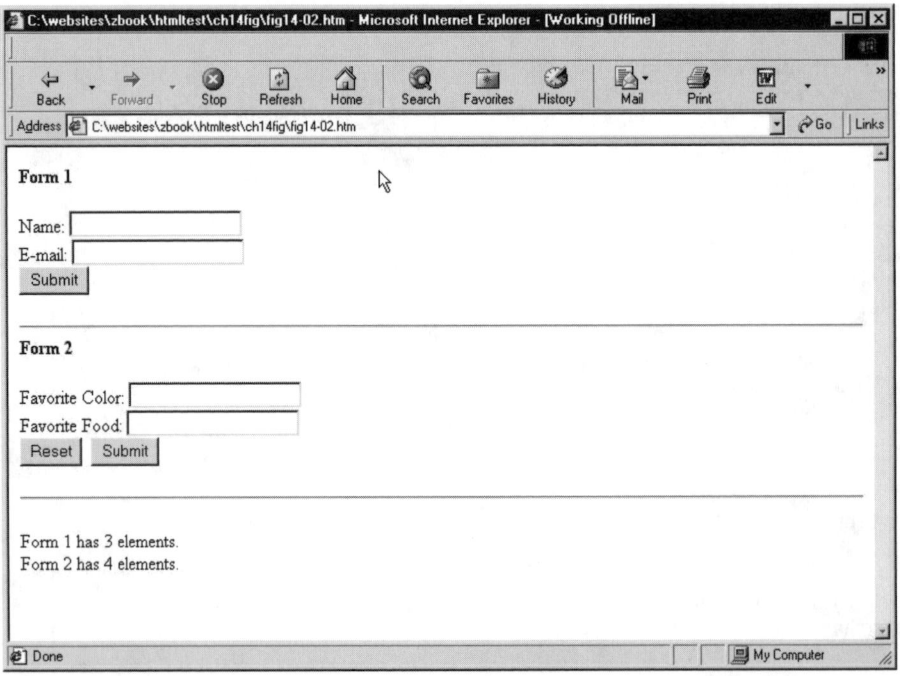

Figure 14-2 The number of elements in each form is displayed

Using Form Names

Using form names allows you to name the forms on the page that you want to access later. This option can help eliminate any confusion between document.forms.length and document.forms[*x*].length because you won't need to use the latter unless you're trying to loop through each element in each form on the page.

To use a form name, you must add a name=*"yourname"* attribute to the opening <FORM> tag on the form you want to access. Replace *yourname* with a name you want to use for the form, as in the following code:

```
<FORM name="info_form">
Name: <INPUT type="text"><BR>
<INPUT type="submit">
</FORM>
```

The name of the form is now info_form, and you can use this name to access the form in your script.

The name of the form allows it to become an instance of the form object that you can access through its name. To use JavaScript to access a form that uses a form name, you can use the syntax shown here:

```
document.yourname
```

Replace *yourname* with the name given to the form in the name= *"yourname"* attribute in its opening <FORM> tag. Thus, if you wanted to write a script to find the number of elements in a named form, you could use the following code:

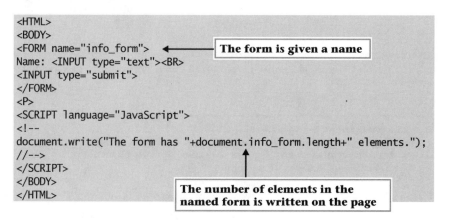

```
<HTML>
<BODY>
<FORM name="info_form">    ◄──── The form is given a name
Name: <INPUT type="text"><BR>
<INPUT type="submit">
</FORM>
<P>
<SCRIPT language="JavaScript">
<!--
document.write("The form has "+document.info_form.length+" elements.");
//-->
</SCRIPT>
</BODY>
</HTML>
```

The number of elements in the
named form is written on the page

14

Notice how the form is accessed in the document.write() statement. Instead of the forms array, the name of the form is in its place. It can now access the properties of the form object and does so by accessing the length property. Figure 14-3 shows the results of this script in a browser.

This technique is useful for accessing forms. It allows you to do so without having to access the HTML code to see which index number each form should have based on the order of the forms in the code. Instead, you can name the form and access it using its name.

1-Minute Drill

● **What form would be accessed by document.forms[1]?**

● **What is the difference between document.forms.length and document.forms[*x*].length?**

● **Where do you add the attribute in your HTML code that gives the form a name that you can use in a script?**

C:\websites\zbook\htmltest\ch14fig\fig

Back   Forward   Stop   Ref

Address C:\websites\zbook\htmltest\ch14fig

Name: [   ]

Submit Query

The form has 2 elements.

Figure 14-3   The number of elements in a named form is shown to the viewer

---

● The second form in the document
● The former finds the number of forms on the page, while the latter finds the number of elements in a specific form (by replacing *x* with a number)
● In the opening <FORM> tag of the form

Properties and Methods of the form Object

The JavaScript form object will help you when you need to access certain elements or attributes of the form in a script. The form object has only a few properties and methods. Let's begin with the properties.

Properties

The form object's properties provide information you might need when working with forms in your scripts. Table 14-1 lists the properties of the form object and their values.

Most of these properties just hold values corresponding to the various attributes in an HTML <FORM> tag. A few of them have different types of values, though.

The action Property

This property allows you to access the value of the action="*url*" attribute in the opening <FORM> tag. This attribute is used to send the form to a

Property	Value
action	The value of the action attribute in the HTML <FORM> tag
elements	An array that includes an array element for each form element in an HTML form
encoding	The value of the enctype attribute, which varies with different browsers
length	The value of the total number of elements in an HTML form
method	The value of the method attribute in an HTML <FORM> tag
name	The value of the name attribute in an HTML <FORM> tag
target	The value of the target attribute in an HTML <FORM> tag

Table 14-1   **Properties of the form Object**

14

server-side script for processing (such as a Perl script). The following example shows how to access the property with a named form:

```
<HTML>
<BODY>
<FORM name="info_form" action="http://someplace.com/cgi-bin/form.cgi">
Name: <INPUT type="text"><BR>
<INPUT type="submit">
</FORM>
<P>
<SCRIPT language="JavaScript">
<!--
document.write("The form goes to "+document.info_form.action);
//-->
</SCRIPT>
</BODY>
</HTML>
```

An action attribute is defined

The value of the action property is written on the page

This script writes the URL on the page given in the action attribute. Figure 14-4 shows the result of this script when run in a browser.

The elements Property (Array)

The elements property is an array that allows you to access each element within a specific form in the same order it appears in the code, starting from 0. It works much like the forms array but has an entry for each element in a given form.

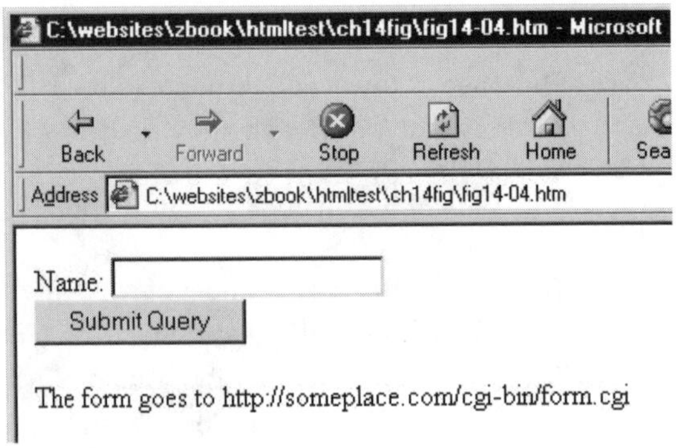

Figure 14-4 The value of the action attribute in the form is printed on the page

To use the elements array to access an element in a form, use the index number for the element you want to access. For instance, the following form has two elements:

```
<FORM name="info_form">
Name: <INPUT type="text"><BR>
<INPUT type="submit">
</FORM>
```

To access the first element (the text box), you can use the syntax shown here:

```
document.info_form.elements[0]
```

Alternatively, if you want to use the forms array (assume this is the first form on the page), you could use this syntax:

```
document.forms[0].elements[0]
```

Yet another option to access the text box is to name it (like with the form) and access it using its name. You can do this with each element, as well as the form itself; you can choose which method is best for accessing a form and its elements in each situation.

The following code gives the form and the text box a name, and allows you to access them using those names:

```
<FORM name="info_form">
Name: <INPUT type="text" name="yourname"><BR>
<INPUT type="submit">
</FORM>
```

In this case, you could access the text box using the form name and the text box name, as in the syntax shown here:

```
document.info_form.yourname
```

To create scripts that use the elements of a form, you must be able to access a property for a form element. Each form element is an instance of an object with its own properties and methods, as shown in Table 14-2.

14

Element Type	Object Name	Properties	Methods
button	button	form, name, type, value	blur(), click(), focus()
check box	checkbox	checked, defaultChecked, form, name, type, value	blur(), click(), focus()
hidden field	hidden	form, name, type, value	none
radio button	radio	checked, defaultChecked, form, name, type, value	blur(), click(), focus()
reset button	reset	form, name, type, value	blur(), click(), focus()
select box	select	form, name, options, selectedIndex, type	blur(), focus()
submit button	submit	form, name, type, value	blur(), click(), focus()
text box	text	defaultValue, form, name, type, value	blur(), focus(), select()
text area	textarea	defaultvalue, form, name, type, value	blur(), focus(), select()

Table 14-2   Form Elements with Their Objects and Methods

The form elements all have their own selection of properties and methods, but many of them are used with most or all of the form elements. To see which properties are used with each type of element, let's look at them in more detail.

The checked Property   This property is used with check boxes and radio buttons. It has a Boolean value, which is true if the box or button is checked and false if it isn't. For instance, use the following code to try it out with a check box:

```
<HTML>
<HEAD>
<SCRIPT language="JavaScript">
<!--
function is_it_checked()
{
 if (document.info_form.yes_no.checked)
  window.alert("Yes! The box is checked!");
 else
  window.alert("No, the box is not checked!");
}
//-->
</SCRIPT>
</HEAD>
<BODY>
<FORM name="info_form">
Check box to say Yes: <INPUT type="checkbox" name="yes_no">
<P>
<INPUT type="button" value= "See the Answer" onClick="is_it_checked();">
</FORM>
</BODY>
</HTML>
```

> The condition of the check box is checked using the checked property

> The form is given a name

> The check box is given a name

> The button starts the function to check the state of the check box

The HTML body has the form named "info_form" with the check box
named "yes_no." A button will call the function is_it_checked() when
it is clicked. The function then checks to see whether the check box is
currently checked using an if/else statement. The if condition uses a
shortcut that allows you to shorten it from this

```
if (document.info_form.yes_no.checked==true)
```

to this:

```
if (document.info_form.yes_no.checked)
```

The checked property will return true or false without needing to test the
value of the checked property against anything. The checked property
already has a value, so the value doesn't need to be compared to anything
(unless you prefer to do it that way, which is also okay).

Figure 14-5 shows the results of this script when the viewer checks the
check box to get the "Yes" alert.

14

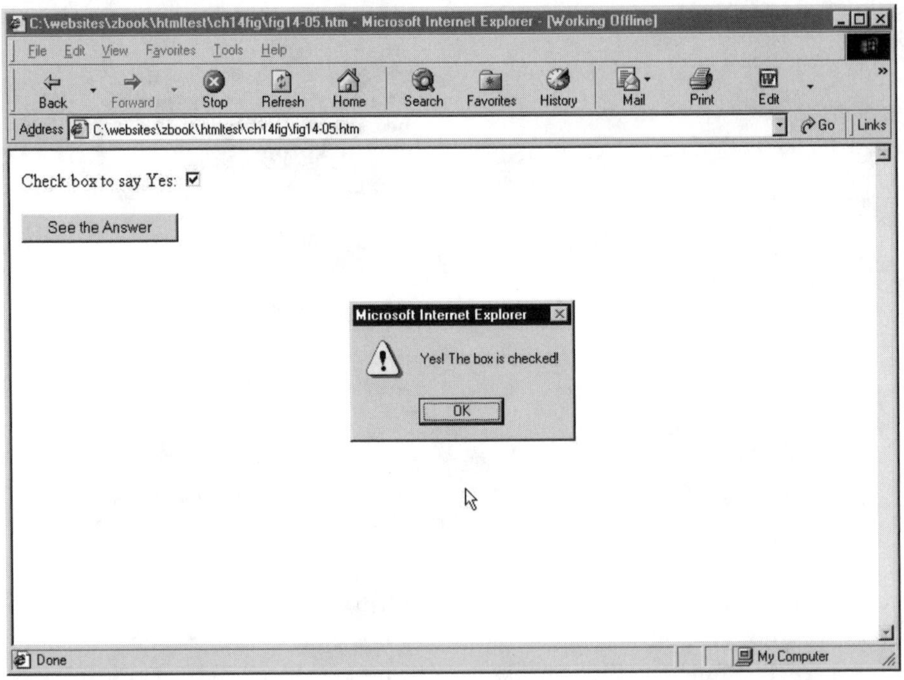

Figure 14-5   The alert shown when the box is checked

The defaultChecked Property   This property is also a Boolean value of true or false. The value depends on whether the check box or radio button has the checked attribute (which sets the element to be checked by default on the page). If the element has the checked attribute, the value is true. If not, the value is false.

For instance, the following code alerts you that the box was checked by default:

```
<HTML>
<HEAD>
<SCRIPT language="JavaScript">
<!--
function was_it_checked()
{
 if (document.info_form.yes_no.defaultChecked)
```

> This time the script determines whether the check box was checked by default

```
  window.alert("Yes! The box was checked by default!");
  else
  window.alert("No, the box was not checked by default!");
}
//-->
</SCRIPT>
</HEAD>
<BODY>
<FORM name="info_form">
Check box to say Yes: <INPUT type="checkbox" name="yes_no" checked>
<P>
<INPUT type="button" value= "See the Answer" onClick="was_it_checked();">
</FORM>
</BODY>
</HTML>
```

Because the check box had the checked attribute, clicking the button will alert the viewer that it was checked by default.

The defaultValue Property   You use this property with text boxes and text areas. It holds the value of the default value set in the value attribute of the form element's tag. This capability can be useful if you set a default value in a text box, the user deletes it, and then he or she decides it would be nice to have the default value back. You could code a button to return that value if clicked by the viewer, as shown in the following code:

```
<HTML>
<HEAD>
<SCRIPT language="JavaScript">
<!--
function back_to_default()
{
  document.info_form.favurl.value= document.info_form.favurl.defaultValue;
}
//-->
</SCRIPT>
</HEAD>
<BODY>
<FORM name="info_form">
Favorite URL:<BR>
<INPUT type="text" name="favurl" value="http://www.yahoo.com">
<P>
<INPUT type="button" value="Reset Default" onClick="back_to_default();">
</FORM>
</BODY>
</HTML>
```

The current value of the check box is changed back to the default value

The text box is assigned a default value

The button calls the function that resets the default value

14

In the HTML code, the value attribute in the <INPUT> tag for the text box is set to http://www.yahoo.com. This gives it a default value. When the function is called, it assigns this default value back to the text box by changing its current value (document.info_form.favurl.value) to the default value (document.info_form.favurl.defaultValue).

The form Property   This property is often used with the keyword "this" to refer to the form that contains the element that uses it. For instance, if you want to change the value of a text box by clicking a button, you could refer to the form by using this.form rather than by using the name of the form:

```
<FORM name="info_form">
Favorite URL:<BR>
<INPUT type="text" name="favurl" value="http://www.yahoo.com">
<P>
<INPUT type="button" value="Change"
 onClick="this.form.favurl.value='http://www.lycos.com';">
</FORM>
```

This code changes the current value of the text box to http://www.lycos.com when the button is clicked. Using this.form.favurl.value allows you to access the same form from an element within it without having to go back and use document.info_form.favurl.value, which is a bit longer.

The name Property   This property holds the value of the name attribute of an element. For instance, the following code prints the value of the name of the first element (the text box) on the page:

```
<HTML>
<BODY>
<FORM name="info_form">
Name: <INPUT type="text" name="yourname"><BR>
<INPUT type="submit">
</FORM>
<P>
<SCRIPT language="JavaScript">
<!--
document.write("The first element is "+document.info_form.elements[0].name);
//-->
</SCRIPT>
</BODY>
</HTML>
```

This is a handy way to find an element name without having to search the code for it.

The options Property (Array)   The options property is an array that contains an element for each option listed in a select box in a form. The index numbers count from 0, and each option is placed in the array in the order in which it is written in the HTML code. The following code shows how you can access the value of an option (this is the value in the value attribute of the <OPTION> tag, not the content of the tag) and write it on the page:

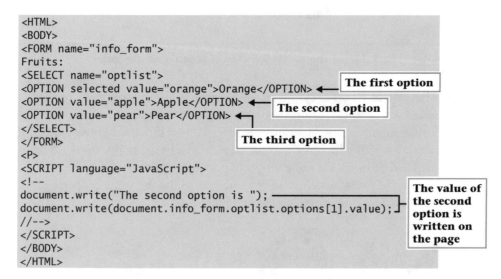

```
<HTML>
<BODY>
<FORM name="info_form">
Fruits:
<SELECT name="optlist">
<OPTION selected value="orange">Orange</OPTION>    ◄── The first option
<OPTION value="apple">Apple</OPTION>    ◄── The second option
<OPTION value="pear">Pear</OPTION>  ◄─┐
</SELECT>                             The third option
</FORM>
<P>
<SCRIPT language="JavaScript">
<!--
document.write("The second option is ");    ──────────   The value of
document.write(document.info_form.optlist.options[1].value); ─┘   the second
//-->                                                            option is
</SCRIPT>                                                        written on
</BODY>                                                          the page
</HTML>
```

Figure 14-6 shows the results of this script when run in a browser. Notice that the value printed is the value contained in the value attribute of the <OPTION> tag (all lowercase), rather than the content of the tag (first letter capitalized).

The selectedIndex Property   This property holds the value of the index number of the option (in the options array just discussed) that the viewer has selected. If the first option is selected, the value is 0. If the second option is selected, the value is 1. We will look at this in more detail when we use it for a navigation script in Module 14.

The type Property   This property holds the value of the type property for a form element, such as type="text" or type="button". The value of the type attributes for these is text and button, respectively.

14

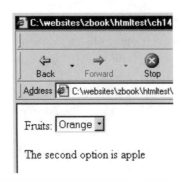

Fruits: Orange

The second option is apple

Figure 14-6 The value of the second option is written on the page

---

The value Property   This property holds the current value of an element. For instance, a text box may have no default value; but when the viewer inputs information into the box, the text box has a current value. If nothing is in the box, the current value would be an empty string. (You used this property for some scripts in previous modules.)

The following example shows one way to use the value property to find out the value of an element and make use of it:

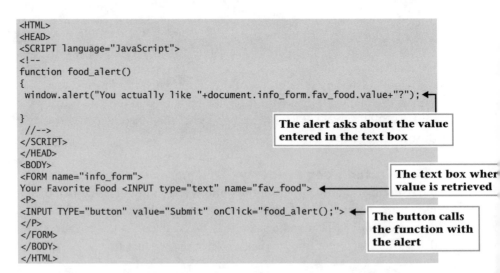

```
<HTML>
<HEAD>
<SCRIPT language="JavaScript">
<!--
function food_alert()
{
 window.alert("You actually like "+document.info_form.fav_food.value+"?");
}
 //-->
</SCRIPT>
</HEAD>
<BODY>
<FORM name="info_form">
Your Favorite Food <INPUT type="text" name="fav_food">
<P>
<INPUT TYPE="button" value="Submit" onClick="food_alert();">
</P>
</FORM>
</BODY>
</HTML>
```

The alert asks about the value entered in the text box

The text box where value is retrieved

The button calls the function with the alert

The alert uses the value of the text box fav_food—which is inside the form info_form—to ask the viewer if the food typed in the text box is really likeable. Figure 14-7 shows the result of this script in a browser when the word "asparagus" is typed into the text box and the button is clicked.

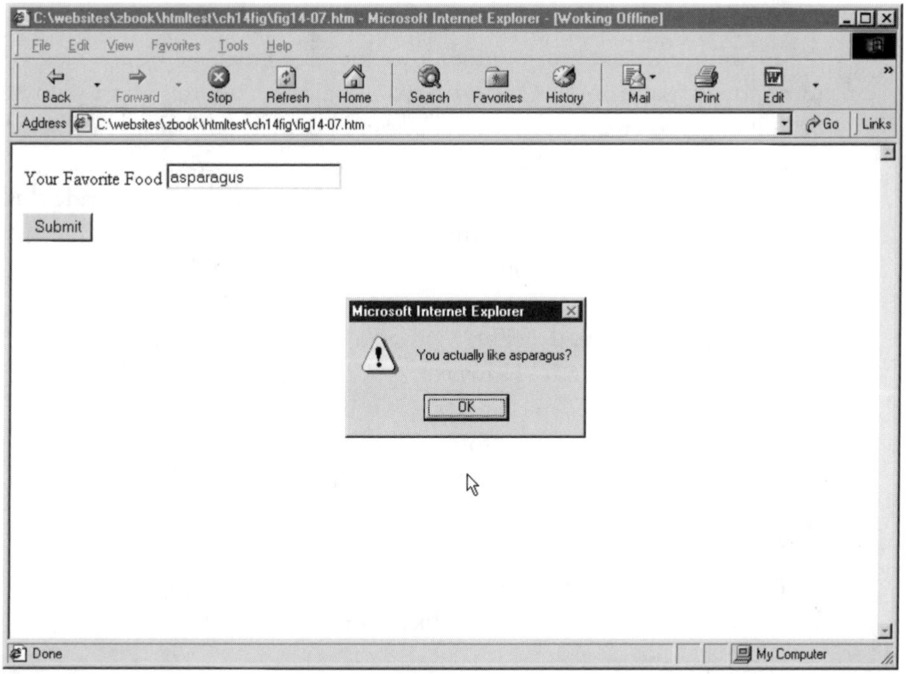

Figure 14-7 Do you really like asparagus, or perhaps it is something else?

You will use this property frequently for information, validation, and navigation with forms. You'll see it a lot more throughout this module.

The blur() Method This method allows you to create a blur event on an element in your code. For example, if you want to keep your default value in a text box from being adjusted by the viewer, you could use the blur() method to remove focus from an element if it receives focus from the viewer. An example of this is shown in the following code:

```
<HTML>
<BODY>
<FORM name="info_form">
Your Favorite Food
<INPUT type="text" name="fav_food" value="Pizza"
 onFocus="this.form.fav_food.blur();">
</FORM>
</BODY>
</HTML>
```

14

Clicking the text box gives it focus, but the onFocus event handler catches the focus on the text box and then uses the blur() method on the element to remove focus from it. Of course, you could also use this script with no default value to create a text box that can't be filled out because it can't receive focus.

The viewer turning off JavaScript in the browser would override this script in either case. (It would ruin any other script as well.) Still, it can be helpful to you in your scripts that use forms.

The click() Method   This method allows you to create a click event on a button in your code. However, a click created this way doesn't activate the onClick event handler if it is used in the button. Thus, the click() method is most useful for activating buttons such as submit and reset, which don't need an onClick event handler to be able to work.

Note

A click created using the click() method doesn't activate the onClick event handler of the button on which the click() method is used to simulate a click.

For instance, a reset button will reset a form when clicked. If you want to reset a form when a field loses focus (and really irritate the viewer), you could use the following code:

```
<HTML>
<BODY>
<FORM name="info_form">
Your Favorite Food
<INPUT type="text" name="fav_food" onBlur="this.form.annoy.click();"><BR>
Drink <INPUT type="text">
<P>
<INPUT type="reset" name="annoy" value="Reset Form">
</FORM>
</BODY>
</HTML>
```

This code uses the onBlur() event to cause the button named "annoy" (the reset button) to be called to action when the viewer removes focus from the first text box.

The focus() Method   The focus() method lets you create a focus event in your code so you can bring a certain form element into focus for the viewer.

For example, you might want to give focus to the first form element on a page (usually a text box) as soon as the page loads so that the viewer doesn't have to click the element to bring it into focus and begin typing. The following code shows how you can do this:

```
<HTML>
<BODY onLoad="document.info_form.fav_food.focus();">
<FORM name="info_form">
Your Favorite Food
<INPUT type="text" name="fav_food" value="Pizza"
 onBlur="this.form.annoy.click();"><BR>
Drink <INPUT type="text">
</FORM>
</BODY>
</HTML>
```

The onLoad event handler in the opening <BODY> tag fires when the page has finished loading. It then uses the focus() method to give focus to the first text box for the viewer.

The select() Method   This method allows you to automatically select (highlight) the contents of a text box or a text area for the viewer. This is useful if you have set a default value for the element and would like the viewer to be able to quickly delete the value to type a new one, or if you want to make it easy for the viewer to copy and paste the contents of the element.

The following code selects the text in a text area when the viewer gives it focus, making it possible to quickly delete or to easily copy the contents to the clipboard:

```
<HTML>
<BODY>
<FORM name="info_form">
<TEXTAREA name="sometext" onFocus="this.form.sometext.select();">
This text is the default text for the text area and is selected
when the text area is given focus by the viewer.
</TEXTAREA>
</FORM>
</BODY>
</HTML>
```

The onFocus event handler causes the call to the method to be executed when the viewer clicks inside the text area. All of the default text within the <TEXTAREA> and </TEXTAREA> tags is selected.

14

That's the end of the properties and methods of the form elements. Now let's return to the properties of the form object.

The encoding Property

This property often holds the value of the enctype attribute of a <FORM> tag. However, the results can be different for each browser.

The length Property

The length property holds the number of elements in a given form on a page. This module has already covered it pretty extensively, so there's no need to discuss it again here.

The method Property

This property holds the value contained in the method attribute of a <FORM> tag. Thus, if you're sending the form to the server to be processed, you might use something similar to the following code:

```
<FORM name="f1" method="post" action= "http://site.com/cgi-bin/form.cgi">
<!-- form contents here -->
</FORM>
```

The value of the method property for this form would be post because it's within the method attribute of the form.

The name Property

This property holds the value of the form's name, which is given to it in the name attribute of the <FORM> tag. You might have some code like this:

```
<FORM name="cool_form">
<!-- form contents here -->
</FORM>
```

Here, the value of the name property is cool_form, because it's the value inside the name attribute of the form.

The target Property

This property holds the value given in the target property in a <FORM> tag. For instance, you might have the following code:

```
<FORM name="cool_form" target="place">
<!-- form contents here -->
</FORM>
```

Here, the value of the target property would be place because it's the value inside the target attribute of the form.

Methods

Now let's look at the form object's methods. The following table lists them.

Method	Function
reset()	Resets the contents of a form, like clicking a reset button
submit()	Submits a form, like clicking a submit button

The reset() Method

This method allows you to reset a form using your script, allowing you to reset the form on any event you like. So, if you want to reset a form after the viewer removes focus from an element, you could use the following:

```
<HTML>
<BODY>
<FORM name="info_form">
Your Favorite Food
<INPUT type="text" name="fav_food" onBlur="this.form.reset();"><BR>
Drink <INPUT type="text">
<P>
<INPUT type="reset" value="Reset Form">
</FORM>
</BODY>
</HTML>
```

The form is reset if this field loses focus

The submit() Method

This method allows you to submit a form without the viewer clicking the submit button. The following code shows how to do this when the viewer removes focus from an element (much the same way as with the reset() method):

```
<HTML>
<BODY>
<FORM name="info_form" action="http://site.com/cgi-bin/form.cgi">
Your Favorite Food
<INPUT type="text" name="fav_food" onBlur="this.form.submit();"><BR>
Drink <INPUT type="text">
<P>
<INPUT type="submit" value="Submit Form">
</FORM>
</BODY>
</HTML>
```

The form is submitted if this field loses focus

14

1-Minute Drill

● **What does the elements array contain?**

● **What does the focus() method do?**

● **Which attribute is used to determine the value of the method property?**

Validation

Validating JavaScript forms is extremely useful. For example, you can validate input before it is submitted to help reduce the number of forms with incomplete or inaccurate information.

However, validating forms with JavaScript alone isn't always smart, because the user might have disabled JavaScript on the client. Still, validation of form data prior to submission to, say, a Common Gateway Interface (CGI) script or a Java servlet can save time and reduce load on the server.

onSubmit and the return Statement

To validate the contents of one or more elements in a form, you need to know when the viewer tries to submit the form. When the viewer clicks the submit button, a submit event occurs, which can be captured with the onSubmit event handler in the opening <FORM> tag.

Thus, the following form would be able to do something when the submit button is clicked, before acting on its action attribute:

```
<FORM name="f1" action="http://site.com/cgi-bin/form.cgi" onSubmit="script">
Name: <INPUT type="text" name="yourname">
<P>
<INPUT type="submit" value="Submit">
</FORM>
```

You would replace *script* here with some JavaScript to be executed when the submit button is clicked. This is often a call to the function that will be run to test one or more of the form fields.

● **It contains an entry for each element in a form**
● **It allows you to bring focus to a form element through your script**
● **The method attribute of the opening <FORM> tag**

For the function to do its work, however, you must be sure the submit button is not able to perform its default action if the viewer's input doesn't pass the validation. This means that you need a return statement in the onSubmit event handler. You want this statement to return true if the validation passes and to return false if the validation fails. Thus, you want an end result to be either

```
onSubmit="return true;"
```

which allows the submission to continue normally, or

```
onSubmit="return false;"
```

which makes the submission void and thus does nothing. (Recall how return false; was added to a link tag in Module 7 to keep a link from changing the page location when clicked.)

For the technique in the preceding code to work with a function, the return statement in the onSubmit event handler must call a function that returns a value of true or false. Thus, you would get a statement like this:

```
onSubmit="return yourfunction();"
```

You would replace *yourfunction()* with a real function name.

The key here is that the function must return a value of true or false so that the previous statement will evaluate to what you need (return true; or return false;). The function itself can do anything else, but it needs to have a return statement that sends back a value of true or false to the event handler.

So, you could perform a validation on a form to be sure a text box is not left completely blank. The following code shows how to do this using a function with the onSubmit event handler:

```
<HTML>
<HEAD>
<SCRIPT language="JavaScript">
<!--
function check_it()
{
 var complete=true;         The variable is declared to hold the
                            true or false value to be returned
 var thename=document.f1.yourname.value;   The variable is given the value
                                           of the contents of the text box
```

14

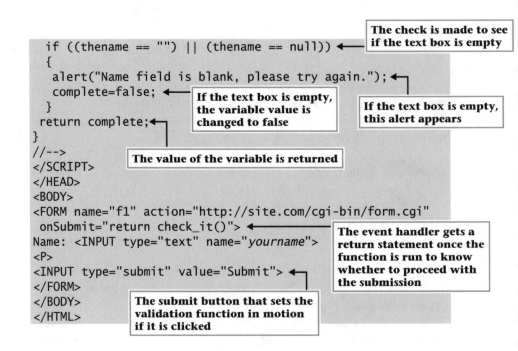

```
if ((thename == "") || (thename == null))
{
  alert("Name field is blank, please try again.");
  complete=false;
}
return complete;
}
//-->
</SCRIPT>
</HEAD>
<BODY>
<FORM name="f1" action="http://site.com/cgi-bin/form.cgi"
  onSubmit="return check_it()">
Name: <INPUT type="text" name="yourname">
<P>
<INPUT type="submit" value="Submit">
</FORM>
</BODY>
</HTML>
```

The check is made to see if the text box is empty

If the text box is empty, the variable value is changed to false

If the text box is empty, this alert appears

The value of the variable is returned

The event handler gets a return statement once the function is run to know whether to proceed with the submission

The submit button that sets the validation function in motion if it is clicked

The function assigns a variable named "complete" with a Boolean value of true. It then checks whether the text field has been left blank with an if statement. If so, an alert tells the viewer to try again and the value of complete is changed to false. The function then returns the value of the complete variable to the onSubmit event handler.

If it returns true, the submission continues. Otherwise, nothing happens and the viewer can try again by entering the necessary information and clicking the submit button again. Keep in mind that the check_it() function invalidates only a totally empty form field. You would need to make the function more complex to eliminate names such as a space, a pound (#) symbol, and so on.

Techniques

For the most part, validation can be as simple or as complex as you need it to be for your purposes. All you need to do is create your own custom functions to validate the form fields of your choice based on the information needed.

For instance, the example in the preceding section checked for an empty text box in a name field. However, for an e-mail address, you could go a bit further by checking to see whether the field contains an at (@) character and a dot (.) character. If not, then you can send an alert telling the viewer the address is invalid and ask for it to be reentered. The following code shows a way to do this:

```
<HTML>
<HEAD>
<SCRIPT language="JavaScript">
<!--
function check_it()
{
 var complete=true;
 var email_ad=document.f1.em.value;
if ((email_ad.indexOf("@")==-1) || (email_ad.indexOf(".")==-1))
{
 alert("Email Address not Valid, please type it again.");
 complete=false;
}
 return complete;
}
//-->
</SCRIPT>
</HEAD>
<BODY>
<FORM name="f1" action=http://site.com/cgi-bin/form.cgi
 onSubmit="return check_it();">
Email: <INPUT TYPE="text" name="em">
<P>
<INPUT type="submit" value="Submit">
</FORM>
</BODY>
</HTML>
```

> **This time the check uses indexOf() to search for characters in the string from the text box**

The code uses the string method indexOf() to see if the correct characters are present in the form field. (Remember that it returns −1 if the character searched for is not present.) If these characters aren't present, then an alert is shown and the function returns false. Otherwise, it returns true.

Keep in mind, though, that this validation is also very basic. An address like a@a.a would pass here. You are, of course, free to adjust the preceding code to your needs or to write your own custom function.

14

As with the e-mail address, other types of input will require different types of validation to check them. Just keep in mind what you need to check to be sure the field is valid.

Hint

One way to find validation scripts is to try checking some JavaScript sites on the Web. A number of them have special functions that are made to validate different types of data. This can save you some work if you can find a function to suit your purposes.

1-Minute Drill

● **Which event handler is used to react to the viewer clicking the submit button?**

● **Why does a function used for validation need to return a value of true or false?**

● **What does the indexOf() method return when it doesn't find the character you need?**

Ask the Expert

Question: All of the elements like text areas and select boxes have too many properties and methods to remember. Any suggestions?

Answer: A number of these properties and methods are used with all of the element types, while only a few are more specific. As you continue to write scripts, you will start to know which elements have which properties and methods and it won't be as confusing. If you notice which properties and methods are used with each element, it will be easier to see when there is one that is specific to a certain type of element.

● **onSubmit**
● **To let the browser know whether it should continue the submission or not**
● **–1**

Question: What types of input can I validate?

Answer: For the most part, you can validate anything you like in the manner you see fit. You can validate dates, names, times, addresses, e-mail addresses, phone numbers, or anything else you might need.

Question: No, I mean, can I validate the selections in a select box or the text in a text area instead? Or maybe some of the other input types?

Answer: In some of these cases, you will already have your own values built into the elements. However, if you can, you should still validate those values against other information to be sure the information you receive matches your needs. You will just need to adjust your function to perform the needed tasks based on the different types of input devices (text areas, radio buttons, and so on). For instance, the next section covers select boxes as they relate to navigation. However, some of the information (such as the selectedIndex property) is useful for validation as well.

Question: I want to validate a form to keep the viewer from submitting a space, a pound character, or something else like you said. But do I really have to keep adding (this) || (that) || (another) to an if statement to do it?

Answer: That's one way to validate a form, but you can improve the validation some by creatively using the string methods. The best way to test values that have been entered in a form field is probably by using a regular expression, but this isn't covered until Module 16. However, regular expressions do offer you quite a few more options for testing input.

pr14_1.html

Project 14-1: What's the Time?

In this project, you'll create a script for basic validation of a time entered by the viewer, such as 2:30, 12:01:21, or other times.

Step-by-Step

1. Create an HTML page, leaving room in the HEAD and BODY sections for code.

14

2. In the BODY section, create a form with a text box that asks

`What time is it?`

Name the form "f1" and name the text box "the_time." Give the form an action of # in the action attribute of the opening <FORM> tag.

3. Give the form a submit button. Because no processing will happen afterward, the submit button shouldn't do anything even if the form passes validation (the action is # from the previous step).

4. In the HEAD section, create a function named "check_it()" that checks to see if the value entered into the text box has at least one colon (:) in it. If it doesn't, send an alert to the viewer that says

`Sorry, the time needs to have a colon (:) to be valid. Try again.`

5. Save the file as pr14_1.html and open it in your browser. See if it works by typing a value with no colon into the text box and submitting the form.

Forms for Navigation

By using JavaScript with forms, you can create some alternatives to the regular text link and image link navigation if you wish. This section discusses ways to create navigation for your site using select boxes and radio buttons. Let's begin with select box navigation.

Select Box Navigation

This type of navigation allows the viewer to choose a destination from a list in a select box, and then go to the new location either by clicking a button or by changing the value. To get started, let's create a navigation drop-down box that will use the click of a button by the viewer to set it in motion.

Button

Creating a select box is pretty straightforward. First, you set up the code for the select box like this:

```
<FORM name="f1">
<SELECT name="s1">
<OPTION SELECTED value="page1.html">Page 1</OPTION>
<OPTION value="page2.html">Page 2</OPTION>
</SELECT>
</FORM>
```

Note that the form and the select box have been given names. The form is named "f1," while the select box is named "s1." These names will be important later when the code for the button is created. Also, notice the value attributes are given URL values (local URLs here).

These are the destinations you want the viewer to go to when he or she chooses the specified option from the list and clicks the button. Finally, the text to be shown for each option is added inside the <OPTION> and </OPTION> tags.

Next, code the button that will set this script in motion. The button needs to perform the action of transferring the viewer to the new destination. To do this, you must be able to access the option that has been selected in the select box and get its value (the URL). Then the browser needs to take the viewer to the new URL.

To access the option that has been selected, you must work your way down to the options array for the select box. Recall that the name of the form is f1, and the name of the select box is s1. So, to get to the options array for this select box, you can use the following syntax:

```
document.f1.s1.options[]
```

The question is, which option do you want to get from the array? You don't want to guess by just inserting an index number of choice, you want the index number of the option that has been selected by the viewer.

This is where the selectedIndex property of a select box becomes useful. Recall that this holds the value of the index number of the option that has been selected by the viewer. By using the value of this property as the index number in the options array, you can access the correct option when the viewer makes a selection. This would get you this syntax:

```
document.f1.s1.options[document.f1.s1.selectedIndex]
```

14

You now have the correct option from the list. Now you must get its value so that the URL in the value attribute is retrieved. To do this, you just need to add the value property on the end of the long line, like this:

```
document.f1.s1.options[document.f1.s1.selectedIndex].value
```

This is now the value you want, which is the URL of the selection made by the viewer.

Next, you must get this syntax into a working form. This value is the URL where you want the browser to go when a button is clicked. Thus, you need a button that will change the window.location property to this value when it is clicked. The following code creates a button to do this:

```
<INPUT type="button" name="go" value="Go!" onClick="window.location=
 document.f1.s1.options[document.f1.s1.selectedIndex].value;">
```

Notice that the onClick event handler sets the code to be executed in motion when the button is clicked. The window.location property is then changed to the new value obtained from the select box.

Be sure this entire tag is placed on one line in your text editor. It takes two lines here because it is so long. There just isn't enough space to write it across the page to get it on one line, so be sure to do so in your text editor.

Next, combine the code so that you have the complete script for the navigational drop-down box. The full code follows:

```
<HTML>
<BODY>
<FORM name="f1">
<SELECT name="s1">
<OPTION SELECTED value="page1.html">Page 1</OPTION>
<OPTION value="page2.html">Page 2</OPTION>
</SELECT>
  
<INPUT type="button" name="go" value="Go!" onClick="window.location=
 document.f1.s1.options[document.f1.s1.selectedIndex].value;">
</FORM>
</BODY>
</HTML>
```

Be sure these lines are placed on only one line in your text editor

The viewer should be able to navigate by making a selection from the box and clicking the Go! button. Figure 14-8 shows the initial drop-down box when viewed in a browser.

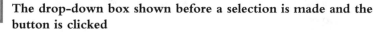

Figure 14-8 The drop-down box shown before a selection is made and the button is clicked

Figure 14-9 shows the result of selecting the option for page 2 and clicking the Go! button. A new page is shown in the browser as a result.

No Button

To create a select box for navigation without a button, you can use the onChange event handler. This change event occurs when the contents of a form field are changed in some way (text is typed, a selection is made, and so on). Thus, to eliminate the button, you could have the browser go to the new page right after the viewer selects the destination.

Figure 14-9 The page displayed after the selection is made and the button is clicked

14

You want to catch the changing of the select box, so you must add the event handler to the opening <SELECT> tag, as shown in the following syntax:

```
<SELECT name="s1" onChange="script">
```

You replace *script* with the action to be performed on the change event. If you want to make the same sort of drop-down box you made earlier, you just need to remove the button and place the code you had in the button's onClick event handler into the onChange event handler in the select box.

The following code shows how this new drop-down box could be scripted:

```
<HTML>
<BODY>
<FORM name="f1">
<SELECT name="s1" onChange="window.location=
document.f1.s1.options[document.f1.s1.selectedIndex].value;">
<OPTION SELECTED value="#">Choose Destination</OPTION>
<OPTION value="page1.html">Page 1
<OPTION value="page2.html">Page 2
</SELECT>
</FORM>
</BODY>
</HTML>
```

Be sure these lines are placed on only one line in your text editor

Notice how the code to change the window.location property is now inside the onChange event handler, and that there is now no need for a button. Also, notice the first option is not active, as it cannot be selected without first selecting something else (which, in this case, changes the page anyway). It is given a value of # just in case, which basically creates a lifeless link.

Radio Button Navigation

Radio button navigation can be a bit tricky because you want only one radio button to be selected, so you must give each radio button the same name to avoid having multiple selections by the viewer. This keeps you from referring to the element by its name, making it more difficult to code the navigation. However, you can use the elements array to find out which radio button has been selected in place of its name.

The following code creates a set of destinations. By choosing a radio button and clicking the Go! button, the viewer is taken to the selected page:

```
<HTML>
<BODY>
<SCRIPT language="JavaScript">
<!--
function gothere()
{
 if (document.f1.elements[0].checked)       The state of the first
  window.location= document.f1.elements[0].value;   radio button is checked
 if (document.f1.elements[1].checked)
  window.location= document.f1.elements[1].value;
}
//-->                                        The state of the second
</SCRIPT>                                    radio button is checked
<FORM name="f1">
Page Resource: <INPUT TYPE="radio" name="r1"       The radio buttons
 value="http://www.pageresource.com">              are given the same
JavaScript City: <INPUT TYPE="radio" name="r1"     name to keep more
 value="http://www.javascriptcity.com">            than one from
<P>                                                being selected
<INPUT type="button" value="Go!" onClick="gothere();">
</FORM>
</BODY>
</HTML>
```

The function checks the checked property for the first two elements in the form (the radio buttons). If the button is checked, the browser takes the viewer to the new location specified in the value attribute of the radio button. The button at the end of the form calls the function into action. If the list of options becomes long, you can use a loop to cycle through and check each element until one is checked instead.

You can also build navigational systems around some other form elements. Just remember to adjust your coding for the various element types.

pr14_2.html

Project 14-2: Select Box Navigation Script

In this project, you will build two navigational select boxes that have five destinations each for the viewer to choose. One select box will have a button, while the other will not.

Step-by-Step

1. Create an HTML document, leaving space in the BODY section for code.

2. First, create a select box with a button for navigation. You can choose the destination sites and descriptions you like. Name the form "f1" and the select box "s1."

3. Place a <P> tag after the end of the form.

4. Create a select box with no button for navigation using your own destination sites and descriptions. Be careful here: *this form must have a different name than the first form!* Otherwise, only one of them will work, if any. Name the form "f2" and the select box "s2."

5. Save the file as pr14_2.html and open it in your browser. Check to see whether both navigation systems work.

☑ Mastery Check

1. Which of the following would access the fourth form on a page?

   A. document.forms[4]

   B. document.forms[3]

   C. document.forms(4)

   D. document.forms(3)

2. Which of the following holds the value of the number of forms in a document?

   A. document.forms[0].length

   B. document.form.length

   C. document.forms.length

   D. document.forms[1].length

☑ Mastery Check

3. Which of the following accesses the value of an element named "e1" in a form named "f1?"

A. document.f1.e1.value

B. document.e1.f1.value

C. document.f1.e2.value

D. document.forms1.e1.value

4. Which type of value should a function return when it is used to validate a form?

A. yes or no

B. true or false

C. maybe so

D. a floating point number

5. What do you use to get the currently selected option in a select box?

A. The length property

B. The reset() method

C. The getSelected() method

D. The selectedIndex property

14

Module 15

JavaScript and Frames

The Goals of This Module

- Understand frame basics
- Access frames with JavaScript
- Frame documents from other frames
- Use JavaScript to improve frame navigation
- Use variables across frames

I n JavaScript, you can perform some helpful tasks with frames. This module provides a basic overview of frames and then explains how you can access frames from other frames. You'll also learn how to change one frame from another frame, and then you'll use some fun frame navigation tricks. Finally, you'll learn to use variables across frames to store and retrieve information.

An Introduction to Frames

Using frames on a Web site is a rather controversial issue. The decision to use them or not is up to you. It depends on your navigational requirements and other Web site issues you might have. If you don't know anything about frames, learning some basic information will help you determine whether they will be useful to you.

If you're already comfortable using frames, you can skim this section or skip it entirely. However, if you have little or no experience with frames, you should read this introduction to frames thoroughly. Frames can get quite messy, especially when you add JavaScript to the picture.

Purpose of Frames

Frames divide a window into two or more separate areas (a *frameset*), each containing different content. This differs from tables in that the divisions in a frameset each contain a separate Hypertext Markup Language (HTML) document, and you can change one of the sections without affecting the other sections.

Note

Each frame shown on a Web page is actually a separate HTML document.

For example, Figure 15-1 shows a Web page with two frames. Each frame is actually a separate HTML document. The HTML document that creates the frames uses a set of <FRAMESET> and </FRAMESET> tags to create a frameset.

C:\websites\zbook\htmltest\ch15fig\fig01\frameset.html - Microsoft Internet Explorer

Back · Forward · Stop · Refresh · Home · Search · Favorites · History · Mail

Address C:\websites\zbook\htmltest\ch15fig\fig01\frameset.html · Go · Links

I am an HTML document!   **I am another HTML document!**

Figure 15-1   A frameset containing two frames

Frames have several applications. For instance, you can use them to create a site-wide navigation system, or you can create a reference system where the table of contents is in one frame and the corresponding content appears in another.

The Code Behind the Frames

The following code contains the frameset element. It puts together the number and structure of the frames that will be shown when the document is opened:

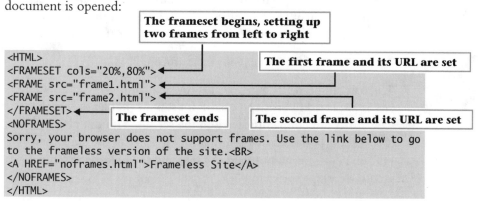

```
<HTML>
<FRAMESET cols="20%,80%">
<FRAME src="frame1.html">
<FRAME src="frame2.html">
</FRAMESET>
<NOFRAMES>
Sorry, your browser does not support frames. Use the link below to go
to the frameless version of the site.<BR>
<A HREF="noframes.html">Frameless Site</A>
</NOFRAMES>
</HTML>
```

This code creates a basic frameset that produces a smaller frame on the left side of the window and a larger frame on the right. Here's how it works:

15

1. The opening <FRAMESET> tag tells the browser that a frameset is to begin. Notice that it replaces the <BODY> tag used in a regular window.

2. The cols attribute of the opening <FRAMESET> tag tells the browser the window will be divided into two columns (which move from left to right). The first column (left) is to take up 20 percent of the screen space, while the second column (right) is to take up 80 percent of the screen space.

3. The first <FRAME> creates the first frame on the page. The browser displays the frames from left to right, top to bottom, in the order that they appear in the source code. Thus, this frame is in the top-left portion of the page—which, in this case, is just the left side of the page.

4. The src attribute tells the browser the URL of the HTML document to display as the contents of the frame, which is actually what the viewer sees on the left side of the window. In this case, the document is a file named "frame1.html."

5. The second <FRAME> tag does the same thing, but the frame is the next one in order from left to right and top to bottom. Again, because there are only two columns, this frame is just on the right side of the window. The src attribute points to the URL of the HTML document to be displayed in this frame. In this case, the document is a file named "frame2.html."

6. The </FRAMESET> tag ends the frameset.

7. The content between the <NOFRAMES> and </NOFRAMES> tags is displayed in browsers that don't support frames so that the viewer has something displayed on the screen. You can place a link to a version of the site with no frames, or you can use any other HTML code you wish. I used the text and the link to keep the section short for the example.

The document created from the previous code is the page you want to open in the browser to display the frames. Save this document as frameset.html so you can use it once you add some code for the documents used in the frames.

Once the frameset is created, you must create the documents that will fill in the frames. First, create a document to be used for the left frame (frame1.html):

```
<HTML>
<BODY>
I am frame1.html, and I am on the left side!
</BODY>
</HTML>
```

This simple code tells you which document is being shown in which frame. (You can make the code as complex as you wish.) Save this as frame1.html in the same directory as frameset.html.

Next, you must supply code for the other frame (frame2.html):

```
<HTML>
<BODY>
I am frame2.html, and I am on the right side!
</BODY>
</HTML>
```

Save this as frame2.html in the same directory as frameset.html and frame1.html.

Now, when you open frameset.html in your browser, it should display the window with two frames, each containing the appropriate HTML document, as shown in Figure 15-2.

Frame Options

As you have seen, the opening <FRAMESET> tag can take on the cols attribute to divide the window into columns. In the same way, it can instead use the rows attribute to divide the page into rows from top

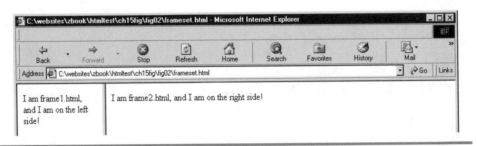

Figure 15-2 A frameset with two frames, one in each column created by the frameset

to bottom. Here is an example of a code that creates a frameset with two rows:

```
<HTML>
<FRAMESET rows="20%,80%">    ◄——  This time the frames go
<FRAME src="frame1.html">          from top to bottom, since
<FRAME src="frame2.html">          the rows attribute is used
</FRAMESET>
<NOFRAMES>
Use the link below to go to the frameless version of the site.<BR>
<A HREF="noframes.html">Frameless Site</A>
</NOFRAMES>
</HTML>
```

This time, the page is divided into two frames, one on top and the other below it. An example of what this might look like if both frame1.html and frame2.html exist is shown in Figure 15-3.

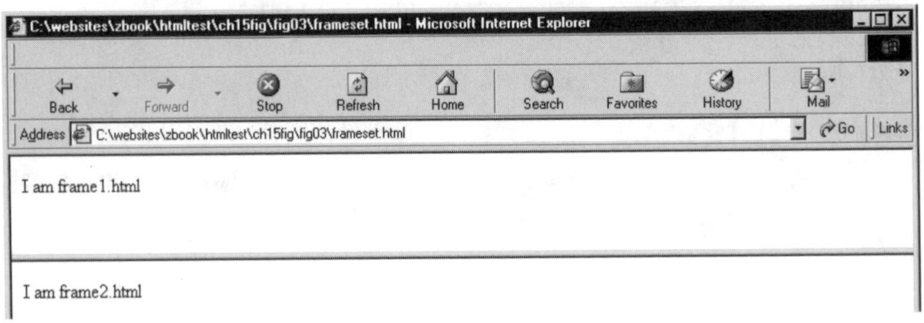

C:\websites\zbook\htmltest\ch15fig\fig03\frameset.html - Microsoft Internet Explorer

Address C:\websites\zbook\htmltest\ch15fig\fig03\frameset.html

I am frame1.html

I am frame2.html

Figure 15-3 A frameset based on rows instead of columns

Rows or Columns

If you prefer, the numbers used in the rows or cols attribute can be in pixels rather than percentages. Also, you can use an asterisk (*) if you want a certain frame to take all of the space remaining after other frames have been set. For example, look at this code:

```
<HTML>
<FRAMESET rows="150,*">
<FRAME src="frame1.html">
<FRAME src="frame2.html">
</FRAMESET>
<NOFRAMES>
Use the link below to go to the frameless version of the site.<BR>
<A HREF="noframes.html">Frameless Site</A>
</NOFRAMES>
</HTML>
```

> The asterisk tells the second frame to take any remaining space not used by the first frame

This time, the first row (top) takes up 150 pixels, while the second row (bottom) takes the rest of the remaining space in the window.

More Than Two Rows or Columns

Of course, you aren't limited to only two rows or two columns. You can have as many rows or columns as you like. For instance, if you want a frameset with three columns, you could use this code:

```
<HTML>
<FRAMESET cols="150,*,150">
<FRAME src="frame1.html">
<FRAME src="frame2.html">
</FRAMESET>
<NOFRAMES>
Use the link below to go to the frameless version of the site.<BR>
<A HREF="noframes.html">Frameless Site</A>
</NOFRAMES>
</HTML>
```

> The asterisk tells the middle frame to use any remaining space not taken by the other frames

Here, the left and right columns have a width of 150 pixels each. The column in the center takes all of the remaining space in the window.

Nesting to Allow Both Rows and Columns

Finally, if you want to have a more complex frameset that includes both rows and columns, you must nest one frameset within another. For instance, you may want a row that spans the top portion of the page that is 100 pixels in height. Then, you might want to have two columns below it: one on the left taking up 150 pixels and one on the right taking the remaining area.

To do this, you need to have a frameset that represents the rows (because the top row must span the entire top portion of the page). Inside the bottom row, you need another frameset that uses columns to divide the lower row into the two areas. The following code shows how this nesting can be done:

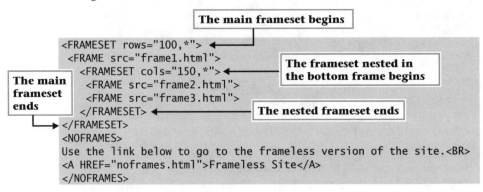

```
<FRAMESET rows="100,*">
  <FRAME src="frame1.html">
    <FRAMESET cols="150,*">
      <FRAME src="frame2.html">
      <FRAME src="frame3.html">
    </FRAMESET>
</FRAMESET>
<NOFRAMES>
Use the link below to go to the frameless version of the site.<BR>
<A HREF="noframes.html">Frameless Site</A>
</NOFRAMES>
```

The main frameset begins

The frameset nested in the bottom frame begins

The nested frameset ends

The main frameset ends

Notice that in place of another <FRAME> tag for the frame in the second (bottom) row, a new frameset is used, dividing the bottom row into two more frames. These frames run in columns and go from left to right.

Hint

Be sure to close each <FRAMESET> tag with a </FRAMESET> tag. As with tables, forgetting one of these can cause the frames to be displayed improperly or not at all.

Figure 15-4 shows an example of how this nested frameset appears in a browser (assuming all the documents and files exist).

```
C:\websites\zbook\htmltest\ch15fig\fig04\frameset.html - Microsoft Internet Explorer        _ □ ×

    ⇦       ⇨       ⊗        ▣        ⌂        ▤         ▦        ◉        ▤▾        »
   Back    Forward   Stop     Refresh   Home     Search    Favorites  History    Mail

  Address  C:\websites\zbook\htmltest\ch15fig\fig04\frameset.html                ▾  ⟳Go   Links

   I am frame 1.html



   I am frame 2.html      I am frame 3.html
```

Figure 15-4   A nested frameset allows both rows and columns to be used in a window

1-Minute Drill

● **What is the general purpose of frames?**

● **What is used as the content of an individual frame?**

● **What types of values are acceptable for the rows and cols attributes?**

Accessing Frames

How do you access a frame in JavaScript? As with forms, you can either use the frames array or name the frame and use the frame name instead. To begin, let's look at how to access a frame using the frames array.

● **To divide a window into two or more separate areas, each containing different content**
● **An HTML document**
● **Numbers in pixels, percentages, and asterisks (*) (to represent the remaining window space)**

15

The frames Array

You use the frames array to access frames based on their order in the source code. You will access one frame from within another frame, so you must be able to find the frame you want to access.

Recall that the frames array comes from the window object. Frames carry most of the same properties and methods as regular windows, but you access them differently. For instance, take a look at this code, which creates a frameset with two frames. We'll name it frameset.html. (This replaces the previous example.)

```
<HTML>
<FRAMESET cols="60%,40%">
<FRAME src="frame1.html">
<FRAME src="frame2.html">
</FRAMESET>
<NOFRAMES>
Use the link below to go to the frameless version of the site.<BR>
<A HREF="noframes.html">Frameless Site</A>
</NOFRAMES>
</HTML>
```

If you're coding some script inside the first frame (frame1.html), and you want to know the value of the location property in the second frame (frame2.html) to display it for the viewer, you must figure out how to access the second frame.

Remember, you're working inside a frameset. You are in the code for one of the documents that will be the content for the first frame within the frameset. Thus, to access the other frame, you need to find a way to get back to the main window and reference the frame. If you remember the window object's properties, you will recall that the top property allows you to access the topmost window in a frameset (the main window).

You can now use the frames array because you have access to that main window, which contains the code for the frameset. The frames array contains an entry for each <FRAME> tag in the code. The count starts at 0 and continues in the order that each <FRAME> tag appears in the source code. Thus, to access the first frame in a frameset, you could use the following syntax:

```
top.frames[0]
```

Using the top property allows you to access the main window and the frameset code. Then, frames[0] is used to access the first frame in the source code. So, if you're coding within the first frame and want to access the second frame, you would use this syntax:

```
top.frames[1]
```

Now, you can make the code in the first frame access the needed information in the second frame for the viewer. The following code is for the first frame (frame1.html) and makes the first frame display the value of the location property of the second frame (frame2.html):

```
<HTML>
<BODY>
The second frame is from: <BR>
<SCRIPT language="JavaScript">
<!--
document.write(top.frames[1].location); ◄─────────────┐
//-->                                    ┌─────────────────────────────────┐
</SCRIPT>                                │ **The value of the location of the** │
</BODY>                                  │ **second frame is printed on the page** │
</HTML>                                  │ **using the frames array to access the** │
                                         │ **information in the frame** │
                                         └─────────────────────────────────┘
```

All the action occurs here in the first frame, but it takes information from the second frame. To complete this script, be sure frame2.html exists. You will probably want it to display some text to know the code is working correctly. You could use the following code for frame2.html:

```
<HTML>
<BODY>
I am frame 2 and the other frame took information from me! How rude!
</BODY>
</HTML>
```

Now you can see the result by opening the main window (frameset.html). The left frame should tell you the location of the document used for the right frame. Figure 15-5 shows how this may appear in a browser. (Your location value will probably be different from the filename.)

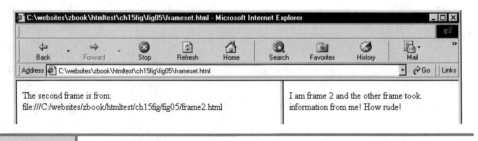

Figure 15-5 The first frame shows information taken from the second frame

The frames array is a good way to access unnamed frames or to access frames if you need to loop through them. If you recall, the length property of the frames array provides the number of frames in a document. Thus, you could loop through the frames array to print the location of each of the frames in one frame for your viewer to see. First, you will need the document containing the frameset to be used.

Again, save this main window as frameset.html. The code for this document is shown here:

```
<HTML>
<FRAMESET cols="20%,80%">
<FRAME src="frame1.html">
<FRAME src="frame2.html">
</FRAMESET>
<NOFRAMES>
Use the link below to go to the frameless version of the site.<BR>
<A HREF="noframes.html">Frameless Site</A>
</NOFRAMES>
</HTML>
```

This time, frame1.html will just have a brief statement:

```
<HTML>
<BODY>
I am frame 1!
</BODY>
</HTML>
```

Now, frame2.html is where the script and results will appear and could be coded as shown here:

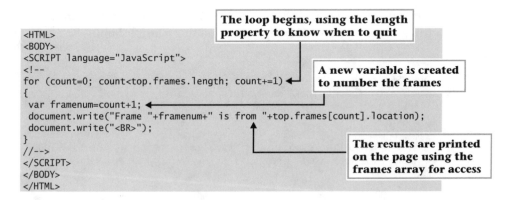

As you've seen in previous scripts, the length property determines when the loop should end. The framenum variable prints out the frame number beginning at 1 rather than its index number in the array (which begins at 0). The frames array is then used in the document.write() statement to print the value of the location property for each frame.

Figure 15-6 shows the results of this script when run in a browser (when frameset.html is opened). Again, your location values will probably differ from the filenames.

Using a Frame Name

Another way to access one frame from another is to use the name of the frame (much like the way you used form names in the previous module).

Figure 15-6   The location value for each frame is printed in one of the frames

For example, this code gives each frame a name by adding the name attribute to the <FRAME> tag (again, call this frameset.html):

```
<HTML>
<FRAMESET cols="50%,50%">
<FRAME src="frame1.html" name="left_side">
<FRAME src="frame2.html" name="right_side">
</FRAMESET>
<NOFRAMES>
Use the link below to go to the frameless version of the site.<BR>
<A HREF="noframes.html">Frameless Site</A>
</NOFRAMES>
</HTML>
```

You can now access one of the frames from the other using the frame name rather than the frames array. Thus, if you want to access the second frame (right_side) from the first one, you could use this syntax:

```
top.right_side
```

In the same way, you could access the first frame from within the second frame with this syntax:

```
top.left_side
```

Now you can make each frame tell the viewer the location of the other frame by coding the frames with a short document.write() statement in each. The document for the first frame (frame1.html) could be coded like this:

```
<HTML>
<BODY>
The second (right) frame is from: <BR>
<SCRIPT language="JavaScript">
<!--
document.write(top.right_side.location);
//-->
</SCRIPT>
</BODY>
</HTML>
```

The name of the right frame is used to print information from it in the left frame

After that, frame2.html could be coded as follows:

```
<HTML>
<BODY>
The first frame (left) is from: <BR>
<SCRIPT language="JavaScript">
<!--
document.write(top.left_side.location); ◄────
//-->
</SCRIPT>
</BODY>
</HTML>
```

> **The name of the left frame is used to print information from it in the right frame**

Each frame now gives out information about the other one. Figure 15-7 shows how the results would look when frameset.html is opened in a browser. (Again, your location values will likely be different.)

1-Minute Drill

● **What are two ways of accessing one frame from another frame?**

● **What is the value of the length property of the frames array?**

● **How do you give a frame a name that you can use to access it later?**

Changing Frames

To change the content of one frame from another frame, you can use the target attribute in HTML for a single change. However, by using the location property in JavaScript, you can change more than one frame at a time. The following sections cover both possibilities.

● **Using the frames array or using a frame name**
● **The number of frames that exist in the main window**
● **By using the name attribute in the <FRAME> tag**

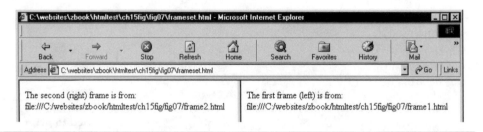

The second (right) frame is from:
file:///C:/websites/zbook/htmltest/ch15fig/fig07/frame2.html

The first frame (left) is from:
file:///C:/websites/zbook/htmltest/ch15fig/fig07/frame1.html

Figure 15-7 Each frame provides information on the other by using a frame name

Change a Single Frame

In HTML, if you want to change one frame from within another, use the target attribute within your link tag and give it the value of the name of the frame. For instance, if you want to change the contents of a frame named "right_side" from another frame in the frameset, you could create a link like this:

```
<A HREF= "nextpage.html" target= "right_side">Next Page</A>
```

This would open nextpage.html in the frame right_side, rather than opening it in the current frame (which is the default for a link).

Hint

Be sure the target matches the frame name exactly. If it doesn't match a frame name or a predefined target, the page to be displayed will open in a new browser window instead of in the frame or window you intended.

To perform the same task with JavaScript, you can use the frame name along with the location property to make it work, as in the following syntax:

```
top.right_side.location="nextpage.html";
```

Here, right_side is the name of the frame to have its contents changed, and nextpage.html is the page that appears in place of the original document. To code this into a link, you could use the return false technique used in previous chapters:

```
<A HREF="n" onClick= "top.right_side.location='newpage.html';return false;">
New Page</A>
```

On the other hand, you could also use a method that allows you to point the href attribute of a link tag to perform JavaScript statements, as shown here:

```
<A HREF="javascript:top.right_side.location='newpage.html'">
New Page</A>
```

Notice the addition of the word "javascript" in lowercase followed by a colon. After that, you can use JavaScript statements as you would use them in an event handler.

The technique in the preceding code also keeps you from needing to add the return false statement to the code. Either method works, although the latter is best used only with newer browsers.

Change Multiple Frames

To change more than one frame at a time, you can use JavaScript. Let's grab the basic frameset again and save it as frameset.html. Here's the code:

```
<HTML>
<FRAMESET cols="20%,80%">
<FRAME src="frame1.html" name="left_side">
<FRAME src="frame2.html" name="right_side">
</FRAMESET>
<NOFRAMES>
Use the link below to go to the frameless version of the site.<BR>
<A HREF="noframes.html">Frameless Site</A>
</NOFRAMES>
</HTML>
```

To change the contents of both frames, you need two additional HTML files so that the two documents in the two frames can be changed to two new documents. Thus, you need a document list similar to the following:

- frameset.html (the main window code)

- frame1.html (document initially shown in the left frame)

- frame2.html (document initially shown in the right frame)

- frame3.html (new document to appear in the left frame)

- frame4.html (new document to appear in the right frame)

You already have the code for frameset.html, so you just need the code for the four remaining documents. The fun occurs in the example in frame1.html, so that's where you'll start.

Frame 1, the Action Frame

This frame contains the link that makes both frames show a new HTML document. To do this, you can use a function and then call the function from the link. Here's the code for frame1.html:

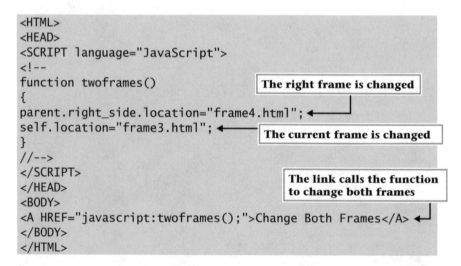

```
<HTML>
<HEAD>
<SCRIPT language="JavaScript">
<!--
function twoframes()
{                                    The right frame is changed
parent.right_side.location="frame4.html";
self.location="frame3.html";         The current frame is changed
}
//-->
</SCRIPT>
</HEAD>                              The link calls the function
<BODY>                              to change both frames
<A HREF="javascript:twoframes();">Change Both Frames</A>
</BODY>
</HTML>
```

The link tag calls the twoframes() function. The function first changes the contents of the right frame by referring to its name (right_side). It then changes the location of its own frame (recall that "self" is a way to refer to the current window or frame, which makes what is being changed in the code a little less ambiguous). When the link is clicked, both documents will change to the new documents.

The Other Frames: Basic Code

In the remaining frames, you can just add some simple code to make the frame identify itself. Here is some code for frame2.html:

```
<HTML>
<BODY>
I am frame 2!
</BODY>
</HTML>
```

Here is some code for frame3.html:

```
<HTML>
<BODY>
I am frame 3!
</BODY>
</HTML>
```

Finally, here is some code for frame4.html:

```
<HTML>
<BODY>
I am frame 4!
</BODY>
</HTML>
```

Once these are all set up, open frameset.html to see the link change both frames. Figure 15-8 shows the initial view of frameset.html before the link is clicked.

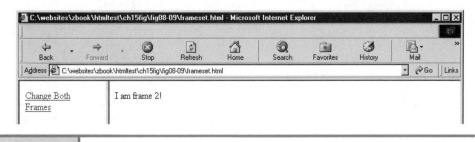

Figure 15-8   The view of the frameset before the link is clicked

15

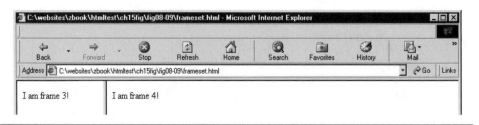

Figure 15-9 After the link is clicked, two new documents appear in the frames

Figure 15-9 shows the page after the link has been clicked and the content of both frames has been changed.

You could certainly use more detailed code if you wanted to. You could set it up with more frames and then change as many of them as you like. You could also code one of the new frames to have a link that takes the viewer back to the original two frames. In addition, you could use the URLs or filenames as parameters to the function.

1-Minute Drill

- **What do you use to change the contents of a frame with HTML?**
- **How do you change a frame's contents using JavaScript?**
- **What is "self"?**

pr15_1.html

Project 15-1: Frame Changing

In this project, you will create framesets and change more than one frame at once. You will also create a frameset that will use one frame to change the contents of two other frames in the document.

- The addition of a target attribute to the <A> tag that points to the frame name to be changed
- You use the name of the frame to be changed along with the location property.
- Another way of referring to the current window that can make window names clearer in the code

Step-by-Step

1. Create an HTML document to serve as the frameset. Create a frameset that contains three frames from top to bottom (rows). The top and bottom frames should each use 33 percent of the available window space, while the middle frame should use the remaining space.

2. Use the following filenames for each frame:

> Top frame: frame1.html
>
> Middle frame: frame2.html
>
> Bottom frame: frame3.html

3. Use these names for each frame:

> Top frame: t_frame
>
> Middle frame: m_frame
>
> Bottom frame: b_frame

4. Save the file as frameset.html.

5. In the code for the top frame (frame1.html), provide a link that causes the two lower frames to receive new content. Use these names for the two new frames: frame4.html and frame5.html.

6. Save the file (frame1.html), and then add any content you like to the remaining files that will be used in frames.

7. Open frameset.html in your browser and try out the link. It should change the lower two frames in the frameset while the top frame remains the same.

Frame Navigation

JavaScript also provides handy frame navigational techniques. For instance, you could adjust the select box navigation created in Module 14 to work from one frame to another.

Or you could create code to allow your viewers to break out of frames or code that sends viewers to your frames if they accidentally enter on a page that should be in a frameset.

Using the Select Box with Frames

If you want the select box in one frame to open a document in another frame, you must alter select box navigation slightly. To do this, you need to change only one part of the code in the select box.

Let's use the standard filename frameset.html to see how the frames will be shown. The code is shown here:

```
<HTML>
<FRAMESET rows="120,*">
<FRAME src="frame1.html" name="t_frame">
<FRAME src="frame2.html" name="b_frame">
</FRAMESET>
<NOFRAMES>
Use the link below to go to the frameless version of the site.<BR>
<A HREF="noframes.html">Frameless Site</A>
</NOFRAMES>
</HTML>
```

In this case, the frames are going from top to bottom using rows. The top frame (t_frame) spans 120 pixels from the top, and the bottom frame (b_frame) takes up the remaining space on the page.

In this case, a select box changes when the viewer makes a choice (no button). The select box is placed in the top frame to allow the viewer to change the document shown in the bottom frame. Thus, you need to see the code in frame1.html, as shown here:

```
<HTML>
<BODY>                          Remember to put these two lines
<FORM name="f1">                on a single line in your text editor
Change the lower frame:
<SELECT name="s1" onChange="top.b_frame.location=
document.f1.s1.options[document.f1.s1.selectedIndex].value;">
<OPTION SELECTED value="#">Choose Destination</OPTION>
<OPTION value="frame3.html">Frame 3</OPTION>
<OPTION value="frame4.html">Frame 4</OPTION>
<OPTION value="frame2.html">Back</OPTION>
</SELECT>
</FORM>
</BODY>
</HTML>
```

Notice that the only major difference in the code for the select box is the first portion of the code in the onChange event handler. Instead of using window.location (which changes the same frame), it uses the name of the bottom frame so that its location is changed (top.b_frame.location).

The three available choices are to go to frame 3 (frame3.html), frame 4 (frame4.html), or back to the frame that was there initially (frame2.html). Choosing one changes the bottom frame to the new page.

The only other task is to add some code to the other frame files (frame2.html, frame3.html, and frame4.html) so there is something to view in the bottom frame. Figure 15-10 shows how frameset.html might look initially, before a choice is made (depending on the code you add to frame2.html).

Figure 15-11 shows an example of how the window might appear if Frame 3 is chosen from the drop box (depending on the code you add to frame3.html).

Breaking Out of Frames

Sometimes another Web site will code links that don't break the user out of the site's frames before arriving at your site. Your site is then left in a smaller portion of the viewer's window with the navigation from the other site still showing in other frames. When this happens, you may want to offer your viewers a way to break out of the other site's frames, or you may want to do it automatically.

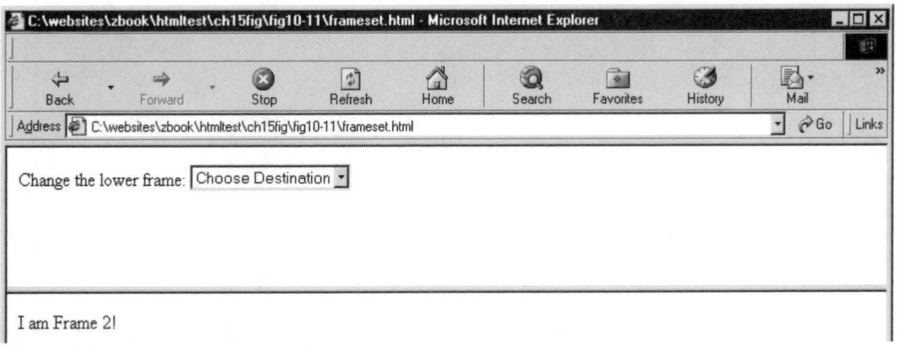

Figure 15-10   **A possible initial appearance of the frameset**

15

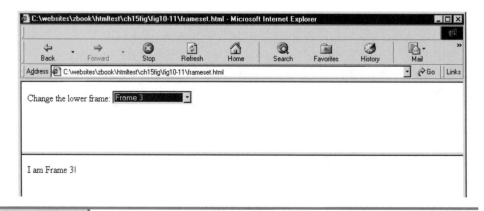

Figure 15-11 | A possible appearance once the Frame 3 option is chosen

Using an Optional Link

You can place a link on your page for viewers to click to break out of frames. You need to add a special target in the <A> tag, as shown here:

```
<A HREF="http://yoursite.com" target= "_top">Break Out of Frames</A>
```

The target of _top tells the browser to use the full window when opening the URL in the link, rather than opening the link inside a frame. You just need to replace the URL in the tag with your own.

Hint

Using a target of _top in an anchor (<A>) tag tells the browser to use the full window when opening the URL in the link, rather than opening the link inside a frame.

If you use frames on your site and want to be sure viewers aren't stuck in your frames when going to a new site, you can use this same target to be sure the new URL is opened in the full window rather than in the frame. The following code shows an example of this:

```
<A HREF="http://www.pageresource.com" target= "_top">Another Site</A>
```

This technique doesn't even require JavaScript (you could do it with JavaScript if you really felt like it), but the next technique does.

Automatically Removing Frames

To remove frames automatically, you must find out if your Web page is inside a frameset when it loads. If your page doesn't use frames, then you can determine whether or not it is stuck in frames from another site pretty easily by using the length property.

If your page is inside a frameset, the value of the length property will be greater than 0 for the frames array in the main window. Thus, you can check for a value greater than 1 in the length property and reload your page in the full window if there are frames. Try this code:

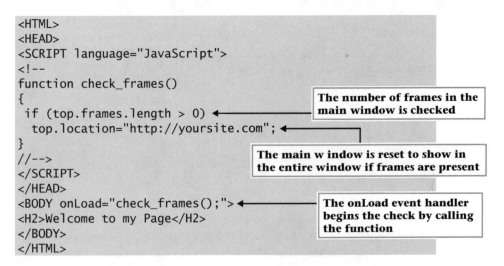

```
<HTML>
<HEAD>
<SCRIPT language="JavaScript">
<!--
function check_frames()
{
  if (top.frames.length > 0)
    top.location="http://yoursite.com";
}
//-->
</SCRIPT>
</HEAD>
<BODY onLoad="check_frames();">
<H2>Welcome to my Page</H2>
</BODY>
</HTML>
```

The number of frames in the main window is checked

The main window is reset to show in the entire window if frames are present

The onLoad event handler begins the check by calling the function

The check_frames() function is called when the page loads. The function checks to see if any frames are in the main window. If so, then the location of the top window is changed to the URL of your page, making your page open in the main window instead of within a frame. You would replace the URL shown in the code with your own URL.

Sending Viewers to Frames

When you use frames, a visitor might enter your site on one of your pages meant to be inside your frameset rather than in the full window. This can happen when a search engine is used, which may index the document and list it. The viewer sees it but may not be able to navigate through the rest of the site because the frames aren't there.

The following code checks to see whether the page is loaded without frames and will redirect the viewer to the main page of the site if the frames have not been loaded:

```
<HTML>
<HEAD>
<SCRIPT language="JavaScript">
<!--
 function check_frames()
 {
 if (top.frames.length==0)    ◄──────  This time the check
  top.location="http://www.yoursite.com";        is to see whether
 }                                                the main window is
 //-->                                            lacking the necessary
</SCRIPT>                                          frames
</HEAD>
<BODY onLoad="check_frames();">
<H2>Some Inner Page</H2>
I should be inside a frameset, the script that is run when this page
loads will check to see if I am.
</BODY>
</HTML>
```

The check_frames() function checks to see whether the length property is 0. If so, your frameset hasn't been loaded. In that case, the viewer is taken to your main page, where your frameset can be loaded. You would replace the URL in the code with the URL for the document containing your frameset (usually your main page).

Ask the Expert

Question: Why do I need to nest framesets to get rows inside columns or columns inside rows? Why can't I just use both the rows and cols attribute on one frameset instead?

Answer: You must nest framesets so that the browser knows where to place all of the rows and columns. If you just tell the browser you want three rows and two columns, it won't necessarily know where to place all of them. For instance, does one of the columns hold the three rows, or does one of the rows hold both of the columns? When the framesets are nested, the browser knows where you want things to appear.

Question: What is that "self" thing again?

Answer: Flip back to Module 10 for a short explanation of this concept. Basically, it's another way to write "window." Instead of window.location, you can write self.location. (You can do this with any of the window properties or methods.) It is just a way to help the code become clearer because with frames, in some cases, it's easier to tell what the code means if you use "self" rather than "window."

Question: Why would I ever want to change more than one frame at a time?

Answer: Some Web sites have so much information that for navigational purposes, changing more than one frame at a time can be helpful. Also, if you have more than two frames, sometimes it's helpful to be able to change all but one of the frames, leaving the lone frame the same for navigation.

Question: I don't like frames and don't plan to use them. Do I really need to read this stuff about them?

Answer: Although you may not use them yourself, learning about frames can help you if you need to code them for someone else, or debug someone's code, or even if you just want to understand what a Web site is doing while you're surfing.

15

Using Variables Across Frames

Another advantage of using frames is that you can use variables stored in one frame in another frame. You could store form information in one frame and use it again in another frame after that frame has loaded a new document, for instance.

The script you'll create now takes information a viewer entered in a form and stores it in the other frame when the viewer clicks the button to send the information. The information can then be used on the page to which the viewer is sent.

First, you need a frameset. You can use a simple two-frame system for this, like the following code:

```
<HTML>
<FRAMESET cols="150,*">
<FRAME src="frame1.html" name="left_side">
<FRAME src="frame2.html" name="right_side">
</FRAMESET>
<NOFRAMES>
Use the link below to go to the frameless version of the site.<BR>
<A HREF="noframes.html">Frameless Site</A>
</NOFRAMES>
</HTML>
```

Save this as frameset.html. You should have a frame on the left (left_side) that spans 150 pixels and a frame on the right (right_side) that takes the remaining window space.

In the left frame, you want a document that contains some variables. This is the frame that won't be changed, so it can keep track of the variable values while the contents in the other frame are changed. For this script, you want to have a variable named "thename" and a variable named "thefood" to hold information the viewer will enter into a form in the other frame. Here is some code for frame1.html:

```
<HTML>
<HEAD>
<SCRIPT language="JavaScript">
<!--
var thename="";
var thefood="";
//-->
```

> Two variables are declared to hold values that will be taken from the other frame

```
</SCRIPT>
</HEAD>
<BODY>
This is frame1.html, it holds the variable values. You can put any
content you like here.
</BODY>
</HTML>
```

The variables are initially given a value of an empty string. The values will be changed when the viewer sends the information from the other frame.

The document shown initially in the right frame contains a form that allows the viewer to enter a name. This name is then stored in the thename variable in the left frame. The code for frame2.html is shown here:

```
<HTML>
<HEAD>
<SCRIPT language="JavaScript">
<!--
function store_info()
{
top.left_side.thename= document.f1.yourname.value;
self.location="frame3.html";
}
//-->
</SCRIPT>
</HEAD>
<BODY>
I'd like to get your name. Please enter it below.
<P>
<FORM name="f1">
Your Name:
<INPUT type="text" name="yourname" size="25">
<P>
<INPUT type="button" value="Continue" onClick="store_info();">
</FORM>
</BODY>
</HTML>
```

> **The variable in the left frame is given a value from the form in the current frame**

> **The document in the frame is changed**

> **The button calls the function to begin the action**

The store_info() function is called when the viewer clicks the button to continue. Notice the use of top.left_side to access the left frame. Then the variable name is added (top.left_side.thename) to access the thename variable in the other frame. The value that has been entered into the text box in the form is then assigned to the thename variable in the left frame. After that, the document in the frame is changed to frame3.html, which will be able to get the information back from the left frame.

15

In the frame3.html document, the viewer's name is written in a greeting. It is also filled into a field in a new form to keep the viewer from writing it over again. (This just shows a use for the stored variable value; you don't really need the name in the form again in this case.) The form also asks for the viewer's favorite food, which the viewer must enter. The code for this page is shown here:

```
<HTML>
<HEAD>
<SCRIPT language="JavaScript">
<!--
  function more_info()
  {
top.left_side.thefood= document.f2.yourfood.value;
self.location="frame4.html";
}
//-->
</SCRIPT>
</HEAD>
<BODY onLoad="document.f2.yourname.value=top.left_side.thename;">
<SCRIPT language= "JavaScript">
<!--
document.write("Hi, "+top.left_side.thename+"!<BR>");
//-->
</SCRIPT>
Now I'd like to get your favorite food, please enter it below:
<P>
<FORM name="f2">
Your Name:
<INPUT type="text" name="yourname" size="25">
<BR>
Favorite Food:
<INPUT type="text" name="yourfood" size="25">
<P>
<INPUT type="button" value="Continue" onClick="more_info();">
</FORM>
</BODY>
</HTML>
```

> The value from the Food field in the form is stored in the variable in the left frame

> The value of the first text box is set using information stored in a variable in the left frame

> The document in the frame is changed

> The value of the variable in the left frame is used to write a greeting as well

> The button calls the function when clicked

Here, the form field for the name is given the value from the left frame when the page loads. The name is also printed in a greeting on the page. After the viewer fills in a food and clicks the button, the value is stored in the thefood variable in the left frame and the document in the frame is changed to frame4.html.

In frame4.html, the values of both of the variables stored in the left frame will just be used to print a special message for the viewer on the page, as shown in the following code:

```
<HTML>
<HEAD>
<SCRIPT language="JavaScript">
<!--
 function print_info()
{
 document.write("Thank you, "+top.left_side.thename+"!");
 document.write("<P>");
 document.write("You must really like "+top.left_side.thefood+"!");
}
//-->
</SCRIPT>
</HEAD>
<BODY>
<SCRIPT language="JavaScript">
<!--
print_info();
//-->
</SCRIPT>
</BODY>
</HTML>
```

> **The information stored in variables in the left frame is printed for the viewer**

> **The function is called here**

The information is just printed out in a message to the viewer in the preceding code. The printed information marks the end of the line for this script because there are no more forms or variables to use. (You could add more forms and variables if you wanted to, though.) Figure 15-12 shows how frameset.html looks initially, before anything is changed.

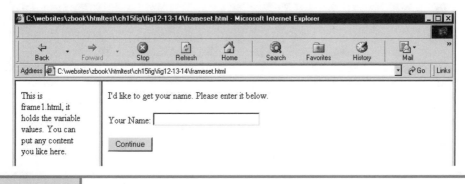

Figure 15-12   The initial appearance of the frameset

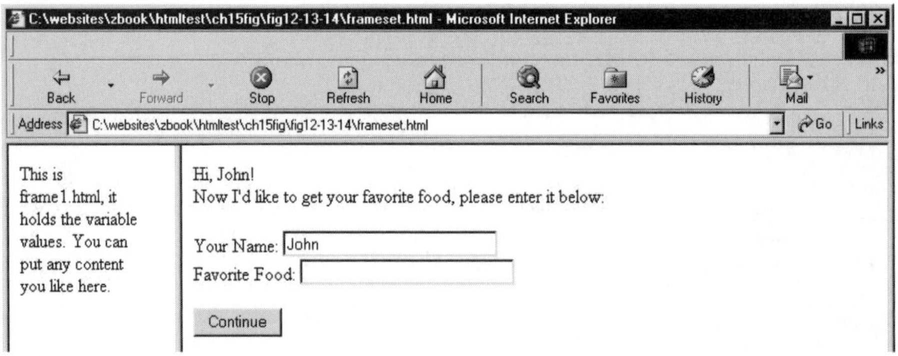

Figure 15-13 The result of entering John into the first form and clicking the button

Figure 15-13 shows how the page looks if the viewer enters **John** as the name in the first form and clicks the button.

Figure 15-14 shows how the page looks if the viewer enters **sandpaper** as the food in the second form and clicks the button. This doesn't sound very tasty.

Remember that even though frames are useful in various contexts, you shouldn't go overboard. Frames require minimal screen real estate and may not be suitable for devices with small screens.

If you do want to use them, just remember to add the tag set <NOFRAMES> and </NOFRAMES> and to offer a frameless version for viewers with smaller screens or screen resolutions.

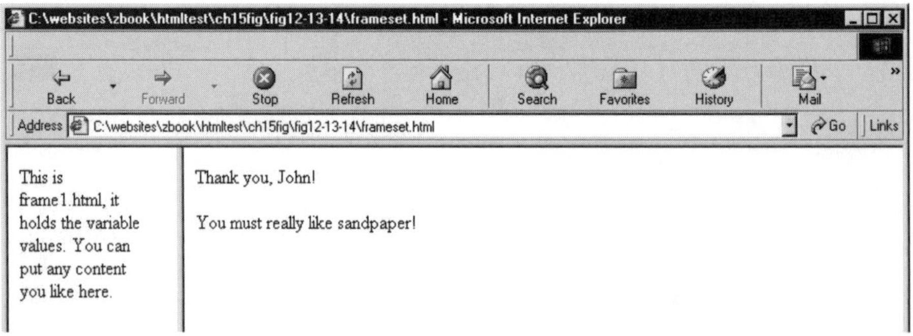

Figure 15-14 Eating sandpaper is not recommended!

pr15_2.html

Project 15-2: Variables Again

In this project, you'll practice storing variable values in a static frame and using them in another frame. You'll create a form that lets the viewer fill in some information and then uses the information when the document in the frame is changed.

Step-by-Step

1. Create a frameset with two frames, one on the left taking up 150 pixels and one on the right that uses the remainder of the window space. Name the left frame left_side and the right frame right_side. The filename for the first frame should be frame1.html, and the filename for the second frame should be frame2.html. Save the frameset file as frameset.html.

2. In frame1.html, create three variables and assign empty strings as their initial values. Use these variable names:

> thename
> thecolor
> thecar

3. In frame2.html, create a form that asks the viewer for a name, a favorite color, and a favorite car. When a button is clicked, the information should be stored in the variables in the left frame and the document should be changed to frame3.html.

4. In frame3.html, the following greeting should be printed on the page for the viewer, using the values stored in the variables in the left frame:

> Hello, *<viewer's name>*! I bet you would really love to have a *<favorite color>* *<favorite car>*! Too bad I can't give you one!

5. Open frameset.html in your browser and try it out.

✓Mastery Check

1. What are two methods that can be used to access frames?

   A. The frames array or a frame name

   B. The frame array or a frame name

☑ *Mastery Check*

    C. The frames array or a special code

    D. There is only one way to do it

2. What is the value of the length property of the frames array?

    A. The length of a specific frame based on its width or height

    B. The number of framesets on a page

    C. The number of frames in a window

    D. The number of arrays in a frame

3. What does an asterisk (*) mean when used in the rows or cols attribute of a frameset?

    A. There's no room for another frame.

    B. The frame should take up any remaining space in the window.

    C. The frame never ends.

    D. The frame is shown in a pop-up window.

4. What is used to access the main window so that you can access another frame?

    A. top

    B. self

    C. window

    D. this

5. Which of these would correctly change the document in a frame named "right_side" to frame3.html from another frame?

    A. self.location="frame3.html";

    B. top.right-side.location="frame3.html";

    C. self.location="frame3.htm";

    D. top.location="frame03.html";

Module 16

An Introduction to Advanced Techniques

The Goals of This Module

- Learn how XML and XHTML affect your code
- Debug troublesome scripts
- Use regular expressions
- Use JavaScript cookies

This module covers several advanced techniques that may affect your JavaScript code. You'll see how XML and XHTML can affect your JavaScript code, you'll learn how to debug troublesome scripts, and you'll learn how to use regular expressions and cookies.

XML and XHTML

Throughout this book, you've been using Hypertext Markup Language (HTML) for your documents. However, as you become a more experienced programmer, you'll want to know about other languages and technologies that can affect your coding. Extensible Markup Language (XML) is where HTML is headed; eventually, XML will influence your documents. In the short term, however, you don't need to worry. HTML will almost surely work for a long time to come. But if you want to stay on the cutting edge, you should at least learn the basics about XML.

XML is a *metalanguage* (a language used to describe another language) that provides a way to separate document structure from its presentation. Recall that in HTML, you can use tables and other tags to present the layout of a Web page. XML provides meaningful tags for better searching ability and allows the data in the page to be extracted more easily. Style sheets manage the layout, while XML manages the data.

How XML Affects Code

XHTML 1.0 is being implemented for the transition between HTML and XHTML. To see how XHTML affects your code, you need to know a few rules about how XML works:

- All tags must be closed

- Elements are case sensitive

- All attributes need quote marks

- All elements must be properly nested

- The name attribute is replaced by the id attribute

All Tags Must Be Closed

This rule applies mainly to empty elements that don't require a closing tag in HTML because they have no content (some data to place between two tags). For example, the img element is empty and doesn't require a closing tag in HTML, as in the following code:

```
<img src="filename.gif">
```

However, in XHTML, it needs to be closed. The good news is that XHTML offers a shortcut to allow you to open and close an empty tag without writing out the closing tag. The following code shows how:

```
<img src="filename.gif" />
```

At the end of the tag, you can add a space and then the forward slash (/) before the greater than (>) character to close the tag using the shortcut. This strategy also works for other similar tags. While this system still requires some extra work, it is still a little less trouble than writing out the closing tag each time.

Also, recall that HTML is lenient, so a tag like the paragraph tag (even though it isn't empty) doesn't require a closing tag. In the new system, the tag now needs to be closed (if used).

Elements Are Case Sensitive

In HTML, you can use any capitalization scheme you like. For instance, you can use <SCRIPT></script>, <script></SCRIPT>, <Script></SCRIPT>, or even <sCRIPT></SCRIPt> if you want to add a script to the page.

In XHTML, however, every element is case sensitive. The opening tag's case must exactly match the closing tag's case. To make a page compliant with the XHTML specification, the tag names and attribute names must also be in all lowercase letters. Thus, the following code would cause problems in XHTML:

```
<SCRIPT LANGUAGE="JavaScript">
var x=1;
</SCRIPT>
```

This code is fine in HTML, but in XHTML, everything other than the content between the tags and the value of the attribute must be lowercase. To fix the previous code, you could use this:

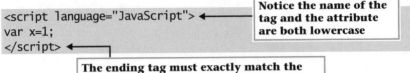

```
<script language="JavaScript">
var x=1;
</script>
```

Notice the name of the tag and the attribute are both lowercase

The ending tag must exactly match the starting tag, so it must be all lowercase

If you want your markup to validate in XHTML, start coding your elements and attribute names in all lowercase to get in the habit.

All Attributes Need Quotation Marks

In XHTML, you also need to be sure each attribute value is enclosed in quotation marks. Recall that in HTML, you can get away with code like the following:

```
<img src="filename.gif" width=100 height=100>
```

In XHTML, all of the attributes must be inside quotes. To fix the previous code, you just need to add quotation marks around the width and height values, as shown here:

```
<img src="filename.gif" width="100" height="100">
```

Another similar point is that you can list attributes as merely the attribute name in HTML, but you must write them out in XHTML.

For example, recall that in HTML, you can have a check box be checked by default by using the checked attribute, as shown here:

```
<input type="checkbox" name="cb1" value="yes" checked>
```

In XHTML, you must write out the checked attribute completely (which may appear a bit redundant, but it's required). The following code shows how to do it with XHTML:

```
<input type="checkbox" name="cb1" value="yes" checked="checked">
```

This practice adds more consistency to the code, like many of these other rules do.

All Elements Must Be Properly Nested

Another rule is that you must nest all of your elements properly. This means that the element that was opened first must be closed last, and the element opened last must be closed first. For instance, you can use this code in HTML with no trouble:

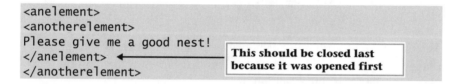

```
<anelement>
<anotherelement>
Please give me a good nest!
</anelement>  ◄──────────  This should be closed last
</anotherelement>              because it was opened first
```

Notice that the font element is the first to be opened but also the first to be closed. In XHTML, closing elements in the wrong order isn't allowed. To fix the problem in the preceding code, you must be sure the inside element is closed first and the outside element is closed last, as shown here:

```
<anelement>
<anotherelement>
Please give me a good nest!
</anotherelement>
</anelement>
```

The entire document must work like this, so you must close the body element before the HTML element and other similar nested elements. In this way, you can avoid having trouble with any nested elements in an XHTML document.

A Name Becomes an ID

This rule is probably the most significant change because it relates to JavaScript. Recall that you have been able to access form elements and other items by using the value inside the name attribute. However, in XHTML, the name attribute is dropped in favor of the id attribute to name an element for reference.

As a result, the following code isn't suitable in XHTML:

```
<form name="f1">
<input type="text" name="t1">
</form>
```

Instead, XHTML requires the code to look like this:

```
<form id="f1">
<input type="text" id="t1">
</form>
```

The use of the id attribute actually makes the code shorter, so it's a positive change. The only trouble with this rule is that browsers that don't recognize the id attribute will ignore it.

So until you feel safe switching completely, you might decide to use both attributes. Some browsers will ignore the name attribute, and others will ignore the id attribute. Thus, you could use the following code:

```
<form name="f1" id="f1">
<input type="text" name="t1" id="t1">
</form>
```

While using both the name and id attributes seems a bit redundant, it can help you if your site receives a lot of visitors with older browsers and you are using scripts that reference the elements. The visitors will at least be glad they aren't getting JavaScript errors.

Where to Learn More About XML and XHTML

An in-depth discussion of XML and XHTML is beyond the scope of this book. If the topic interests you, you can find more information and specifications by visiting the World Wide Web Consortium Web site. For XML, use this URL: http://www.w3.org/XML/.

For XHTML, use this URL: http://www.w3.org/TR/xhtml1/.

In addition, other sites have tutorials on the subject, including these: http://tech.irt.org/articles/js192/index.htm and http://www.webmonkey.com.

1-Minute Drill

- **Is XHTML case sensitive?**
- **Does XHTML allow you to use empty tags without closing them, like you can with HTML?**
- **Which attribute replaces the name attribute to reference an element through scripting?**

Debugging Scripts

Even though JavaScript is fun, sometimes it can also be quite frustrating. One error in the code can cause an entire script to run incorrectly or not to run at all. Debugging a script can be quite annoying, but the process is easier with a little knowledge. The first step in debugging a script is to figure out what type of error is likely to be causing the problem.

Types of Errors

The two main types of errors are syntax errors and logical errors. A syntax error occurs when the coder forgets to add a semicolon, forgets a quotation mark, misspells a word, and so on. A logical error occurs when the code is implemented incorrectly.

For example, a while loop could go on infinitely if the condition for executing the loop never becomes false. While it may be coded with the correct syntax, the results won't be what the programmer expected.

Find the Syntax Errors

A syntax error could be as simple as leaving out a necessary semicolon. For example, the following code is missing a semicolon between statements:

```
<INPUT type="button" value="Click" onClick="analert() analert2()">
```

- Yes
- No
- The id attribute

In this case, the semicolon is very important because the two statements (function calls) are on the same line. To fix this, you just need to add the needed semicolon, as shown here:

```
<INPUT type="button" value="Click" onClick="analert();analert2()">
```

Syntax errors often cause the browser to display an error message so you can debug the script. For example, you might see a message like the one in Figure 16-1.

These messages can help you figure out what's causing the problem. The line number shown in the error message often tells you where the error is.

For instance, if the message says the error is on line 15, you would start at the 15th line from the top of your document and see what's there. The rest of the message might tell you what's missing or what has been placed improperly.

However, some times the line stated in the message is not the line where the actual problem is located. It could be on the preceding line, a few lines away, or it could even be somewhere else entirely. You will need to do a little searching to figure out where the problem started. (The upcoming sectin "Scanning the Script" covers this in more detail.)

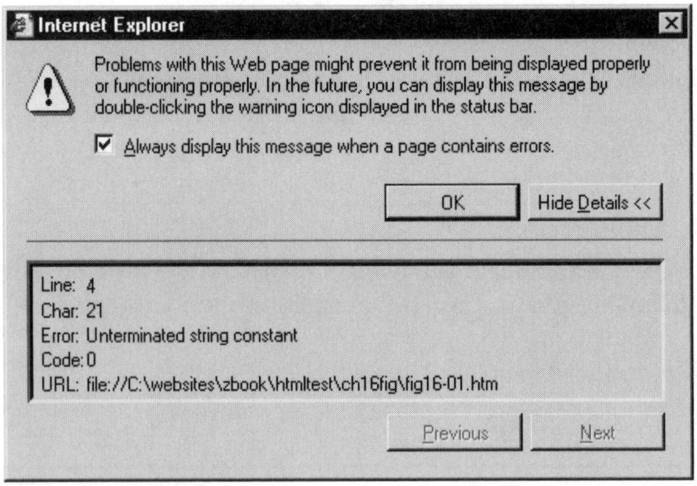

Figure 16-1 A JavaScript error message

Use the Error Message   If you get an error message, it can either make the problem easier to find or give you a bigger headache. Some messages are just better than others. First, go to the line given in the error message. If the text in the message makes any sense (such as "Expected ';'"), then look to see if the message is leading you in the right direction. For example, if it tells you it was expecting a semicolon, then look to see if a semicolon is missing on that line or on a line near it.

If you don't see a problem in the near vicinity, you'll have to search for it. If the line in question is calling a function or using a variable from another part of the script, take a look at where the function or variable was defined. Go to the function or variable to see if the name is the same as what you used to call it. If so, see if all the syntax is correct (such as the curly brackets, quotation marks, and parentheses). For instance, look at the following code:

```
<HTML>
<HEAD>
<SCRIPT language="JavaScript">
<!--
function cool()
window.alert("Cool!");          Notice the opening bracket that
}                               is missing between these lines
//-->
</SCRIPT>
</HEAD>
<BODY>
<INPUT type="button" value="Click" onClick="cool();"></input>
</BODY>
</HTML>
```

The code will produce an error message in Internet Explorer saying "Object Expected" when you click the Click button, and it points to the line in the code where the button is placed on the page (line 12, in this case). If you look at that line, nothing appears to be wrong.

However, if you go back to the function cool() that is called on that line, you will notice that the opening curly bracket is missing. The missing bracket is the problem, and adding it in will fix the code.

Scanning the Script If the error message doesn't help you locate the problem, try scanning the script for errors on your own. This solution can be more tedious, but it may help you find the problem if the error message isn't helpful. Table 16-1 shows some items you should try to find.

The following code is riddled with errors; see how many of them you can find.

```
<SCRIPT language="JavaScript">
<!--
var mycar="Mustang";
function send_alert()
 window.alery("You like+mybar+"!");
 window.alert("Cool";
}
var somearray= neq Array(2)
somearray[0]="Me";
somearray1]="Me2";
for count=0;count<somearray.length;count+=1)
{
 document.write(somearray[0+"and"+somearray[1]);
//-->
</SCRIPT>
```

The code is missing a number of necessary items. Following is the list of items you should have found:

- Between lines 4 and 5: The function is missing its opening curly bracket.

- Line 5: The word *alert* is misspelled as *alery*; the double quote mark is missing after the word *like*; the mycar variable is misspelled as *mybar*.

Item(s)	Appearance
Missing semicolon	;
Missing curly or square brackets	{ } [ ]
Missing parenthesis	( )
Missing single or double quote	' ' " "
Misspelling	*coool* instead of *cool*, for example

Table 16-1   Items to Look for When Scanning a Script for Errors

- Line 6: The alert method is missing a closing parenthesis.

- Line 8: The word *new* is misspelled as *neq*.

- Line 10: The array index number is missing its opening square bracket.

- Line 11: The opening parenthesis for the loop is missing.

- Line 13: The index number for somearray[0] is missing its closing square bracket.

- Between lines 13 and 14: The closing curly bracket to end the loop is missing.

You probably won't make that many errors, but the example provides a nice way to see how to catch them while scanning a script. After you become more experienced with locating these small errors, you'll be able to find them quickly when you have a problem in a script.

Find the Logical Errors

Logical errors are often tougher to find because the syntax of the code is correct. You will be trying to find a mistake in how the code was implemented. For example, look at the following code (but do not run it!):

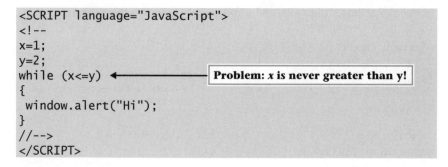

```
<SCRIPT language="JavaScript">
<!--
x=1;
y=2;
while (x<=y)          Problem: x is never greater than y!
{
 window.alert("Hi");
}
//-->
</SCRIPT>
```

The code has no syntax errors. All of the semicolons and quote marks are where they should be. The problem here is that the variable *x* is never greater than the variable *y*. This situation would cause an infinite loop, possibly crashing the browser.

You can fix the code by adding a line inside the loop to increase the value of *x*, decrease the value of *y*, or both increase *x* and decrease *y*. The important point is that something must be done to make the condition false. The following code shows a possible fix for this problem:

```
<SCRIPT language="JavaScript">
<!--
x=1;
y=2;
while (x<=y)
{
  window.alert("Hi");
  x+=1;  ◄──────────   Increasing x within the loop
}                       will allow x to become
//-->                   greater than y over time
</SCRIPT>
```

The techniques described in the following sections can help you find logical errors.

Alert Technique for Problem Variables   One way to find the problem in the previous example is to go back and rerun it with an alert to test the value of one or both variables each time through the loop (assuming it didn't crash the browser). An alert can be an excellent way to find out what is happening, and it can give you an idea of how to fix the problem.

For example, let's take the previous example (before the fix) and add an alert that shows the values of *x* and *y* each time the loop is run:

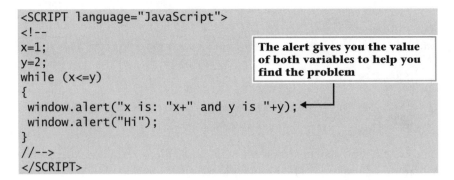

```
<SCRIPT language="JavaScript">
<!--
x=1;                      The alert gives you the value
y=2;                      of both variables to help you
while (x<=y)              find the problem
{
  window.alert("x is: "x+" and y is "+y); ◄──
  window.alert("Hi");
}
//-->
</SCRIPT>
```

Provided the script doesn't crash the browser, you will be able to see what the problem is. Each time the alert shows up, it will say the same thing: "x is 1 and y is 2." Therefore, you'll know you need to make an adjustment in the loop to fix it.

This technique is quite helpful when you have a variable that goes through numerous reassignments and calculations in a script. By using a well-placed alert, you can find out where the problem starts. For example, take a look at this code:

```
<SCRIPT language="JavaScript">
<!--
var item1="10";
var item2=20;
var total=item1+item2;        This calculation does not
upcharge=5;                   give the expected result
total+=upcharge; ◄────────────┘
window.alert("The total is $"+total);
//-->
</SCRIPT>
```

The variable total is assigned on the fifth line and then reassigned by adding another variable to it on line 7. The alert with the total after all the calculations gives a funny result of 10205. Do you see the problem? If not, you could place an alert after the first assignment to see if the calculation of item1+item2 works correctly:

```
<SCRIPT language="JavaScript">
<!--
var item1="10";
var item2=20;
var total=item1+item2;
window.alert(total); ◄──────  The alert allows you to see
upcharge=5;                    whether the first calculation
total+=upcharge;              is working correctly
window.alert("The total is $"+total);
//-->
</SCRIPT>
```

When you run the script again, the first alert gives a result of 1020. Now the problem becomes a bit clearer. For some reason, the script is adding item1 and item2 as strings and not as numbers, causing the two numbers to be combined instead of adding them mathematically.

Looking back at the assignment for item1, notice that it was assigned as a string accidentally. Removing the quotation marks around the 10 fixes the script and gives you the expected final result of 35.

The Hard Way: Trace Everything or Make Changes   If all of the shortcuts fail, then the final option is to try to run through the entire script piece by piece again to see if you can detect an error. If not, see if you can find another way to code the task. For example, try using a different type of loop. Hopefully, a new strategy will help you clear up the problem and complete the script.

Ask the Expert

Question: The error message I get says something I don't understand. What should I do?

Answer: Error messages don't always make sense and don't always point to the right line in the code. You may need to trace any variables or functions you have called on the line the message gave you or check the lines near it for errors. Once you've seen an error message a few times, it becomes easier to guess its meaning.

Question: Something in my code crashed the browser when I tried to run it, and I can't try adding alerts to help find the problem because it crashes every time! What should I do?

Answer: If the script crashes the browser, look closely at your variables, loops, objects, and functions. As a last resort, write some new code from scratch.

Question: An error in my code not only crashed the browser, but also the computer! What do I do?

Answer: Restart the computer but *do not* run the code again. Check it very carefully and see if you can find the problem.

16

> **Question:** Can any other strategies help me debug my scripts?
>
> **Answer:** Some text editors use color coding to mark HTML tags, JavaScript code, or other types of code. Color coding helps you see the code more clearly and makes it easier to detect an error. (Try VIM or NoteTab.)

Regular Expressions

Regular expressions give you much more power to handle strings in a script. They allow you to form patterns that can be matched against strings, rather than trying to use the string object's methods, which make it more difficult to be precise.

For example, you may want to know whether the value entered in a text box included at least three characters at the beginning, followed by an at (@) symbol, followed by at least three characters and a dot (.), followed by at least three more characters (matching a traditional e-mail address like jon@jon.com).

The string object's methods don't provide a neat and clean way to perform this task (although with enough tinkering, it may be possible). However, a regular expression can shorten the task or even turn a match that seemed impossible with the string object's methods into one that can be completed.

Creating Regular Expressions

To create regular expressions, you must create an instance of the JavaScript RegExp object. You can do this almost exactly the same way as you would create a string literal. To create a RegExp literal, you just assign the regular expression to a variable. Instead of using quotation marks to surround the expression, you use forward (/) slashes, as shown here:

```
var varname=/your_pattern/flags;
```

You replace *varname* with the name you want to use for a variable and *your_pattern* with the regular expression pattern of your choice. You can follow the last slash with one or more flags (which are discussed in the upcoming section "Adding Flags").

The easiest regular expression pattern to create is one that looks for an exact match of characters. For instance, if you wanted to see if the sequence *our* is present in a string, you could create the following regular expression pattern:

```
var tomatch=/our/;
```

The preceding code creates a RegExp literal named "tomatch." Now you need a string against which to test the pattern. If you test the word *our* against the expression, it's a match.

If you test *your, sour, pour,* or *pouring* against it, then it's a match. If you test *cool, Our, oUR, OUR,* or *souR,* then it won't be a match. So how do you perform this test?

Testing Strings Against Regular Expressions

To test a regular expression against a string, you can use the test() method of the RegExp object. The basic syntax is as follows:

```
regex_name.test(string_to_test);
```

This syntax is similar to using a string method. You replace *regex_name* with the name of the regular expression and replace *string_to_test* with a string or a string variable name. For instance, look at the following example:

```
var tomatch=/our/;
tomatch.test("pour");
```

This code will test the "pour" string against the regular expression named "tomatch." It doesn't make use of the result, though.

The "test()" method returns a Boolean value of true or false. It returns true when any portion of the string matches the regular expression pattern.

Using the test() method, you can already write a short script, as
shown here:

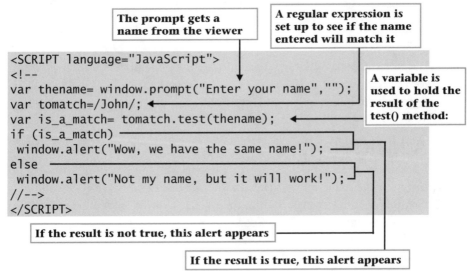

> **The prompt gets a
> name from the viewer**

> **A regular expression is
> set up to see if the name
> entered will match it**

> **A variable is
> used to hold the
> result of the
> test() method:**

```
<SCRIPT language="JavaScript">
<!--
var thename= window.prompt("Enter your name","");
var tomatch=/John/;
var is_a_match= tomatch.test(thename);
if (is_a_match)
 window.alert("Wow, we have the same name!");
else
 window.alert("Not my name, but it will work!");
//-->
</SCRIPT>
```

> **If the result is not true, this alert appears**

> **If the result is true, this alert appears**

The prompt gathers a name and holds the value in a variable. The pattern
to match is John, and it is case sensitive. Thus, only an entry containing
John with a capital J followed by lowercase o, h, and n will create a match
and return true when it is tested.

The result of the test() method is assigned to a variable named
"is_a_match." The variable is then used as the condition for the if
statement. If the variable holds a value of true, then the viewer gets the
"Wow, we have the same name!" alert. If it holds a value of false, the
viewer gets the "Not my name, but it will work!" alert instead.

If you want to shorten the script, you can just make the result of the
test() method the condition for the if statement rather than creating another
variable, as in the following code:

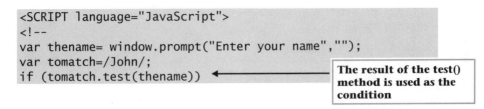

```
<SCRIPT language="JavaScript">
<!--
var thename= window.prompt("Enter your name","");
var tomatch=/John/;
if (tomatch.test(thename))
```

> **The result of the test()
> method is used as the
> condition**

```
 window.alert("Wow, we have the same name!");
else
 window.alert("Not my name, but it will work!");
//-->
</SCRIPT>
```

Because the method returns true or false, it can be placed as the condition for the if statement on its own. (You could make it (tomatch.test(thename)==true) if you wanted to, though.)

Adding Flags

Flags allow you to make the match case insensitive or to look for every match in the string rather than just the first one (a global test). To add a flag, place it after the last slash in the regular expression. You can use three options, as shown in Table 16-2:

If you wanted to adjust the name script used previously to be case insensitive, you could add an i flag to the regular expression, as shown in the following code:

```
<SCRIPT language="JavaScript">
<!--
var thename= window.prompt("Enter your name","");
var tomatch=/John/i;  ◀──────────
if (tomatch.test(thename))
 window.alert("Wow, we have the same name!");
else
 window.alert("Not my name, but it will work!");
//-->
</SCRIPT>
```

> The i flag makes this regular expression case insensitive

Flag(s)	Purpose
i	Makes the match case insensitive
g	Makes the match global
ig	Makes the match case insensitive and global

Table 16-2   Regular Expression Flags

The test() method will now return true as long as the pattern of John is in the string. It can be in any case, so now John, JOHN, john, and even JoHn are all matches and will cause the test() method to return true.

The g flag is also able to replace a portion of the string when the match occurs a number of times.

Creating Powerful Patterns

Although it's nice to be able to create such an exact pattern, you won't always be looking for a match so precise. In many cases, you will be looking to match a more general pattern, such as an entry needing to have at least three characters or needing to have two characters of any type followed by a special character.

By using special characters in your expressions, you can create the type of patterns you need to match a given sequence you want. JavaScript regular expressions use the syntax of Perl regular expressions as a model. Thus, if you've used regular expressions in Perl, much of this material will be familiar. Table 16-3 lists a number of the characters to help you create your patterns.

Character	Purpose	Example
^	Matches only from the beginning of a line	/^c/ matches c in *corn* /^c/ does not match c in *acorn*
$	Matches only at the end of the line	/r$/ matches r in *Car* /r$/ does not match t in *Cat*
*	Matches the character preceding it if the character occurs zero or more times	/co*/ matches co or c /co*/ does not match *pi*
+	Matches the character preceding it if it occurs one or more times	/co+/ matches co or *cooooo* /co+/ does not match *ca*
?	Matches the character preceding it if it occurs zero or one time	/o?l/ matches *style* or *column* /o?l/ does not match *cool*
.	Matches any individual character, excluding the newline character	/.l/ matches *al* or *@l* /.l/ does not match *\nl* or *l*

Table 16-3   **Regular Expression Codes**

Character	Purpose	Example
(x)	By replacing x with characters, matches that sequence and keeps it in memory to be used later	/(a)/ matches *a* /(cool)/ matches *cool* /(cool)/ does not match *coal*
|	Used as a logical OR symbol to allow a match of what is on the left of the symbol OR what is on its right	/cool|bad/ matches *cool* /cool|bad/ matches *bad* /cool|bad/ does not match *car*
{x}	Using a number to replace x, matches when there are exactly x occurrences of the character preceding it	/n{1}/ matches *n* /nn{2}/ matches *nn* /nn{1} does not match *nn*
{x,}	Using a number to replace x, matches when there are x or more occurrences of the character preceding it	/n{1,}/ matches *n* /n{1,}/ matches *nnnnn* /n{3,}/ does not match *nn*
{x,y}	Using numbers to replace x and y, matches when there are at least x occurrences of the character preceding it but no more than y occurrences of it	/n{1,2}/ matches *n* /n{1,2}/ matches *nn* /n{1,3}/ does not match *nnnn* /n{1,2}/ does not match *nnn*
[]	Matches a character set of your choice; will match when any one of the characters in the brackets (such as [abc]) or any one of a range of characters (such as [a-k]) is present	/abc/ matches *a* /abc/ matches *b* /abc/ matches *c* /a-k/ matches *j* /a-k/ does not match *n*
[^]	Matches when the characters in your character set are *not* present; may be a set (such as [abc]) or a range (such as [a-k])	/^abc/ matches *d* /^abc/ does not match *b* /^a-k/ matches *n* /^a-k/ does not match *j*
\	Used to escape special characters or to make a normal character special	\@ escapes the @ character \n represents a newline character
[\b]	Matches a backspace keystroke	/[\b]/ matches a backspace
\b	Matches when the character before or after it is located at a word boundary, such as before or after a space character; to match the beginning of a word, place the character to the right of the symbol (\bc); to match the end of a word, place the character to the left (c\b)	/\bc/ matches *c* in *my car* /\bm/ matches *m* in my *car* /\bc/ does not match *c* in *ace* /\bm/ does not match *m* in *Sam* /m\b/ matches *m* in *Sam* /c\b/ matches *c* in *Mac W* /m\b/ does not match *m* in *emu* /c\b/ does not match *c* in *my car*
\B	Matches a character that is not located at a word boundary	/\Ba/ matches *a* in *car* /\Bc/ does not match *c* in *car*

Table 16-3   Regular Expression Codes *(continued)*

Character	Purpose	Example
\cX	Using a letter character to replace *X*, matches when the user presses the CTRL key followed by typing the letter *X*	/cX/ matches *Ctrl+X* /cV/ matches *Ctrl+V* /cS/ does not match *Ctrl+Z*
\d	Matches if the character is a single numeric character	/\d/ matches *4* /\d/ does not match *s*
\D	Matches a single character if it is *not* a numeric character	/\D/ matches *s* /\D/ does not match *4*
\f	Matches if there is a form feed	/\f/ matches a form feed
\n	Matches if there is a new line	/\n/ matches a new line
\r	Matches if there is a carriage return	/\r/ matches a carriage return
\s	Matches a single character if it represents white space (such as a space or a new line)	/\s/ matches the space in *b c* /\s/ matches the tab in *b c* /\s/ does not match *bc*
\S	Matches a single character if it does *not* represent white space	/\S/ matches *d* /\S/ does not match the space in *b c*
\t	Matches if there is a tab	/\t/ matches the tab in *b c*
\v	Matches if there is a vertical tab	/\v/ matches a vertical tab
\w	Matches any single character that is a letter, number, or underscore	/\w/ matches *4* /\w/ does not match *@*
\W	Matches any single character that is *not* a letter, number, or underscore	/\W/ matches *@* /\W/ does not match *g*

Table 16-3   Regular Expression Codes *(continued)*

As you can see, extensive options exist for creating the pattern you need. Now you could easily verify an e-mail address according to the standards you decide to set.

Thus, if you want to accept an e-mail address in a form that includes at least three characters, followed by an at (@) character, followed by at least three characters, followed by a dot (.), and ending with three more characters, you could use a regular expression to validate the information. Three is an arbitrary number: some addresses end with a two-character extension or have less than three characters in one of the other areas, so use what you feel is appropriate.

You could use the following code:

```
<HTML>
<HEAD>
<SCRIPT language="JavaScript">
<!--
function check_it()
{
var tomatch=/[A-Za-z0-9]\w{2,}@ [A-Za-z0-9-]{3,}\.\[A-Za-z]{3}/
var emadd= document.f1.t1.value;
if (tomatch.test(emadd))
{
window.alert("E-mail Address OK");
return true;
}
else
{
  window.alert("E-mail Address invalid. Please Try Again");
  return false;
}
}
//-->
</SCRIPT>
</HEAD>
<BODY>
<FORM name="f1" id="f1"   action="http://yoursite.com/cgi-bin/form.cgi"
 onSubmit="return check_it()">
Enter your e-mail address:<br />
<INPUT type="text" name="t1" id="t1" /><br />
<INPUT type="submit" />
</FORM>
</BODY>
</HTML>
```

The pattern to be matched is set as a regular expression

The value of the entry in the text field is placed in a variable

The if/else block determines which alert should be sent and whether the information has been validated

Because you know how the validation works, you will want to look more closely at the regular expression pattern that is used. Use the information in Table 16-3 to decipher the meaning of the following code:

```
var tomatch=/[A-Za-z0-9]\w{2,}@ [A-Za-z0-9-]{3,}\.\[A-Za-z]{3}/
```

The first character should be a letter or a number, so a set of ranges is used. Notice that each range has nothing separating it from the next range; they are just placed one after another. The characters allowed for the first character include letters and numbers within these ranges.

Next, the rest of the first segment of the address can be letters, numbers, or underscores (sometimes more types of characters are allowed, though), so the \w is used. It is followed with {2,} to make sure that this type of character occurs at least twice. (With the first character, this ensures that the first part of the address has at least three characters.)

Next, the at (@) sign requires an at character to be present. (In Perl, the at sign is a special character that must be written as \@). Next, there is another range, this time allowing letters, numbers, and the hyphen (-). It is followed by the {3,} to ensure that at least three characters are in that range.

Finally, the last range includes only letters and must have exactly three characters within that range.Thus, any of the following entries are acceptable:

- efg@efg.com

- efghij@efghijklm.net

- e2bd_f443@fg45-cool.net

The following entries are not acceptable:

- $fg@ghi.org

- gbs#ghi.com

- rad@bad

- rad@bad.2om

- rad@cool.jj

Note

Regular expressions can be quite powerful for validation because they allow less erroneous information to be accepted.

The pattern used in the example was rather strict. You could change it to accept domain extensions that are only two letters or accounts that allow more special characters than just underscores. You can decide how strict or lenient you want to be when creating your pattern to be matched.

Client-side validation of form submissions with data such as e-mail addresses or phone numbers can save unnecessary trips to the server. A JavaScript validation solution is not ideal for validating sensitive cases (such as credit card numbers).

Furthermore, users can often disable JavaScript support and perhaps make form submissions directly. Therefore, client-side validation could support server-side validation (by a CGI script or a Java servlet, for example), but should not replace it.

Replacing Information

To replace information in a string, you can use regular expressions and the replace() method of the string object (which was not covered in Module 13 because of its need for a regular expression). The syntax for using the replace() method is as follows:

```
varname= stringname.replace(regex,newstring);
```

You replace *varname* with the name of the variable that will hold the new string value once the information has been replaced. You replace *stringname* with the name of the string variable that will undergo the replacement. You replace *regex* with the name of the regular expression to be used to match against the string. Finally, you replace *newstring* with the string or string variable to replace any matched values in the string.

As an example, the following code replaces the first instance of "car" in mystring with bar:

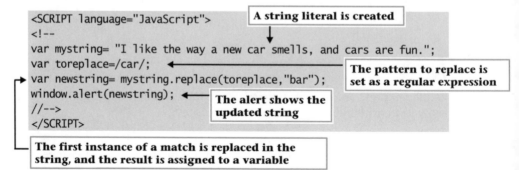

The preceding code replaces only the first instance of car, giving the alert "I like the way a new bar smells, and cars are fun." If you want to change every instance of "car" instead, the g flag is helpful at the end of the regular expression, as shown in the following code:

```
<SCRIPT language="JavaScript">
<!--
var mystring= "I like the way a new car smells, and cars are fun.";
var toreplace=/car/g;
var newstring= mystring.replace(toreplace,"bar");
window.alert(newstring);
//-->
</SCRIPT>
```

> Adding the g flag causes all matches of the pattern to be replaced when the replace() method is run

The g flag will match every instance of the regular expression it finds in the string. Thus, when the replace() method is run, all instances of "car" will be replaced with "bar." The viewer will see this alert: "I like the way a new bar smells, and bars are fun."

You could also use the replace() method to make a name-changing script that is shorter and somewhat less complex than the one in Module 13. By using the replace() method with a regular expression, the first letter of the first and last name can be changed more easily. The following code shows how:

```
<SCRIPT language="JavaScript">
<!--
function getname()
{
 var tomatch=/[A-Za-z]{2,}\s[A-Za-z]{2,}/;
 var toreplace=/\b[A-Za-z]/gi;
 var thename=window.prompt("Enter your first and last name","");
 if (tomatch.test(thename))
 {
 newname=thename.replace(toreplace,"Z");
 window.alert("Now your name is "+newname);
 }
 else
 {
  window.alert("Name invalid. Please Try Again");
  getname();
 }
}
getname();
//-->
</SCRIPT>
```

> Regular expressions are used to validate and change the viewer's entry

This script changes the first letter of the first and last name to Z regardless of what it was before. The regular expression for the replacement simply looks for a letter at the beginning of a word using the word boundary (\b) code. Each time a letter is at the beginning of a word, it is replaced.

The validation of the input keeps the script from getting more than two names and one space, and it also ensures that at least two letters are in each name, with no numbers or special characters. The illustration shows the result of the script if the viewer enters **Debra Loo** at the prompt: the viewer's name is changed.

> Microsoft Internet Explorer
>
> ⚠ Now your name is Zebra Zoo
>
> [OK]

1-Minute Drill

- **What's the name of the object used for regular expressions?**
- **Which method is used to test a string against a regular expression?**
- **Which string method can you use to replace information based on a regular expression match?**

`pr16_1.html`

Project 16-1: Validating a Web Address

To practice using regular expressions, in this project, you'll create a script that validates information from a form.

Step-by-Step

1. Create an HTML document, leaving room in the HEAD and BODY sections for code.

- **The RegExp object**
- **The test() method**
- **The replace() method**

2. Create a form in the BODY section with a text box named "t1" and a submit button. Have it call a function named "check_it()" when it is submitted. Set the action value to # to avoid submission.

3. In the HEAD section, create a function named "check_it()" that uses a regular expression to validate the URL the viewer entered. Assume that you need the URL to contain the following:

● It must begin with http://.

● The characters in between need to be dots (.), hyphens (-), letters, or numbers.

● It must end with a dot (.) and no more than three letter characters.

4. If the information validates, send an alert saying "URL OK" and return true. If the information does not validate, send an alert saying "URL invalid: Try again" and return false.

5. Save the file as pr16_1.html in your browser and try entering different URL addresses to see the results.

Cookies

A *cookie* is a small text file that is stored on the end user's computer. It can be referenced any time the viewer returns to your site, provided the cookie hasn't been deleted or expired. Of course, if the viewer doesn't accept cookies, then a cookie won't be able to be set or referenced later. Keep the following points in mind when using cookies:

● Cookies must be 4K each or less

● A browser can accept up to only 20 cookies from a single domain

● If a number of viewers don't accept cookies, this eliminates any advantages of your cookie(s) to those viewers

Netscape invented cookies to help users browse your site more effectively. For instance, if you use a script on your main page that sends one or more alerts while the page is loading, you won't want that to happen every time the viewer goes to another page on your site and then comes back to the home page. It would likely be so aggravating that you wouldn't have a visitor after it happened a few times.

The alerts pop up each time the page loads because HTTP lacks state persistence. Cookies fill that gap. With cookies, you can fix problems like these for any viewers who have cookies enabled.

Setting a Cookie

Setting a basic cookie is as easy as giving a value to the cookie property of the document object. The only restriction is that you can't have spaces, commas, or semicolons inside the string. For example, you can set a cookie that will store a name so that you can identify it if you set more than one cookie later. The following code sets a basic cookie:

```
function set_it()
{
  document.cookie="name=tasty1";
}
```

Caution

Remember when setting a cookie not to use spaces, commas, or semicolons inside the string that sets the cookie data.

The preceding code sets a cookie with a value of name=tasty1 when the function is called. You can set any delimiter you want, though, so the following code would work as well:

```
function set_it()
{
  document.cookie="name:tasty1";
}
```

The only problem is that you may need to use a space, comma, or semicolon in your cookie at some point. For instance, you might want to add in some text that tells what your favorite kind of cookie is.

Adding the additional information isn't very difficult as long as the value does not need a space, as shown in the following code:

```
function set_it()
{
  document.cookie="name=tasty1&fav=Sugar";
}
```

As you can see, the value of the cookie is being formatted in name=value pairs, and each pair is separated with an ampersand (&). Again, you can choose any type of separators you want. The following code is fine as well:

```
function set_it()
{
  document.cookie="name:tasty1|fav:Sugar";
}
```

In this case, the names and values are separated with colons, while the pipe (|) symbol separates them into pairs. You can use anything that makes you comfortable.

The escape() Method

If you want to use spaces, commas, or semicolons in your cookie, you need a way to "escape" them so that they are translated into something a cookie accepts.

A cookie will accept character codes like a CGI program often does. They may look like %20, %41, or something similar. To turn spaces, commas, and semicolons into these codes, you must use the JavaScript escape() method. It is a top-level method, so you don't need to specify an object.

The following code shows how you could use the escape() method to set a cookie with a space in it:

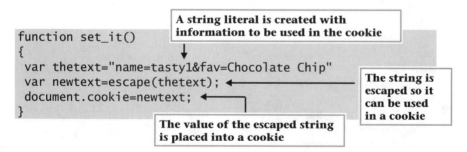

```
function set_it()
{
  var thetext="name=tasty1&fav=Chocolate Chip"
  var newtext=escape(thetext);
  document.cookie=newtext;
}
```

A string literal is created with information to be used in the cookie

The string is escaped so it can be used in a cookie

The value of the escaped string is placed into a cookie

The thetext variable is set to include the string you want to use in the cookie. The newtext variable is set to hold the result of using the escape() method on thetext. The escaped text is then used as the string for the cookie, which will now have the code for the space character in it.

Allowing User Input

By using the escape() method, you can prompt the viewer for the information, escape it, and then use it in the cookie. The following code shows how to do this to get the viewer's favorite type of cookie:

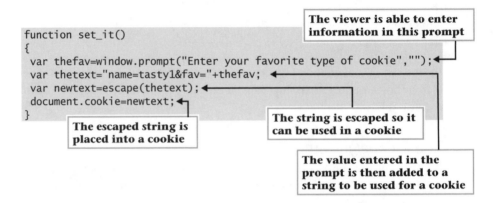

```
function set_it()
{
  var thefav=window.prompt("Enter your favorite type of cookie","");
  var thetext="name=tasty1&fav="+thefav;
  var newtext=escape(thetext);
  document.cookie=newtext;
}
```

The viewer is able to enter information in this prompt

The string is escaped so it can be used in a cookie

The escaped string is placed into a cookie

The value entered in the prompt is then added to a string to be used for a cookie

Now the viewer can help decide the information that will be set in the cookie, and you can use the information your viewers enter on your site on their next visit.

Setting an Expiration Date

Adding an expiration date to a cookie will keep it from being deleted once the browser is closed, or it can be used to expire a cookie you no longer want to use. To set an expiration date, add a little more to your string for the cookie, as shown in the following code:

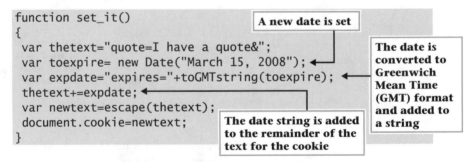

```
function set_it()
{
  var thetext="quote=I have a quote&";
  var toexpire= new Date("March 15, 2008");
  var expdate="expires="+toGMTstring(toexpire);
  thetext+=expdate;
  var newtext=escape(thetext);
  document.cookie=newtext;
}
```

A new date is set

The date is converted to Greenwich Mean Time (GMT) format and added to a string

The date string is added to the remainder of the text for the cookie

Basically, you are adding on another name/value pair that adds an expiration date. It needs to be in this form:

```
expires=date (in GMT format)
```

In the code, an expiration date for the cookie was added by creating a new date object and setting the date to be used as the expiration date. A new variable is created to add the string "expires=" to the result of changing the date to GMT format using the toGMTstring() method.

The toGMTformat() method transforms a regular date into one in GMT format, so you don't have to make the conversion yourself. Then the result is added to the variable that will be used to set the string for the cookie.

If you want a cookie to last a long time, you can set the date far into the future. If you want to expire a cookie you have decided not to use anymore, set a date in the past and the cookie will expire.

Reading a Cookie

Reading cookies is fairly simple if you have only a single cookie set and want to read it. To read the cookie, you just need to get the value of the document.cookie property from the browser:

```
function read_it()
{
 var mycookie=document.cookie;
}
```

However, the preceding code will only give you a long and possibly messy string for the value of the mycookie variable. It might look like this:

```
name=tasty1&fav=Chocolate%20Chip
```

The %20 got in the code when the input for the cookie was escaped using the escape() method. To fix that, use the unescape() method to get the data in a more readable format.

Thus, the following code would provide the string you need:

```
function read_it()
{
 var mycookie=document.cookie;
 var fixed_cookie= unescape(mycookie);
}
```

Next, you must find a way to extract the information you need from the cookie. Assuming the cookie contained the string just used as an example (name=tasty1&fav=Chocolate%20Chip), the string would now look like this:

```
name=tasty1&fav=Chocolate Chip
```

Notice that the text is divided in two different ways. The ampersand (&) divides the string into name/value pairs, while the equal signs divide the name/value pairs into their names and values.

Assuming the string name=tasty1&fav=Chocolate Chip is what is now in the fixed_cookie variable from the code, you could use that variable to create a new array by splitting the string on the ampersand character:

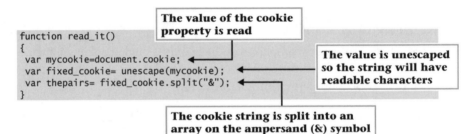

The preceding code splits the string into two array values:

```
thepairs[0] with a value of name=tasty1
```

```
thepairs[1] with a value of fav=Chocolate Chip
```

You split each of these into a new array that will have a name and a value. Therefore, you need some code like this:

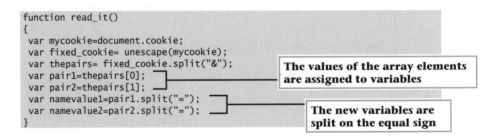

Now you have all the information you need using the namevalue1[]
and namevalue2[] arrays:

```
namevalue1[0] with a value of name
namevalue1[1] with a value of  tasty1
namevalue2[0] with a value of fav
namevalue2[1] with a value of  Chocolate Chip
```

You can use them in any way you like, such as placing them in alerts:

```
function read_it()
{
 var mycookie=document.cookie;
 var fixed_cookie= unescape(mycookie);
 var thepairs= fixed_cookie.split("&");
 var pair1=thepairs[0];
 var pair2=thepairs[1];
 var namevalue1=pair1.split("=");
 var namevalue2=pair2.split("=");
 window.alert("The cookie's "+namevalue1[0]+" is "+namevalue1[1]);
 window.alert("My "+namevalue2[0]+"orite type of cookie is "+namevalue2[1]);
}
```

**The values obtained
from the cookies are used**

You might want to be sure *document.cookie* exists before trying to run
all the code in the function. Any cookie you set to expire later can be
read, but those without the cookie may get an error. By making the
check, you can ensure the existence of the cookie or send the viewer to
the function that sets the cookie. To do that, add an if/else block around
the code in the function, as shown here:

```
function read_it()
{
 if (document.cookie)
 {
 var mycookie=document.cookie;
 var fixed_cookie= unescape(mycookie);
 var thepairs= fixed_cookie.split("&");
 var pair1=thepairs[0];
 var pair2=thepairs[1];
 var namevalue1=pair1.split("=");
 var namevalue2=pair2.split("=");
 window.alert("The cookie's "+namevalue1[0]+" is "+namevalue1[1]);
 window.alert("My "+namevalue2[0]+"orite type of cookie is "+namevalue2[1]);
 }
 else
 {
  set_it();
 }
}
```

The preceding code assumes that the set_it() function exists and will set the cookie so it can be used.

Project 16-2: Remember a Name

pr16_2.html

In this project, you'll use a cookie to remember a name when a visitor returns to the page.

Step-by-Step

1. Create a new HTML document and leave room in the HEAD and BODY sections for code.

2. In the HEAD section, create a function named "set_it()" that will set a cookie. Set the expiration to a future date. Allow the viewer to enter a name in a prompt and use it in the cookie.

3. Create a function named "read_it()" that will check to see whether the cookie exists; and, if so, read the cookie and send an alert to the viewer with the name in it, in the following format (replace *<name>* with the name read from the cookie):

   Welcome, *<name>*!

4. If the cookie doesn't exist, call the set_it() function.

5. Call the read_it() function inside the <SCRIPT></SCRIPT> tags, but after the two function definitions. It should begin execution while the page is loading.

6. Save the file as pr16_2.html and open it in your browser. Enter your name. Close your browser and open the page again. This time, you should get an alert with your name rather than the prompt.

☑ *Mastery Check*

16

1. Which attribute replaces the *name* attribute in XHTML?

A. The nickname attribute

B. The ref attribute

C. The id attribute

D. The callit attribute

2. Which of the following is valid in XHTML?

A. <INPUT TYPE="text">

B. <input type="text">

C. <input type=text \>

D. <input type="text" \>

3. Which of the following lines does not create a JavaScript syntax error?

A. var myvar="cool;

B. function cool()

C. document.write("Is there an error?");

D. window.alert "what is this?");

4. Which of the following would validate when tested against the regular expression of /pep/?

A. Peep

B. pepper

C. pop

D. Pep

☑ Mastery Check

5. Which property is used to set and read a cookie?

   A. The cookie property of the window object

   B. The cookie property of the document object

   C. The cook property of the document object

   D. The set_or_read_cookie property of the document object

Module 17

More Advanced Techniques

The Goals of This Module

- Create image rollover effects using scripts with the image object
- Use cascading style sheets
- Create DHTML scripts that move elements on the page
- Learn about JavaScript security

This module introduces some more advanced—and fun—JavaScript capabilities. First, you'll learn about the image object and use it to create rollover effects. You'll also learn about cascading style sheets and how they can be combined with JavaScript to create dynamic HTML (DHTML) effects. Finally, you'll learn about JavaScript security. If you'd like to explore any of these topics further on your own, this module also provides some sources where you can find additional information.

Images

JavaScript uses the image object to preload images, create rollover effects, and even create slide shows or animations. The image object's properties will help when you want to create such scripts. Table 17-1 lists the image object's properties.

The src property is used the most in this module because it allows the source of an image to be changed to create a rollover effect.

Preloading

When you code your Web pages, sometimes you may want to preload your images. *Preloading* an image allows it to be in the browser's cache before it is called in the HTML or JavaScript code in the browser. This

Property	Purpose
name	Holds the value of the image's name from the name attribute
src	Holds the value of the URL from the src attribute
width	Holds the value of the width from the width attribute
height	Holds the value of the height from the height attribute
border	Holds the numeric value of the border property from the border attribute
hspace	Holds the numeric value of the hspace property from the hspace attribute
vspace	Holds the numeric value of the vspace property from the vspace attribute
lowsrc	Holds the value of the URL from the lowsrc attribute
complete	Indicates whether an image has finished loading

Table 17-1 Properties of the Image Object

way, the image will show up much more quickly when it is called and will keep the viewer from having to wait for an image to load.

One technique for preloading is to load an image on your main page that will be used on other pages in your site. The image will be in the browser's cache on each of the other pages and will load instantly. For example, you may want your Web site's logo to appear on every page of the site. When it is loaded on the first page, the other pages will load it instantly.

Of course, you can do this with HTML because you are likely to want the logo to appear on the main page as well as all the other pages. Therefore, when you code the img element, the image is loaded into the cache.

In some cases, you may want to preload images that will appear later on the same page. This practice is common when using rollovers or other scripts that call images after the page has finished loading. In such a case, you don't want the viewer to be stuck waiting on a new image to load because it keeps the script from working as well as it should.

For instance, if you have set a new image to appear when the viewer moves the mouse over an image, you want the new image to show up immediately. If the viewer has to wait a few seconds for the image to load, it can ruin the intended effect.

With JavaScript, you can create a new instance of the image object in the HEAD section and then give its src property the URL of the image you want to preload, as shown in the following code:

```
<HEAD>
<SCRIPT language="JavaScript">
<!--
if (document.images)
{
 var pic1= new Image(120,35);
 pic1.src="image1.gif";
 var pic2= new Image();
 pic2.src="image2.gif";
}
//-->
</SCRIPT>
</HEAD>
```

Recall a similar bit of code in Module 9 when the images array was discussed. The first instance (pic1) of the image object defines a width and height for the image. The second (pic2) does not, but it will get those values from the actual width and height of the image from the image.

You don't have to use both methods. You can choose the method you prefer and use it for all of the images you want to preload.

The full page with the img elements could look something like this:

```
<HEAD>
<SCRIPT language="JavaScript">
<!--
if (document.images)
{
 var pic1= new Image(120,35);
 pic1.src="image1.gif";
 var pic2= new Image();
 pic2.src="image2.gif";
}
//-->
</SCRIPT>
</HEAD>
<BODY>
<H1>Some Images</h1>
<IMG src="image1.gif" width="120" height="35">
<P>
<IMG src="image2.gif" width="50" height="75">
</BODY>
</HTML>
```

Of course, the preloading really isn't serving a purpose in this case. To give the technique of preloading a purpose, you want a script that shows a new image when an event occurs, such as in a rollover script.

Rollovers

Image *rollovers* (also known as hover buttons, image flips, and other similar names) can add some zest to your navigational images. The viewer moves the mouse over a linked image and the image changes. This change could be anything from a simple color to a completely different image of the same size, which can create more interest in the navigational system.

The effect described in the last two sentences is a simple rollover, but you can also change an image from a mouseover event on another linked image or text link, or even change more than one image at a time.

A Simple Rollover

A simple rollover just changes one image to another when the mouse moves over the initial image. First, you create two images of the same size and make the second image different in some way. For example, examine the two images shown, giving the first image the filename image1.gif and the second, image1_c.gif.

Note

For each rollover effect you create, you will need to have two separate images.

Once you have two images, you can begin working on the code for the image rollover. First, you preload the images so your rollover won't need to call the second image when the viewer moves the mouse over the first image. Technically, you need to preload only the second image, but it is handy (as you will soon see) to have both images set as instances of the image object. You can use the following code to preload the two images:

```
<HEAD>
<SCRIPT language="JavaScript">
<!--
if (document.images)
{
  // Preload original image (to show when page loads)
  var pic1_init= new Image();
  pic1_init.src="image1.gif";
  //Preload image that will show on the mouseover event
  var pic1_new= new Image();
  pic1_new.src="image1_c.gif";
}
//-->
</SCRIPT>
</HEAD>
```

The initial image is used as an image object and is preloaded

The second image is used as an image object and is preloaded

Notice the names of the image objects both begin with pic1, they both have an underscore (_) character, and they use either init (initial) or new. Using the naming convention for the image objects described in the previous sentence, you can add more images to the script later with a system to let you know which images are paired together. Also, the naming convention will help when the functions are written for the actual rollover.

Rather than write the function right now, let's insert the HTML code for the image rollover into the BODY section. In the case of a simple rollover, you could use the following code:

> **The "a" element does most of the work by creating a link and calling the necessary functions**

```
<BODY>
<H1>The image below changes! Move your mouse over it!</H1>
<A href="somepage.html" onMouseOver="change_it('pic1')"
onMouseOut="change_back('pic1')">
<IMG src="image1.gif" name="pic1" id="pic1" border="0"></A>
</BODY>
```

> **Notice that the img element is given a name and id**

The "a" element is used around the image element so that the image can be used as a navigational link, and also so the onMouseOver and onMouseOut event handlers can be used. (Some newer browsers are beginning to support these event handlers in the img element, though, which may be nice if you don't require a link.)

Both event handlers call functions (which you will create soon) to make the image change to the new image on the mouseover event, and then back to the initial image on the mouseout event. Each function is sent a parameter that will be the name (id) of the image to be changed. The <IMG> tag then gives the source of the initial image (image1.gif) and gives the image a name (pic1). Recall that pic1 was conveniently used as part of the object name for both images.

The functions will help clear up all of the naming that has been done. The following code shows the functions that you should add into the HEAD section to create the rollover effect:

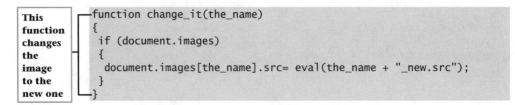

> **This function changes the image to the new one**

```
function change_it(the_name)
{
  if (document.images)
  {
    document.images[the_name].src= eval(the_name + "_new.src");
  }
}
```

```
function change_back(the_name)
{
 if (document.images)
 {
  document.images[the_name].src= eval(the_name + "_init.src");
 }
}
```

This function changes the image back to the initial one

Notice that the parameter each function takes in is going to be the name of the image sent to it when the function is called in an event handler in the HTML code. A check for the images array is made within the function to be sure the browser can do the task.

In the change_it() function, you will see this long line:

```
document.images[the_name].src= eval(the_name + "_new.src");
```

To understand the meaning of all of it, let's break it down into parts.

The part on the left side of the equal (=) sign is using the images array of the document object. You can use it as an associative array by placing the name (id) of the image inside the square brackets. Recall that the_name will have the value of the image name that was sent to the function as a parameter.

In this case, pic1 is sent as the name of the image (because it is the only image) and the_name will have a value of pic1. Thus, this part of the statement would evaluate like this:

```
document.images['pic1'].src
```

Therefore, the source URL of the image named "pic1" will be assigned a new value based on what is on the right side of the equal (=) sign.

The right side introduces a new top-level function eval(). The eval() function evaluates an expression sent as its parameter as a string value. In other words, if you put in eval("1+1"), the expression returns 2 rather than the 1+1 string. (If you want the string to be returned, you must use the string object constructor function. See Module 13 for more information.) The eval() function can also evaluate a string value and use it as a JavaScript statement. This means you could use code similar to the following:

```
var todo="alert";
eval("window."+todo+"('Hey!');");
```

The end result is an alert popping up on the screen. While messy, the fact that this code works means that you can combine unknown variable values with a regular JavaScript statement and the statement will execute. If you add all of the values as a regular string, it is not executed, but combined as a regular string value.

How does that help here? Look at the eval() call again:

```
eval(the_name + "_new.src");
```

The preceding code combines the value of the the_name variable with the string _new.src and allows the result to be a JavaScript statement. The src property of an image object is a value that can be accessed and used with JavaScript. Essentially, the entire line boils down to making an assignment like this:

```
document.images['pic1'].src= pic1_new.src;
```

See something familiar? Yes, pic1_new is the name of the instance of the image object used for the image that will replace the initial image. The value of its src property (image1_c.gif) is being assigned to the image named pic1 (the initial image), changing the image that appears in that position on the page.

The change_back() function reverses the process when the mouse moves off of the image. It assigns the src property of the image to the one used for the initial image. The full code for the page looks like this:

```
<HTML>
<HEAD>
<SCRIPT language="JavaScript">
<!--
if (document.images)
{
 // Preload original image (to show when page loads)
 var pic1_init= new Image();
 pic1_init.src="image1.gif";
 //Preload image that will show on the mouseover event
 var pic1_new= new Image();
 pic1_new.src="image1_c.gif";
}
function change_it(the_name)
```

```
{
 if (document.images)
 {
  document.images[the_name].src= eval(the_name + "_new.src");
 }
}
function change_back(the_name)
{
 if (document.images)
 {
  document.images[the_name].src= eval(the_name + "_init.src");
 }
}
//-->
</SCRIPT>
</HEAD>
<BODY>
<H1>The image below changes! Move your mouse over it!</H1>
<A href="somepage.html" onMouseOver="change_it('pic1')"
 onMouseOut="change_back('pic1')">
<IMG src="image1.gif" name="pic1" id="pic1" border="0"></A>
</BODY>
</HTML>
```

The closest you can get to seeing the results here is to see a before and after set of images. Figure 17-1 shows the initial image, while Figure 17-2 shows the result when the mouse is moved over the image.

Figure 17-1 The initial image

Figure 17-2 The new image appears when the mouseover event occurs

Why code the preceding script in such a complex way? Well, if you want the rollover effect for more than one pair of images, you can now call the same functions. The only additions you need to make are to preload the new images and keep the names consistent.

For example, if you decided you wanted to have three rollover effects, you would need three pairs of images, and each would need to have either _init or _new at the end of its name when it is created as an instance of the image object. You could use the following code if you decided to name the images pic1, pic2, and pic3 in their <IMG> tags:

```
<HTML>
<HEAD>
<SCRIPT language="JavaScript">
<!--
if (document.images)
{
 // Preload original images (to show when page loads)
 var pic1_init= new Image();
 pic1_init.src="image1.gif";
 var pic2_init= new Image();
 pic2_init.src="image2.gif";          The extra initial images
 var pic3_init= new Image();          are added
 pic3_init.src="image3.gif";

//Preload images that will show on the mouseover event
 var pic1_new= new Image();
```

```
   pic1_new.src="image1_c.gif";
   var pic2_new= new Image();
   pic2_new.src="image2_c.gif";
   var pic2_new= new Image();
   pic2_new.src="image3_c.gif";
   }
   function change_it(the_name)
   {
    if (document.images)
    {
     document.images[the_name].src= eval(the_name + "_new.src");
    }
   }
   function change_back(the_name)
   {
    if (document.images)
    {
     document.images[the_name].src= eval(the_name + "_init.src");
    }
   }
   //-->
   </SCRIPT>
   </HEAD>
   <BODY>
   <H1>The images below change! Move your mouse over one!</H1>
   <A href="somepage.html" onMouseOver="change_it('pic1')"
    onMouseOut="change_back('pic1')">
   <IMG src="image1.gif" name="pic1" id="pic1" border="0"></A>
   <BR>
   <A href="somepage.html" onMouseOver="change_it('pic2')"
    onMouseOut="change_back('pic2')">
   <IMG src="image1.gif" name="pic2" id="pic2" border="0"></A>
   <BR>
   <A href="somepage.html" onMouseOver="change_it('pic3')"
    onMouseOut="change_back('pic3')">
   <IMG src="image1.gif" name="pic3" id="pic3" border="0"></A>
   </BODY>
   </HTML>
```

The extra new images are added

17

Notice how all of the names of the objects correspond to the image names in the HTML code and the function parameters. In this way, you can continue adding as many images as you want to use the rollover effect.

Changing a Different Image

To change an image from another linked image or a plain text link, you need to change only the calls to the functions in the HTML code and add either a text link or a linked image to set everything in motion. For instance, you could use the following HTML code in the BODY section:

```
<BODY>
<H1>Place your mouse over the image link to change the image!</H1>
<A href="somepage.html" onMouseOver="change_it('pic2')"
 onMouseOut="change_back('pic2')">
<IMG src="static_image.gif" name="pic1" id="pic1" border="0"></A>
<P>
<IMG src="image1.gif" name="pic2" id="pic2">
</P>
</BODY>
```

> **Notice that the functions are called with the name of the other image as the parameter**

Notice that instead of calling the functions from an <A> tag surrounding the image to be changed, they are called from another static linked image. The call sends the name "pic2" to each function, telling each function to change the image named "pic2" (which is the second image).

By sending the name of the second image, the first image remains the same while the second is changed when a mouseover event occurs on the first image. Thus, you need a third image for this one, static_image.gif, as seen in the code.

In this case, you don't need to change the code in the HEAD section because it works the same way as before. You're just telling it to do the same effect but on a different image. If you put it all together, the code would look like this:

```
<HTML>
<HEAD>
<SCRIPT language="JavaScript">
<!--
if (document.images)
{
// Preload original image (to show when page loads)
 var pic2_init= new Image();
 pic2_init.src="image1.gif";
//Preload image that will show on the mouseover event
 var pic2_new= new Image();
 pic2_new.src="image1_c.gif";
}
```

```
function change_it(the_name)
{
 if (document.images)
 {
  document.images[the_name].src= eval(the_name + "_new.src");
 }
}
function change_back(the_name)
{
 if (document.images)
 {
  document.images[the_name].src= eval(the_name + "_init.src");
 }
}
//-->
</SCRIPT>
</HEAD>
<BODY>
<H1>Place your mouse over the image link to change the image!</H1>
<A href="somepage.html" onMouseOver="change_it('pic2')"
 onMouseOut="change_back('pic2')">
<IMG src="static_image.gif" name="pic1" id="pic1" border="0"></A>
<P>
<IMG src="image1.gif" name="pic2" id="pic2">
</P>
</BODY>
</HTML>
```

Now the mouse can move over a static linked image and change a different image. Figures 17-3 and 17-4 show another set of before and after screens.

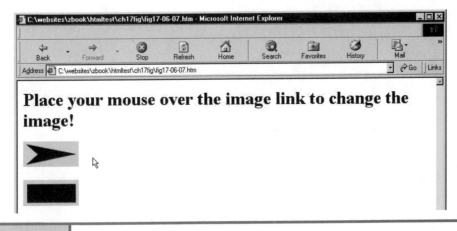

Figure 17-3 | The images shown before the mouseover event

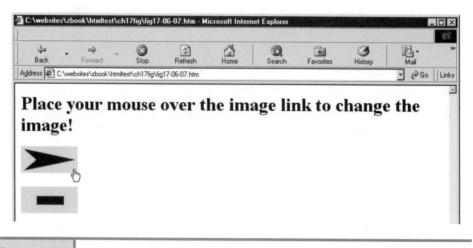

Figure 17-4   The images shown after the mouseover event

Changing Multiple Images

To change more than one image at a time, you need to have even more images. You also need to change the number of parameters sent to the functions, as well as some code in the functions themselves.

For simplicity, let's use only two pairs of images. The code we create will cause a mouseover event on the first image to change both itself and the second image on the page at the same time. The images used for this script are shown in the next four illustrations, which we will call, respectively, image1.gif, image1_c.gif, image2.gif, and image2_c.gif.

The additions to the HTML code produce the following code in the BODY section:

```
<BODY>
<H1>Place your mouse over the image link to change the image!</H1>
<A href="somepage.html" onMouseOver="change_it('pic1','pic2')"
 onMouseOut="change_back('pic1','pic2')">
<IMG src="image1.gif" name="pic1" id="pic1" border="0"></A>
<P>
<IMG src="image2.gif" name="pic2" id="pic2">
</P>
</BODY>
```

> **The functions now take two parameters, the name of each image**

The major difference is in the function calls. They now have two parameters, which are the names of both images that will be changed. Now you need to make some additions to the functions.

The new code for the HEAD section is shown here. Notice how the functions take an additional parameter and then make two image changes:

```
<HEAD>
<SCRIPT language="JavaScript">
<!--
if (document.images)
{
// Preload original images (to show when page loads)
 var pic1_init= new Image();
 pic1_init.src="image1.gif";
 var pic2_init= new Image();
 pic2_init.src="image2.gif";
//Preload images that will show on the mouseover event
 var pic1_new= new Image();
 pic1_new.src="image1_c.gif";
 var pic2_new= new Image();
 pic1_new.src="image2_c.gif";
}
function change_it(the_name,the_name2)
{
 if (document.images)
 {
  document.images[the_name].src= eval(the_name + "_new.src");
  document.images[the_name2].src= eval(the_name2 + "_new.src");
 }
}
function change_back(the_name,the_name2)
{
 if (document.images)
 {
```

> **The additional line allows the second image to be changed**

```
  document.images[the_name].src= eval(the_name + "_init.src");
  document.images[the_name2].src= eval(the_name2 + "_init.src");
  }
}
//-->
</SCRIPT>
</HEAD>
```

The additional line allows the second image to change back

All you need to do is take in an additional parameter and then simply repeat the same statement using the second parameter rather than the first in each function. This allows both images to change at the same time.

By putting the HEAD and BODY sections together into an HTML document, you get the following code:

```
<HTML>
<HEAD>
<SCRIPT language="JavaScript">
<!--
if (document.images)
{
// Preload original images (to show when page loads)
 var pic1_init= new Image();
 pic1_init.src="image1.gif";
 var pic2_init= new Image();
 pic2_init.src="image2.gif";
//Preload images that will show on the mouseover event
 var pic1_new= new Image();
 pic1_new.src="image1_c.gif";
 var pic2_new= new Image();
 pic2_new.src="image2_c.gif";
}
function change_it(the_name,the_name2)
{
 if (document.images)
 {
  document.images[the_name].src= eval(the_name + "_new.src");
  document.images[the_name2].src= eval(the_name2 + "_new.src");
 }
}
function change_back(the_name,the_name2)
{
 if (document.images)
 {
  document.images[the_name].src= eval(the_name + "_init.src");
  document.images[the_name2].src= eval(the_name2 + "_init.src");
 }
}
//-->
</SCRIPT>
</HEAD>
```

```
<BODY>
<H1>Place your mouse over the image link to change the image!</H1>
<A href="somepage.html" onMouseOver="change_it('pic1','pic2')"
 onMouseOut="change_back('pic1','pic2')">
<IMG src="image1.gif" name="pic1" id="pic1" border="0"></A>
<P>
<IMG src="image2.gif" name="pic2" id="pic2">
</P>
</BODY>
</HTML>
```

When the code is run, you will see something like the before and after screens shown in Figures 17-5 and 17-6.

1-Minute Drill

- **What is the value of the src property of an image object?**
- **Is it a good idea to preload images when you create a rollover script?**
- **How can you use the images array as an associative array?**

Figure 17-5 | The images before the mouseover event

- The value of the URL from the src attribute in the <IMG> tag or the value of the URL set by setting this property using JavaScript
- Yes
- By using the name of the image from the name or id attribute in the <IMG> tag as a string value inside the square brackets

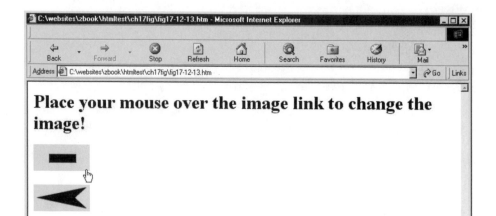

Figure 17-6 The images after the mouseover event

pr17_1.html

Project 17-1: Create a Navigational System of Images

In this project, you'll produce a simple rollover effect by creating a navigational system of images for a Web page.

Step-by-Step

1. Create four pairs of images. The images should contain the following text:

> Home
> About
> Help
> Links

The first image in each pair should have the text in blue, and the second image in each pair should have the text in red.

2. Based on what you have learned, place these images on the page so that each one will have a rollover effect. You can link them to anything you like.

3. When you have it set up, save the file as pr17_1.html and open it in your browser. You should have a set of linked images with rollover effects.

DHTML Introduction

Once you've learned JavaScript, DHTML is an interesting topic to explore. However, you need a basic knowledge of cascading style sheets as well. By combining the layout abilities of cascading style sheets with JavaScript to allow elements to be moved and resized, DHTML allows Web pages to be even more dynamic than they were with just HTML and JavaScript.

By using DHTML, you can also create some new navigational options that aren't available with just JavaScript and HTML. Note, though, that cascading style sheets and the scripts used with them work only in the major browsers (Microsoft Internet Explorer and Netscape Navigator) in version 4 or later. You can access a nice table indicating browser support for Cascading Style Sheet (CSS) levels 1 and 2 at http://www.webreview.com/style/css1/charts/mastergrid.shtml.

Cascading Style Sheets

Using cascading style sheets give you more control over page layout, colors, fonts, and other aspects of a Web page. Using cascading style sheets also allows you to specify certain properties for elements over an entire page, a set of pages, or an entire site.

Setting a Style Inline

The easiest type of style to set is one that you set on an individual element by adding a style attribute. The following code shows the syntax for this:

```
<div style= "color:red">This is red</div>
```

The style attribute allows one or more style properties to be added to anything inside the div element. Notice the syntax of the style property:

```
property:value
```

This syntax uses a colon (:) rather than an equal (=) sign to assign a value. The color property is used to assign a color. You can then give the color property a value of a color name or a red-green-blue (RGB) code.

This module only covers the style properties used to create the two DHTML scripts in this section.

The Necessary Properties

Table 17-2 shows the properties you must know to create the scripts in this module.

─┤Note

You can use many other properties as well. To learn more about cascading style sheets, see the "Ask the Expert" section later in this module.

Setting Styles in the HEAD Section

In addition to setting style properties inline, you can set them in the HEAD section of a document, and they will work for every instance of an element in the document.

Element Styles   To set up a style sheet in the HEAD section, you first need to add a set of <STYLE> and </STYLE> tags. These are separate from the <SCRIPT> and </SCRIPT> tags, but they also go in the HEAD section. The following code shows an example:

```
<STYLE type="text/css">
<!--
H1 { color:red }
-->
</STYLE>
```

Property	Possible Values
color	Color name or RGB code
font-family	Name of the font face to be used
position	Value of absolute, relative, or static
left	Number of pixels from the left of the browser window
top	Number of pixels from the top of the browser window
z-index	Number representing which element will have higher precedence if more than one element occupies some of the same space on the page. The element with the highest number is shown on top, while the element with the lowest number is shown on the bottom.

Table 17-2   The Cascading Style Sheet Properties Needed for the Scripts in This Module

Notice that the type attribute is set to text/css to let the browser know a cascading style sheet will be used. Notice also that the HTML comment tags are used as well in case an older browser comes across the script.

The style property that is set up is the color property. The property is being set for all H1 elements on the page. Thus, every heading 1 on the page will be in red font. Notice the syntax of the style sheet used in the preceding code:

```
element { property:value }
```

The element (such as H1) is listed, and then any properties are set inside the two curly brackets.

If you want to set more than one property at a time, you can separate each property:value pair with a semicolon. Thus, you could use the following code if you wanted all of the H1 elements on the page to be red and to use the Verdana font:

```
<STYLE type="text/css">
<!--
H1 { color:red; font-family:Verdana }
-->
</STYLE>
```

Adding the preceding code to a page with H1 elements changes all of those elements. For example, the following HTML document would have both H1 elements shown in a gray, Verdana font:

```
<HTML>
<HEAD>
<STYLE type="text/css">
<!--
H1 { color:gray; font-family:Verdana }
-->
</STYLE>                        ┌────────────────────────┐
</HEAD>                         │ This heading has a     │
<BODY>                         │ gray Verdana font      │
<H1>My Stamp Collection</H1> ◄─└────────────────────────┘
OK, I lied, I don't have any stamps!    ┌──────────────────────────┐
<H1>My Book Collection</H1> ◄───────────│ This heading also has a  │
No time to write all of them, so let's  │ gray Verdana font        │
                                        └──────────────────────────┘
just say I have a lot!
</BODY>
</HTML>
```

Figure 17-7 shows the results of this script when run in a browser. Notice that both of the headings have the same properties.

Using Classes   Sometimes you won't want all of the elements of the same type to have the same properties. For instance, you might wish to have certain div elements in a Verdana font, but others in an Arial font. Assigning the style to all the div elements on the page just won't do in this case. To add this flexibility, you can use classes.

A class is set up as shown in the following syntax:

```
.classname { property:value }
```

Notice that the class name begins with a dot (.) character. You replace *classname* with a unique name for the class being assigned. Then you give it the properties and values you want to use in that class.

Thus, to set up two classes for different elements, you can use the code shown here:

```
<STYLE type="text/css">
<!--
.mytext1 { font-family:Verdana }
.mytext2 { font-family:Arial }
-->
</STYLE>
```

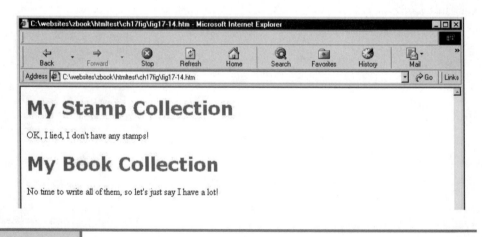

Figure 17-7   The result of the style sheet on the H1 elements

Next, add a class attribute to any element you want to have use a class inside the HTML code:

```
<BODY>
<DIV class="mytex1">
This is in a Verdana font!
</DIV>
<DIV class="mytext2">
This is in an Arial font!
</DIV>
</BODY>
```

Now you will have two div elements using two different styles when you put it all together:

```
<HTML>
<HEAD>
<STYLE type="text/css">
<!--
.mytext1 { font-family:Verdana }
.mytext2 { font-family:Arial }
-->
</STYLE>
</HEAD>
<BODY>
<DIV class="mytex1">
This is in a Verdana font! ◄——— This line will use a Verdana font
</DIV>
<DIV class="mytext2">
This is in an Arial font! ◄——— This line will use an Arial font
</DIV>
</BODY>
</HTML>
```

The following illustration shows the results of the preceding code when run in a browser. Notice the two different fonts that appear on the page because the classes allow elements of the same type to use different styles.

```
C:\websites\zbook\htmltest\ch17

      ⇦              ⇨
     Back          Forward

Address  C:\websites\zbook\htmltest\

This is in a Verdana font!
This is in an Arial font!
```

Moving Elements

For your first DHTML script, you will simply place an image on top of some text using style sheets, and then move it away to reveal the text, using JavaScript to access the image's style properties.

First, set up a style sheet in the HEAD section that puts two images in the same place. Use two classes, as shown here:

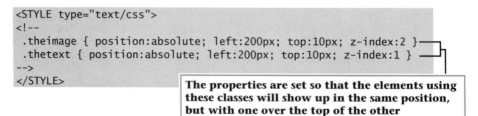

```
<STYLE type="text/css">
<!--
 .theimage { position:absolute; left:200px; top:10px; z-index:2 }
 .thetext { position:absolute; left:200px; top:10px; z-index:1 }
-->
</STYLE>
```

The properties are set so that the elements using these classes will show up in the same position, but with one over the top of the other

Notice that the classes in the preceding code use the position property and that it is set to absolute. Therefore, you can give the element an exact position on the page using pixel values.

You perform this task by using the left and top properties (notice the px for pixels). Both classes begin at the same position on the page, 200 pixels from the left and 10 pixels from the top of the browser window. The z-index property decides which element will be shown and which will be left underneath. Because the theimage class has a higher number set for this property, it is shown over the top of the thetext class, hiding whatever content is used in the element using that class.

Next, set up the code for the BODY section so that you can see which elements are going to use which class:

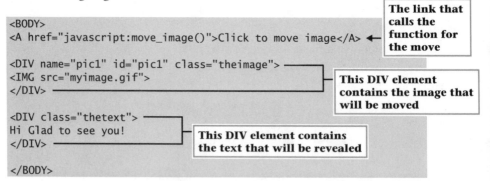

The link that calls the function for the move

```
<BODY>
<A href="javascript:move_image()">Click to move image</A>

<DIV name="pic1" id="pic1" class="theimage">
<IMG src="myimage.gif">
</DIV>

<DIV class="thetext">
Hi Glad to see you!
</DIV>

</BODY>
```

This DIV element contains the image that will be moved

This DIV element contains the text that will be revealed

The first element to appear on the page is a link that calls a JavaScript function (which you will create soon). The function will be used to move the image elsewhere and reveal the text.

The DIV element that contains the image is next. Notice that it uses the the image class for its positioning. Thus, it will show up 200 pixels from the left and 10 pixels from the top of the browser window. Also notice it is given the name "pic1" so that you can use JavaScript to access its style properties later.

Inside the <DIV> and </DIV> tags is the code for the image. You can use any image you like, as long as it is big enough to cover the text. Finally, the DIV element that contains the text is placed. Notice that it uses the class thetext and thus will be in the same position as the other DIV element, but below it.

Now you need a script so that you can move the image away from the text and reveal what has been hidden under the image. The following code shows how:

```
<SCRIPT language="JavaScript">
<!--
function move_image()
 {
 if (document.layers)
 {
  if (document.pic1.left<400)
    document.pic1.left=400;
 }
 if (document.all)
 {
  if (document.all.pic1.style.left<400)
    document.all.pic1.style.left=400;
 }
}
//-->
</SCRIPT>
```

Note

Notice that there are two tests to ensure that the browser can handle the script. If the browser has the layers array, then it is likely to be Netscape Navigator 4 or later. If the browser has the all property, then it is likely to be Microsoft Internet Explorer 4 or later. The only trouble is that the use of the mentioned arrays in a specific browser could change when newer browsers come out, so you may need to adjust the code to check for different objects or to check the browser version and type.

In the first if block, you need to go only from the document object to the element name to the style property name to access the left property. If it is less than 400, it is changed to 400. Thus, the DIV element containing the image is moved from its original position at 200 pixels from the left to a new position at 400 pixels from the left.

In the second if block, you need to follow a longer path to get to the style property. Otherwise, it performs the same task as the if block that preceded it, moving the DIV element to its new destination. The differences that occur are due to the different way each browser handles the document object model.

While a detailed discussion on the document object model is beyond the scope of this book, "Ask the Expert" provides more resources later in this module.

Next, you just need to put all the code together, as shown here:

```
<HTML>
<HEAD>
<STYLE type="text/css">
<!--
 .theimage { position:absolute; left:200px; top:10px; z-index:2 }
 .thetext { position:absolute; left:200px; top:10px; z-index:1 }
-->
</STYLE>
<SCRIPT language="JavaScript">
<!--
function move_image()
 {
 if (document.layers)
 {
  if (document.pic1.left<400)
    document.pic1.left=400;
 }
 if (document.all)
 {
  if (document.all.pic1.style.left<400)
    document.all.pic1.style.left=400;
 }
 }
//-->
</SCRIPT>
</HEAD>
<BODY>
<A href="javascript:move_image()">Click to move image</A>

<DIV name="pic1" id="pic1" class="theimage">
<IMG src="myimage.gif">
</DIV>
```

```
<DIV class="thetext">
Hi Glad to see you!
</DIV>

</BODY>
</HTML>
```

Once complete, you can test it out by clicking the link. The following two illustrations show what the page looks like before and after the link is clicked.

Animating Objects

If you want the image to move over gradually rather than to just reappear at the new destination, edit the code to make it animate by using a parameter and a timed interval. The following code shows the adjustments:

```
<HTML>
<HEAD>
<STYLE type="text/css">
<!--
.theimage { position:absolute; left:200px; top:10px; z-index:2 }
```

```
.thetext { position:absolute; left:200px; top:10px; z-index:1 }
-->
</STYLE>
<SCRIPT language="JavaScript">
<!--
function move_image(theplace) ◄──────
 {
 if (document.layers)
 {
  if (theplace<400)
  {
   document.pic1.left= theplace;
   theplace+=5;
   setTimeout('move_image('+theplace+')',100);
  }
 }
 if (document.all)
 {
  if (theplace<400)
  {
   document.all.pic1.style.left= theplace;
   theplace+=5;
   setTimeout('move_image('+theplace+')',100);
  }
 }
}
//-->
</SCRIPT>
</HEAD>
<BODY>
<A href="javascript:move_image(200)">Click to move image</A>

<DIV name="pic1" id="pic1" class="theimage">
<IMG src="myimage.gif">
</DIV>

<DIV class="thetext">
Hi Glad to see you!
</DIV>

</BODY>
</HTML>
```

> **The function takes a parameter each time so the script knows whether to continue the animation**

The function now takes in a parameter called "theplace" (which, when called, is initially set to 200, the value of the left property). The value is increased by 5, and the function is run again after a set amount of time. When the value of theplace reaches 400, the movement stops and the animation is complete.

1-Minute Drill

- **What syntax is used to separate property names and values in a style sheet?**
- **What syntax is used to separate property/value pairs if you have more than one pair?**
- **What syntax is used in front of a class name when defining a class?**

JavaScript Security

You may have noticed that when you try to use the window.close() method on the main browser window, a confirmation box appears asking if you really want to allow the window to be closed. This situation is one of the issues of JavaScript security.

The browser does not want a site to close a window the viewer opened without permission from the viewer. If that were allowed, the programmer would have some control of the viewer's computer, which could be a problem.

Another aspect of security is the thought that you can "protect" Web pages with passwords or keep the source code of the page from being viewed by a user.

Security and Signed Scripts

To get permission to close the main browser window or to use certain properties or methods in JavaScript, you must use signed scripts. Signed scripts will open up some additional JavaScript features, but you must do some additional work.

Basically, you digitally sign the script using a special tool. The viewer then gets a message when entering the page asking whether to allow the signed script, with some information about the signed script. If the viewer accepts, then you will be able to use the additional features. If not, you'll need to have an alternative code ready to avoid JavaScript errors.

- A colon (:) character
- A semicolon (;) character
- A dot (.) character

For further information about this subject, go to the Web site http://developer.netscape.com/docs/manuals/communicator/ jsguide4/sec.htm.

Page Protection

Many scripts attempt to keep viewers out in some way, such as by using password protection or by using a "no-right-click" script to keep the source code of the page from being viewed. I even have some examples of these scripts on my Web sites

However, these security strategies are largely ineffective because these "no-right-click" scripts can often be bypassed by turning off JavaScript or by doing a little extra work.

Passwords

Some password systems are better than others, but none really seem to offer true Web page security. If you don't want someone to view a page, much better methods exist than using a JavaScript system, such as using server-side languages or using certain setups on your Web server.

If you are on a free Web-hosting service, the better methods may or may not be available. However, keep in mind that a JavaScript password system is unlikely to be foolproof and that you should not protect anything important with such a system.

Hiding Web Page Source Code

Many people would love to hide the source code of a Web page. However, JavaScript isn't going to do the trick. A number of scripts try various means of disabling the right-click. Basically, these strategies don't work because they can be bypassed in a couple of ways:

- If the right-click is disabled, you can always try the View menu and select View Source.

- If the preceding method does not work, you can always turn off JavaScript or look in your cache directory on your computer. The browser must have the code to display the page, so a copy of it goes into the browser's cache.

In the long run, these scripts just make viewing the source code more difficult (and they can be annoying). For more information about this topic, go to http://webhome.idirect.com/~bowers/copy/copy1.htm.

Ask the Expert

Question: Where can I find free cut-and-paste JavaScript code on the Web?

Answer:
http://www.javascriptsource.com
http://www.javascripts.com
http://www.javascriptcity.com

Question: Where can I learn more about JavaScript?

Answer:
http://www.wsabstract.com
http://tech.irt.org/articles/script.htm
http://www.pageresource.com/jscript/

Question: Where can I learn more about cascading style sheets?

Answer:
http://home.cnet.com/webbuilding/
0-7258.html?tag=st.bl.3880.dir.7258
http://hotwired.lycos.com/webmonkey/authoring/stylesheets/
http://www.devshed.com/Client_Side/CSS/

Question: Where can I learn more about DHTML?

Answer:
http://webreference.com/dhtml/
http://www.dynamicdrive.com
http://hotwired.lycos.com/webmonkey/authoring/
dynamic_html/

pr17_2.html

Project 17-2: Use DHTML Animation

In this project, you will use DHTML animation to move some text on the screen.

Step-by-Step

1. Set up a style sheet with a class named "mytext" that will be positioned 100 pixels from the left and 10 pixels from the top of the browser window.

2. Set up the BODY code so that there is a DIV element named "cool" and use the following text between the <DIV> and </DIV> tags: "I'm moving over!"

3. Create a link that calls a function named "move_text()" when clicked.

4. In the HEAD section, add a script that will move the text until it is 500 pixels from the left of the browser window using the move_text() function.

5. Save the file as pr17_2.html and open it in your browser. Try out the link to see the text move.

☑ Mastery Check

1. Which property of the image object sets the width of an instance of the image object?

   A. width

   B. height

   C. img_width

   D. src

2. In which type of script would you want to preload images on a page?

   A. Status bar text change

   B. Rollover effect

   C. Animating text

   D. Disabling a right-click

☑ *Mastery Check*

3. Which style sheet property is used to define the font color of an element?

   A. font-face

   B. font-family

   C. fontcolor

   D. color

4. Is it effective to try to hide the source code of a page using JavaScript?

   A. Of course!

   B. Why not?

   C. No, but it can make it more difficult or annoying.

   D. Works every time!

5. Is JavaScript fun?

   A. Yes!

   B. No!

   C. I was forced to learn this by my boss, so it can never be fun!

   D. Before I read this it was awful, but now it is extremely fun!

Appendix A

Answers to Mastery Checks

Module 1: Introduction to JavaScript

1. You must know which of the following to be able to use JavaScript?

   C. HTML

2. Which of the following is something you should have to use JavaScript?

   A. A Web browser

3. How can a client-side language help when using forms on a Web page?

   B. It can validate the information before it is sent to the server.

4. How is JavaScript added to a Web page?

   D. It is added to an HTML document.

Module 2: Placing JavaScript in an HTML File

1. What is the purpose of the <SCRIPT></SCRIPT> tags?

   D. All of the above

2. Why would you use HTML comments within the <SCRIPT></SCRIPT> tags?

   B. To keep the JavaScript code inside the tags from rendering as plain text in older Web browsers

3. When would it be a good idea to use an external JavaScript file?

   C. When the script is very long or needs to be placed in more than one HTML document

4. JavaScript comments can be very useful for the purpose of **documenting** or **debugging** your code.

Module 3: Using Variables

1. Which of the following declares a variable named *pagenumber* and gives it a value of 240?

   C. var pagenumber=240;

2. Which of the following variable declarations uses a variable with a valid variable name in JavaScript?

   B. var my_house;

3. Which of the following string declarations is invalid?

   C. var mytext= "Here is some text!';

4. Which of the following statements would be valid in JavaScript?

   D. document.write("John said, \"Hi!\"");

5. Which of the following successfully prints a variable named "myhobby" by adding it to a set of strings?

   B. document.write("I like to "+myhobby+" every weekend");

Module 4: Using Functions

1. In general, a function is a little **script** within a larger **script** that is used to perform a single **task** or a series of **tasks**.

2. Which of the following would be a valid function name in JavaScript?

   C. function get_text()

3. Which of the following is a valid use of the window.alert() method?

   D. window.alert("This is text");

4. Which of the following correctly calls a function named *some_alert()* and sends it two string values as parameters?

   B. some_alert("some","words");

5. Which of the following correctly assigns the result of a function named *get_something()* to a variable named *shopping?*

   A. var shopping=get_something();

Module 5: JavaScript Operators

1. Which of the following is not a JavaScript operator?

   D. $#

2. What does an assignment operator do?

   A. Assigns a new value to a variable

3. What does a comparison operator do?

   C. Compares two values or statements, and returns a value of true or false

4. Which of the following statements will return true?

   B. !(17>=20)

5. Which of the following statements will return false?

   B. (4>=4)&&(5<=2)

Module 6: Conditional Statements and Loops

1. Which of the following would be valid as the first line of an if/else statement?

   B. if (y<7)

2. What do we use to enclose the blocks of code in conditionals and loops?

C. Curly brackets

3. Which of these would be valid as the first line of a for loop?

A. for ($x=1;x<6;x+=1$)

4. Which of these would not be valid as the first line of a while loop?

B. while ($x=7$)

5. How many times can you nest a code block within another?

D. As many times as you like

Module 7: Event Handlers

1. Event handlers are useful because they enable us to gain **access** to the **events** that may occur on the page.

2. Which of the following correctly codes an alert on the click event?

C. <INPUT type="button" onClick="window.alert('Hey there!');">

3. The onLoad event handler is placed inside the opening **<BODY>**tag.

4. A mouseover event occurs when

D. The viewer moves the mouse cursor over a link, linked image, or linked area of an image map.

5. Which of the following calls a function named "major_alert()" inside the onFocus event handler correctly?

E. <INPUT type="text" onFocus= "major_alert();">

Module 8: Objects

1. In JavaScript, we access object properties through the use of the

B. Dot operator

2. What could we say about the following code:

```
var x=myhouse.kitchen;
```

C. Assuming the myhouse object exists, it assigns the value of the kitchen property of the myhouse object to the variable x.

3. Which of the following lines correctly creates a method named "cost" from a function named "get_cost()," if this line is within a constructor function?

D. his.cost=get_cost;

4. Which of the following would send an alert to the viewer that tells the name of the browser being used?

B. window.alert("You are using "+navigator.appName);

5. What could we say about the following code:

```
myhouse.kitchen="big';
```

C. Assuming the myhouse object exists, the kitchen property is assigned a new string value.

A

Module 9: The Document Object

1. Which of the color properties allows us to change its value on the fly?

B. bgColor

2. Which property returns the complete URL of the current document?

C. URL

3. How does the writeln() method differ from the write() method?

C. It adds a JavaScript new line character at the end of the line.

4. How is a formName type property created in JavaScript?

A. When a form is given a name, the name of the form becomes the property name.

5. What statements are allowed between a document.open() and a document.close() statement?

B. document.write() and document.writeln() statements

Module 10: Window Object

1. The calls to properties and methods of the window object can often be shortened because

A. The browser typically assumes the window object exists.

2. Why would this code not work?

C. A change in the status property in an onMouseOver event must return true afterward.

3. What value is returned by the confirm() method if the viewer clicks the OK button?

A. true

4. When setting the toolbar attribute as part of the third parameter in the open() method, what values may the attribute have?

D. yes, no, 1, and 0

5. What is the difference between the setInterval() method and the setTimeout() method?

B. The setInterval() method is used to repeat a function at a set time interval, while setTimeout() executes a function only once after a set time delay.

Module 11: Arrays

1. Which of the following does not correctly create an array?

D. var if= new Array[10];

2. Which of the following will correctly access the fifth element of an array named "cool?"

D. cool[4];

3. What property of the Array object will return the numeric value of the length of an array?

A. The length property

4. By default, how does the sort() method sort the contents of an array?

C. It sorts the contents alphabetically

5. What is used in place of an index number in an associative array?

D. A string value

Module 12: Math and Date Objects

1. What do the properties and methods of the Math object enable us to do?

B. Perform mathematical calculations

2. Which of the following would correctly write the value of pi on a Web page?

C. document.write(Math.PI);

3. Which of the following would correctly generate a random number between 0 and 7?

C. var rand_int= Math.floor(Math.random()*8);

4. What must be created in most cases before the Date object's properties and methods can be used?

D. An instance of the Date object

5. Which of the following correctly assigns the day of the week for an instance of the Date object named "rightnow" to a variable named "weekday"?

B. var weekday= rightnow.getDay();

Module 13: Handling Strings

1. What are the two ways in which we created string objects?

A. Creating an instance of the string object and creating a string literal

2. Which properties of the *string* object can you use with both string objects and string literals?

   C. length

3. Which of the following correctly creates a string literal?

   B. var the_text= "Look at me!";

4. Which method of the string object can you use to find which character is at a given position in a string?

   B. charAt()

5. Which of the following statements is true?

   D. The indexOf() method returns a numeric value that is the position of a character sent as a parameter, but only the position of the first occurrence of that character.

Module 14: JavaScript and Forms

1. Which of the following would access the fourth form on a page?

   B. document.forms[3]

2. Which of the following holds the value of the number of forms in a document?

   C. document.forms.length

3. Which of the following would access the value of an element named "e1" in a form named "f1?"

   A. document.f1.e1.value

4. What type of value should a function return when it is used to validate a form?

   B. true or false

5. What is used to get the currently selected option in a select box?

   D. The selectedIndex property

Module 15: JavaScript and Frames

1. What are two methods that can be used to access frames?

   A. The frames array or a frame name

2. What is the value of the length property of the frames array?

   C. The number of frames in a window

3. What does an asterisk (*) mean when used in the rows or cols attribute of a frameset?

   B. The frame should take up any remaining space in the window.

4. What is used to access the main window so that you can access another frame?

   A. top

5. Which of these would correctly change the document in a frame named "right_side" to "frame3.html" from another frame?

B. top.right_side.location="frame3.html";

Module 16: An Introduction to Advanced Techniques

1. Which attribute replaces the name attribute in XHTML?

C. The id attribute

2. Which of the following is valid in XHTML?

D. <input type="text" />

3. Which of the following lines does not create a JavaScript syntax error?

C. document.write("Is there an error?");

4. Which of the following would validate when tested against the regular expression of /pep/?

B. pepper

5. Which property is used to set and read a cookie?

B. The cookie property of the document object

Module 17: More Advanced Techniques

1. What property of the image object sets the width of an instance of the image object?

A. width

2. In which type of script would you want to preload images on a page?

B. Rollover effect

3. Which style sheet property is used to define the font color of an element?

D. color

4. Is it effective to try to hide the source code of a page using JavaScript?

C. No, but it can make it more difficult or annoying

5. Is JavaScript fun?

Opinion question; all answers are acceptable!

Index

W

INTERNATIONAL CONTACT INFORMATION

AUSTRALIA
McGraw-Hill Book Company Australia Pty. Ltd.
TEL +61-2-9417-9899
FAX +61-2-9417-5687
http://www.mcgraw-hill.com.au
books-it_sydney@mcgraw-hill.com

CANADA
McGraw-Hill Ryerson Ltd.
TEL +905-430-5000
FAX +905-430-5020
http://www.mcgrawhill.ca

**GREECE, MIDDLE EAST,
NORTHERN AFRICA**
McGraw-Hill Hellas
TEL +30-1-656-0990-3-4
FAX +30-1-654-5525

MEXICO (Also serving Latin America)
McGraw-Hill Interamericana Editores S.A. de C.V.
TEL +525-117-1583
FAX +525-117-1589
http://www.mcgraw-hill.com.mx
fernando_castellanos@mcgraw-hill.com

SINGAPORE (Serving Asia)
McGraw-Hill Book Company
TEL +65-863-1580
FAX +65-862-3354
http://www.mcgraw-hill.com.sg
mghasia@mcgraw-hill.com

SOUTH AFRICA
McGraw-Hill South Africa
TEL +27-11-622-7512
FAX +27-11-622-9045
robyn_swanepoel@mcgraw-hill.com

**UNITED KINGDOM & EUROPE
(Excluding Southern Europe)**
McGraw-Hill Education Europe
TEL +44-1-628-502500
FAX +44-1-628-770224
http://www.mcgraw-hill.co.uk
computing_neurope@mcgraw-hill.com

ALL OTHER INQUIRIES Contact:
Osborne/McGraw-Hill
TEL +1-510-549-6600
FAX +1-510-883-7600
http://www.osborne.com
omg_international@mcgraw-hill.com